EUROPE'S SECOND CONSTITUTION

The process of European constitutionalization is met with extensive scepticism in current national legal and political spheres and in broader circles of public opinion across Europe. By shedding light on these concerns, this book reveals the widespread misunderstanding of constitutional federalism that permeates the Member State courts, popular media and many academic communities. A failure to address confusion over this fundamental concept is leading us towards impoverished development of the EU's 'Second Constitution', and even ensuring that the role of both domestic and European courts in enriching the constitutionalization process is overlooked and undervalued. In a bid to avoid such consequences, this book explores how federalism and further constitutionalization – rightly understood in a dialogue of the European courts – may actually change this process and allow a clearer advance towards Europe's Second Constitution for, but also with, the people of Europe.

MARKUS W. GEHRING, JSD (YALE), MA (CANTAB), LLM (YALE), DR IUR (HAMBURG), is a lecturer in law at the Faculty of Law, University of Cambridge. He serves as an affiliated lecturer in European and international law at Politics and International Studies (POLIS), University of Cambridge. He is an expert in the Centre for European Legal Studies (CELS), a fellow and Director of Studies in Law at Hughes Hall and a fellow of the Lauterpacht Centre for International Law. Dr Gehring is also an affiliated lecturer in the Department of Land Economy and a fellow of the Centre for Environment, Energy and Natural Resources Governance (C-EENRG). He also serves as Lead Counsel for Trade in the Centre for International Sustainable Development Law (CISDL). He co-edits a book series on Treaty Implementation for Sustainable Development with Cambridge University Press and is author of several publications on EU, international and sustainable development law.

CAMBRIDGE STUDIES IN CONSTITUTIONAL LAW

The aim of this series is to produce leading monographs in constitutional law. All areas of constitutional law and public law fall within the ambit of the series, including human rights and civil liberties law, administrative law, as well as constitutional theory and the history of constitutional law. A wide variety of scholarly approaches is encouraged, with the governing criterion being simply that the work is of interest to an international audience. Thus, works concerned with only one jurisdiction will be included in the series as appropriate, while, at the same time, the series will include works which are explicitly comparative or theoretical – or both. The series editor likewise welcomes proposals that work at the intersection of constitutional and international law, or that seek to bridge the gaps between civil law systems, the US, and the common law jurisdictions of the Commonwealth.

Books in the series

A.V. Dicey and the Common Law Constitutional Tradition: A Legal Turn of Mind Mark D. Walters

Legal Sabotage: Ernst Fraenkel in Hitler's Germany Douglas Morris

Proportionality in Action: Comparative and Empirical Perspectives on the Judicial Practice Edited by Mordechai Kremnitzer, Tayla Steiner and Andrej Lang

Constitutional Dialogue: Democracy, Rights, Institutions Edited by Geoffrey Sigalet, Grégoire Webber and Rosalind Dixon

The Veiled Sceptre: Reserve Powers of Heads of State in Westminster Systems Anne Twomey

Vigilance and Restraint in the Common Law of Judicial Review Dean Knight

The Alchemists: Questioning Our Faith in Courts as Democracy-Builders Tom Gerald Daly

Australia's Constitution after Whitlam Brendan Lim

Building the Constitution: The Practice of Constitutional Interpretation in Post-apartheid South Africa James Fowkes

Dimensions of Dignity: The Theory and Practice of Modern Constitutional Law Jacob Weinrib

Reason of State: Law, Prerogative, Empire Thomas Poole

Bills of Rights in the Common Law Robert Leckey

The Guardian of the Constitution: Hans Kelsen and Carl Schmitt on the Limits of Constitutional Law Translated by Lars Vinx, with an introduction and notes by Lars Vinx

Parliamentary Bills of Rights: The Experiences of New Zealand and the United Kingdom Experiences Janet L. Hiebert and James B. Kelly

Lawyering for the Rule of Law: Government Lawyers and the Rise of Judicial Power in Israel Yoav Dotan

Balancing Constitutional Rights: The Origins and Meanings of Postwar Legal Discourse Jacco Bomhoff

Judges on Trial: The Independence and Accountability of the English Judiciary Shimon Shetreet and Sophie Turenne

Proportionality and Constitutional Culture Moshe Cohen-Eliya and Iddo Porat

The Politics of Principle: The First South African Constitutional Court, 1995–2005 Theunis Roux

The New Commonwealth Model of Constitutionalism: Theory and Practice Stephen Gardbaum

Searching for the State in British Legal Thought: Competing Conceptions of the Public Sphere Janet McLean

Judging Social Rights Jeff King

Proportionality: Constitutional Rights and Their Limitations Aharon Barak

Parliamentary Sovereignty: Contemporary Debates Jeffrey Goldsworthy

EUROPE'S SECOND CONSTITUTION

Crisis, Courts and Community

MARKUS W. GEHRING
University of Cambridge

CAMBRIDGE
UNIVERSITY PRESS

CAMBRIDGE
UNIVERSITY PRESS

University Printing House, Cambridge CB2 8BS, United Kingdom

One Liberty Plaza, 20th Floor, New York, NY 10006, USA

477 Williamstown Road, Port Melbourne, VIC 3207, Australia

314–321, 3rd Floor, Plot 3, Splendor Forum, Jasola District Centre, New Delhi - 110025, India

79 Anson Road, #06–04/06, Singapore 079906

Cambridge University Press is part of the University of Cambridge.

It furthers the University's mission by disseminating knowledge in the pursuit of education, learning, and research at the highest international levels of excellence.

www.cambridge.org
Information on this title: www.cambridge.org/9781108487962
DOI: 10.1017/9781108768399

First published 2020

A catalogue record for this publication is available from the British Library.

Library of Congress Cataloging-in-Publication Data
Names: Gehring, Markus W., author.
Title: Europe's second constitution : crisis, courts and community / Markus W. Gehring, University of Cambridge.
Description: Cambridge, United Kingdom ; New York, NY, USA : Cambridge University Press, 2020. | Series: Cambridge studies in constitutional law | Includes bibliographical references and index.
Identifiers: LCCN 2020006013 | ISBN 9781108487962 (hardback) | ISBN 9781108768399 (epub)
Subjects: LCSH: Constitutional law – European Union countries – Philosophy. | European Union countries – Politics and government.
Classification: LCC KJE4445 .G44 2020 | DDC 342.24–dc23
LC record available at https://lccn.loc.gov/2020006013

ISBN 978-1-108-48796-2 Hardback

CONTENTS

PREFACE

In both the court of public opinion and modern legal scholarship, the Europe of today appears to lurch from crisis to crisis, driven by socio-political, environmental and economic challenges. How might the European Union overcome these crises? Which obstacles should become Europe's central concerns? Which opportunities should be explored? To date, many political debates focus on the next feeble incremental steps to be taken towards formal inter-governmental amendments of the Constitutional Treaties. Yet to overcome what are, in their foundations, a series of constitutional crises shaking the EU, a more considered approach to further constitutionalization is required. In this book, I turn to an under-researched dimension of EU constitutionalization, one that not only provides opportunities to help overcome the current series of crises but also presents a new approach to integration that takes seriously the perceptions and understandings of European jurisprudence with regard to federalism and the European public sphere.

Through a detailed analysis of Member State court jurisprudence and associated literature, the study evaluates the most important *demos*, *civitas* and *ius* dimensions of European constitutionalization. *Demos* focuses on the populace of a democracy, as a self-perceived, aware and organized political unit, and the European *demos* dimension of European constitutionalization concerns the political cohesion of the people of the Union. It also concerns the potential for Europe to develop a common European citizenship, rely on common values and develop a common attitude towards religion. The analysis highlights the lack of a common European public space for deliberation and effective communications through discussions in intelligible working languages. *Civitas* stands for the collection of citizenship duties attributed to a member of a community, and in later years more broadly to a state, and the *civitas* dimension of European constitutional development invokes the potential for a functioning EU institutional citizenship as characterized by EU democratic elections, European political parties, the role of the president in the EU, the function of the Council and the European Parliament, and the role of a foundational document. *Ius* refers to the rule of law and respect for rights, which also includes more broadly the mandates of legal authorities and the effective functioning of courts of justice, taking into consideration common structures in the law based on EU law, any general principles *Ius Commune Europaeum*, and the collection of rules and rule-making in Europe. In this sense, the *ius* dimension of European constitutionalization discusses the potential for a single rule of law in Europe, the structure of the EU court system, the criminal law and police force, the system of human rights protection and external relations law in the EU.

In these three dimensions, EU constitutionalization has been judged by many periphery courts to be either non-existent or deficient. At the root of these opinions, my research has revealed an impoverished understanding of federalism and its potential role in further European constitutionalization. Through case law analysis, it is revealed that many Member State courts on the periphery do not fully appreciate either the constitutional nature of federations or the lived experiences of federalism in other jurisdictions. This work demonstrates that the litany of obstacles commonly raised by Member State courts and academics have nearly all been overcome, or were never challenges in the first place.

Once many common concerns have largely been dismissed, my research identifies the most significant and potentially fatal remaining obstacle to EU constitutionalization: the absence of a strong and vibrant trans-European public sphere in which transparent, legitimate policy debates can occur, and corollary challenges such as lack of a pragmatic number of working languages, lack of unitary elections, and important gaps in the European central court's *Kompetenz-Kompetenz*. Overcoming *this* obstacle and its related challenges would do much to address the constitutional crisis and set Europe on a healthier path towards further constitutionalization.

This research leads me to further conclude that while a European 'constitutional moment' might be the most straightforward next step, it is not currently on the political horizon. Other constitutional adaptive mechanisms do, however, offer certain opportunities. Incremental formal treaty amendments and fundamentally changed constitutional practices have helped to address certain early obstacles. However, given embedded Member State privileges, they are unlikely alone to be effective in addressing *this* remaining hurdle. Rather, in conclusion it is argued that there is a crucially decisive challenge to be taken up in the jurisprudence itself. Further constitutionalization can, in essence, be *prepared* by the concerted efforts of more courageous centre and periphery courts, through engaged and legitimate dialogues between the Courts of Europe themselves. Only by enabling and strengthening a vibrant pan-European public policy debate can Europe's Second Constitution one day become a reality.

ACKNOWLEDGEMENTS

This book is dedicated to my wife, Professor Marie-Claire Cordonier Segger, and to our sons, Jona and Nico, with thanks for their patience and inspiration, as well as to Ulli and Peter, Maike, Marit and their families whose support has been deeply appreciated.

Thanks are due to Professor Bruce Ackerman at the Yale Law School for his wise advice and for being a shining light of liberalism in the law, and to many colleagues from the University of Cambridge, especially Professor Catherine Barnard at the Centre for European Legal Studies, who has been an essential part of this project; also Dr Martin Steinfeld and Professor Antje Wiener from Hughes Hall, whose help allowed me to advance the final manuscript during a sabbatical. As a Fellow of the Lauterpacht Centre for International Law, I also appreciate the advice of excellent public-law-spirited international lawyers, especially Professor Michael Waibel and Professor Freya Baetens as well as Professor James Crawford. Thanks are also due to public law colleagues such as Professor Alison Young and Professor Paul Daly for their attempts to explain parts of the UK Constitution, which remain a mystery, and to colleagues from POLIS, especially Baroness Dr Julie Smith, and from Land Economy, especially Professor David Howarth, who challenged my continental black-letter legal understandings. I have benefited from a Jean Monnet ad personam Chair at the University of Ottawa, where I had the pleasure of collaborating with the Honourable Judge Sébastien Grammond, Professor Pascale Fournier and others. Colleagues from the Centre for International Sustainable Development Law (CISDL), especially Dr Ashfaq Khalfan, Professor Alexandra Harrington and Freedom-Kai Phillips, and also outside Cambridge, especially fellow EU constitutional lawyer Professor Robert Schütze, have been very encouraging.

Thanks are also due to heads of two Cambridge colleges, Professor David Yates of Robinson College and Dr Anthony Freeling of Hughes Hall who opened the space and time needed to finalize this research; I strongly value their support. I am also grateful to several student legal research assistants, especially Jacquelyn Veraldi, who helped in the final stretches of the project, and to my fourteen successful PhD students who endured countless discussions of these issues throughout their studies in Cambridge, EUI, Kisangani and Ottawa.

Finally, I am deeply indebted to the law team of Cambridge University Press, especially Finola O'Sullivan, for their encouragement, and also to the reviewers for their helpful comments. This book is about crises inside the European Union and now for the first time outside it, too. The Brexit process in the UK, that is, the process of one Member State leaving the Union, remains in my view one of the strongest expressions of the constitutionalization obstacles discussed in the volume. It serves as both a warning and a reminder that most constitutional structures change over time.

TABLE OF CASES

Dimensions / Obstacles	Cases EU	Cases Member States	Notes
Demos			
No homogeneity of citizenship	Case C-184/99, *Rudy Grzelczyk* v. *Centre public d'aide sociale d'Ottignies-Louvain-la-Neuve* [2001] ECR I-06193 Case C-109/01, *Secretary of State for the Home Department* v. *Hacene Akrich* [2003] ECR I-09607 Case C-209/03, *The Queen (on the application of Dany Bidar)* v. *London Borough of Ealing and*	US Supreme Court, *Dred Scott* v. *Sandford*, 60 U. S. 393 [1857]	In *Dred Scott* v. *Sandford*, the US Supreme Court ruled that African Americans could not be citizens and that the federal government could not regulate slavery in the new states. In *Grzelczyk*, the Court pointed out that EU citizenship was 'destined' to provide the foundation statute for Member State nationals in other Member States.

(*cont.*)

Dimensions / Obstacles	Cases EU	Cases Member States	Notes
	Secretary of State for Education and Skills [2005] ECR I-02119 Case C-158/07, *Jacqueline Förster* v. *Hoofddirectie van de Informatie Beheer Groep* [2008] ECR I-08507 Case C-135/08, *Janko Rottmann* v. *Freistaat Bayern* [2010] ECR I-01449 Case C-256/11, *Murat Dereci and Others* v. *Bundesministerium für Inneres* [2011] ECR I-11315 Case C-85/96, *María Martínez Sala* v. *Freistaat Bayern* [1998] ECR I-02691 Case C-34/09, *Gerardo Ruiz Zambrano* v.		In *Martínez Sala, Ruiz Zambrano, Akrich, Bidar, Förster, Rottmann* and *Dereci*, the Court elaborated on 'genuine enjoyment of substance of citizenship rights'.

(*cont.*)

Dimensions / Obstacles	Cases EU	Cases Member States	Notes
	Office national de l'emploi (ONEm) [2011] ECR I-01177		
No religious homogeneity	Case 41/74, *Yvonne van Duyn* v. *Home Office* [1974] ECR 01337 Case C-159/90, *The Society for the Protection of Unborn Children Ireland Ltd* v. *Stephen Grogan and others* [1991] ECR I-04685		In *van Duyn* and *Grogan*, the Court defended the right to religious tolerance.
No homogeneity of values	Case 294/83, *Parti écologiste 'Les Verts'* v. *European Parliament* [1986] ECR 013391 Case C-280/11 P, *Council of the European Union* v. *Access Info Europe*, Judgment of the Court (First Chamber) of 17		*Les Verts* suggests that homogeneity is not required, in contradiction of some national constitutional scholars. In *Access Info Europe*, the Court ruled in a straightforward way that democracy and transparency are

(*cont.*)

Dimensions / Obstacles	Cases EU	Cases Member States	Notes
	October 2013, not yet reported Case 29/69, *Erich Stauder* v. *City of Ulm – Sozialamt* [1969] ECR 00419 Case 4/73, J. *Nold, Kohlen- und Baustoffgroßhandlung* v. *Commission of the European Communities* [1974] ECR 00491 Joined Cases C-92/09 and C-93/09, *Volker und Markus Schecke GbR (C-92/09) and Hartmut Eifert (C-93/09)* v. *Land Hessen* [2010] ECR I-11063 Case C-236/09, *Association Belge des Consommateurs Test-Achats ASBL and Others* v. *Conseil des*		constitutional values of Europe. In *Stauder* and *Nold*, the Court ruled that 'the court is bound to draw inspiration from constitutional traditions common to the Member states'. In *Volker and Eifert* and *Test-Achats*, the Court ruled that the Charter of Fundamental Rights serves as a basis to engage in legislative review of EU norms. In *Kadi*, the Court decided that even UN Security Council Resolutions and the UN Charter cannot trump the priority of fundamental rights in the EU system.

(cont.)

Dimensions / Obstacles	Cases EU	Cases Member States	Notes
	ministres [2011] ECR I-00773 Joined Cases C-402/05 P and C-415/05 P, *Yassin Abdullah Kadi and Al Barakaat International Foundation* v. *Council of the European Union and Commission of the European Communities* [2008] ECR I-06351 T-112/98, *Mannesmannröhren-Werke* v. *Commission*, 20 February 2001, [2001] ECR II-729		
No social and linguistic homogeneity	Case C-361/01 P, *Christina Kik* v. *Office for Harmonisation in the Internal Market (Trade Marks and Designs)*		In *Christina Kik*, the Court of Justice defended a pragmatic approach to languages where a balance between official languages and

(*cont.*)

Dimensions / Obstacles	Cases EU	Cases Member States	Notes
	(OHIM) [2003] ECR I-08283		economic expense for translation services could be struck. In other words, the Court of Justice here embarked on a centralizing trend in language policy that was previously known only at the level of nation states.
	Joined Cases C-274/11 and C-295/11, *Kingdom of Spain and Italian Republic* v. *Council of the European Union*, Judgment of the Court (Grand Chamber) of 16 April 2013, not yet reported		In *Spain and Italy* v. *Council*, thc Court resoundingly rejected the notion that the exclusion of Italian and Spanish in an EU patent could constitute a misuse of powers or violation of the enhanced cooperation powers in Art. 20 TEU.
	Case C-281/98, *Roman Angonese* v. *Cassa di Risparmio di Bolzano SpA* [2000] ECR I-04139		In *Angonese*, the Court decided on the basis that linguistic diversity is a protected
	Case No 51/2006, 19 April 2006, Belgian Constitutional Court, www.const-court.be/public/f/2006/2006-051f.pdf.		
	Case C-212/06, *Government of*		

(*cont.*)

Dimensions / Obstacles	Cases EU	Cases Member States	Notes
	Communauté française and Gouvernement wallon v. *Gouvernement flamand*, [2008] ECR I-01683		right in Europe that the requirement to use a particular language could be a restriction on free movement. In *Wallonia* v. *Flanders*, the Belgian Constitutional Court had made a preliminary reference to the CJEU, but the latter stated that constitutional decisions of linguistic politics should be left to national courts.
No common European public space for political debate	Case C-280/11 P, *Council of the European Union* v. *Access Info Europe*, Judgment of the Court (First Chamber) of 17 October 2013, not yet reported Case C-518/07, *European Commission* v. *Federal*	GFCC, *Lisbon Treaty*, BVerfG, 2 BvE 2/08 of 30 June 2009 GFCC, *Solange I*, BVerf 37 of 29 May 1974 GFCC, *Maastricht Treaty*, BVerfGE 89, 155 of 12 October 1993 GFCC, *European Stability*	In his Opinion in *Access Info Europe*, AG Cruz Villalon put forward a very participatory model of democracy for the EU. In the federal interplay between the Union and its Member States, Member States are not permitted

(*cont.*)

Dimensions / Obstacles	Cases EU	Cases Member States	Notes
	Republic of Germany (Personal data processing) [2010] ECR I-01885 Opinion of AG Bot in Case C-300/11, *ZZ* v. *Secretary of State for the Home Department*, not yet reported	*Mechanism Treaty*, Decision of 12 September 2012 in 2 BvR 1390/12, 2 BvR 1421/12, 2 BvR 1438/12, 2 BvR 1439/12, 2 BvR 1440/12, 2 BvE 6/12, etc. Applications for the issue of a temporary injunction GFCC, *OMT*, 2 BvR 2728/13 of 14 January 2014 Polish Constitutional Tribunal, *Lisbon Treaty*, Case K 32/09	to argue that they should be treated as foreign sovereigns. In *Lisbon Treaty*, the GFCC expressed a more traditional view of representative democracy. In *Personal data processing*, the Court considered that it sufficed that an institution is bound by law to be considered democratic as long as independent courts can review its decisions, in contradiction to the view of Germany. In *ZZ*, AG Bot confirmed that democratic values should be given primacy to the extent that this would not result in 'suicide of democracy itself'.

(*cont.*)

Dimensions / Obstacles	Cases EU	Cases Member States	Notes
			Solange I and *Maastricht* are relevant as to whether a homogenous European *demos* is required for constitutionalization of the EU. In the *Polish Lisbon Treaty* case, the Court warned that the Treaty must not undermine the identity of the Polish Constitution. In the *German Lisbon Treaty* case and the *ESM* case, the GFCC reiterated its conviction that real democratic legitimacy can only stem from the national legal order. In *OMT*, the GFCC referred a question to the CJEU for the first time.

(*cont.*)

Dimensions / Obstacles	Cases EU	Cases Member States	Notes
Civitas			
Lack of unitary elections	Joined Cases C-393/07 and C-9/08, *Italian Republic and Beniamino Donnici* v. *European Parliament* [2009] ECR I-03679 Case C-370/12, *Thomas Pringle* v. *Government of Ireland*, Judgment of the Court (Full Court) of 27 November 2012, not yet reported Case C-208/03 P, *Jean-Marie Le Pen* v. *European Parliament* [2005] ECR I-06051 Case C-145/04, *Kingdom of Spain* v. *United Kingdom of Great Britain and Northern*	GFCC, *5% Hurdle European Election*, 2 BvC 4/10 of 9 November 2011 ECtHR, *Matthews* v. *United Kingdom* (Application No. 24833/94) (1991) 28 E.H. R.R. 361 French Conseil d'Etat, *Nicolo* [1990] 1 Common Market Law Review 173; French Conseil d'Etat, Assemblée, du 20 octobre 1989, No. 108243 English High Court, *The Queen on the application of Chester* v. *(1) Secretary of State for Justice and (2) Wakefield*	In *5% Hurdle European Election*, the GFCC doubted the ability of the polity to develop constitutionally, given that only rudimentary EU legislation is in place for EU elections, which are largely governed by Member State rules. However, given that the European Parliament does not have many important or relevant government functions, a lack of cohesion engendered by fragmentation of voting rules and systems should not really prevent it from fulfilling its limited role at present. The specific functions of

(*cont.*)

Dimensions / Obstacles	Cases EU	Cases Member States	Notes
	Ireland [2006] ECR I-07917 Case C-300/04, *M. G. Eman and O. B. Sevinger* v. *College van burgemeester en wethouders van Den Haag* [2006] ECR I-08055	*Metropolitan District Council* [2009] EWHC 2923 (Admin)	the European Parliament are not such as to require a stable majority. In *Donnici*, the CJEU clarified that the European Parliament has no power to challenge the administration of these elections, even when it believes that the Member State in question did not follow its own procedures. In *Pringle*, the Court stated that it had jurisdiction to ensure that the conditions for the simplified Treaty amendment procedure are observed. It seems that the post-Lisbon Court is at least willing to engage with the problem of the EU still

(*cont.*)

Dimensions / Obstacles	Cases EU	Cases Member States	Notes
			being largely driven as an elite project in which mainly governments have the overall and final decision-making power. In *Le Pen*, the Court maintained that it is the Member State decision in election matters that binds the EU institutions. *Matthews* v. *UK* in the European Court of Human Rights declared the lack of organizing EU European Parliament elections in Gibraltar to be a human rights violation. In the *Gibraltar Election* case, the Court held that it was part of the constitutional tradition of the UK to grant nationals of the

(*cont.*)

Dimensions / Obstacles	Cases EU	Cases Member States	Notes
			Commonwealth the right to vote; thus, any exclusion would pose significant questions concerning discrimination. In *Eman*, the Court confirmed that Member State nationals in overseas countries and territories enjoy full EU citizenship rights, but then left it to the Member States to decide if those EU citizens had the right to vote in EU elections. However, the Court highlighted the strong impact of the principle of non-discrimination meaning that citizens in similar situations would have to be treated in an equal way. In *Nicolo*, the Conseil d'Etat, in

(*cont.*)

Dimensions / Obstacles	Cases EU	Cases Member States	Notes
			a ruling concerning EU elections, concluded that international treaties that are applied equally by the treaty partners take precedence over ordinary national law, thus recognizing supremacy. In *ex parte Chester*, the English High Court rejected an application by a prisoner on whole life tariff to be admitted to elect in the European Election, indirectly reaffirming the importance of European elections.
No European-wide parties	Case 294/83, *Parti écologiste 'Les Verts'* v. *European Parliament* [1986] ECR 01339		In *Les Verts*, the ECJ recognized the special role that political parties play in the European Parliament and

(*cont.*)

Dimensions / Obstacles	Cases EU	Cases Member States	Notes
	Joined Cases T-222/99, T-327/99 and T-329/99, *Jean-Claude Martinez, Charles de Gaulle, Front National, and others* v. *Parliament* [2001] ECR II-02823 Case C-267/08, *SPÖ Landesorganisation Kärnten* v. *Finanzamt Klagenfurt* [2009] ECR I-09781		in the EU political process. In *Front National,* the Court highlighted the importance of political parties in the decision-making process and took again a very federal decision indicating that, even though a mixed party grouping was not allowed for the Front National, the party as a national party was not affected. In *SPÖ Landesorganisation Kärnten,* the Court of Justice concluded that the party was not liable for VAT because of political party privilege.
Lack of one real president	Case C-77/11, *Council of the European Union* v. *European Parliament*	GFCC Cases	The *Budget signature* case suggested that politically the Court does not

(*cont.*)

Dimensions / Obstacles	Cases EU	Cases Member States	Notes
	(*Budget signature*) Judgment of the Court (Grand Chamber) of 17 September 2013, not yet reported		have any appetite for a strong president in the European Union.
The European Parliament is not the only law-maker	Case 294/83, *Parti écologiste 'Les Verts'* v. *European Parliament* [1986] ECR 01339 Case C-176/03, *Commission of the European Communities* v. *Council of the European Union* (Environmental Crimes) [2005] ECR I-07879	GFCC, *5% Hurdle European Election*, 2 BvC 4/10 of 9 November 2011 GFCC, *Zuwanderungsgesetz 2002*, 2 BvF 1/02 of 18 December 2002 English High Court, *The Queen on the application of Chester* v. *(1) Secretary of State for Justice and (2) Wakefield Metropolitan District Council* [2009] EWHC 2923 (Admin)	In *5% Hurdle European Election*, the GFCC ruled that a 5% hurdle for political parties was unconstitutional in EU elections, because the European Parliament does not require functioning like a Member State parliament that elects a government. The European Parliament participates only in the law-making of the Union and thus does not

(*cont.*)

Dimensions / Obstacles	Cases EU	Cases Member States	Notes
		Irish High Court, *Redmond* v. *Minister for the Environment* [2001] IEHC 128 (31st July, 2001)	require a stable majority. In *Zuwanderungsgesetz 2002*, the GFCC decided that the federal institution has a different legal status from Länder and the law of the federal level does not intrude on the Länder level. In other words, federal institutions develop their own characteristics that are not derived from Länder law. *Les Verts* shows that the Parliament has an elevated position within the constitutional order of the European Union. In the *Environmental Crimes* case, the Court decided that Member States have an obligation to

(*cont.*)

Dimensions / Obstacles	Cases EU	Cases Member States	Notes
			adopt a measure under the Community Pillar competences if that is possible, thus strengthening the Parliament's competences. In *ex parte Chester*, the English High Court decided that the European Parliament cannot be treated as a lesser institution and thus its elections were of high importance to the judge. The Irish High Court in *Redmond* decided that a deposit of 1,000 EUR to stand in Irish and European elections was unconstitutional because the European Parliament had to be treated as a

(*cont.*)

Dimensions / Obstacles	Cases EU	Cases Member States	Notes
			representation of the people.
The Council of the European Union cannot serve as a senate	Case C-246/07, *European Commission* v. *Kingdom of Sweden (PFOS)* [2010] ECR I-03317 Case C-370/12, *Thomas Pringle* v. *Government of Ireland*, Judgment of the Court (Full Court) of 27 November 2012, not yet reported	GFCC, *Zuwanderungsgesetz 2002*, 2 BvF 1/02 of 18 December 2002 GFCC, *Lisbon Treaty*, BVerfG, 2 BvE 2/08 of 30 June 2009 GFCC, *OMT*, 2 BvR 2728/13 of 14 January 2014	In *Zuwanderungsgesetz 2002*, the GFCC found that the Bundesrat respects the constitutional order of the Länder 'without itself resorting to guidance or determination which would undermine the constitutional space of a Länder. In *Lisbon Treaty* before the GFCC, it was argued that the views of opposition parties are not receiving any representation in the Council and that, where a majority voting applies, a minister cannot be held accountable to the Council's decisions by his national

(*cont.*)

Dimensions / Obstacles	Cases EU	Cases Member States	Notes
			parliament when he has been outvoted. In *PFOS*, the ECJ stated that the EU principle of loyalty mandated that Sweden must refrain from making a submission without support in the Council when the EU and all its Member States participated in the negotiation of an international environmental instrument. In *Pringle*, the CJEU highlighted that Member States are free to conclude international agreements among themselves in Council in areas outside of EU competences and they are free to attribute further functions to the

(*cont.*)

Dimensions / Obstacles	Cases EU	Cases Member States	Notes
			EU institutions if they so decide. In *OMT*, the GFCC criticized the open-ended nature of Council mandates, requiring increased involvement not just of the government but also of the German Bundestag when financial expenditure is involved in Council decisions.
The foundational documents of the Union are international treaties, not a constitution	Case 41/74, *Yvonne van Duyn* v. *Home Office* [1974] ECR 01337 Case 149/77, *Gabrielle Defrenne* v. *Société anonyme belge de navigation aérienne Sabena* [1978] ECR 01365	GFCC, *Lisbon Treaty*, BVerfG, 2 BvE 2/08 of 30 June 2009 GFCC, *European Stability Mechanism Treaty*, 2 BvR 1390/12, 2 BvR 1421/12, 2 BvR 1438/12, 2 BvR 1439/12, 2 BvR 1440/12, 2 BvE 6/12, etc. of 12 September 2012	In *van Duyn* and in *Defrenne*, the Court concluded that citizens can rely directly on the treaties before national and EU courts and these provisions also apply horizontally between private citizens. It thus recognized the importance of the treaty and applied it as a

(*cont.*)

Dimensions / Obstacles	Cases EU	Cases Member States	Notes
		Czech Constitutional Court, *Slovak Pensions* case	Constitutional Court would apply a constitution. In the *Lisbon Treaty* and *ESM* cases, however, the GFCC considered the EU Treaties as special international treaties that require for their operation special democratic legitimacy granted by an informed and consulted German Parliament, rather than as a Constitution.
Ius			
No single rule of law	Case 6/64, *Flaminio Costa* v. *E.N.E.L.* [1964] ECR 00585 Case 106/77, *Amministrazione delle Finanze dello Stato* v.	Czech Constitutional Court Decision footnote 754 US Supreme Court, *Ware* v. *Hylton*, 3 U.S. (3 Dall) 199 (1796)	The cases *Ware* v. *Hylton*, *McCulloch* v. *Maryland*, *Martin* v. *Hunter's Lessee*, *Cohens* v. *Virginia*, and *Ableman* v. *Booth*

(*cont.*)

Dimensions / Obstacles	Cases EU	Cases Member States	Notes
	Simmenthal SpA. [1978] ECR 00629 Case C-285/98, *Tanja Kreil* v. *Bundesrepublik Deutschland* [2000] I-00069 Case C-399/09, *Marie Landtová* v. *Česká správa socialního zabezpečení* [2011] ECR I-05573 Case C-127/07, *Société Arcelor Atlantique et Lorraine and Others* v *Premier ministre*, Ministre de l'Écologie et du Développement durable and Ministre de l'Économie, des Finances et de l'Industrie [2008] ECR I-09895	US Supreme Court, *McCulloch* v. *Maryland*, 17 U.S. (4 Wheat) 316 (1819) US Supreme Court, *Martin* v. *Hunter's Lessee*, 14 U.S. 304 (1816) US Supreme Court, *Cohens* v. *Virginia*, 19 U.S. 264 (1821) US Supreme Court, *Ableman* v. *Booth*, 62 U.S. 506 (1859) US Supreme Court, *Marbury* v. *Madison*, 5 U.S. (1 Cranch) 137 (1803) GFCC, *Hochschulrahmengesetz 2*	demonstrate the ability of the US Supreme Court to overturn state laws. In *Marbury* v. *Madison*, it was determined by the US Supreme Court that constitutional review by the judiciary against the will of a legislature was possible in the US. In *Martin* v. *Hunter's Lessee*, the US Supreme Court said that states were sovereign but that 'every state had lost part of its sovereignty when it accepted the Constitution and therefore all states were subject to the rulings of the Supreme Court'.

(*cont.*)

Dimensions / Obstacles	Cases EU	Cases Member States	Notes
	Case C-399/11, *Stefano Melloni* v *Ministerio Fiscal*, Judgment of the Court (Grand Chamber) of 26 February 2013, not yet reported	BvF 2/02 of 27 July 2004 Canada, Privy Council, *The Attorney General of Canada* v. *The Attorney General of Ontario and others* [1937] UKPC 6 Czech Constitutional Court, Decision of 31 January 2012, Pl. ÚS 5/12, Slovak Pensions	In *McCulloch* v. *Maryland*, the US Supreme Court established its right to review state governmental acts. In *Hochschulrahmengesetz*, the GFCC interpreted Article 70 of the Grundgesetz as giving reserve powers to the federated level. The ILO Labour Conventions Case in the Privy Council established a certain respect for the jurisdiction of the provincial governments and their right to be consulted even in international affairs that concern their constitutional competences.

(*cont.*)

Dimensions / Obstacles	Cases EU	Cases Member States	Notes
			In *Costa*, the Court stated that 'the executive force of community law cannot vary from one State to another in deference to subsequent domestic laws, without jeopardizing the attainment of the objectives of the treaty'. In *Simmenthal*, the Court decided that any deviation from a common project, no matter at what level inside the Member State, cannot be accepted in an autonomous legal order. In *Tanja Kreil*, the Court ruled that the non-discrimination Directive trumped a German Constitutional provision.

(*cont.*)

Dimensions / Obstacles	Cases EU	Cases Member States	Notes
			In *Slovak Pensions,* the Czech Constitutional Court declared the Landtová CJEU decision to be ultra vires and thus decided that it should not be followed in the Czech Republic. The CJEU had required the referring court to set aside important decisions of the Czech Constitutional Court. In *Arcelor*, the Court acknowledged the historic occasion of having the highest French public law court refer a case, but ruled the Emission Trading Scheme to be legal. In *Melloni*, the CJEU did not pay particular attention to the fact that a constitutional

(*cont.*)

Dimensions / Obstacles	Cases EU	Cases Member States	Notes
			court asked a question. Rather, it oddly decided that, in the end, it was for Spanish constitutional law to decide the issue.
No powerful unitary federal Court system	Case C-459/03, *Commission of the European Communities* v. *Ireland* [2006] ECR I-04635 Case 283/81, *Srl CILFIT and Lanificio di Gavardo SpA* v. *Ministry of Health* [1982] ECR 03415 Case 244/80, *Pasquale Foglia* v. *Mariella Novello* [1981] ECR 03045	US Supreme Court, *Bush* v. *Gore*, 531 U.S. 98 (2000)	In *Bush* v. *Gore*, the Supreme Court majority decided that a state Supreme Court cannot arrogate to itself power that violates the equal protection rights of citizens, even if a citizen is a candidate for president of the United States. In *Commission* v. *Ireland*, it was confirmed that Member States are barred from engaging in any other international dispute resolution than the CJEU in areas that fall within EU competence.

(*cont.*)

Dimensions / Obstacles	Cases EU	Cases Member States	Notes
			In *CILFIT*, it was found that (with small exceptions) there is a general obligation for EU Member States and their applicable courts to refer cases involving interpretation of the EEC Treaty or EU Community law to the European Court. The Court also extensively discussed the question of discretion to hear cases, both on the side of the Member State court and by the Court of Justice. In *Foglia* v. *Novello*, the Court claimed the power to review the admissibility of all cases. The court at the centre thus forced the courts at the periphery to

(*cont.*)

Dimensions / Obstacles	Cases EU	Cases Member States	Notes
			facilitate its centre role.
No clear procedures for selection of Justices	Case F-112/06, *Erika Krcova* v. *Court of Justice of the European Communities* [2007] ECR FP-I-A-1-00305; FP-II-A-1-01723 Case T-498/07 P, *Erika Krcova* v. *Court of Justice of the European Communities* [2009] ECR FP-I-B-1-00035; FP-II-B-1-00197		The *Erika Krcova* case is an example of non-retention of a lawyer-linguist after an initial trial period. The function of the Court and the appointment of judges have not yet been part of a Court proceeding.
No federal Court powers of constitutional review	Case 6/64, *Flaminio Costa* v. *E.N.E.L.* [1964] ECR 00585 Case 26/62, *NV Algemene Transport – en Expeditie Onderneming van Gend & Loos* v. *Nederlands Administratie de Belastingen*	US Supreme Court, *Marbury* v. *Madison*, 5 U.S. (1 Cranch) 137 (1803) Czech Constitutional Court, Decision of 31 January 2012, Pl. ÚS 5/12, Slovak Pensions	In *Marbury* v. *Madison*, the US Supreme Court found constitutional review to be a 'natural' consequence of the existence of a written constitution. It claimed the right in principle to strike down laws adopted by the

(*cont.*)

Dimensions / Obstacles	Cases EU	Cases Member States	Notes
	[1963] ECR 00003 Case 283/81, *Srl CILFIT and Lanificio di Gavardo SpA* v. *Ministry of Health* [1982] ECR 03415 Case 240/78, *Atalanta Amsterdam BV* v. *Produktschap voor Vee en Vlees* [1979] ECR 02137 Case 114/76, *Bela-Mühle Josef Bergmann KG* v. *Grows-Farm GmbH & CO. KG* [1977] ECR 01211 Case C-375/96, *Galileo Zaninotto* v. *Ispettorato Centrale Repressione Frodi – Ufficio di Conegliano – Ministero delle risorse agricole, alimentari e*	GFCC, *Mobilcom*, 2 BvR 2661/06 of 6 July 2010	democratic institutions. In *Costa*, the Court found that EU Member States had created a new legal order that could not be unilaterally altered by a single Member State. In *van Gend*, the Court found that EU rules had direct effect and thus could be relied upon by individuals directly in the national courts and the EU courts. In *CILFIT*, the Court stated that supremacy means that the EU courts, and by extension Member State courts after a preliminary reference, have the power to set aside national

(*cont.*)

Dimensions / Obstacles	Cases EU	Cases Member States	Notes
	forestali [1998] ECR I-06629 Case C-144/04, *Werner Mangold* v. *Rüdiger Helm* [2005] ECR I-09981		law that is found to be in violation of EU law. In *Atalanta, Bela-Mühle*, and *Galileo*, the CJEU reviewed the legality of acts against the treaties and against general principles such as proportionality, legal certainty and predictability. In *Slovak Pensions*, the Czech Constitutional Court seemed to be unhappy with the way the CJEU exercised its power of judicial review. The Czech Court in particular criticized the fact that its own determination was set aside by the CJEU. In its view, this was considered an ultra vires act because the Czech Court

(*cont.*)

Dimensions / Obstacles	Cases EU	Cases Member States	Notes
			considered that the CJEU has no competence to review Member State constitutional court decisions. The GFCC decided in *Mobilcom* that *Mangold* was not ultra vires because it followed normal standards of interpretation. This ruling was strongly criticized by a dissenting opinion in the case.
Court jurisdiction vis-à-vis the Member States is undetermined	Case 22/70, *Commission of the European Communities* v. *Council of the European Communities (European Agreement on Road Transport (ERTA)* [1971] ECR 00263 Opinion 1/94, Opinion of the Court of 15	US Supreme Court, *National League of Cities* v. *Usery*, 426 U. S. 833 (1976) US Supreme Court, *Garcia* v. *San Antonio Metropolitan Transit Authority*, 469 U.S. 528 (1985) US Supreme Court, *New*	*National League of Cities* v. *Usery* was the only case prior to the 1990s in which the US Supreme Court chose to strike down a federal statute because it was seen to violate states' rights to regulate – and even this one case was expressly overturned in

(*cont.*)

Dimensions / Obstacles	Cases EU	Cases Member States	Notes
	November 1994 on the Competence of the Community to conclude international agreements concerning services and the protection of intellectual property, [1994] ECR I-05267 Case C-376/98, *Federal Republic of Germany* v. *European Parliament and Council of the European Union (Tobacco Advertising)* [2000] ECR I-08419 Case C-380/03, *Germany* v. *European Parliament and Council (Tobacco Advertising II)* [2006] ECR I-11573	*York* v. *United States*, 505 U.S. 144, 157 (1992) US Supreme Court, *Mack and Printz* v. *United States*, 521 U.S. 898 (1997) US Supreme Court, *Reno* v. *Condon*, 528 U. S. 149 (2000) US Supreme Court, *State of Missouri* v. *Holland*, 252 U. S. 416 (1920) Environmental Code Case [1999] footnote 889	*Garcia* v. *San Antonio*. The Tenth Amendment later took on greater importance for cases such as *New York* v. *United States* and *Printz* v. *United States*. In the case of Reno, the US Supreme Court upheld the federal statute, but only because it did not compel state authorities to act. In the *ERTA* case, the Court confirmed the Commission's opinion that an internal competence that was exercised had to be mirrored by an external competence so as not to allow Member States to undermine internal Union rules through

(*cont.*)

Dimensions / Obstacles	Cases EU	Cases Member States	Notes
	Case C-84/94, *United Kingdom of Great Britain and Northern Ireland* v. *Council of the European Union (Working Time)* [1996] ECR I-05755 Case C-399/11, *Stefano Melloni* v. *Ministerio Fiscal*, Judgment of the Court (Grand Chamber) of 26 February 2013, not yet reported Case C-617/10, *Åklagaren* v. *Hans Åkerberg Fransson*, Order of the Court (Grand Chamber) of 7 May 2013, not yet reported Opinion 1/09, Opinion of the Court (Full Court) of 8		international treaties. This has been considered to be an expansive interpretation. In Opinion 1/94, the Court added the caveat that there could be mixed agreements where both the Union and Member States shared competences and that these had to be negotiated and ratified by both. *Tobacco Advertising I* is a rare case where the Court struck down a legislative act for complete lack of competence. This did not occur, however, in *Tobacco Advertising II*. In the *Working Time* case, the CJEU decided that if the Council came to

(*cont.*)

Dimensions / Obstacles	Cases EU	Cases Member States	Notes
	March 2011 on the draft agreement for the creation of a unified patent litigation system – European and Community Patents Court [2011] ECR I-01137 Case 6/64, *Flaminio Costa* v. *E.N.E.L.* [1964] ECR 00585 Case 26/62, *NV Algemene Transport – en Expeditie Onderneming van Gend & Loos* v. *Nederlands Administratie de Belastingen* [1963] ECR 00003		the political conclusion that the objectives of the action could not be sufficiently achieved by Member States, it was not for the Court to second guess this assessment. The Court therefore gave only lip service to subsidiarity. In *Melloni* and *Akerberg Fransson*, the Court decided that Charter rights were applicable whenever Member States act in the sphere of EU law. In Opinion 1/09, the CJEU went a step further, declaring that Member State courts have to be regarded as EU courts when they apply EU law. In *State of Missouri* v. *Holland*, the

(*cont.*)

Dimensions / Obstacles	Cases EU	Cases Member States	Notes
			US Supreme Court demonstrated that a constitutional polity does not require clearly defined competences or division thereof at the moment of founding. These competences could develop over time and can be part of a living constitution. In *van Gend*, the Court created the common ground for EU Member States to apply and thus rely on EU law directly, rather than merely through implementation of EU legal norms into their own legal order. In *Costa* v. *E.N.E.L.*, the Court further strengthened a core of European rule of law by

(*cont.*)

Dimensions / Obstacles	Cases EU	Cases Member States	Notes
			assigning supremacy to European rules where they existed.
No federal Court kompetenz-kompetenz		GFCC, *Mobilcom*, 2 BvR 2661/06 of 6 July 2010 GFCC, *Lisbon Treaty*, BVerfG, 2 BvE 2/08 of 30 June 2009	In *Mobilcom*, the GFCC decided that the 'Mangold judgment of the European Court of Justice does not transgress Community competence in a constitutionally objectionable manner'. In the *Lisbon Treaty* judgment, the GFCC stated that the Grundgesetz does not permit the transfer of Kompetenz-Kompetenz to the EU.
No common criminal law or police force	Case C-176/03, *Commission of the European Communities* v. *Council of the European Union (Environmental*	GFCC, *Lisbon Treaty*, BVerfG, 2 BvE 2/08 of 30 June 2009	In the *Lisbon Treaty* judgment, the GFCC drew the connection between criminal law and democracy. It noted that it is not clear that

(*cont.*)

Dimensions / Obstacles	Cases EU	Cases Member States	Notes
	Crimes) [2005] ECR I-07879		the EU does have a common criminal law. In the *Environmental Crimes* case, the Court sided with the Commission against no fewer than sixteen Member States, addressing the case of environmental crimes by deciding that a legislative act under consideration should have been adopted under the Environmental competence, not the Justice and Home Affairs competence.
Lack of a common and effective system to protect human rights	Case 11/70, *Internationale Handelsgesellschaft mbH* v. *Einfuhr- und Vorratsstelle fur Getreide und Futtermittel* [1970] ECR 01125	GFCC, *Solange I*, BVerf 37 of 29 May 1974 GFCC, *Solange II*, BVerfGE 73 of 22 October 1986	In *Internationale Handelsgesellschaft*, the CJEU denied reliance on the fundamental rights of a Member State. The GFCC, in *Solange I*, however,

(*cont.*)

Dimensions / Obstacles	Cases EU	Cases Member States	Notes
	Case 29/69, *Erich Stauder* v. *City of Ulm – Sozialamt* [1969] ECR 00419 Case 4/73, J. *Nold, Kohlen- und Baustoffgroßhandlung* v. *Commission of the European Communities* [1974] ECR 00491 Case T-112/98, *Mannesmannröhren-Werke AG* v. *Commission of the European Communities* [2001] ECR II-00729 Joined Cases C-92/09 and C-93/09, *Volker und Markus Schecke GbR (C-92/09) and Hartmut Eifert (C-93/09)* v. *Land Hessen* [2010] ECR I-11063		contradicted the CJEU in finding that 'the guarantee of fundamental rights in the Constitution prevails as long as the competent organs of the Community have not removed the conflict of norms in accordance with the Treaty mechanism'. In *Solange II*, the GFCC held that the Union, through the jurisprudence of the CJEU, had now reached such a level of human rights protection that the GFCC would refrain from reviewing EU acts so as to establish their human rights compatibility. In *Stauder* v. *Ulm*, the Court decided that it could read

(*cont.*)

Dimensions / Obstacles	Cases EU	Cases Member States	Notes
	Case C-399/11, *Stefano Melloni* v. *Ministerio Fiscal*, Judgment of the Court (Grand Chamber) of 26 February 2013, not yet reported		human rights protection into the treaties by way of general principles 'as they result from the constitutional traditions common to the Member States'.
	Case C-617/10, *Åklagaren* v. *Hans Åkerberg Fransson*, Order of the Court (Grand Chamber) of 7 May 2013, not yet reported Joined Cases C-411/10 and C-493/10, *N.S. (C-411/10)* v. *Secretary of State for the Home Department and M.E. and Others (C-493/10)* v. *Refugee Applications Commissioner and Minister for Justice, Equality and Law*		In *Stauder*, *Internationale Handelsgesellschaft* and *Nold*, the Court recognized that many different human rights are protected in the constitutions of Member States, and found that the CJEU will only recognize those rights that are truly 'common' to the Member States. In *Mannesmannröhren-Werke*, the Court stated that though companies enjoy the right to privacy in the German

(*cont.*)

Dimensions / Obstacles	Cases EU	Cases Member States	Notes
	Reform [2011] ECR I-13905		Constitution, it is not clear that such a right should be protected in the entire EU. In *Volker and Eifert*, the CJEU for the first time struck down an EU legislative act for breach of the Charter of Fundamental Rights. *Melloni* and *Åckerberg Fransson* strongly confirmed the impression that fundamental rights remain valid and applicable when Member States act in the sphere of EU law. In the *Saeedi (N.S.)* case, the CJEU said that the Protocol on the Application of the Charter in the United Kingdom

(*cont.*)

Dimensions / Obstacles	Cases EU	Cases Member States	Notes
			and Poland does not provide for a carve-out, simply a clarification.
No foreign relations according to the rule of law	Case C-91/05, *Commission of the European Communities* v. *Council of the European Union (ECOWAS)* [2008] ECR I-03651	GFCC, *Lisbon Treaty*, BVerfG, 2 BvE 2/08 of 30 June 2009 US Supreme Court, *Rasul* v. *Bush*, 542 U.S. 466, 487 (2004) US Supreme Court, *Boumediene* v. *Bush*, 128 S Ct 2229, 2248 (2008)	In the *Lisbon Treaty* case, the GFCC declared that decision-making in the CFSP area had a very close link to the realization of democracy. The GFCC considered foreign relations, such as deployment of the military, as one of the core elements of a sovereign State. *Rasul* v. *Bush* and *Boumediene* v. *Bush* in the US Supreme Court demonstrate that when it comes to foreign relations in the US, which are at their core an executive function, any type of judicial review is hard fought and even harder won.

(*cont.*)

Dimensions / Obstacles	Cases EU	Cases Member States	Notes
			In the *ECOWAS* case, the Court decided that it had the power to review compliance with Art. 40 TEU. In other words, it played the role of guardian against encroachment of the Union competences on CSFP measures adopted exclusively by the Member States in Council.

TABLE OF LEGISLATION

Source	Components Cited (if any)
European Union	
Treaties and Protocols	
Treaty establishing the European Coal and Steel Community, ECSC Treaty, 18 April 1951	Article 9
Treaty establishing the European Economic Community (EEC), 25 March 1957	Articles 4(1), 138(3), 191, 223, 226, 227 and 234
Single European Act 1985 (OJ 1987 L 169 p.1)	
Treaty of Maastricht on European Union (OJ 1992 C 191 p.1)	Preamble, 3b
Treaty of Amsterdam amending the Treaty on European Union, the Treaties establishing the European Communities and certain related acts (OJ 1997 C 340 p.1)	Title I section 9 (amending Title I), Title VII Article 3(10)
Charter of Fundamental Rights of the European Union (OJ 2000 C 364 p.1)	Articles 10, 12(2), 29–32, 39, 51 and 53
Protocol on the Application of the Charter of Fundamental Rights of the European Union to Poland and to the United Kingdom (OJ 2012 C 326 p.313)	
Treaty of Nice Amending the Treaty on European Union (OJ 2001 C 80 p.1)	Article 1(1)
Treaty establishing a Constitution for Europe (OJ 2004 C 310 p.1)	Articles I-6 and I-8

(*cont.*)

Source	Components Cited (if any)
Treaty of Lisbon amending the Treaty on European Union and the Treaty establishing the European Community (OJ 2007 C 306 p.1)	Articles 1(Preamble) and 1(158)
Protocol on the Role of National Parliaments in the European Union OJ 2007 C 306 p.148)	
Protocol on the Application of the Principles of Subsidiarity and Proportionality (OJ 2007 C 306 p.150)	
Lisbon Treaty Declaration by the Kingdom of Belgium, the Republic of Bulgaria, the Federal Republic of Germany, the Hellenic Republic, the Kingdom of Spain, the Italian Republic, the Republic of Cyprus, the Republic of Lithuania, the Grand-Duchy of Luxembourg, the Republic of Hungary, the Republic of Malta, the Republic of Austria, the Portuguese Republic, Romania, the Republic of Slovenia and the Slovak Republic on the symbols of the European Union (OJ 2007 C 306 p.267)	
Treaty establishing the European Stability Mechanism (OJ 2011 L 91 p.1)	
Treaty on the Functioning of the European Union (OJ 2012 C 326 p.1)	Articles 2(6), 20, 45(4), 51, 88, 207(2), 207(3), 218(6), 228, 253, 255, 258, 259, 267, 311, 352 and Part 5, Title II
Treaty on European Union (OJ 2012 C 326 p.1)	Articles 1, 2, 3, 4, 5, 6(1), 6(3), 7, 9, 10, 14(1), 14(2), 14(3), 15, 16(9), 17(2), 19(2), 20, 40, 48(6), 48(7), 49 and 50

(*cont.*)

Source	Components Cited (if any)
Regulations and Directives	
Regulation No. 1/1958 determining the languages to be used by the European Economic Community (OJ L 17, 6.10.1958, p.385)	
Regulation (EU) No. 1219/2012 of the European Parliament and of the Council of 12 December 2012 establishing transitional arrangements for bilateral investment agreements between Member states and third countries (OJ 2012 L 351 p.40)	
Council Directive No. 76/207/EEC of 9 February 1976 on the implementation of the principle of equal treatment for men and women as regards access to employment, vocational training and promotion, and working conditions (OJ 1976 L 39 p.40)	
Directive No. 95/46/EC of the European Parliament and of the Council of 24 October 1995 on the protection of individuals with regard to the processing of personal data and on the free movement of such data (OJ 1995 L 281 p.31)	
Directive No. 2003/88/EC of the European Parliament and of the Council of 4 November 2003 concerning certain aspects of the organization of working time (OJ 2003 L 299 p.9)	
Directive No. 2009/12/EC of the European Parliament and of the	

(cont.)

Source	Components Cited (if any)
Council of 11 March 2009 on airport charges (OJ 2009 L 70 p.11)	
Directive No. 2009/29/EC of the European Parliament and of the Council amending Directive 2003/87/EC so as to improve and extend the greenhouse gas emission allowance trading scheme of the Community (OJ 2009 L 140 p.63)	
Other Legal Sources	
Resolution of the European Council on the Stability and Growth Pact Amsterdam, 17 June 1997 (OJ 1997 C 236 p.1)	
Rules of Procedure of the European Parliament (OJ 1999 L 202 p.1)	Rule 29(1)
The Laeken Declaration on the Future of the European Union, Laeken, 15 December 2001, European Union Document SN 273/01	
Act concerning the election of the representatives of the Assembly by direct universal suffrage (OJ 1976 L 278 p.1) as amended by Council Decision of 25 June 2002 and 23 September 2002 amending the Act concerning the election of the representatives of the European Parliament by direct universal suffrage, annexed to Decision 76/787/ECSC, EEC, EURATOM (OJ 2002 L 283 p.1)	Articles 1, 2, 7(2) and 12
Preliminary draft Constitutional Treaty, drawn up by the Praesidium, which the President presented at the European Convention's Plenary session on 28 October 2002, CONV 369/02	Article 19

(*cont.*)

Source	Components Cited (if any)
The European Convention, Secretariat, Contribution by members of the Convention, 'Initiative for the incorporation of the Charter of Fundamental Rights into the European Constitution', 11 March 2003, CONV 607/03	
The European Convention, Proposal of the Polish members of the European Convention – Mr. Edmund Wittbrodt, Mrs. Danuta Huebner, Mr. Jozef Oleksy, Mrs. Genowefa Grabowska, Mr. Janusz Trzciński and Mrs. Marta Fogler	
Council of Europe	
The Convention for the Protection of Human Rights and Fundamental Freedoms of 4 November 1950 [European Convention on Human Rights]	
Draft revised agreement on the accession of the European Union to the Convention for the Protection of Human Rights and Fundamental Freedoms	
United Nations	
Charter of the United Nations of 26 June 1945	
Argentina	
The Constitution of the Argentine Nation: Approved by the National Constituent Assembly, March 11th, 1949	

(*cont.*)

Source	Components Cited (if any)
Canada	
Constitution Act 1867	
Canadian Bill of Rights 1960	
Canadian Charter of Rights and Freedoms, Constitution Act 1982	
Quebec Charter of Values [Charte des valeurs québécoises], Proposed Bill 60, 2013, Quebec National Assembly	
Czech Republic	
Constitution of the Czech Republic of 16 December 1992; Constitutional Law No. 1/1993 Coll. as amended by Act No. 347/1997 Coll. 300/2000 Coll., 448/2001 Coll. 395/2001 Coll., 515/2002 Coll. and 319/2009 Coll.	Article 10a
Germany	
Nationality Law of the German Empire and States of 22 July 1914 [Reichs- und Staatsangehörigkeitsgesetz]	
Basic Law for the Federal Republic of Germany of 23 May 1949 [Grundgesetz]	Articles 20(4), 21, 30, 51(1), 51(3), 53a (1), 70, 72(2), 79(3), 93, 146 and the emergency clauses of 1969
Lindau Agreement of 14 November 1957	
Switzerland	
Federal Constitution of the Swiss Confederation of 12 September 1848	
Federal Constitution of the Swiss Confederation of 18 April 1999	Articles 3 and 47
Federal Supreme Court Act of 17 June 2005	Article 95
United Kingdom	
Magna Carta of 15 June 1215	
Acts of Union 1707	

(*cont.*)

Source	Components Cited (if any)
European Union Act 2011	Section 4
United States of America	
Declaration of Independence of 4 July 1776	
Articles of Confederation 1777–1781	
Constitution of the United States 1787	Articles I, II, VI and IX and Amendments X, XIV, XV, XVII and XXVII and Amendments I–X (Bill of Rights)
Judiciary Act of 1789, 1 Stat 73 (1789)	
National Security Act of 1947, PL 80–235, 61 Stat 496 (1947)	

ABBREVIATIONS

AC	Appeal Cases Law Reports
AfD	*Alternative für Deutschland*
AG	Advocate General
BBC	British Broadcasting Corporation
BIT	bilateral investment treaty
BVerfG	*Bundesverfassungsgericht*
BVerfGE	*Entscheidungen des Bundesverfassungsgerichts*
CFR	Charter of Fundamental Rights
CFSP	Common Foreign and Security Policy
CIA	Central Intelligence Agency
CJEU	Court of Justice of the European Union
CONV	The European Convention
EC	European Community
ECB	European Central Bank
ECHR	European Convention on Human Rights
ECJ	European Court of Justice
ECOWAS	Economic Community of West African States
ECR	European Court Reports
ECSC	European Coal and Steel Community
ECtHR	European Court of Human Rights
EEC	European Economic Community
EHRR	European Human Rights Reports
EJIL	*European Journal of International Law*
EP	European Parliament
ESM	European Stability Mechanism
ETS	Emission Trading Scheme
EU	European Union
EUR	euro
EURATOM	European Atomic Energy Community
EWHC	High Court of Justice of England and Wales
FBI	Federal Bureau of Investigation
FCC	Federal Constitutional Court

FDI	foreign direct investment
FN	*Front National*
FRG	Federal Republic of Germany
FTA	free trade agreement
GFCC	German Federal Constitutional Court
GG	*Grundgesetz*
GHG	greenhouse gas
GNP	gross national product
IEHC	High Court of Ireland
IGC	intergovernmental conference
ILO	International Labour Organization
ILSA	International Law Students Association
IMF	International Monetary Fund
ITLOS	International Tribunal for the Law of the Sea
LSE	London School of Economics and Political Science
LTF	*Loi sur le Tribunal fédéral*
MEP	Member of the European Parliament
OECD	Organisation for Economic Co-operation and Development
OJ	Official Journal
PPU	*Procédure préjudicielle d'urgence*
RuStAG	*Reichs- und Staatsangehörigkeitsgesetz*
TCE	Treaty establishing a Constitution for Europe
TEC	Treaty establishing the European Community
TEU	Treaty on European Union
TFEU	Treaty on the Functioning of the European Union
UACES	University Association for Contemporary European Studies
UK	United Kingdom
UKIP	UK Independence Party
UKPC	Privy Council of the United Kingdom
UKSC	Supreme Court of the United Kingdom
UN	United Nations
US	United States
USA	United States of America
VAT	value-added tax
WTO	World Trade Organization

1

Introduction

1.1 European Constitutionalization Questioned

1.1.1 *Crisis and Constitutional Order in Europe*

In both the court of public opinion and modern legal scholarship, our Europe of today appears to lurch from crisis to crisis.[1] These crises are political, cultural, social, environmental and now also economic. A severe financial crash has sent shockwaves around the continent, exposing the fault lines in Europe's institutions and constitution.[2] After the near-collapse of Greece's national economy, the EU focused heavily on inventing new mechanisms to provide economic stability for the euro-currency countries. However, deeper issues with the broader European project, which had festered in the dark for years, were revealed and thrown into stark relief

[1] M. Dawson and F. de Witte, 'Constitutional Balance in the EU after the Euro-Crisis' (2013) 76 *Modern Law Review* 817–44; J.-C. Piris, *The Future of Europe: Towards a Two-Speed EU?* (New York 2012); F. Laursen (ed.), *The EU and the Eurozone Crisis: Policy Challenges and Strategic Choices* (Farnham 2013); M. Beblavý, D. Cobham and L. u. Ódor, *The Euro Area and the Financial Crisis* (Cambridge 2011); P. Arestis and M. Sawyer, *The Euro Crisis* (Basingstoke 2012); P. R. Lane, 'The European Sovereign Debt Crisis' (2012) 26 *The Journal of Economic Perspectives* 49–67; A. Georgosouli, 'The Financial Crisis in Constitutional Perspective: The Dark Side of Functional Differentiation' (2012) 10(4) *International Journal of Constitutional Law* 1174–7; P. F. Kjaer, G. Teubner and A. Febbrajo, *The Financial Crisis in Constitutional Perspective: The Dark Side of Functional Differentiation* (Oxford 2011); S. Deakin, 'Social Policy, Economic Governance and EMU: Alternatives to Austerity', Cambridge Working Papers (Cambridge 2013); A. Blundell-Wignall, 'Solving the Financial and Sovereign Debt Crisis in Europe' (2012) 2011(2) *OECD Journal: Financial Market Trends* 201; H. Hofmeister, 'To Bail Out or Not to Bail Out? Legal Aspects of the Greek Crisis' (2011) 13 *Cambridge Yearbook of European Legal Studies* 113.

[2] F. Chaltiel, 'Les crises de l'Europe' (September 2011) No. 551 Revue de l'Union européenne 485.

by the financial floodlights. Most recently the COVID-19 global health crisis also challenged the EU with Member States initially reacting unilaterally but realising that by collaborating the crisis could be more effectively addressed. The 'quick fixes' sought by European decision-makers addressed only their perception of victimization in the hands of global financial markets and neglected to establish a longer-term solution for troublesome questions of governance. While the European public was informed about the near-disintegration of their economic and social system,[3] these events unfolded almost without their support or even their engagement. Bruce Ackerman rightly argues that the EU's crisis is constitutional in nature. He argues that there are three different paths of constitutional contestation and fundamental law-making: the French tradition by which revolutionaries enshrine in the constitution the values that inspired their struggle, the UK tradition of elite reform preventing revolutionary movements before they happen and the German tradition of constitutionalization inspired by outsiders or foreign influences. He thus calls the EU's constitutional crisis cultural and perhaps Brexit is one expression of the level of utter dissonance between these different constitutional pathways inside the EU.[4] This work tries to follow his call and 'provoke Europeans to think more deeply about the distinctive mix of constitutional cultures currently prevailing on the continent'.[5]

The crises are also constitutional in nature because of the response to answer them each chosen by the institutions. This allows us to refer back to David Dyzenhaus, who aptly argued that the Constitution of Law, especially in times of crisis, has to rely on the courts more than the other branches of government. He explained:

> I will respond to that challenge in arguing that judges have a constitutional duty to uphold the rule of law even, perhaps especially, in the face of indications from the legislature or the executive that they are trying to withdraw from the rule-of-law project. Indeed, the legislature and the executive have that same duty to uphold the rule of law in emergency times no less than in ordinary times, which is why judges are entitled to assert the rule of law in the face of what seem to be legislative or executive indications to the contrary.[6]

[3] T. Risse, *European Public Spheres* (Cambridge 2014).
[4] B. A. Ackerman, 'Three Paths to Constitutionalism – and the Crisis of the European Union' (2015) 45 *British Journal of Political Science* 705.
[5] Ibid. 716.
[6] D. Dyzenhaus, *The Constitution of Law: Legality in a Time of Emergency* (Cambridge 2006) 4.

In other words, the reaction by the courts to overcome crisis is increasingly important.

A new dimension of crisis was added in 2016 when the British Prime Minister first attempted to re-negotiate some of the fundamentals of the European economic integration project and then lost a referendum vote in which the Leave campaign blamed virtually all economic ills of the UK on the European Union. This new constitutional crisis could perhaps trigger a renewed reflection in the EU and it is thus timely to discuss European constitutionalization.

One answer, pushed in particular by Germany, was provided through a new wave of constitutionally balanced budget provisions. In a December 2011 Intergovernmental Conference (IGC) in Brussels, the European Council, comprising the Heads of State and Governments of the EU's then twenty-seven Member States, agreed to adopt yet another reform treaty, enshrining the balanced budget ideology and imposing very tight controls on national budgets. During a further January 2012 EU Summit in Brussels, a Stability and Growth Pact was adopted by twenty-five EU Member States. The Pact added yet another chapter to the step-by-step incremental governance building book, which is being written by and for the EU over the last sixty years. At the same time, it re-obscured, and perhaps even evaded, concerted efforts to understand the more fundamental problems in the EU's constitutionalization process.

How should the European Union overcome these crises? Which opportunities should be explored? Which obstacles should become Europe's central concerns? To date, the political discussions have focused upon the next feeble steps to be taken in Europe's policy of incrementalism,[7] characterized by formal intergovernmental amendment of the Constitutional Treaties.[8] Yet to overcome the succession of financial, institutional and constitutional crises shaking the EU, a more considered approach to further constitutionalization is required. The debate is deliberately shifted towards a previously under-researched dimension of EU constitutionalization,

[7] On this 'step-by-step process of constitution-making' seen with the Amsterdam Treaty, Wiener and Neunreither wrote that '[t]he 1996–7 IGC demonstrated that the heads of the EU member states and governments were in no mood for radical changes, neither "forward" towards a state-like European centre of decision-making, nor indeed in any other distinguishable direction. On the contrary, the overall approach was rather incremental; it resembled a repair shop more than a design centre': A. Wiener and K. Neunreither, 'Introduction: Amsterdam and Beyond' in K. Neunreither and A. Wiener (eds.), *European Integration after Amsterdam: Institutional Dynamics and Prospects for Democracy* (Oxford 2000) 10.

[8] See D. Cameron, 'EU Speech at Bloomberg' [on the future of the EU and the UK's relationship with it] (23 January 2013), www.number10.gov.uk/news/eu-speech-at-bloomberg/.

which not only provides opportunities to help overcome the current series of crises but also presents a new approach to integration that takes seriously the perceptions and understandings of European jurisprudence with regard to federalism and the EU public sphere.[9]

The process of European constitutionalization is met with extensive scepticism, both in current national legal and political spheres and in broader circles of public opinion across Europe. By shedding light on these concerns, this book reveals a widespread misunderstanding of constitutional federalism, which permeates the Member State courts, popular media and many academic communities. A failure to address confusion over this fundamental concept is leading us towards an impoverished development of the EU's 'Second Constitution' and even ensuring that the role of both domestic and international European courts in enriching the constitutionalization process is overlooked and undervalued. In a bid to avoid such consequences, this book explores how federalism and further constitutionalization – rightly understood in a dialogue of the European courts – may actually change this process and allow a clearer advance to Europe's Second Constitution for, but also with, the people of Europe.

While the primary method is based on juridical analysis of over 240 court decisions between the centre European Courts and the periphery Member State courts over the past three decades, discussions are illustrated with examples from a number of other jurisdictions, to flesh out the concepts that are currently so misconceived in Europe.

Certainly, there is nothing very straightforward about the EU integration project and it does present some particular issues. Indeed, this book was originally inspired by the EU Constitutional Treaty process, which arguably did more harm to further constitutional development than it contributed to our advance.[10] EU constitutionalization is clearly no simple replica of US constitutionalization, transposed to a different continent 200 years later. Further, while the study of EU constitutional law

9 On existing integration theories, see the various contributions in A. Wiener, T. A. Börzel and T. Risse, *European Integration Theory*, 3rd ed. (Oxford 2018).

10 On the Constitutional Convention, see P. Craig, 'Constitutional Process and Reform in the EU: Nice, Laeken, The Convention and the IGC' (2004) 10 *European Public Law* 635; P. Norman, *The Accidental Constitution: The Making of Europe's Constitutional Treaty* (Brussels 2005); M. Rosenfeld, 'The European Convention and Constitution Making in Philadelphia' (2003) 1 *International Journal of Constitutional Law* 373–8; F. Galinas and L. Sirota, 'Constitutional Conventions and Senate Reform' (2013) 5 *Revue québécoise de droit constitutionnel* 107.

has become more common over time in continental Europe,[11] the use of comparative federalism tools continues to risk inaccurate or superficial analogies.[12] These errors are even more serious when they enter and influence what currently passes for European public policy discourse across key Member States and their allies. For instance, it caught both European and American headlines when Valéry Giscard d'Estaing, President of the Constitutional Convention, reviewed a biography of John Adams to prepare for his Convention tasks.[13] However, every standard text on EU law now contains a chapter on the constitutional

[11] W. Halstein, H. H. Götz and K.-H. Narjes, *Der unvollendete Bundesstaat – Europäische Erfahrungen und Erkenntnisse* (Dusseldorf 1969); R. Bieber, 'Verfassungsentwicklung und Verfassungsgebung in der Europäischen Gemeinschaft' in R. Wildenmann (ed.), *Staatswerdung Europas? Optionen für eine Europäische Union* (Baden-Baden 1991) 393; M.-T. Bitsch, *Histoire de la construction européenne de 1945 à nos jours* (Brussels 1999); A. Augustin, *Das Volk der Europäischen Union. Zu Inhalt und Kritik eines normativen Begriffs* (Berlin 2000); H.-J. Blanke, 'Der Unionsvertragvon Maastricht–EinSchrittaufdem Wegzueinem europäischen Bundesstaat' (1993) Die Öffentliche Verwaltung 412; P. Häberle, *Europäische Rechtskultur* (Baden-Baden 1994) 33. On European Constitutional law, see K. Bahlmann, 'Europäische Grundrechtsperspektiven' in B. Börner and K. Carstens (eds.), *Einigkeit und Recht und Freiheit – Festschrift für Karl Carstens zum 70* (Cologne 1984) 17; K. von Beyme, 'Fischers Griffnacheiner EuropäischenVerfassung' in C. Joerges, Y. Mény and J. H. H. Weiler (eds.), *What Kind of Constitution for What Kind of Policy? Responses to Joschka Fischer* (Cambridge, MA 2000) 61; P. Häberle, 'Gemeineuropäisches Verfassungsrecht' (1991) Europäische Grundrechte Zeitschrift 261; I. Pernice, 'Europäisches und nationales Verfassungsrecht' (2001) Veröffentlichungen der Vereinigung der Deutschen Staatsrechtslehrer 60, 148; I. Pernice, 'The European Constitution' (May 2001), paper presented at the 16th Sinclair House Talks in Bad-Homburg; H. Quandt Stiftung, *Europe's Constitution: A Framework for the Future of the Union* (Bad Homburg 2001) 18; I. Pernice, 'Multilevel Constitutionalism in the European Union' (2002) 27 *European Law Review* 511; A. Peters, *Elemente einer Theorie der Verfassung Europas* (Berlin 2001); A. Peters, 'Global Constitutionalism Revisited' (2005) 11 *International Legal Theory* 39; J. H. H. Weiler, 'The Transformation of Europe' (1991) 100 *Yale Law Journal* 2403; J. H. H. Weiler, 'Does Europe Need a Constitution? Reflections on Demos, Telos and the German Maastricht Decision' (1995) 1 *European Law Journal* 219; J. H. H. Weiler, 'European Neo-constitutionalism: In Search of Foundations for the European Constitutional Order' (1996) 44 *Political Studies* 517; J. H. H. Weiler, *The Constitution of Europe: 'Do the New Clothes Have an Emperor?' and Other Essays on European Integration* (Cambridge 1999); J. H. H. Weiler and M. Winds, *European Constitutionalism beyond the State* (Cambridge 2003); P. Costanzo, L. Mezzetti and A. Ruggeri, *Lineamenti di Diritto costituzionale dell'Unione Europea: Quarta edizione* (Torino 2014); A. Rosas and L. Armati, *EU Constitutional Law: An Introduction* (London 2018); S. Kadelbach (ed.), *Verfassungskrisen in der Europäischen Union* (Baden-Baden 2018).

[12] See for example a lecture given at Humboldt University, Berlin, 6 June 2002 by G. Burghardt, 'Die Europäische Verfassungsentwicklung aus dem Blickwinkel der USA' in A. Golze and E. Lenski (eds.), *Die europäische Verfassung im globalen Kontext* (Baden-Baden 2004) 41.

[13] L. Dembart, 'Giscard's Summer Reading: Federalism in the U.S.: The Future Europe Takes Form' (3 September 2002), *New York Times*.

dimension of integration.[14] And the Union's highest court, the Court of Justice (ECJ), decided in *Les Verts* that the founding treaties of the European Union can be described as '*la charte constitutionnelle de base*'.[15] Further, in the Advocate General Opinion in *Government of the French Community and Walloon Government* v. *Flemish Government* case,[16] AG Leo Sharpston not only described a Member State Constitution as a devolutionary cousin but also framed the Constitution in question as the result of a series of incremental adaptive changes similar to the EU itself.[17]

Of course, the European project remains far from being completely unique and immune to any comparison. The history of federal thought is rich, and thus far most works still focus on factual similarities without highlighting the history of ideas behind the polity. The

[14] See C. Barnard and S. Peers, *European Union Law* (Oxford 2014); or see P. Craig and G. de Búrca, *EU Law: Text, Cases, and Materials*, 5th ed. (Oxford 2011), whose discussion of constitutional pluralism at 297 is worth reviewing in detail.

[15] Case C-294/83, *Parti écologiste 'Les Verts'* v. *European Parliament* [1986] ECR 01339, at para. 23. Reflecting on the impact of the case decades later, see: K. Lenaerts, 'The Basic Constitutional Charter of a Community Based on the Rule of Law' in M. P. Maduro and L. Azoulai (eds.), *The Past and Future of EU Law: The Classics of EU Law Revisited on the 50th Anniversary of the Rome Treaty* (Oxford 2010) 295; A. Boerger and B. Davies, 'Imagining the Course of European Law?' in F. Nicola and B. Davies (eds.), *EU Law Stories: Contextual and Critical Histories of European Jurisprudence* (Cambridge 2017) 83–102.

[16] Case C-212/06, *Government of the French Community and Walloon Government* v. *Flemish Government*, Judgment of the Court (Grand Chamber) of 1 April 2008 [2008] ECR I-01683.

[17] Opinion of Advocate General Sharpston delivered on 28 June 2007, *Government of the French Community and Walloon Government* v. *Flemish Government*, C-212/06: The Belgian federal system, rather like a devolutionary cousin of the Community [K. Lenaerts, 'Constitutionalism and the Many Faces of Federalism' (1990) 38(2) *American Journal of Comparative Law* 205], did not come about as a result of a single plan. [See the well-known excerpt from the Schuman Declaration of 9 May 1950: 'Europe will not be made all at once, or according to a single plan. It will be built through concrete achievements which first create a de facto solidarity.' Press Conference, Robert Schuman, French Foreign Minister (May 9, 1950) (transcript available at www.robert-schuman.eu/declaration_9 mai.php).] It is the result of incremental changes, originally driven by the Flemish desire to gain cultural autonomy, which took form in the Communities, and the Walloon desire for economic autonomy, which was achieved through the Regions. For further enlightenment in English on the rather labyrinthine Belgian federal structure, see P. Peeters, 'The Federal Structure: Kingdom, Regions and Communities' in G. Craenen (ed.), *The Institutions of Federal Belgium: An Introduction to Belgian Public Law* (Leuven 1996) 55. For an in-depth analysis of the Belgian federal structure, see: A. Alen and K. Muylle, *Compendium van het Belgisch staatsrecht, Diegem* (The Hague 2004), 239–499 and M. Uyttendaele, *Précis de droit constitutionnel belge. Regards sur un système institutionnel paradoxal*, 3rd ed. (Brussels 2005) 815–1071.

primary contribution of this book, however, is its focus upon judicial decisions and what they can reveal to us. Somewhat akin to a common law approach to constitutional thought, this examination proves that, while in several key dimensions the critics of constitutionalization are wrong, a crucial obstacle remains to be overcome.

This chapter, by way of introduction, explains the central argument, rationale, assumptions and context of this work, outlines the methodology and data set studied, and provides a brief road map. Specifically, it begins by stating and explaining the central idea and its rationale. Second, it introduces current constitutional debates in the European Union, identifying current obstacles to three key dimensions of further constitutionalization. Third, it explains the legal research methodology, combining a 'common law' analysis of European jurisprudence with evocations of illustrative examples from other early federal projects. Fourth, it also outlines the structure and remaining progression of the volume.

1.1.2 Central Idea

Through a detailed analysis of Member State court jurisprudence and associated literature, I have evaluated the most important *demos*, *civitas* and *ius* dimensions of the European Constitutional project.

The term '*demos*' was coined to describe the political identity of the common people of an ancient Greek state. Today, the concept of *demos* is equally relevant, referring as it does to the populace of a democracy as a self-perceived, aware and organized political unit.[18] At its core, the term highlights that 'any type of majoritarian-based government would need a *demos* for such a system to be democratically legitimate. Thus, although a *demos* is a prerequisite for a democracy, the extent to which a *demos* is a prerequisite for democratic decision-making will depend on how it is intended that the making of certain decisions is going to be legitimized.'[19] The European *demos* dimension of European constitutionalization concerns the political cohesion of the people of the Union, the potential for Europe to develop a common European citizenship, values or attitude towards religion. *Demos* can also encompass a common European public space for deliberation and

[18] A. Stevenson (ed.), *Oxford Dictionary of English*, 3rd ed. (Oxford 2010).
[19] M. Jolly, *The European Union and the People* (New York 2007) 71.

effective communications through discussions in intelligible working languages.[20]

The term '*civitas*', also originally Latin, stands for the collection of rights attributed to a citizen or community, and in later years more broadly to a state.[21] Samuel von Pufendorf, often credited as the founder of modern constitutional law scholarship,[22] highlighted the importance of this dimension of constitutionalization as early as 1668, reflecting on *civitas composita* or the composite commonwealth of the Holy Roman Empire.[23] The *civitas* dimension of European constitutional development invokes the potential for a functioning EU institutional law, as highlighted by several courts and academics.[24] Important elements of *civitas*, for Europe, include EU democratic elections, European political parties, the role of the president in the EU, the function of the Council and the European Parliament, and the role of a foundational document.

Finally, the term '*ius*', in Latin, refers to the rule of law and respect for rights, which also includes more broadly the mandates of legal authorities and the functioning of effective courts of justice.[25] The term *ius* describes this dimension of constitutionalization, inspired by discussions in Europe of common structures in the law based on EU law and, in particular, general principles said to form a new kind of *Ius Commune*

[20] See Jolly, ch. 3; A. Moravcsik, 'In Defense of the "Democratic Deficit": Reassessing Legitimacy in the European Union' (2002) 40(4) *Journal of Common Market Studies* 603; D. M. Curtin, *Postnational Democracy: The European Union in Search of a Political Philosophy* (London 1997); A. Sbragia, 'Post-National Democracy as Post-National Democratization' in S. Fabbrini (ed.), *Democracy and Federalism in the European Union and the United States: Exploring Post-National Governance* (Abingdon/New York 2005) 167; A. D. Smith, 'National Identity and the Idea of European Unity' (1992) 68(1) *International Affairs* 55; German Federal Constitutional Court ['GFCC'], *Maastricht Treaty*, BVerfGE 89, 155 of 12 October 1993 ['*Maastricht Decision*'].

[21] J. Morwood (ed.), *Oxford Latin Dictionary: Latin–English*, 3rd ed. (Oxford 2012).

[22] R. M. Hatton, R. Oresko, G. C. Gibbs and H. M. Scott, *Royal and Republican Sovereignty in Early Modern Europe: Essays in Memory of Ragnhild Hatton* (Cambridge 1997) 456.

[23] S. Pufendorf, *Dissertatio de Republica irregulari* (Heidelberg 1668) ch. IV para. 9.

[24] See T. Kostakopoulou, 'Democracy-Talk in the European Union: The Need for a Reflexive Approach' (2003) 9 Columbia Journal of European Law 411; Y. Devuyst, 'The European Union's Constitutional Order? Between Community Method and Ad Hoc Compromise' (2000) 18 *Berkeley Journal of International Law* 1; M. Nettesheim, 'A Tribute to Professor Richard M. Buxbaum: Developing a Theory of Democracy for the European Union' (2005) 23 *Berkeley Journal of International Law* 358; M. Zuleeg, 'What Holds a Nation Together? Cohesion and Democracy in the United States of America and in the European Union' (1997) 45 *American Journal of Comparative Law* 505; GFCC, *Lisbon Treaty*, BVerfG, 2 BvE 2/08 of 30 June 2009 ['*Lisbon Decision*'], www.bverfg.de/entscheidungen/es20090630_2bve000208en.html.

[25] Morwood.

Europaeum, a common law uniting Europe,[26] as outlined in one of the most influential EU law book collections.[27] The term highlights the distinction between common law and civil law, but refers to the entire collection of rules and rule-making in Europe. In this sense, the *ius* dimension of European constitutionalization discusses the potential for a single rule of law in Europe, the structure of the EU Court System, the criminal law and police force, the system of human rights protection, as well as external relations law in the EU.[28]

I argue that it is in these three dimensions that EU constitutionalization has been judged by many periphery Courts to be either non-existent or deficient. At the root of these opinions is an impoverished understanding of federalism and its potential role in further European constitutionalization. This work demonstrates that the litany of obstacles commonly raised by Member State courts and academics have nearly all been overcome or were never challenges in the first place. Through case law analysis, it is also revealed that many Member State courts on the periphery do not fully appreciate either the constitutional nature of federations or the lived experiences of federalism in other jurisdictions.[29] The term 'obstacle' was chosen because the nature of the criticisms of European constitutionalization is manifold. Some include denial of the legal or doctrinal prerequisites of a federal structure' other reasons include empirical or socio-legal arguments. Some might term what this work calls 'obstacle' just a source of scepticism towards further integration, but, arguably, most constitutionalists go further and outright deny that constitutionalization can take place at the EU level. The term 'obstacle' captures this more fundamental scepticism. It is less a critique and more an outright denial that a supranational structure could be anything other than a (perhaps constitutional) order of sovereign states.[30]

Once many concerns have largely been dismissed, the most significant and potentially fatal remaining obstacle to EU constitutionalization can be

[26] X. Groussot, *Creation, Development and Impact of the General Principles of Community Law: Towards a Ius Commune Europaeum?* (Lund 2005).

[27] *Ius Commune Europaeum* book series Intersentia, https://intersentia.com/en/product/series/show/id/9164/.

[28] See the GFCC repeatedly in *Solange I*, BVerf 37 of 29 May 1974, *Solange II*, BVerfGE 73 of 22 October 1986, *Maastricht Decision* and *Lisbon Decision*. With an emphasis on fundamental rights (similar to *Solange I*), see D. Grimm, *Braucht Europa eine Verfassung?*, vol. 60 Siemens Stiftung (Munich 1995).

[29] See M. Burgess, *Comparative Federalism: Theory and Practice* (New York 2006).

[30] See A. Arnull, C. Barnard, M. Dougan and E. Spaventa (eds.), *A Constitutional Order of States? Essays in EU Law in Honour of Alan Dashwood* (Oxford/Portland, OR 2011).

identified: the absence of a strong and vibrant trans-European public sphere in which transparent, legitimate policy debates can occur. Corollary challenges such as lack of a pragmatic number of working languages, lack of unitary elections and important gaps in the central court's *Kompetenz-Kompetenz* also remain to be addressed. Overcoming this obstacle and its related challenges would do much to address the constitutional crisis and set Europe on a healthier path towards further constitutionalization.

My research further leads me to conclude that while a European constitutional moment might be the most straightforward step forward, it is currently not really on the political horizon. Other constitutional adaptive mechanisms offer further options. While incremental formal treaty amendments and fundamentally changed constitutional practices have helped to address certain other obstacles, given embedded Member State privileges, they are unlikely alone to be effective in addressing this remaining hurdle. Rather, I argue that there is a crucially decisive challenge to be taken up in the jurisprudence itself. Further constitutionalization can, in essence, be prepared by the concerted efforts of more courageous centre and periphery courts, through engaged and legitimate dialogues between the Courts of Europe themselves. Only by enabling and strengthening a vibrant pan-European public policy debate can Europe's Second Constitution one day become a reality.

1.1.3 Rationale and Scope of the Volume

By combining a 'common law constitutional approach' – the analysis of recent constitutional debates in Europe through the lens of the last three decades of jurisprudence from the European Courts in dialogue with national courts – with a comparison of several federal jurisdictions during the early stages of their federal development, this book provides a novel approach to the constitutionalization process in Europe. After analysing over 60 national court decisions and 180 decisions of the European Courts between 1952 and 2014, drawing examples from the comparative constitutional development of Germany, the United States, Canada, Argentina and Switzerland during their federal formative periods, I am convinced that many of the usual obstacles named for further EU constitutional development either have been overcome through radically different constitutional praxis (such as the '*Spitzenkandidaten*') or were founded on misconceptions. Through this research and analysis, I hope to show that certain obstacles to the *demos* dimension of European constitutionalization, such as the lack of certain forms of homogeneity as demanded by certain courts, are not actually needed for a federal structure. I found that for homogeneity of citizenship, homogeneity of values and religious homogeneity, much has already been established to a necessary degree through ECJ jurisprudence and law. Further, I argue that there is a stronger European *civitas* than several courts and academics believe. As developed by the Courts, it is observed that EU institutional law has begun to integrate democratic principles in its processes, including in the Commission, the presidents, the Council, the European Parliament, and it is clear that the lack of a foundational document has not hindered other constitutional processes. Finally, I observe that there already exists a fairly strong respect for the European *ius*, or rule of law. While much remains to be done, human rights protections are growing stronger in the EU and there are a corresponding hierarchy of norms for EU rule of law, a strong federal court, strong constitutional review powers and sufficient jurisdiction vis-à-vis the Member States.

The lack of a common European public space for democratic deliberations, however, clearly remains a significant obstacle to the further constitutionalization of Europe. Its corollary, lack of recognition for a functional number of working languages, hampers the *demos* dimension. European elections and the lack of EU-wide political parties, similarly, are corollary challenges for a truly European *civitas*. And I find a further corollary in the *ius* dimension in that the Union is still missing a forceful pronunciation of its own *Kompetenz-Kompetenz* and a European selection of judges. The obstacle that remains is the most important missing precondition for Europe's Second Constitution and thus is key to a comprehensive solution of the constitutional crisis.

1.2 Framing European Constitutionalization

1.2.1 Constitutional Foundations of Europe

Even the term 'European constitutionalization' seems to start controversial debates by its very use, in many Member States of the EU. It is impossible to understand the most recent episodes in the EU constitutionalization process, or what might be constructed in the future, without considering its original character. It has also been recognized, however, that there is a profoundly political, if not constitutional, dimension to these processes, even using these black-letter approaches.[31]

[31] See A. Stone Sweet, *The Judicial Construction of Europe* (Oxford 2004).

Originally, the EU was characterized entirely as an intergovernmental organization, agreed in a treaty of Member States, and from this perspective, many 'intergovernmentalists' view the trajectory of the EU as almost wholly determined by its Member State governments.[32] From a related perspective, the 'internationalists' have argued for the EU to be viewed as a very special international organization, such as Stein and Weiler in the early 1980s.[33] Variations of this approach are taken extremely seriously in continental European legal scholarship, though some followers all too often characterize their work with black-letter legal interpretation of EU rules,[34] coupled with a continuing underlying sentiment that Member States could easily change the rules if they disagreed with an outcome of an ECJ decision.[35]

From the intergovernmental perspective, prominent constitutional scholars, such as former German Federal Constitutional Court (GFCC) Judge Dieter Grimm, have raised fundamental objections to the constitutionalization process and to the idea of an EU constitutionalization in general.[36] Their main arguments can be summarized as follows: EU lawyers have negligently adopted the term 'constitution' for the EU

[32] A. Moravcsik, 'Negotiating the Single European Act' in R. Keohane and S. Hoffman (eds.), *The New European Community: Decisionmaking and Institutional Change* (Boulder, CO 1991) 41; G. Garrett, 'International Cooperation and Institutional Choice: The European Community's Internal Market' (1992) 46(2) *International Organization* 533; A. Moravcsik, 'Preferences, Power and Institutions in 21st-Century Europe' (2018) 56 *Journal of Common Market Studies* 1648; M. Kleine and M. Pollack, 'Liberal Intergovernmentalism and Its Critics' (2018) 56 *Journal of Common Market Studies* 1493. In recent years, a 'new intergovernmentalism' theory has also gained traction: C. J. Bickerton, D. Hodson and U. Puetter (eds.), *The New Intergovernmentalism: States and Supranational Actors in the Post-Maastricht Era* (Oxford 2015) 39; D. Hodson and U. Puetter, 'The European Union in Disequilibrium: New Intergovernmentalism, Postfunctionalism and Integration Theory in the Post-Maastricht Period' (2019) 26 *Journal of European Public Policy* 1153.

[33] E. Stein, 'Lawyers, Judges and the Making of a Transnational Constitution' (1981) 75 *American Journal of International Law* 1; Weiler, 'The Transformation of Europe', 2405.

[34] See the introduction to K. J. Alter, *The European Court's Political Power: Selected Essays* (Oxford 2009) 5.

[35] See A. Moravcsik, 'Preferences and Power in the European Community: A Liberal Intergovernmentalist Approach' (1993) 31(4) *Journal of Common Market Studies* 473.

[36] D. Grimm, 'Braucht Europa eine Verfassung?' (1995) 50 *Juristenzeitung* 581; D. Grimm, 'The European Court of Justice and National Courts: The German Constitutional Perspective after the Maastricht Decision' (1997) 3 *Columbia Journal of European Law* 229. Contradicting him is J. Habermas, *Die Einbeziehung des Anderen. Studien zur politischen Theorie* (Frankfurt 1996) 185. See also G. Hirsch, 'Kein Staat, aber eine Verfassung' (2000) Neue Juristische Wochenschrift 46; see more references in C. Dorau and P. Jacobi, 'The Debate over a "European Constitution": Is It Solely a German Concern?' (2000) 6(3) *European Public Law* 413, highlighting the very distinguished authors Grimm, Koenig, Isensee and Kirchhoff. For a more recent critique by Grimm, see D. Grimm, *The Constitution of European Democracy* (Oxford 2017) 81.

founding treaties, while the EU is actually best defined as an international organization *sui generis* that is constructed from the authority of the constitutional orders of Member States.[37]

On a more fundamental level, from this view, there is no possibility for the EU to develop a Constitution in the future and thus formal reform attempts are preordained to failure. The GFCC, in the *Lisbon Decision*, came to its determinations in the same spirit, focusing on the limits of EU constitutional development.[38] This perspective on federalism and the future of the constitutionalization process is seriously considered in this book. Dieter Grimm essentially raises three main sets of obstacles. First, he notes that Europe's founding treaties remain in treaty form and are much more detailed in their institutional arrangements than a 'real' constitution. He notes also that these are based on the principle of conferral, which, in Grimm's view, limits the possibility of the EU ever having a constitution.[39] His second and strongest argument, which also forms the primary reason for his belief that an EU Constitution would be undesirable, is the lack of a real democracy at the EU level, in particular the lack of a common society.[40] He argues that a 'common people' is required for constitutionalization, throwing into stark relief the absence of truly pan-European political parties, one common language, a single media and a unifying culture/history.[41] These rather surprising objections from a leading constitutional thinker have sparked interest. How can a legal scholar, one otherwise known for deeply liberal views, deny even the future possibility of an EU Constitution?[42] While these arguments inspired the study, it should be

[37] Grimm, *Braucht Europa eine Verfassung?*, vol. 60 Siemens Stiftung, 12.

[38] *Lisbon Decision*. On this case, see D. Halberstam and C. Mollers, 'The German Constitutional Court Says "Ja zu Deutschland!"' (2009) 10 *German Law Journal* 1241; G. Beck, 'The Lisbon Judgment of the German Constitutional Court, the Primacy of EU Law and the Problem of Kompetenz-Kompetenz: A Conflict between Right and Right in Which There Is No Praetor' (2011) 17 *European law Journal* 470; S. Theil, 'What Red Lines, If Any, Do the Lisbon Judgments of European Constitutional Courts Draw for Future EU Integration?' (2014) 15 *German Law Journal* 599, 602–4, 609–10; T. Drinoczi, 'Constitutional Identity in Europe: The Identity of the Constitution: A Regional Approach' (2020, forthcoming) *German Law Journal*, https://ssrn.com/abstract=3448407.

[39] Grimm, *Braucht Europa eine Verfassung?*, vol. 60 Siemens Stiftung, 12, 30–1.

[40] Ibid., 46.

[41] Ibid., 39, 41.

[42] There is an important debate as to the final objective of European integration: Is it to create the United States of Europe or has the EU in Lisbon reached the depth and width of possible integration between sovereign nations? See the seminal political science article M. Forsyth, 'The Political Objectives of European Integration' (1967) 43(3) *International Affairs* 483.

highlighted that Grimm published a book in 2017 in which he applies some of these critiques to the European Union that he argues has become over-constitutionalized.[43] He highlights the need for 'Europeanized elections and political parties' and sees greater involvement of Member State parliaments and Courts as answers to the legitimacy question, but his most fundamental objections, for example, are that 'decisions of extraordinary political importance continue to be made through a non-political mechanism. In many political decisions, the Commission and the Court continue to go it alone.'[44] This study attempts to show that similar dynamics exist in early federal polities and that a dialogue between centre and periphery courts can overcome such deficits.

1.2.2 *Failure of the European Constitutional Convention*

In the first decade of 2000, the EU entered a new phase of constitutional development. At first, a Constitutional Convention had led to a proposed European Constitutional Treaty in 2004.[45] After early enthusiasm about a Constitutional Treaty and a relatively successful Convention that agreed a draft text in June 2003, challenges began to emerge when several IGCs could not agree on the final treaty until June 2004 in Brussels. A sense of crisis began to build in the literature and among observers.[46] The proposed treaty was one of the most controversial documents adopted by the European Union and its Member States.[47] This treaty famously failed in two referenda, in France and the Netherlands, having been unable to overcome political and other concerns raised in the national public spheres of these countries.[48] As several commentators had predicted, a political

[43] D. Grimm, *The Constitution of European Democracy* (Oxford 2017).

[44] Ibid., 12.

[45] *Treaty Establishing a Constitution for Europe*, 16 Dec. 2004, 2004 O.J. (C 310) 1 ['*Constitutional Treaty*'].

[46] See *The Economist*, 'European Union: The Right Verdict on the Constitution: European Voters Should Reject the New Constitutional Treaty and Demand Something Better' (24 June 2004), www.economist.com/leaders/2004/06/24/the-right-verdict-on-the-constitution (a referee's red card covered the front as a sign by the European electorate).

[47] C. Eisgruber and J. H. H. Weiler, 'Preface' (2005) 3 *International Journal of Constitutional Law* 163.

[48] It has been argued by Craig that 'the rationale for the French and Dutch rejection of the Constitutional Treaty in national referenda had scant connection to anything novel in the Constitutional Treaty': P. Craig, 'Treaty Amendment, the Draft Constitution and European Integration' in N. W. Barber, M. Cahill and R. Ekins (eds.), *The Rise and Fall of the European Constitution* (Oxford 2019) 51.

crisis ensued in which the French and Dutch electorates rendered clearly negative votes on the treaty in referenda of May 2005.[49]

The failed Constitutional Convention did not result in the European Constitution for which many had hoped, but it did serve to completely restructure the 'constitutional arrangement' at the European level.[50] As *The Economist* concluded:

> For those who fancied that they were building a United States of Europe, a combined power with more people and a bigger economy than the United States of America, the double 'no' to the European Union's constitution from France on May 29th and the Netherlands on June 1st has been a cruel collision with reality. . . . The first [lesson from the negative vote] is that rejection of the constitution signals that the dream of deeper political integration and, in the 1957 Treaty of Rome's famous phrase, 'ever closer union', is over. Instead the EU should move in the direction of being a looser, less federalist and more decentralised club.[51]

There had been hopes that a possible 'no' vote would not be quite so definitive. After all, the Danish and the Irish had said 'no' in referenda regarding Europe before, then had eventually joined the consensus of other Member States.[52] But the political fall-out was significant and was seized upon by opponents to Europe, without adequate opportunity for the proponents to reply or even for an adequate public discussion to be held across the EU. It was the first time that two founding members of the European Union had rejected a further step in its integration. Many countries had predicted that the Polish and UK plebiscites would be the most difficult, and these countries eagerly agreed that they would not even hold referenda.[53] Of course, fifteen Member States plus two accession countries did actually agree to ratify the Treaty establishing a Constitution for Europe (TCE), including Spain, Germany and Luxemburg after

[49] *The Economist*, 'The Future of Europe: The Europe that Died; And the One that Should Live On' (2 June 2005), www.economist.com/leaders/2005/06/02/the-europe-that-died; *The Economist*, 'The European Union Constitution: Dead, but Not Yet Buried: Voters in France and the Netherlands Have Killed the EU Constitution' (2 June 2005), www.economist.com/europe/2005/06/02/dead-but-not-yet-buried.

[50] European Council, *The Future of The European Union: Laeken Declaration*, Presidency Conclusions, European Council Meeting in Laeken 14 and 15 December 2001, www.consilium.europa.eu/media/20950/68827.pdf ['*Laeken Declaration*'].

[51] Ibid.

[52] L. van Middelaar, *The Passage to Europe: How a Continent Became a Union* (New Haven, CT 2013).

[53] See A. Duer and N. Konstantinidis, 'Ratifying International Treaties by Referendum: The Case of the EU's Constitutional Treaty', LSE Working Paper (2012).

a successful referendum.[54] However, this was not sufficient for entry into force and, after a further period of nervous reflection, the least problematic elements of the TCE were transposed into the Treaty of Lisbon, which was duly adopted in December 2007 and entered into force on 1 December 2009.[55] In essence, many of the constitutional ideas discussed during the Convention later resurfaced in a slimmed-down Reform Treaty, the so-called Lisbon Treaty.[56] The Treaty of Lisbon brought a new constitutional reality; it sets a yardstick by which we can measure earlier developments.

After all these treaty amendments and failed constitutional treaty attempts, the questions remained: What is the best way forward for further constitutionalization? Is it even necessary? Is a Second Constitution desirable? Given the introduction of a 'referendum lock' for further changes to the European treaties in the UK European Union Act 2011, further fundamental changes are becoming increasingly improbable, and an adoption such as the Treaty of Lisbon as a 'mere amendment' to existing treaties without a series of popular votes (except in Ireland) appears less likely in the foreseeable future.[57] Unsurprisingly then, in this context, the comfortable familiarity of incrementalism

[54] European Foundation (the official EU foundation), Treaty establishing a Constitution for Europe, www.eurofound.europa.eu/observatories/eurwork/industrial-relations-dictionary/treaty-establishing-a-constitution-for-europe.

[55] P. Birkinshaw and M. Varney (eds.), *The European Union Legal Order after Lisbon* (Alphen aan den Rijn 2010).

[56] Treaty of Lisbon amending the Treaty on European Union and the Treaty establishing the European Community, 13 December 2007, 2007 OJ (C306) 1 ['Lisbon Treaty'].

[57] **Section 4: Cases where treaty or Article 48(6) decision attracts a referendum**

> Subject to subsection 4, a treaty or an Article 48(6) decision falls within this section if it involves one or more of the following – (a) the extension of the objectives of the EU as set out in Article 3 of TEU; (b) the conferring on the EU of a new exclusive competence; (c) the extension of an exclusive competence of the EU; (d) the conferring on the EU of a new competence shared with the Member States; (e) the extension of any competence of the EU that is shared with the Member States; (f) the extension of the competence of the EU in relation to – (i) the co-ordination of economic and employment policies, or (ii) common foreign and security policy; (g) the conferring on the EU of a new competence to carry out actions to support, co-ordinate or supplement the actions of Member States; (h) the extension of a supporting, co-ordinating or supplementing competence of the EU; (i) the conferring on an EU institution or body of power to impose a requirement or obligation on the United Kingdom, or the removal of any limitation on any such power of an EU institution or body; (j) the conferring on an EU institution or body of new or extended power to impose sanctions on the United Kingdom; [etc]. See www.legislation.gov.uk/ukpga/2011/12/contents/enacted.

became the go-to policy in further crises. As a response to the recent financial crisis, twenty-five of twenty-seven governments agreed on a separate European Fiscal Compact on 30 January 2012,[58] using the same incremental method of constitutional reform that appeared successful in the past.[59] It was a clear attempt to insulate constitutional change in a separate instrument, divorced from the main treaties. The problems with such an approach are numerous, and constitutional challenges to the Stability Pact have been threatened by the European Parliament and other parts of EU society. I could almost characterize the Stability Pact as a constitutional text adopted in times of crisis but without the necessary ingredients for fundamental change or the popular support that would bring democratic legitimacy.

This period of rapid constitutional flux, which has progressed from Convention, adoption, failure, to re-negotiation and finally adoption as Treaty, provides an excellent example of the strengths but also the weaknesses of European constitutional development. Indeed, while constitutions are dynamic and federal balances of power evolve over time, the starting point mattered.

Many reasons can be offered for the failure of this endeavour,[60] but, from a constitutional development perspective, the elite composition of the Constitutional Convention itself and its lack of deeper trans-European public engagement were not helpful for constitutional development.[61] Many commentators are clear that the Laeken

[58] On the Pact, see: A. Aumaitre, 'From the SGP to the TSCG through the Lenses of European Integration Theories' (2018) Bruges Political Research Papers 67/2018, aei.pitt.edu/97356/1/wp67_aumaitre.pdf; M. Kukk, 'Enhanced Fiscal Governance in the European Union: The Fiscal Compact' (2018) 5 *Baltic Journal of European Studies* 73; L. Besselink and J. H. Reestman, 'The Fiscal Compact and the European Constitutions: "Europe Speaking German"' (2012) 8 *European Constitutional Law Review* 1.

[59] On the becoming of the Fiscal Compact, see: B. Laffan and P. Schlosser, 'Public Finances in Europe: Fortifying EU Economic Governance in the Shadow of the Crisis' (2016) 38 *Journal of European Integration* 237, 243–5; S. Smeets and D. Beach, 'Political and Instrumental Leadership in Major EU Reforms: The Role and Influence of the EU Institutions in Setting-Up the Fiscal Compact' (2019) 27(1) *Journal of European Public Policy* 63, https://doi.org/10.1080/13501763.2019.1572211.

[60] It is perhaps because the stakes were so high and the title 'Constitution' carried so many connotations that significant questions were raised from the beginning. With such important issues being decided, it became crucial to determine if and how the Convention process would function and how its outcomes could lead to a successful and lasting Constitution.

[61] K. Nicolaidis, 'A View from the Ground Up' in N. W. Barber, M. Cahill and R. Ekins (eds.), *The Rise and Fall of the European Constitution* (London 2019) 41, 45–8;

mandate[62] served to pre-empt any significant constitutional development in the Convention, thus ensuring that the Convention ultimately amounted to little more than a run-of-the-mill treaty amendment.[63] Some feared from the beginning that the process would create only a paper tiger, unable to deliver substantive change, while others saw the Constitutional Convention as a key moment in European history.[64] The Convention was composed of the main parties involved in the debate on the future of the European Union.[65] The Laeken Declaration even provided for candidate States to take a full part in the proceedings without, however, being able to prevent any consensus that may emerge among the Member States. This composition extended beyond the Convention for the European Charter of Fundamental Rights, placing emphasis on the participation of European Parliamentarians. Further, in the Secretariat of the Convention, government experts and 'Eurocrats' were well represented. And in recognition of this new moment in European history, other important stakeholders were provided with spaces for participation, including the Eastern European accession states. This process failed, at least in terms of the 105 people who met to determine the fate of Europe. From this alone we can see that, going forward, securing and facilitating the involvement of the European People is critical.

N. Scicluna, 'When Failure Isn't Failure: European Union Constitutionalism after the Lisbon Treaty' (2012) 50 *Journal of Common Market Studies* 441, 445.

[62] European Council, 'The Laeken Declaration on the Future of the European Union', Annex 1 to the Presidency Conclusions of the European Council Meeting in Laeken, Brussels, 14–15 December 2001.

[63] J. H. H. Weiler, 'On the Power of the Word: Europe's Constitutional Iconography' (2005) 3 *International Journal of Constitutional Law* 173.

[64] Rosenfeld, 'The European Convention'.

[65] In addition to its Chairman and two Vice-Chairmen, the Convention was composed of fifteen representatives of the Heads of State or Government of the Member States (one from each Member State), thirteen representatives of the Heads of State or Government of the candidate States (one per candidate State), thirty representatives of the national parliaments of the Member States (two from each Member State), twenty-six representatives of the national parliaments of the candidate States (two from each candidate State), sixteen members of the European Parliament and two representatives of the European Commission. In addition, three eminent European politicians were appointed to the secretariat of the Convention by the European Council (Mr Valéry Giscard d'Estaing as Chairman of the Convention and Mr Giuliano Amato and Mr Jean-Luc Dehaene as Vice-Chairmen). The Economic and Social Committee (three representatives), the Committee of the Regions (six representatives), the social partners (three representatives) and the European Ombudsman were invited to attend as observers.

Some remained sceptical that integration by constitution would be possible.[66]

These debates to greater or lesser extent took place, and continue to take place, in each of the European Member States, rather than across the Union as a whole, though they were certainly heard on a global level.[67] The failure of the Treaty Establishing a Constitution for Europe appears to confirm the views of the constitutional critics and underscores the sense of European crisis.

The design of an otherwise-promising attempt of formal higher law-making in the EU was problematic from the beginning, arguing for the need to explore a more 'common law'-inspired approach to overcoming obstacles. The Convention was not directly elected but rather selected by European Member State parliaments. It was vested with a mandate from European governments. Public participation was thus stifled and, as such, it can be suggested that the European Union was not able to

[66] D. Grimm, 'Integration by Constitution' (2005) 3 *International Journal of Constitutional Law* 193, 194.

[67] G. A. Bermann, 'Executive Power in the New European Constitution' (2005) 3 *International Journal of Constitutional Law* 440–7; D. Chalmers, 'Judicial Authority and the Constitutional Treaty' (2005) 3 *International Journal of Constitutional Law* 448–72; P. Craig, 'European Governance: Executive and Administrative Powers under the New Constitutional Settlement' (2005) 3 *International Journal of Constitutional Law* 407–39; D. M. Davis, 'Constitutional Borrowing: The Influence of Legal Culture and Local History in the Reconstitution of Comparative Influence: The South African Experience' (2003) 1 *International Journal of Constitutional Law* 181–95; Eisgruber and Weiler, 'Preface', 163–4; Grimm, 'Integration by Constitution', 193–208; R. Hirschl, 'Preserving Hegemony? Assessing the Political Origins of the EU Constitution' (2005) 3 *International Journal of Constitutional Law* 269–91; M. Kumm and V. F. Comella, 'The Primacy Clause of the Constitutional Treaty and the Future of Constitutional Conflict in the European Union' (2005) 3 *International Journal of Constitutional Law* 473–92; M. P. Maduro, 'The Importance of Being Called a Constitution: Constitutional Authority and the Authority of Constitutionalism' (2005) 3 *International Journal of Constitutional Law* 332–56; F. C. Mayer, 'Competences – Reloaded? The Vertical Division of Powers in the EU and the New European Constitution' (2005) 3 *International Journal of Constitutional Law* 493–515; G. Palombella, 'Whose Europe? After the Constitution: A Goal-Based Citizenship' (2005) 3 *International Journal of Constitutional Law* 357–82; O. Pfersmann, 'The New Revision of the Old Constitution' (2005) 3 *International Journal of Constitutional Law* 383–404; Rosenfeld, 'The European Convention', 373–8; A. Sajó, 'Constitution without the Constitutional Moment: A View from the New Member States' (2005) 3 *International Journal of Constitutional Law* 243–61; A. von Bogdandy, 'The European Constitution and European Identity: Text and Subtext of the Treaty Establishing a Constitution for Europe' (2005) 3 *International Journal of Constitutional Law* 295–315; N. Walker, 'Europe's Constitutional Momentum and the Search for Polity Legitimacy' (2005) 3 *International Journal of Constitutional Law* 211–38; Weiler, 'On the Power of the Word', 173–90.

experience an overt liberal revolution[68] – there was no groundswell of public involvement and, arguably, discussion of the process was predominantly contained within expert and elite-led circles.[69] This is not to say that Constitutional Conventions should play no role in constitutional development. Part of constitutional development may well need to take place through Constitutional Conventions, whether or not they are constitutionally legitimate. As James Madison himself admitted, in certain instances the Philadelphia Convention 'departed from the tenor of their commission'.[70] For instance, he sought to justify the ratification through Conventions in the States, instead of the State legislators, and by only three-quarters of the States (instead of all) by referring to the will of the majority of all Americans.

Similar issues occurred for the European Constitutional Convention. Although the European Council (Art. 15 Treaty of European Union (TEU))[71] had decided that a Convention process on the Future of the

[68] B. A. Ackerman, *We the People: Vol. 1: Foundations* (Cambridge, MA 1991).

[69] J.-C. Piris, *The Constitution for Europe: A Legal Analysis* (Cambridge 2006) 22.

[70] J. Madison, 'The Federalist No. 40' in *The Federalist Papers* (1787–1788).

[71] Art. 15 TEU:

1. The European Council shall provide the Union with the necessary impetus for its development and shall define the general political directions and priorities thereof. It shall not exercise legislative functions.
2. The European Council shall consist of the Heads of State or Government of the Member States, together with its President and the President of the Commission. The High Representative of the Union for Foreign Affairs and Security Policy shall take part in its work.
3. The European Council shall meet twice every six months, convened by its President. When the agenda so requires, the members of the European Council may decide each to be assisted by a minister and, in the case of the President of the Commission, by a member of the Commission. When the situation so requires, the President shall convene a special meeting of the European Council.
4. Except where the Treaties provide otherwise, decisions of the European Council shall be taken by consensus.
5. The European Council shall elect its President, by a qualified majority, for a term of two and a half years, renewable once. In the event of an impediment or serious misconduct, the European Council can end the President's term of office in accordance with the same procedure.
6. The President of the European Council:
   (a) shall chair it and drive forward its work;
   (b) shall ensure the preparation and continuity of the work of the European Council in cooperation with the President of the Commission, and on the basis of the work of the General Affairs Council;
   (c) shall endeavour to facilitate cohesion and consensus within the European Council;

Union should develop the foundations of the European Union,[72] the Convention sought to be almost hyper-textualist. While the short text of the Laeken Declaration may have given the European Convention enough room for manoeuvre, it may also have tried too hard to respect boundaries set by the European Council.[73] There was a strong call from most Convention members, including its Chairman, for the proclamation and later ratification of the new European Constitution.[74] Yet the door to a Constitutional Convention has been firmly closed by the failure to ratify the CTE and the dynamism of any 'new beginning' after the EU's Constitutional Convention was lost.[75] Expectations were high, as can be seen from the arguments on terms. Some continued to describe the process as the drafting of a 'European Constitutional Treaty' or *Verfassungsvertrag*, while others referred clearly to the framing of a 'European Constitution' or *Europäische Verfassung*.[76]

Much depended on the subsequent debates, especially whether optimal federal structures could be chosen and developed for the new union and its federated members. The dynamism was shattered when the final draft resembled closely the existing European Union rather than adopting notable changes that served to accelerate integration. Discussions did

(d) shall present a report to the European Parliament after each of the meetings of the European Council.

The President of the European Council shall, at his level and in that capacity, ensure the external representation of the Union on issues concerning its common foreign and security policy, without prejudice to the powers of the High Representative of the Union for Foreign Affairs and Security Policy.The President of the European Council shall not hold a national office.

[72] In the words of the Heads of State, the task of the convention is 'to consider the key issues arising for the Union's future development and try to identify the various possible responses'; see *Laeken Declaration*. On the background leading up to the Convention, see: Craig, 'Treaty Amendment'.

[73] The fact that the mandate is formulated in questions does not make the limits of the mandate clearer; see *Laeken Declaration*: 'The question ultimately arises as to whether this simplification and reorganisation [of the existing four EU Treaties] might not lead in the long run to the adoption of a constitutional text in the Union. What might the basic features of such a constitution be? The values which the Union cherishes, the fundamental rights and obligations of its citizens, the relationship between Member States in the Union?'

[74] Piris, *The Constitution for Europe*, 42.

[75] Piris, *The Future of Europe*, 7; D. Hodson and I. Maher, 'EU Treaty Making and the Partial Eclipse of the IGC' in D. Hodson and I. Maher (eds.), *The Transformation of EU Treaty Making* (Cambridge 2018) 57, 78.

[76] See the European Convention, Secretariat, Contribution by members of the Convention, 'Initiative for the incorporation of the Charter of Fundamental Rights into the European Constitution', 11 March 2003, CONV 607/03.

include concern for what the ECJ would do with provisions with significantly greater scope, but it appears that there was next to no comparative analysis or analysis of the existing case law in preparation for the Constitutional Treaty provisions.

My key observation from this study's review of the literature is that failure has become the single most recurring theme across historical examples of constitutionalization, even as it also characterizes recent attempts to advance the European process. Most commentators agree that the failed Constitution triggered the first fundamental constitutional crisis in the EU. The elite-driven Constitutional Convention process failed to deliver on the objectives of constitutional development for Europe and, given the high stakes, it is understandable that this failed constitutionalization process triggered a constitutional crisis that to this day remains to be overcome. However, the history of most federal entities is full of failures and new beginnings. It is clear not only that a failed project can contain valuable lessons but also that there are very diverse ways to advance a constitutionalization process. Public constitutional debates take place on multiple levels, both raising and assisting in overcoming obstacles to constitutional development, through these processes. I believe, and will argue in this book, that a better understanding of the dynamics between central and periphery courts, particularly as they address Europe's capacity for broader public debates, could have facilitated attempts to address the real (as opposed to presumed) obstacles to European constitutionalization.

If deeper integration is, indeed, the best answer to the continuing crisis, what are the key dimensions at play in laying the preconditions for a real 'constitutional moment' for Europe?

According to certain jurists, such as Joseph Weiler, Neil Walker and Kalypso Nicolaidis, what was needed was not a decisive Constitutional Convention – instead, they assert that further constitutional development of the Union was and is possible within the existing constitutional framework.[77] I suggest that this is only partially wrong. To a great extent, obstacles identified by the Member State courts can be overcome when interpreted in the light of a more informed understanding of federalism, but this alone is insufficient. As I will discuss in the rest of this work, some very significant obstacles remain. This discussion is of key importance because if the EU could address all crisis problems within the existing,

[77] See N. Walker, J. Shaw and T. Stephen, *Europe's Constitutional Mosaic* (Portland, OR 2011).

un-amended framework, then understanding the courts' perspective on federalism and addressing the remaining obstacles to further constitutionalization would be less relevant. Given the prevalence of crisis language and analysis explained so far in this chapter, it is unlikely that a 'business as usual' scenario will be successful.

1.2.3 Europe in Crisis

After the failure of the Convention, the question of a second constitution arises because Europe is far from working to the best of its abilities. Indeed, to a certain extent Europe could better be described as simply surviving from crisis to crisis.[78] Such questions constitute the background against which this analysis is conducted. Great challenges have arisen for the European constitutionalization process, especially in the context of the failed ratification for a European Constitution[79] and the recent financial, political and legitimacy troubles.[80] This book has neither scope nor space to speculate on all causes or reasons for Europe's successive financial and other crises. But to address only the economic or political problems that Europe faces, one by one, would be a Band-Aid solution. They conceal a more insidious dilemma. The recent series of political, economic, financial and even legitimacy challenges is founded, at least in part, in a deeper European constitutional crisis.

[78] For a detailed timeline, see The Guardian, www.theguardian.com/business/debt-crisis.

[79] *Laeken Declaration.*

[80] L. Papadopoulou, I. Pernice and J. H. H. Weiler (eds.), *Legitimacy Issues of the European Union in the Face of Crisis: Dimitri Tstsos in Memoriam* (Baden-Baden 2018); D. Innerarity, *Democracy in Europe* (Cham 2018) 21 ff; R. Rose, 'Referendum Challenges to the EU's Policy Legitimacy – and How the EU Responds' (2018) 26 *Journal of European Public Policy* 207; V. A. Schmidt, 'The Political Dynamics of EU Governance in Response to Crisis: Toward More or Less EU Legitimacy?' (2017), www.democratic-anxieties.eu/wordpress/wp-content/uploads/2017/10/Berlin-Paper-EU-political-dynamics-and-legitimacy.pdf; M. Kleine, 'Informal Governance and Legitimacy in EU Politics' (2018) 40 *Journal of European Integration* 873; T. Barber, 'Europe Must Confront Crisis of Legitimacy' (23 April 2012), *Financial Times*, www.ft.com/content/4e2c793c-8d50-11e1-8b49-00144feab49a; *The Economist*, 'Charlemagne: A Flawed Temple: The Loss of Legitimacy May Now Be the Biggest Threat to the European Project' (16 March 2013), www.economist.com/europe/2013/03/16/a-flawed-temple; *The Economist*, 'The Euro Crisis: An Ever-Deeper Democratic Deficit: The Level of Further Integration Necessary to Deal with the Euro Crisis Will Be Hard to Square with the Increasing Cantankerousness of Europe's Voters' (26 May 2012), www.economist.com/briefing/2012/05/26/an-ever-deeper-democratic-deficit; P. Eeckhout and M. Lopez-Escudero, 'Introduction' in P. Eeckhout and M. Lopez-Escudero (eds.), *The European Union's External Action in Times of Crisis* (London 2016).

It is not the case, however, that observers are ignorant of the constitutional dimensions of Europe's plight. The reality of the constitutional aspects of Europe's challenges is nearly common knowledge across various Member States of the EU and in the United States of America as well, although the risk that the different and interrelated layers of the ongoing crisis may bring about the fall of Europe is not yet fully appreciated. From these debates, a sense of the underlying constitutional elements of the successive European crises has lingered. Suddenly, the path forward in pursuit of constitutionalization does not seem as certain. Among European commentators, questions are being asked loudly as to where Europe should go from here, with most of the ongoing discussion centred upon many of the un-transposed proposals from the TCE, alongside other obstacles that, I suggest, are actually serving to cloud the key debates.

In a sense, it is as though the actual electorates themselves in key EU Member States no longer agree with certain tenets of the economic and socio-political direction of the Union, raising very significant underlying questions as to the legitimacy of the entire European agenda.[81] Such debates reflect a growing Constitutional discontent that is at the heart of Europe's crisis. The underlying constitutional foundations of these crises have not yet been overcome. Important obstacles to further constitutionalization remain, especially given that many feel that the EU is quite distant from popular democracy, as is common in most federal polities.

1.2.4 Reaching for Europe's Second Constitution

This study builds on important concepts of constitutional development and federalism to identify possible paths for Europe's next constitutional steps. A few key terms and concepts provide foundations for the analysis.

First, 'constitutional development' refers to the evolution of constitutional practice, taking into account political and social changes and how those changes influence constitutional practice.[82] Putting it slightly differently, as Paul Kahn explains, constitutionalism (at the State level) can be defined as an 'ongoing debate about the meaning of the rule of law in a democratic political order'.[83] This democratic theory of constitutional

[81] A. Hinarejos, 'The Euro Area Crisis and Constitutional Limits to Fiscal Integration' (2011–2012) 14 *Cambridge Yearbook of European Legal Studies* 243.

[82] M. Rosenfeld and A. Sajó, *The Oxford Handbook of Comparative Constitutional Law* (Oxford 2012) 12.

[83] P. W. Kahn, 'Interpretation and Authority in State Constitutionalism' (1993) 106 *Harvard Law Review* 1147, 1148.

development is useful because it highlights that there is rarely just one understanding of constitutionalism; rather, there exists a set of enablers and obstacles to constitutional development. In essence, constitutional development is the conscious process of a constitutional practice responding to political and social changes, which can result in small, significant or fundamental changes to the constitutional landscape of a given polity. This is particularly pertinent for my research as it frames and influences my study of the European Union and its constitutionalization. In this work, the EU is analysed not as an international organization or a *sui generis* entity but as a constitutional polity that is subject to constitutional development.[84] And the forms of constitutional development themselves are diverse. There can be periods of higher law-making that fundamentally change the constitutional polity or adaptive mechanisms such as Constitutional Conventions for treaty amendment or fundamental changes in constitutional practice or, indeed, judicial constitutional changes. Further, if Europe can be said to be governed by its 'First Constitution', the European Constitutional Convention failed to deliver a 'constitutional moment' that would have facilitated further constitutional development to the extent required for Europe's 'Second Constitution'.

Constitutional development has a strong historical dimension, especially in the Common Law tradition. Most constitutional development is path dependent.[85] This is close to obvious for judicial developments that rely heavily on precedent, but its relevance to constitutional documents and negotiations is often underplayed. Constitutional texts also have a rich history and build upon historical antecedents.[86] As such, we have seen, for example, that German constitutional development in the post-war period was heavily influenced by the Weimar experience and by US Constitutional law.[87] Many pivotal decisions are taken in that formative

[84] Wiener calls it 'the world's leading "non-state polity"': A. Wiener, 'The EU's Unbound Constitutional Quality' in S. Champeau, C. Closa, D. Innerarity and M. P. Maduro (eds.), *The Future of Europe: Democracy, Legitimacy and Justice after the Euro Crisis* (London 2015) 111.

[85] A. Stone Sweet, *Governing with Judges: Constitutional Politics in Europe* (Oxford 2000).

[86] A. J. Rosenthal and L. Henkin, *Constitutionalism and Rights: The Influence of the United States Constitution Abroad* (New York 1990); V. C. Jackson, 'Constitutional Comparisons: Convergence, Resistance, Engagement' (2005) *Harvard Law Review* 109; Davis, 'Constitutional Borrowing', 181.

[87] K. Rabl, C. Stoll and M. Vasold, *From the U.S. Constitution to the Basic Law of the Federal Republic of Germany [Von der amerikanischen Verfassung zum Grundgesetz der Bundesrepublik Deutschland]* (Munich 1988).

period of constitutional development that is often referred to as 'infancy' or 'young constitution'. This early constitutional period can shape a polity for many years.[88] These early periods are thus particularly significant for those wishing to analyse constitutional development as they provide not only fertile ground for analysis of an era full of federal development but also insight into what it takes to develop a successful federal entity. After all, it is the key constitutional features introduced into these early federal constitutions that have laid the foundations for further federal constitutional development.

Given that history plays such a central role in all aspects of constitutional development, noting the age of a given polity when evaluating its evolution is key. Indeed, when comparing constitutional development across different jurisdictions, one of the main challenges is selecting the relevant periods for comparison. It is extremely problematic to compare the constitutional development of a new constitution with that of one that is centuries old. With this in mind, while most contemporary federalism studies compare the EU and the current state of federations, this study aims to look towards the beginnings of federal democratic structures.

Further, lawyers from civil and common law backgrounds differ in their approach to the historical dimension of constitutional development. Common lawyers often have to explain constitutional history because most cases they rely on can be explained only with a relevant understanding of the constitutional realities existing at the time of the decision. Civil lawyers sometimes assume that they have an easier task, since their legal system tends to be less dependent on a given historical context. However, with growing numbers of court decisions interpreting and applying the constitution within a civil law jurisdiction, this vantage point becomes less tenable over time.

Courts participate fully in constitutional development. Alec Stone Sweet explains: 'As time passes, the constitution will become heavily supplemented by the jurisprudential corpus, which itself comes to look increasingly like a theory – or set of theories – about the constitution. Considered in this way, constitutional politics generate the ongoing construction, or development, of the normative basis of the state itself.'[89] Many theories on development focus on this sort of

[88] For an early plea to take history seriously, see J. Goebel, Jr., 'Constitutional History and Constitutional Law' (1938) 38 *Columbia Law Review* 555, 556.

[89] Stone Sweet, *Governing with Judges*, 29.

constitutional interpretation. One of the most far-reaching theories on this form of interpretative development is the notion of a living constitution, which allows interpreters to move beyond the original meaning of constitutional terms.[90] As Jed Rubenfeld explains, constitutional development can be reached through the idea of revolution by judiciary. This idea, in contrast to the doctrine of a living constitutional text, is an interpretive, pragmatic account for radical change.[91] This expands upon the notion that even more radical change is possible through interpretative means by the judiciary. Constitutional development can occur in even more fundamental terms, equating to constitutional amendment through Bruce Ackerman's 'constitutional moments', after which Courts are asked to synthesize the new meaning with previous constitutional meanings. Developments of this nature are not restricted in their form but rather characterized by an extraordinary political engagement of the People.[92]

Certainly, then, a study of constitutional development cannot just be based upon the original constitutional text; rather, it must take institutional, judicial and political developments into account.[93] As noted by Robert Schütze, Neil Walker, Georg Nolte, Anne Peters, Robert Howse and Kalypso Nicolaidis, Joseph Weiler, and Jan Erick Fossum and Agustín José Menendez among others, the constitutional development and constitutionalization of Europe is no longer an argumentative position but, rather, a recognition of transformation based on judicial and other important developments in the EU.

Constitutional development, as explained by Ackerman, means, in an ideal world, that '[w]e cannot remain comfortable with the status quo; the challenge is to build a constitutional order more just and free than the one we have inherited'.[94] As summarized by Choudhry, the Ackerman contribution is

> his view that the transitions between constitutional regimes have taken place through a process of 'higher law-making' involving intense and

[90] H. L. McBain, *The Living Constitution: A Consideration of the Realities and Legends of Our Fundamental Law* (1927).

[91] J. Rubenfeld, *Revolution by Judiciary: The Structure of American Constitutional Law* (Cambridge, MA 2005) 11.

[92] Ackerman, *We the People: Vol. 1: Foundations.*

[93] G. Nolte (ed.), *European and US Constitutionalism* (Cambridge 2005) 3.

[94] B. A. Ackerman, 'Constitutional Politics/Constitutional Law' (1989) 99 *Yale Law Journal* 453, 455.

> relatively brief periods of focused and public-spirited deliberation by the American people. These transitional periods have other defining features: a complex but determinate pattern of interaction between America's governing institutions, which is recognized by both those institutional actors and the public as unique to transitions between constitutional regimes; and, most arrestingly, a failure to comply with the written legal rules governing constitutional amendment.[95]

The judicial dimension of constitutional change is of paramount importance. Some of the constitutionalization scholars in the EU seem to rely firmly on a civilian approach, not highlighting the role of courts in constitutionalization.[96]

Ackerman forcefully defends his view of an American 'dualist democracy'[97] in which citizens largely rely on representative forms of government but are also able to trigger fundamental regime changes at a time of great popular uprising, which is when constitutional moments occur. These moments are defined by clear criteria signalling proposal, mobilized popular deliberation and synthesis and are discernible from ordinary constitutional development, especially given their reliance upon great popular support. As several authors have suggested from a comparative perspective, in a dualist democracy, constitutional moments are central as they constitute times of higher law-making.[98] These 'moments' are part of constitutional development but constitute special leaps driven by the people of a polity. While some of Ackerman's theory regarding dualist democracies is particular to the US Constitution, which makes constitutional change very cumbersome or impossible, it also offers a powerful argument to develop adaptive mechanisms in

[95] S. Choudhry, 'Ackerman's Higher Lawmaking in Comparative Constitutional Perspective: Constitutional Moments as Constitutional Failures?' (2008) 6(2) *International Journal of Constitutional Law* 193.

[96] On the constitutionalizing role of the ECJ: J. Shaw and A. Wiener, 'The Paradox of the "European Polity"' in M. G. Cowles and M. Smith (eds.), *The State of the European Union: Risks, Reform, Resistance, and Revival* (Oxford 2000) 81.

[97] Compared e.g. to Rousseau's model of a legitimate polity: S. White, 'Rousseau and the Meaning of Popular Sovereignty' in D. Satz and A. Lever (eds.), *Ideas that Matter: Democracy, Justice, Rights* (Oxford 2019) 72.

[98] See N. Walker, 'After the Constitutional Moment' in I. Pernice and M. Maduro (eds.), *A Constitution for the European Union: First Comments on the 2003 Draft of the European Convention* (Baden-Baden 2004); P. L. Lindseth, 'Law, History and Memory: "Republican Moments" and the Legitimacy of Constitutional Review in France' (1996–1997) 3 *Columbia Journal of European Law* 49; S. Levinson, 'Transitions' (1999) 108 *Yale Law Journal* 2215; Sajó, 'Constitution without the Constitutional Moment', 243; M. V. Tushnet, 'Misleading Metaphors in Comparative Constitutionalism: Moments and Enthusiasm' (2005) 3 *International Journal of Constitutional Law* 262.

constitutions that allows new realities to be integrated into constitutional practice.

There remains a question about constitutional moments in the EU. Ackerman himself suggested that the creation of the EU through the Maastricht Treaty might be characterized as a constitutional moment.[99] Some commentators saw the *Van Gend en Loos* decision itself as monumental, although it was not accompanied by broad popular support.[100]

As noted above, a possible 'missed' moment was the failed Constitutional Convention process in the early 2000s,[101] as some commentators have suggested.[102] But given the design of the Constitutional Convention and the controversy leading to failed referenda, this can hardly be seen as a moment for regime change or higher law-making. In this sense, it is correct if, for commentators, it was 'not quite Philadelphia'[103] or, as Ackerman called it, 'idle chatter' or a 'negative constitutional moment'.[104] Most constitutional law scholars would agree that a real constitutional moment, one that fundamentally changes the EU's constitutional structure, is still outstanding and that, despite significant developments in the jurisprudence, there remains the potential for further higher law-making by the People.

As noted, two differing but apt approaches have characterized the foundational state of constitutional development in Europe. From one viewpoint, the EU is viewed as a creature of international law, albeit a special one.[105] From the other viewpoint, the EU is identified as

[99] B. A. Ackerman, 'The Rise of World Constitutionalism' (1996) 83 *Virginia Law Review* 771.

[100] Case 26/62, *NV Algemene Transport – en Expeditie Onderneming van Gend & Loos* v. *Nederlands Administratie de Belastingen* [1963] ECR 00003; J. H. H. Weiler, 'Van Gend en Loos: The Individual as Subject and Object and the Dilemma of European Legitimacy' (2014) 12 *International Journal of Constitutional Law* 94, 101; M. Rasmussen, 'Law Meets History: Interpreting the Van Gend en Loos Judgment' in F. Nicola and B. Davies (eds.), *EU Law Stories: Contextual and Critical Histories of European Jurisprudence* (Cambridge 2017) 103, 108.

[101] Ackerman, *We the People: Vol. 1: Foundations.*

[102] Walker, 'Europe's Constitutional Momentum', 211.

[103] Scicluna, 'When Failure Isn't Failure', 441, 442.

[104] B. A. Ackerman, 'The Holmes Lectures: The Living Constitution' (2007) 120(7) *Harvard Law Review* 1737.

[105] E.-J. Mestmacker, 'On the Legitimacy of European Law' (1994) *The Rabel Journal of Comparative and International Private Law* 615; D. Chalmers, 'The Single Market: From Prima Donna to Journeyman' in J. Shaw and G. More (eds.), *New Legal Dynamics of European Union* (Oxford 1996) 55; H.-P. Ipsen, 'Europäische Verfassung – Nationale Verfassung' (1987) *Europarecht* 195.

a constitutional polity *ab initio*.[106] There are good reasons for both of these principal approaches to the constitutional status of Europe. Indeed, some have suggested that, given Europe's diversity of governance, some sort of combination of the two approaches is actually required to fully understand the European reality.[107] There is a further scholarly approach to the constitutional status of Europe that is worthy of brief note. In short, some argue that it is best to conceptionalize the EU as an administrative legal entity with the core constitutional elements retained by the Member States.[108] Indeed, rather than applying constitutional concepts to the case law, many Member State courts initially applied the old internationalist, that is, intergovernmental, view of European integration. Taking more recent jurisprudence into account, however, this view becomes difficult to reconcile with reality. The growing case law of the CJEU actually rules on fundamental relationships within the EU and in the Member States, rather than merely influencing administrative matters. Indeed, after the Lisbon Treaty, most Member State courts have abandoned this view and recognize the purported dual natures of the European Union.[109]

Indeed, at first glance, both initial approaches can be firmly rooted in the jurisprudence of Europe's courts. The view of the EU as an international organization is presented in certain case law of the ECJ such as *International Fruit*,[110] *First Corporate Shipping*[111] and the *ATAA*[112] cases, where the ECJ reiterated the mantra that the EU was a child of international law and thus could be viewed as bound by and friendly

[106] R. Schütze, *From Dual to Cooperative Federalism: The Changing Structure of European Law* (New York 2009); Weiler, *The Constitution of Europe*; K. Nicolaidis and R. Howse, *The Federal Vision: Legitimacy and Levels of Governance in the United States and the European Union* (Oxford 2001).

[107] As R. Schütze explains [in *From Dual to Cooperative Federalism*], initially the EEC was probably better conceptionalized using the international law conception of federalism as another word for international organization. In his view, both conceptions retain certain validity.

[108] P. L. Lindseth, *Power and Legitimacy: Reconciling Europe and the Nation-State* (New York 2010).

[109] See GFCC, *OMT*, 2 BvR 2728/13 of 14 January 2014.

[110] Joined Cases 21–24/72, *International Fruit Company NV and Others* v. *Produktschap voor Groenten en Fruit* [1972] ECR 1219.

[111] Case C-371/98 *The Queen* v. *Secretary of State for the Environment, Transport and the Regions, ex parte First Corporate Shipping Ltd* [2000] ECR I-09235.

[112] Case C-366/10 *Air Transport Association of America and Others* v. *Secretary of State for Energy and Climate Change* [2011] ECR I-13755.

towards public international law. On the other hand, from the 'constitutional' perspective, the seminal cases of *Les Verts*,[113] *Beate Weber*[114] and *Kadi*[115] demonstrate instances where the ECJ actually declared the Treaties to be the 'constitutional charter' of the Union.[116]

The question thus becomes can the two positions be reconciled? Theorists such as Walker have explained EU constitutionalization as 'post-constituent constitutionalism'. From this perspective, it is necessary to consider the 'general question of the relationship between constituent power and constitutional form in the context of new or shifting non-state political configurations, and specifically in the case of the constitutionalisation of the European Union'.[117] It is possible to defend this post-constituent constitutionalism as 'one that nurtures at least some "constituent" qualities without undermining the continuing constituent authority of states'.[118] While from this approach there is a regrettable tendency to downplay the constitutionalizing force of the ECJ and the power of EU citizens collectively in Europe,[119] there is also a useful recognition that constitutionalization is a correct analytical starting point.

My compromise position is to argue that the current European integration process contains elements of a federation, a constitution and an international organization. Some fundamental EU provisions are still intergovernmental. Others are more characteristic of federal states. But there is a clear tendency, over the last forty years, away from intergovernmental structures and towards federalism. This process can best be described as constitutionalization. To the ongoing debates, in this research I add the complex dimension of the Member States' courts'

[113] Case 294/83, *Parti ecologiste 'les Verts'* v. *European Parliament* [1986] ECR 1339.

[114] Case C-314/91, *Beate Weber* v. *European Parliament*, [1993] ECR I-01093.

[115] Joined cases C-402/05 P and C-415/05 P, *Yassin Abdullah Kadi and Al Barakaat International Foundation* v. *Council of the European Union and Commission of the European Communities*, [2008] ERC I-06351, para. 181.

[116] P. Faraguna, 'Constitutional Identity in the EU: A Shield or a Sword?' (2017) 18 *German Law Journal* 1617, 1623; F. Fabbrini and M. P. Maduro, 'Supranational Constitutional Courts', iCourts Working Paper Series, No. 98 (2017) 14, https://papers.ssrn.com/sol3/papers.cfm?abstract_id=2990277.

[117] N. Walker, 'Post-Constituent Constitutionalism? The Case of the European Union' in M. Loughlin and N. Walker (eds.), *The Paradox of Constitutionalism: Constituent Power and Constitutional Form* (Oxford 2007) 247.

[118] Ibid.

[119] Indeed, at least to a certain extent, 'European constitutionalism has always contained strong elements of a constitutionalism "from below"': A. Wiener and S. Oeter, 'Introduction: Who Recognizes the Emperor's Clothes Anymore?' (2016) 14(3) I•CON 608, 620.

decisions and discourse to the constitutional terrain of the EU. As research by Alec Stone Sweet has shown, it is important to build our understanding of the mechanisms behind constitutionalization, by invoking a comprehensive analysis of jurisprudence in the ECJ.[120] Building on this previous literature, to which I was fortunate to make an initial contribution,[121] in this work I undertake a substantive analysis of leading cases at both the centre and Member State levels.

In my view, the Court of Justice of the EU (CJEU) has begun to follow and even deepen the work of the ECJ in developing a constitutionalizing tradition.[122] In its first years, the CJEU has already adopted several decisions with far-reaching constitutional effects. For instance, in the *Pringle* (C-370/12) case, the Court, led by Judge Laenerts, concluded that EU Member States could engage in deeper integration even outside the formal EU institutional framework and still rely on EU institutions for its implementation.[123] Several other cases in the area of fundamental rights further advanced the EU's integration. For example, in *Melloni* (C-399/11) the CJEU concluded that Art. 53 of the Charter of Fundamental Rights and primacy of EU law 'confirms that, where an EU legal act calls for national implementing measures, national authorities and courts remain free to apply national standards of protection of fundamental rights, provided that the level of protection provided for by the Charter, as interpreted by the Court, and the primacy, unity and effectiveness of EU law are not thereby compromised'.[124] The seminal case of *Akerberg*

[120] See Stone Sweet, *Governing with Judges*; A. Stone Sweet, 'Judicialization and Supranational Governance' in M. Shapiro and A. Stone Sweet (eds.), *On Law, Politics and Judicialization* (Oxford 2002) 224; A. Stone Sweet and J. Caporaso, 'From Free Trade to Supranational Polity: The European Court and Integration' in W. Sandholtz and A. Stone Sweet (eds.), *European Integration and Supranational Governance* (New York 1998); A.-M. Burley and W. Mattli, 'Europe before the Court: A Political Theory of Legal Integration' (1993) 47(1) *International Organization* 41; G. F. Mancini, 'The Making of a Constitution for Europe' in R. Keohane and S. Hoffman (eds.), *The New European Community: Decisionmaking and Institutional Change* (Boulder, CO 1991).

[121] A. Stone Sweet and M. Gehring, 'Environmental Protection' in A. Stone Sweet, *The Judicial Construction of Europe* (Oxford 2004) 199.

[122] Birkinshaw and Varney, *The European Union Legal Order.*

[123] Case C-370/12, *Thomas Pringle* v. *Government of Ireland, Ireland and the Attorney General*, Judgment of the Court (Full Court) of 27 November 2012. P. Craig, 'Pringle and Use of EU Institutions Outside the EU Legal Framework: Foundations, Procedure and Substance' (2013) 9 *European Constitutional Law Review* 263.

[124] Case C-399/11, *Stefano Melloni* v. *Ministerio Fiscal*, Judgment of the Court (Grand Chamber) of 26 February 2013; L. S. Rossi, '"Same Legal Value as the Treaties"? Rank, Primacy, and Direct Effects of the EU Charter of Fundamental Rights' (2017) 18 *German Law Journal* 771, 785; A. T. Perez, 'The Federalizing Force of the EU Charter of

Fransson (C-617/10) on Art. 51 of the Charter and the scope of EU law was rendered on the same day, confirming that 'the Charter applies to Member States whenever they are within the scope of EU law, rather than only when implementing it (i.e., Art. 51 is to be interpreted in line with the Court's earlier case law on the scope of EU fundamental rights)'.[125] With regard to EU citizenship, the CJEU decided in *Ruiz Zambrano* (C-34/09) that parents of EU citizens have the right to work and reside in EU Member States just like EU citizens because otherwise the 'full enjoyment of EU citizenship rights' would be curtailed.[126] In its December 2014 Opinion 2/13 on the *Accession to the European Convention on Human Rights (ECHR Opinion)*, the full Court (CJEU) emphasized the EU's unique constitutional order.[127] It highlighted that 'the EU has a new kind of legal order, the nature of which is peculiar to the EU, its own constitutional framework and founding principles, a particularly sophisticated institutional structure and a full set of legal rules to ensure its operation . . . .'[128] Indeed, analysis of the growing body of case law demonstrates that the decisions and dialogue of courts are developing and interpreting this constitutional order towards a further constitutionalization that respects distinctly European values and principles. The precise nature of this EU constitutional order, however, remains surprisingly unclear, comprising a complex organizational structure with highly trusted institutions such as the Court of Justice at its centre.

The CJEU has recently embarked upon some notable constitutional development in areas that have been traditionally viewed as 'intergovernmentalist' and facilitated a high level of involvement by Member States. This can be seen, for instance, in the realm of the Art. 259 Treaty on the Functioning of the European Union (TFEU) (former Art. 227 TEC and former Art. 170 EC) procedures before the CJEU. This form of state-to-state litigation appears to be intergovernmental but recently the Court clarified its character as a European form of litigation, not unlike the Länder dispute in

Fundamental Rights' (2017) 15 *International Journal of Constitutional Law* 1080, 1089–90, 1094.

[125] Case C-617/10, *Åklagaren* v. *Hans Åkerberg Fransson*, Judgment of the Court (Grand Chamber) of 26 February 2013.

[126] Case C-34/09, *Gerardo Ruiz Zambrano* v. *Office national de l'emploi (ONEm)* Judgment of the Court (Grand Chamber) of 8 March 2011 [2011] ECR I-01177.

[127] Opinion 2/13 of the Court (Full Court) of 18 December 2014 on the draft agreement providing for the accession of the European Union to the Convention for the Protection of Human Rights and Fundamental Freedoms (ECHR), para. 156. Reiterated e.g. in Opinion 1/17, *CETA* [2019] EU:C:2019:341 and Case C-284/16, *Slovak Republic* v. *Achmea* [2018] EU:C:2018:158.

[128] Ibid., paras. 157–8.

the German Constitution.[129] The Court held, in a dispute between Hungary and the Slovak Republic, that the Art. 259 TFEU procedure was applicable only in so far as EU law was relevant to the situation.[130] In that case, Hungary's President had been prevented from entering Slovakia, which Hungary saw as a violation of the freedom to travel for EU citizens. The CJEU sided with Slovakia, showing that the Head of State of a Member State enjoys special rights and immunities in international law and thus cannot be treated as an ordinary EU citizen. The Advocate General had argued that the case was inadmissible because EU law did not apply to the situation, but the Court ruled that EU law did apply and it was simply the case that international law created a special exception.

1.3 Research Methodology

This research is focused upon European and Member State case law, as informed by a comparative analysis of federalist systems while taking into account illustrative examples from a diversity of constitutionalization processes. This 'common law' approach to constitutionalization combines previously under-researched and fragmented aspects of the existing debates. Most existing literature is based on examination of the treaty texts and relevant scholarly literature, on the one hand, or on analysis of the findings in particular cases and their implications for constitutional development, on the other. Only very rarely does European constitutionalization scholarship also consider Member State jurisprudence, which constitutes a key part of this book.

Eric Stein and Joseph Weiler were the first to argue prominently that the European Community was more than just a special international organization and that the EC had embarked upon a deliberate process of constitutionalization.[131] Many others followed.[132] This hypothesis also gradually entered the more popular literature and a constitutional discourse began to filter into public debates.[133] In 2011, J. E. Fossum and Agustín José Menéndez successfully revived the debate by identifying

[129] See Art. 93 IV 2 alt, *German Grundgesetz*.

[130] Case C-364/10, *Hungary* v. *Slovak Republic (Hungarian President)*, Judgment of 16 October 2012, not yet reported.

[131] Stein, 1; Weiler, 'The Transformation of Europe'.

[132] Schütze, *From Dual to Cooperative Federalism*; Weiler, *The Constitution of Europe*; Nicolaidis and Howse.

[133] J. Rifkin, *The European Dream: How Europe's Vision of the Future Is Quietly Eclipsing the American Dream* (New York 2004).

a process of European constitutional synthesis.[134] Their proposal was that the EU, through the use of constitutional law, is building a veritable EU Constitution through a synthesis of ideas drawn from the diverse Constitutions of EU Member States. The authors employ Bruce Ackerman's theory of founding and transformation to track further constitutionalization of the EU, but they are not able to identify, as yet, sufficient popular mobilization and change that could be characterized as Europe's 'constitutional moment'.[135] While their assessment of EU constitutionalization answers many questions about the current state of European integration theory, it does not attempt to identify the theoretical limits to constitutionalization. Further, without a critical frame to their assessment of Europe's current incrementalist approach, their work does not focus on identifying the missing pieces required to complete the puzzle that is Europe's Second Constitution.[136]

It would be misleading to suggest that these missing pieces can simply be uncovered by a study of the growing literature concerning comparative federalism, reasoning from analogy.[137] Traditionally, and at the beginning

[134] J. E. Fossum and A. J. Menéndez, *The Constitution's Gift: A Constitutional Theory for a Democratic European Union* (Lanham, MD 2011) 45.

[135] Ibid., 126.

[136] Though they extensively review the failed process of constitutionalization through the Treaty Establishing a Constitution for Europe; see ibid., 126.

[137] Nolte; F. Laursen, *The EU and Federalism: Polities and Policies Compared* (Farnham 2011); L. F. Goldstein, *Constituting Federal Sovereignty: The European Union in Comparative Context* (Baltimore, MD 2001); Beaud, O., 'Fédéralisme et souveraineté. Notes pour une théorie constitutionnelle de la Fédération' (1998) 1 *Revue du droit public* 83; G. A. Bermann, 'Taking Subsidiarity Seriously: Federalism in the European Community and the United States' (1994) 94 *Columbia Law Review* 331; T. A. Börzel, 'What Can Federalism Teach Us about the European Union? The German Experience' (2005) 15 *Regional and Federal Studies* 245–7; J. Brown and C. Lloyd, *Federal-Type Solutions and European Integration* (Lanham, MD 1993); M. Burgess, *Federalism and European Union: The Building of Europe, 1950–2000* (London 2000); Burgess, *Comparative Federalism*; M. Burgess, *In Search of the Federal Spirit: New Comparative Empirical and Theoretical Perspectives* (Oxford 2012); M. Burgess and A.-G. Gagnon (eds.), *Comparative Federalism and Federation: Competing Traditions and Future Directions* (London 1993); E. Cloots, G. de Baere and S. Sottiaux (eds.), *Federalism in the European Union* (Oxford/Portland, OR 2012); B. de Villers, *Evaluating Federal Systems* (Cape Town/London 1994); J. Erk, *Explaining Federalism: State, Society and Congruence in Austria, Belgium, Canada, Germany and Switzerland* (New York 2007); S. Fabbrini (ed.), *Democracy and Federalism in the European Union and the United States: Exploring Post-National Governance* (Abingdon/New York 2005); A. Glencross, *What Makes the EU Viable? European Integration in the Light of the Antebellum US Experience* (Basingstoke/New York 2009); D. Halberstam and M. Reimann, 'Federalism and Legal Unification: Comparing Methods, Results, and Explanations across Twenty Systems' in D. Halberstam and M. Reimann (eds.), *Federalism and Legal Unification: A Comparative Empirical Investigation of Twenty Systems*, Vol. 28 of the Ius Gentium: Comparative Perspectives on

of its development, many of the 'constitutionalising judgments'[138] of the ECJ, now the CJEU, remained beneath the radar screen of most observers.[139] It was a US scholar, Eric Stein, who clearly identified the 'judicial construction' of Europe by the Court. In his seminal article 'Lawyers, Judges and the Making of a Transnational Constitution',[140] he identified a number of milestone rulings. These have come to be understood as establishing many foundational principles for EU constitutionalization. First, he noted the cases establishing 'direct effect', whereby nationals of Member States can directly rely on EU rules in national courts; second, he identified the cases establishing the supremacy of EU law – the concept that holds that the EU law at issue will have priority of application over the relevant domestic law in areas where it applies;[141] and third, he discussed the cases establishing fundamental rights protection in the EU. As Stein argued, the ECJ has been rendering constitutional judgments for over sixty years, since the early 1960s,[142] or earlier, according to some.[143] It was the Court that had identified and given life to the three most important factors for the constitutionalization of Europe.

Law and Justice book series (Berlin/Heidelberg 2014), 3; A. Heinemann-Gruder, *Federalism Doomed? European Federalism between Integration and Separation* (New York/Oxford 2002); J. J. Hesse and V. Wright, *Federalizing Europe? The Costs, Benefits and Preconditions of Federal Political Systems* (Oxford 1996); T. O. Hueglin and A. Fenna, *Comparative Federalism: A Systematic Inquiry* (Toronto 2006); D. H. McKay, *Designing Europe: Comparative Lessons from the Federal Experience* (New York 2001); Nicolaidis and Howse; Schütze, *From Dual to Cooperative Federalism*; R. Schütze, 'From Rome to Lisbon: "Executive Federalism" in the (New) European Union' (2010) 47 *Common Market Law Review* 1385; E. T. Swaine, 'Subsidiarity and Self-Interest: Federalism at the European Court of Justice' (2000) 41 *Harvard International Law Journal* 1; J. H. H., Weiler, *Federalism and Constitutionalism: Europe's Sonderweg* (2000), https://jeanmonnetprogram.org/archive/papers/00/001001.html; J. E. Fossum and M. Jachtenfuchs, 'Federal Challenges and Challenges to Federalism: Insights from the EU and Federal States' (2017) *Journal of European Public Policy* 467; L. Thorlakson, 'Representation in the EU: Multi-level Challenges and New Perspectives from Comparative Federalism' (2017) 24 *Journal of European Public Policy* 544.

138 Craig, P. and de Búrca, G. (eds.), *The Evolution of EU Law*, 2nd ed. (Oxford 2011); C. Mac Amhlaigh, 'The Anatomy of Constitutional Pluralism in the European Union' in G. Davies and M. Avbelj (eds.), *Research Handbook on Pluralism and EU Law* (Cheltenham/Northampton, MA 2018) 59, 60.

139 H. P. Ipsen, *Europäisches Gemeinschaftsrecht* (Heidelberg 1972) 311.

140 Stein, 1.

141 This was identified as particularly decisive in the view of the preliminary reference procedure that allows national courts to refer questions to the ECJ.

142 L. Besselink and M. Bonelli, 'Back and Forth between Sovereignty and Constitutionalism: The Court of Justice's Constitutional Case Law' (2018) 14 *European Constitutional Law Review* 665, 668.

143 Alter, *The European Court's Political Power*.

Building on this approach, a legal research methodology is adopted for this book. To address existing criticisms that imply that any form of constitutionalization of the EU should be negated, this research reviews the European and Member State cases that shaped sixty years of EU constitutional development, taking into account the constitutional development of other early federal polities. Specifically, three dimensions of constitutionalization are addressed; obstacles to *demos*, *civitas* and *ius* are analysed to evaluate precisely what elements may actually prove pertinent in denying the future of constitutionalization in the EU. It is the dialogues that occur within these threads of jurisprudence that cast light on what is important to the European constitutionalization project. With this more comprehensive understanding of the actual and perceived obstacles to constitutionalization, and while avoiding the dangers of straight comparison or a historical analysis, I have then incorporated insights by use of illustrative examples from different visions of federalism and constitutionalism from across the globe. This generates a clearer analysis of precisely at which stage along the path of constitutionalization the EU's constitutional development is currently found, as well as providing indication of where opportunities lie for further constitutionalization.

Supplementing the civilian treaty text and constitutional synthesis analysis, this study adopts a more 'common law' approach to constitutionalization, giving the constitutional debates occurring in the case law at the centre and the periphery of the polity the attention they deserve. Essentially, this work seeks to complement the existing legal scholarship, which focuses on comparing written constitutional laws, with a tailored *sui generis* examination of the key dimensions of European constitutionalization, which takes treaty law and comparative constitutional law scholarship into account but also includes a fresh analysis of jurisprudential dialogues between the centre and periphery courts of Europe through over 240 recent cases.

1.3.1 Analysing Three Key Dimensions of European Constitutionalization

While many civilian and other scholars in Europe have focused on treaty rules and written constitutions, in my research I have followed a more 'common law'-inspired approach to constitutional law research, taking the role of the highest court seriously and evaluating its interaction with Member State courts as a constitutionalizing factor.[144]

In addition to key cases in the ECJ and its successor, the CJEU, there are important decisions being taken by the Constitutional Member State courts of Europe. These Constitutional Courts, as dispute settlement bodies, are seen as the great achievement of post-war Europe.[145] Although the need for such Courts was identified as early as 1920 by Hans Kelsen, it was not until the establishment of the GFCC that their greater prevalence was assured. Institutional mandates included (as in the US context) constitutional judicial review of legislation and, later, constitutional complaints by individuals.[146] Given their relatively recent establishment, this study makes it a priority to analyse the interactions between Constitutional Member State courts and the central European Courts.[147] The decisions of the European Courts and the Courts of the Member States serve to supplement the traditional analysis of treaty texts and related scholarly literature. Alongside this, additional insight is gained from a comparative approach, drawing legal and historical constitutional comparisons to critically engage with the dialogues espoused by the European Courts.

Primarily, I focus on how important obstacles have been raised and/or resolved in the interactional dialogues of the courts, throughout the judicial construction of Europe. To do this, I selected and analysed a set of key European case law decisions, as documented from 1962 to

144 K. Alter, *The European Court's Political Power*; A. M. Bickel, *The Least Dangerous Branch: The Supreme Court at the Bar of Politics* (Indianapolis, IN 1962); A.-R. Brewer Carías, Constitutional *Courts* as *Positive Legislators: A Comparative Law Study* (New York 2011); L. Brown and T. Kennedy, *The Court of Justice of the European Communities*, 4th ed. (London 1994); T. Brunell and A. Stone Sweet, 'The European Court, National Judges and Legal Integration: A Researcher's Guide to the Data Base on Preliminary References in European Law, 1958–98' (2000) 6 *European Law Journal* 117; S. Douglas-Scott, 'A Tale of Two Courts: Luxembourg, Strasbourg and the Growing European Human Rights Acquis' (2006) 43 *Common Market Law Review* 629; M. Höreth, *Die Selbstautorisierung des Agenten: der Europäische Gerichtshof im Vergleich zum U.S. Supreme Court* (Baden-Baden 2008); M. Shapiro, 'The European Court of Justice' in P. Craig and G. de Búrca (eds.), *The Evolution of EU Law* (Oxford 1999) 321; A.-M. Slaughter, A. Stone Sweet and J. Weiler, *The European Court and the National Courts: Doctrine and Jurisprudence: Legal Change in Its Social Context* (Oxford 1998); Stone Sweet, *The Judicial Construction of Europe*; Stone Sweet and Caporaso; Fabbrini and Maduro.

145 Nicolaidis and Howse.

146 I. von Munch, *Grundgesetz-Kommentar* (Munich 1975) Art. 20.

147 R. C. van Ooyen, 'Die Staatstheorie des Bundesverfassungsgerichts und Europa' in *Von Solange über Maastricht zu Lissabon* (2010).

2018 in the Courts Digest for the CJEU.[148] I selected this fifty-year period because it was during these years that key institutions were constructed and principles were established for Europe's 'First Constitution'. In this study, the cases from key constitutional courts were selected on the substance of the decisions in question; in particular, I looked to how they raise or address obstacles related to *demos*, *civitas* and *ius*, the three key dimensions of European constitutionalization that are the focus of this research. Though a full, in-depth analysis of the case law at different phases will be conducted, for the time being it suffices for this introduction to the methodology to merely provide an overview of the most significant cases.

It is mainly the Courts of the Member States that have been at the forefront questioning EU constitutional development to date.[149] While there are several dimensions to their criticisms, my research proceeds on the insight that most of the obstacles identified by periphery Member State courts evoke the three important dimensions of constitutionalization: *demos*, *civitas* and *ius*.

Undoubtedly, the most important obstacles to constitutionalization that have been highlighted in the case law of European Member State courts, and that also resonate in related academic literature, revolve around the accusation that Europe lacks sufficient *demos* to constitutionalize further. In my research, I analysed the critiques raised in the cases and legal scholarship with regard to *demos*. Broadly, *demos*-related critiques concern the cohesive nature, or lack thereof, of European citizens, and often also concern the identification of individuals as such, instead of merely existing as citizens of a particular state. In the *demos* dimension of constitutionalization, the primary concern is that the European People(s) have no common attachment to a single European entity. This has been prominently raised as problematic by numerous European Member State courts. The GFCC, for example, was extremely cynical of the concept of a 'European People', denying their existence and submitting that it was not possible for a European People to ever exist in the future. It was confident that all constitutional matters would be left for each European Member State to resolve, often in their domestic

148 The analysis did not focus on the jurisprudence of the European Court of Human Rights, as it is not technically considered part of the European Union *constitutional* order; G. de Búrca, 'The Evolution of EU Human Rights Law' in P. Craig and G. de Búrca (eds.), *The Evolution of EU Law*, 2nd ed. (Oxford 2011) ch. 16.

149 Indeed, '[n]ational courts occupy a pivotal hinge position in relation between European and national law. Their referrals for preliminary rulings contribute to the judicial development of European law': K. Tuori, *European Constitutionalism* (Cambridge 2015) 53.

constitutional courts.[150] In particular, in its *Maastricht* decision, the GFCC submitted that only a State could have a people (*Staatsvolk*) and only a people with a certain level of 'homogeneity' (*Homogenität*)[151] can form the basis for decision-making in a democratic polity. Quite simply, it noted that the power currently possessed by each State comes with democratic legitimacy from the people of that State and so, as the EU was only ever endowed with power from national legislators, its powers derive from and are limited by the Member States. Further, the GFCC noted that any state had to meet certain requirements to be democratically legitimate. Importantly for the GFCC, this included the ability for the citizens of that state to form and express a political will with the aim of giving 'legal expression to those matters which concern that people on a relatively homogenous basis spiritually, socially, and politically'. The disparity between the cultures and histories of Member States makes it impossible, the Court argued, for the requisite level of homogeneity to exist. However, the focus upon the spiritual, social and political hardly delineates clearly the precise degree of homogeneity that is required. In the *Lisbon* decision, the GFCC addressed this question, submitting that European integration and an increasing will to identify as a 'joint European public' would be insufficient. Something more would be required. The issues discussed within any democratic entity and the political leaders participating in those debates would still be viewed from extremely disparate positions; citizens from across the Union, with their differing 'nation-state, language, history and culture', would find agreement elusive. These sentiments have been echoed and, to an extent, amplified by the Polish and Czech Constitutional Courts.[152]

The second dimension that is examined invokes a European *civitas*. In the jurisprudence of European Member State courts, there has been an attempt to question the potential for further constitutionalization of Europe due to serious deficits in European *civitas*. According to several periphery courts, constitutional development, which is so closely interrelated with governance structure, is impossible in Europe. Among the issues identified is the absence of a representative democracy within the EU, which is, itself, more symptomatic of deeper problems of representation, including the lack of EU-wide political parties, the absence of an identifiable 'head of

[150] *Maastricht Decision.*

[151] It references H. Heller, *Gesammelte Schriften*, Vol. 2 (Leiden 1971), 421, 427ff, in *Maastricht Decision.*

[152] Craig and de Burca, *The Evolution of EU Law*, 31; A. Sajó, 'On Constitutional Identity and the Loyalties of the Constitutional Judge' (2019) 40 *Cardozo Law Review* 3253, 3271–2.

state' equivalent and the limited role of the European Parliament. Most recently, the GFCC reiterated these concerns, identifying the secondary status of European elections and the restricted role of the European Parliament, with its supportive and not legislative function. Further, in the *Lisbon Treaty* case, the GFCC pointed to the complex treaty structure of the EU as an additional reason for Europe's limited prospects of constitutionalization.[153] In these decisions, the GFCC initially struck down the minimum threshold for the allocation of seats, which is generally 5 per cent of votes cast in Germany.[154] In 2014, the Court then invalidated the remaining 3 per cent threshold, with the result that the European elections in Germany, as in several other Member States, took place without any threshold.[155] The main justification for this threshold in Germany's proportionate representation system is that such a threshold generally ensures governability and stable majorities in the parliament. The GFCC rejected such arguments for European elections because in its eyes there was no possibility that the German members of the European Parliament might disrupt its constitutional function, in which case the equal weight of each vote prevails as an important constitutional principle. The GFCC concluded that the argument that the 'European Parliament's ability to function would be impaired by the abolition of the five per cent barrier clause cannot rely on a sufficient factual basis and does not adequately take account of the European Parliament's specific working conditions and its duties'.[156] In other words, the GFCC found that the European Parliament does not have many important or relevant government functions, and hence a lack of cohesion engendered by fragmentation of voting rules and systems should not really prevent it from fulfilling its limited role at present, given gaps in European *civitas*. The Italian Constitutional Court has decided on such matters in very similar terms.[157]

[153] GFCC, *Lisbon Decision* and GFCC, *European Stability Mechanism Treaty*, 2 BvR 1390/12, 2 BvR 1421/12, 2 BvR 1438/12, 2 BvR 1439/12, 2 BvR 1440/12, 2 BvE 6/12, etc. of 12 September 2012 ['*ESM Decision*'].

[154] GFCC, *5% Hurdle European Election*, 2 BvC 4/10 of 9 November 2011, www.bundesverfassungsgericht.de/SharedDocs/Pressemitteilungen/EN/2011/bvg11-070.html.

[155] GFCC, *3% Hurdle European Election*, 2 BvE 2/13 of 26 February 2014, 61; see also M. Gehring, 'The German Constitutional Court's Latest Decision on European Elections: No Protection Needed', International Journal of Constitutional Law blog (28 February 2014) www.iconnectblog.com/2014/02/the-german-constitutional-courts-latest-decision-on-european-elections-no-protection-needed.

[156] Ibid.

[157] See Reuters, 'Italy's Top Court to Rule on European Parliament Electoral Law' 9 May 2014, www.reuters.com/article/2014/05/09/us-eu-election-italy-courts-idUSBREA480KM20140509.

The study of case law further helps to identify several key obstacles with regard to a third *ius* dimension of European constitutional development. Certain *ad hoc* constitutional developments by the European Courts may have added to these problems. The EU's legal system, with its backbone concepts such as direct effect and supremacy – themselves the product of the ECJ's own jurisprudence – does not present an easy task for *sui generis* constitutionalization. Many of the key domestic players across European Member States understand that constitutional polities require a common legal system,[158] which, of course, is not present within the EU, creating a potentially insurmountable obstacle.[159] Without one single, shared legal system, it is possible to argue that there is and will never be a common rule of law. And this creates problems as soon as any European Court exercises its functions. With doubt hanging over what is meant by the rule of law within any given system, the most senior court risks overstepping the mark when exercising many of its key functions, including its appellate powers, adding substance to the rules of constitutional review, determining its jurisdiction with regard to Member States[160] and delineating its own legal authority (*Kompetenz-Kompetenz*).[161] This has been highlighted in

[158] With an emphasis on fundamental rights (similar to *Solange I*), see Grimm, *Braucht Europa eine Verfassung?*, vol. 60 Siemens Stiftung.

[159] See the GFCC repeatedly in *Solange I*, BVerf 37 of 29 May 1974, *Solange II*, BVerfGE 73 of 22 October 1986, *Maastricht Decision* and *Lisbon Decision*.

[160] For a very long time it was usual for constitutional courts to engage with the ECJ through the preliminary reference procedure, but after the Italian Constitutional Court referred to the CJEU most recently, it is now mainly the GFCC that does not engage in a direct dialogue with the European Court. However, of late the GFCC is considering a reference to the European Court for the very first time with regard to the main proceedings concerning the constitutional challenge for the European Stability Mechanism ['ESM']; see GFCC, *ESM Decision*. See also A. Hinarejos, *The Euro Area Crisis in Constitutional Perspective* (Oxford 2015) and 'The Euro Area Crisis and Constitutional Limits', 243–68.

See more recently: *OMT*: ECJ case: Case C-62/14, *Gauweiler et al.* v. *Deutscher Bundestag* [2015] EU:C:2015:400 and BVerfG response: Judgment of 21 June 2016 in 2 BvR 2728/13, 2 BvR 2729/13, 2 BvR 2730/13, 2 BvR 2731/13, 2 BvE 13/13. And *WEISS* Referral: Order of 18 July 2017 in 2 BvR 859/15, 2 BvR 1651/15, 2 BvR 2006/15, 2 BvR 980/16. Case C-493/17, *Weiss and Others* [2018] EU:C:2018:1000.

See: A. Hinarejos, 'El diálogo judicial en curso y los poderes del Banco Central Europeo: la sentencia Weiss' (2019) 23 *Revista de Derecho Comunitario Europeo* 651.

[161] The GFCC in its *Lisbon Decision* highlighted its own competence to review the transfer of competence to the EU while the Court of Justice has repeatedly exercised its own exclusive competence to interpret the EU Treaties, including the competence provisions. See also *Lisbon Decision* ibid., at para. [193] ('The Basic Law not only prohibits the transfer of competence to decide on its own competence (*Kompetenz-Kompetenz*) to the European Union or to institutions created in connection with the European Union (see

the *Pension* decision before the Czech Constitutional Court. The lack of a single legal system and the problems created by its absence is also mirrored in other areas. For example, there is still no current, cohesive system of human rights protection.[162] Similar issues arise with the absence of a shared criminal law and a European-wide police force with comparable methods and powers of enforcement.[163] The GFCC, along with other Member State judicial bodies, has expressed a real reluctance to surrender jurisdictional decisions to the European Courts. Indeed, it has viewed it as its role to keep such decisions firmly within its own sphere of responsibility, at least until an impossible 'European People' demand that it relinquishes it.[164] It should also not be omitted that the Danish Supreme Court recently ruled that the CJEU had acted ultra vires in *Ajos*.[165]

Essentially, this study identifies a series of 'constitutional dialogues' on three key dimensions of European constitutionalization – *demos*, *civitas* and

Maastricht Decision BVerfGE 89, 155 <187–188, 192, 199>; see also *Eurocontrol I Decision* BVerfGE 58, 1 <37>; *NATO-Konzept* 104, 151 <210>; 123, 267 <349>). Blanket empowerments for the exercise of public authority may also not be granted by the German constitutional bodies (see BVerfGE 58, 1 <37>; 89, 155 <183–184, 187>; 123, 267 <351>). It is therefore constitutionally required not to agree dynamic treaty provisions with a blanket character, or if they can still be interpreted in a manner that respects the responsibility for integration, to establish, at any rate, suitable safeguards for the effective exercise of such responsibility. Accordingly, the Act of assent and the national accompanying laws must therefore be capable of permitting European integration continuing to take place according to the principle of conferral without the possibility for the European Union, or for institutions created in connection with the European Union, of taking possession of *Kompetenz-Kompetenz* or of otherwise violating the Basic Law's constitutional identity, which is not open to integration. For borderline cases of what is still constitutionally admissible, the German legislature must, where necessary, make effective arrangements in its legislation accompanying the Act of assent to ensure that the responsibility for integration of the legislative bodies can sufficiently develop (*Lisbon Decision*, BVerfGE 123, 267 <353>)").

162 Refer to the Czech Constitutional Court's ruling that the right to a fair trial was not guaranteed in the Court of Justice, rendering its decision in Case C-399/09, *Marie Landtová* v. *Česká správa socialního zabezpečení* [2011] ECR I-05573 *ultra vires*. The early *Solange* jurisprudence by the GFCC was based on this criticism.

163 Grimm, *Braucht Europa eine Verfassung?*, vol. 60 Siemens Stiftung.

164 *Lisbon Decision*, at para. [233].

165 Ajos: ECJ ruling: Case C-441/14, *Dansk Industri* v. *Rasmussen* [2016] ECLI:EU:C:2016:27.
Danish response: Case no. 15/2014 *Dansk Industri (DI) acting for Ajos A/S* v. *The estate left by A*; see M. R. Madsen, H. P. Olsen and U. Šadl, 'Competing Supremacies and Clashing Institutional Rationalities: The Danish Supreme Court's Decision in the Ajos Case and the National Limits of Judicial Cooperation' (2017) 23 *European Law Journal* 140; R. Holdgaard, D. Elkan and G. K. Schaldemose, 'From Cooperation to Collision: The ECJ's Ajos Ruling and the Danish Supreme Court's Refusal to Comply' (2018) 55 *Common Market Law Review* 17.

ius – which are, even now, the key subjects of debate between the EU's central Courts and the 'periphery' highest Courts of its Member States. These judicial dialogues are, with varying degrees of success, both raising and, in some cases, resolving key obstacles to further constitutional development in the European Union. A thorough understanding of these dialogues provides insights to detail and evaluate the validity of the perceived obstacles to European constitutionalization. Through the analysis of the jurisprudence of the federal entity that is the European Union, a process becomes visible that is at times messy and non-linear, but it is clearly constitutionalizing in its character and effect. Drawing upon pan-European case law from both centre and periphery courts, decisions are analysed and their approach to these fundamental objections evaluated.

With regard to these three dimensions of European constitutionalization, periphery Member State courts have highlighted many of the key obstacles to further EU constitutionalization. There are obviously nuances, as will be discussed, and not all obstacles are seen as such by all courts or in all jurisprudence. Nor are obstacles necessarily viewed in the same way between the various courts. However, as the current study of the last thirty years of jurisprudence in European and Member State courts will reveal throughout the next three chapters, there are clear trends in the impoverished understanding of federalism that can be tracked with regard to these *demos*, *civitas* and *ius* dimensions of constitutionalization in Europe at this crucial moment of the region's history, politics and identity as European people(s), their government(s) and their law(s).

1.3.2 *Illustrations from Other Early Federal Experiences*

This analysis is undertaken with the aid of several simple illustrative examples. A legal and historical analysis of early federalist projects reveals the important experiences that can be gained from other democratic federal unions, particularly by a close examination of the constitutional developments undertaken in the lead up to the formation of a union between differing peoples. I go on to highlight how these experiences offer an alternative perspective on federalism, contrary to the views advanced in certain judgments analysed in the book. While the US Early Republic plays a pivotal role in the creation of federal polities,[166] it is not the only relevant example. The comparable periods can be summarized in the following table.

[166] G. S. Wood, *Empire of Liberty: A History of the Early Republic, 1789–1815* (New York 2009).

	United States	Canada	Germany	Switzerland	Argentina
Time period	1789–1815 From the new US Federal Constitution of 1789 to the end of the 1812 War in 1815 (the 'Early Republic').[167]	1967–1981 From the Constitution Act of 1867, which was originally enacted as the British North America Act 1867, to the 1982 Repatriation of the Constitution of Canada.[168]	1949–1969 From the new Federal Republic of Germany and its 1949 *Grundgesetz* to the 'Grand Coalition' institution of the Emergency Constitution in 1968.[169]	1848–1891 From the 1848 Swiss Federal Constitution to the introduction of direct democracy elements in 1891 that partially revised the Constitution.[170]	1949–1955 From the 1949 Argentine Constitution (Perron's Constitution), which was the first explicit federal constitution, to the Revolucion Libertadora (military coup) of 1955.[171]

167 B. A. Ackerman, *The Failure of the Founding Fathers: Jefferson, Marshall, and the Rise of Presidential Democracy* (Cambridge, MA 2005); Wood, *Empire of Liberty*.

168 P. W. Hogg, *Constitutional Law of Canada*, 6th ed. (Toronto 2013); P. Oliver, P. Macklem and N. des Rosiers (eds.), *The Oxford Handbook of the Canadian Constitution* (Oxford 2017).

169 D. Junker, *Cornerstone of Democracy: The West German Grundgesetz, 1949–1989* (Washington, DC 1995); Rabl, Stoll and Vasold; L. R. Reuter, *Constitutional Developments in Germany since 1945* (Hamburg 1994); E. Spevack, *Allied Control and German Freedom: American Political and Ideological Influences on the Framing of the West German Basic Law (Grundgesetz)* (Münster/Piscataway, NJ 2001).

170 T. Fleiner, A. Misic and N. Töpperwien, *Constitutional Law in Switzerland* (Alphen aan den Rijn 2012); F. Sager and C. Zollinger, 'The Swiss Political System in a Comparative Perspective' in C. Trampusch and A. Mach (eds.), *Switzerland in Europe* (New York 2011) 27–42; K. W. Kobach, *The Referendum: Direct Democracy in Switzerland* (Aldershot 1993) 15; C. H. Church and P. Dardanelli, 'The Dynamics of Confederalism and Federalism: Comparing Switzerland and the EU' (2005) 15 *Regional and Federal Studies* 163–85.

171 Argentina, *The Constitution of the Argentine Nation: Approved by the National Constituent Assembly, March 11th, 1949* (Buenos Aires 1949); J. R. Barager, *Why Perón Came to Power: The Background to Peronism in Argentina* (New York 1968); J. M. Miller, *Constitution of Argentina: A Contextual Analysis* (Oxford 2010); A. M. Hernández, *Sub-national Constitutional Law in Argentina* (Alphen aan den Rijn 2011); L. S. Grosman, 'Argentine Constitutional Law: An Overview' (2015) 43 *International Journal of Legal Information* 1, 2.

The illustrations are provided to support a straightforward insight: the EU's path towards federalism is not unique. The development of the EU process of integration has not yet reached the level of integration where such a close union is forged that the Member States play a secondary role and the federal level takes the most important decisions. Crucially, this is normal, rather than unusual, for federalism.

The current level of integration is the product of many incremental changes over a number of decades.[172] There are still significant debates about the constitutional nature of the European Union despite the Lisbon Treaty's aim to create an 'ever closer union among the peoples of Europe, in which decisions are taken as openly as possible and as closely as possible to the citizen'.[173]

Though this research was conceived during the EU Constitutional Convention, at the high water mark of quick and often misleading comparisons,[174] its purpose is not to superficially compare processes or even their intellectual underpinnings in constitutional thought. Rather, I define and characterize a constitutional process and its limits through the lens of EU case law and the views of federalism propounded by judges, as revealed in their judgments. This analysis of the recent cases allows, first, for the identification of the remaining obstacles to EU constitutionalization and, second, for consideration of how they may be overcome. As such, this research takes a further, nuanced step. It seeks to uncover opportunities to address the most important remaining obstacle and its corollaries towards further constitutional development that could eventually lead to 'Europe's Second Constitution'.

[172] The foundations of the current EU were established as early as 1951 with the European Coal and Steel Community (ECSC), which in 1957 was expanded through further treaties to form the European Economic Community and EURATOM. The different institutions were harmonized into one in 1965. The Communities were further strengthened through the Single European Act of 1986, which established the common internal market in 1992. This was also the year that the Maastricht Treaty was adopted. After reforms through the treaties of Amsterdam (1997) and Nice (2001), it was concluded that a new 'constitutional foundation' was necessary. The Treaty establishing a Constitution for Europe was adopted in 2004, rejected by the French and Dutch referenda in 2005 and then, after several reforms, adopted in the Lisbon Treaty, which was signed in 2007 and entered into force in 2009. See further D. Dinan, *Europe Recast: A History of European Union*, 2nd ed. (London 2017).

[173] Art. 1 TEU, C 115/15 OJ of 9 May 2008.

[174] As Ackerman judged it, 'talk at Brussels of the Philadelphia Convention was idle chatter'; 'The Holmes Lectures', 1737. He later called it a negative constitutional moment. I disagree because it did not actually lead to widespread public debate and discussion (twenty-four out of twenty-seven Member States ratified the Constitutional Treaty in the end).

With regard to the first element of this book, in considering obstacles to EU constitutionalization, the main body of this research considers three particular dimensions of the theoretical and practical concerns voiced in the European jurisprudence on EU federalism and echoed by legal scholars such as Grimm and others. It suggests that, while many obstacles are no longer relevant, one remaining obstacle in particular, and related challenges, continues to block further EU constitutionalization today, hampering efforts to move beyond the simple, timid and ineffectual steps that currently characterize the response to the ongoing series of crises in the EU.

The first important dimension of research analyses an important set of obstacles to EU constitutionalization concerning the lack of a single 'European people', *Staatsvolk* or *demos*. This part explains the nature of these *demos*-related obstacles, with particular reference to how they are elucidated and discussed in the jurisprudence of Europe's Courts. This European experience is then briefly contrasted with the Early American Republic and other early federal democratic experiences, drawing upon recent legal and comparative constitutional law studies. For instance, while there was a certain level of homogeneity in the Early American Republic, it is argued that there was much greater diversity in terms of values than during the 'founding' of the European integration project. The study has identified the 'basket' of conditions existing in the Early Republic and in other constitutional polities such as Canada, Switzerland and Germany. This provides context for analysis of further European constitutional developments in light of recent Member State and central jurisprudence, and consideration of how these conditions interacted. This study argues that while a common society is not necessary for constitutionalization, an important common political space is, and is not yet in existence in the EU.

A second important dimension of obstacles to further European constitutionalization concerns the apparent lack of a single democratic system and state-like institutions. These *civitas* obstacles to EU constitutionalization are also contrasted with other early federal experiences, at a point when most of the fundamental institutions that are easily identified today did not exist in their present form. Again, a 'basket' of specific constitutional elements is carefully analysed. For example, although the Early Republic in the United States might have initially lacked a strong presidency, features may have allowed for a balance that mitigated this deficiency. Similarly, other early federal experiences were much more decentralized than they are today. Through further study of current case law in Europe, both from the CJEU and its predecessors as well as the Member State highest courts, these *civitas* debates are further untangled. The presence of certain elements strengthens the claim that further constitutionalization of the European Union is possible.

A third dimension of constitutional obstacles involves the lack of a single law governing every aspect of the EU, or *ius*. By examining the obstacle of form, especially the particular problem of having a constitutional document with detailed institutional provisions but a lack of *Kompetenz-Kompetenz* governed by the principle of conferral unlike other countries, the chapter underscores the fundamental differences between the Member States and their legal systems. This legal research does not just focus on the critique, which is largely centred on a range of selected obstacles, but also provides a careful analysis of recent developments and debates in the evolving jurisprudence of Europe. In considering and addressing the *ius* obstacles to further constitutionalization, the interaction of different features is analysed. For instance, while the experience in early federal polities might have been diverse, the Courts rapidly exerted their jurisdiction and helped integrate the federal polity.

In aiming to identify the court's own understanding of a federal polity, illustrative examples from other early federal experiences can be useful.[175] Comparison can help to understand theoretical and practical criticism of a legal regime, while contributing a certain element of distance that offers perspective. Certainly, intellectual debates that surround the founding of the United States, including how the process is viewed and analysed today, offer interesting insights without underestimating the fundamental differences. As such, rather than a historical comparison, this research includes illustrative examples from the history of ideas about constitutionalization and their limits, between several distinct polities at specific moments in their constitutional development. It considers which real-world preconditions are necessary for a living constitution to develop and what are the ingredients still lacking for a Constitution in Europe. As a result, the illustrations that I reference shed light on whether some factors that actors in Europe believe to be critical for the success of a European federalist project are actually critical or simply misconceptions – Panglossian constitutional 'pies in the sky' that few federal entities today have ever actually needed to attain.

[175] See H. P. Glenn, *Legal Traditions of the World: Sustainable Diversity in Law* (Oxford 2000).

The Early Republic is particularly significant for this research because it is the period of US history where 'political institutions were established, political parties were developed, and a political economy was worked out'.[176] There are differing definitions of the Early Republic. Some include constitutional developments up to the Civil War, but, as with Wood, this study focuses on the time from the first federal Constitution in 1789 to the end of the 1812 war in 1815.[177] If it was the Early Republic that established political institutions, then it might be most apposite to compare that particular moment in time with the modern European Union. Great caveats are necessary for such comparisons, but it is wrong to reject the potential insights to be gained from this type of intellectual and legal analysis because: 'The great challenge for constitutional law is to develop historically sensitive categories for understanding these developments [of changing constitutional institutions in the light of developing national conciseness].'[178] Projecting this thought forward to EU constitutionalism, illustrative examples from modern-day American federalism are severely constrained for utility.[179] With regard to the Early Republic, however, it is particularly interesting to examine a process that Professor Joanne Freeman of Yale University has described as a 'giant shift in the mindset',[180] whereby colonists changed completely how they thought about themselves in the process of revolution and how this reinvention of identity was consolidated in the Early Republic. She describes how people in the different States were not united. Each colony found it more straightforward to communicate with their different mother countries and, indeed, many had closer direct ties with England than with other neighbouring colonies. In essence, it may take a long time for Europeans to see themselves as European and not just as German, Swedish or even British.[181]

While in this research I draw examples from the US Early Republic, I also access illustrations from other early-stage federal projects, such as

[176] Ibid.

[177] G. S. Wood, 'The Significance of the Early Republic' (1988) 8(1) *Journal of the Early Republic* 1.

[178] Ackerman, 'The Holmes Lectures', 1737, 1743.

[179] Though some interesting insights can sometimes be gained, as the book by Nicolaidis and Howse shows.

[180] See J. Freeman, *Affairs of Honor: National Politics in the New Republic* (New Haven, CT 2002).

[181] See recent survey: 'the largest percentage of people declaring that they are European above other identities is observed in Luxembourg (20%), followed by Switzerland (7%)' etc.); D. Ballas, D. Dorling and B. Hennig, *The Social Atlas of Europe* (Bristol 2014) 24.

the early experience of Canada after the Constitution Act 1867, which was originally enacted as the British North America Act 1867. I refer to the first years of the 1848 Swiss Federal Constitution, which was adopted following the twenty-nine-day Swiss civil war (*Sonderbund* War). I also review more modern constitutions, such as the first years of the new Federal Republic of Germany and its 1949 *Grundgesetz*, until the first significant constitutional amendment, also known as the emergency constitution, in 1969. Finally, I examine the 1949 Argentine Constitution (Peron's Constitution), which introduced modern concepts into the federal constitution but was then abolished following a military coup in 1955.

By addressing the key obstacles in comparison to similar problems in early experiences of federal polities, and in light of recent European case law, we are been able to distil and derive an analysis of the most significant remaining impediments to EU constitutionalization. This lays a foundation for analytical insights, particularly in terms of how these impediments could be overcome. For instance, I conclude that the EU remains today an elite project, in a manner that was overcome in the United States, at the latest, by the end of the Early Republic and in other countries. The most important commentators on the US Constitution rightly argue that the US Constitution was rooted in the American Revolution, which thus meant that there is a strong claim that the Constitution could be seen as the expression of popular sovereignty from the very beginning.[182] This is not necessarily a problem in normal times, but, during a crisis that is more than just a momentary affair, the lack of popular understanding and support is revealed and proves destabilizing.[183] This is one of the most pressing and fundamental problems for EU constitutionalization at present.

Additionally, through the unique analysis undertaken, the stark reality of the current driving force behind EU constitutionalization is revealed. It can be seen that the EU constitutional project is not yet driven by popular demand but rather by executive decisions of EU Member States,

182 It should be noted that this view defended by Ackerman and others is not shared by all and remains somewhat controversial to this day; see C. G. Fritz, *American Sovereigns: The People and America's Constitutional Tradition before the Civil War* (Cambridge 2007).

183 One of the most appalling examples was the fall of the Greek government over the proposal to hold a referendum on the austerity measures. EU institutions played a doubtful yet decisive role in convincing the Greek political elite not to submit the measures to a referendum and solicit popular support.

even in terms of treaty changes, through their respective hierarchies. By shedding light on the supposed obstacles to federalism, it is this lack of popular support that becomes more clearly identifiable as one of the fundamental impediments for further constitutionalization. The complexity of the polity and its governance continue to ensure that the EU is difficult for the general population to understand. If the EU continues to be dominated by elite decision-making, I suggest that further constitutionalization will continue to be elusive. If comparative federal history provides one lesson, it is in the identification of indications for a 'shift in mindset', similar to the one that occurred in the US Early Republic when colonists became American republicans.

To date, the EU has also lacked a real 'constitutional moment' in its history.[184] No popular uprising and no fundamental change of the existing constitutional order has yet occurred. This research lays theoretical and analytical foundations, through a careful study of important recent European jurisprudence, to recommend adaptive mechanisms, mainly through a dialogue of centre and periphery courts, that could be enabled to address the most important remaining obstacle for constitutionalization and build more secure foundations for this future EU constitutional moment. Going forward, the key dimensions provide benchmarks for future scholarship, while the recommendations offer new steps to encourage further EU constitutional development.

1.3.3 Considering Constitutional Law in the Context of Constitutional Politics and Governance

There are several diverging approaches to the key constitutional development questions of intergovernmentalism versus constitutionalism in the characterization of European constitutionalization. As the late Eric Stein wrote: 'There are indeed three "schools" among the academic-political elites on what EU is or should be: intergovernmentalists, federalists and "sui generis" supranationalists. The federalist vs. anti-federalist issue is likely to become a subject in the public debate particularly in the U.K., the Nordic countries, in Poland and in the Czech Republic.'[185]

[184] Some might describe the failed Brussels Convention as a negative constitutional moment. But besides some attention in referendum states, its deliberations did not spark widespread popular disagreement or uprising. It is in this regard that the current financial crisis has already brought EU issues closer to the people than the French 'non' in 2005.

[185] Discussions of 10 October 2003, on file with author.

These are questions for law but also for political science. Overall, this volume builds on Ackerman's theory of constitutional development and Stone Sweet's arguments on judicial construction, in examining the early stages of a regional process of 'Second Constitutionalization' between current existing sovereign Member States in Europe. However, I also take into account an ever-expanding body of political science literature documenting the continuing elitist nature of the European integration project, projecting existing low levels of broad popular support for EU integration and identifying the weaknesses in the European common public sphere.

Absurdly, many legal scholars are nearly unaware of the political dimension of their own work, as Karen Alter illustrates in her accounts of the consternation evinced by eminent EU law professors at a conference in Germany when their roles in a political rather than legal integration project were posited.[186] As part of the debates, modern European legal and political scholarship searches for an adequate response to the failed TCE. In this endeavour, they often cast a more diverse constitutional picture of a constitutional mosaic in Europe, in which different constitutional perspectives are present and valid. For example, as Walker explains, there has been 'much debate concerning the constitutional future of Europe, focusing mainly upon the EU in the context of the (failed) Constitutional Treaty of 2003–5 and the Treaty of Lisbon . . .[. T]his focus offers only a partial vision of the complex constitutional terrain of contemporary Europe.'[187] In light of these historical and constitutional law concerns, in addition to scholarly calls for a radically re-conceived administrative praxis,[188] a more nuanced understanding of federalism among judiciaries might be more than useful for further successful constitutionalization. As such, this research is grounded in a thorough search of recent legal and scholarly literature, focusing on the concepts of constitutionalization, the constitutional moment and modern conceptions of federalism in both common law and civil law systems.

Further to this, the methodology adopted in this book is primarily aligned to track the 'judicial dialogues' among the centre and periphery courts for each key dimension of constitutionalization, taking illustrative examples of other federal experiences into account where relevant.[189] As

[186] Alter, *The European Court's Political Power*, 3.
[187] Walker, Shaw and Stephen.
[188] B. Kingsbury, *The Emergence of Global Administrative Law* (Durham, NC 2005).
[189] See, for further references, Burgess, *In Search of the Federal Spirit*.

such, I undertook substantive legal research and analysis to examine the most important obstacles to the construction of a European *demos, civitas* and *ius*, in turn. I examined the comparable constitutional experiences as developed in a multitude of recent studies of the United States, Switzerland, Canada and Argentina with regard to each set of obstacles, drawing on the primary constitutional documents, historical accounts, early case decisions and reports, and related legal treatises and scholarly analysis. Then, I analysed European jurisprudential dialogues with regard to these obstacles. In particular, I examined compilations of the European Court's decisions and case materials on each dimension, as discussed in detail in Chapters 2, 3 and 4. Debating these elements, I also selected several key cases of EU Member States, again based on legal analysis and surveys of the scholarly literature. This involved analysis of the decisions, case materials and reports of cases identifying obstacles to the constitutional development of European *demos, civitas* and *ius* in turn. For each key factor and related set of fundamental objections identified in the literature, through case analysis, comparison with other constitutionalization processes and analysis of existing legal scholarship, I either found the obstacles invalid or recognized them as significant. Although my analysis found that many concerns were invalid, it recognized one particular element and its corollaries as significant. Indeed, perhaps one of the most significant contributions of this research is my identification of the most important remaining obstacle and its corollary weaknesses in the European constitutionalization process.

As such, after disproving most of the obstacles, this book focuses on this most significant remaining obstacle to constitutionalization – the absence of a European public sphere. While even this obstacle could be addressed as certain public spheres are being Europeanized,[190] it is a problem that arises both in practical legal analysis and in the study of broader governance systems. Through combined legal and political science analysis, this study considers how this remaining constitutional obstacle has been particularly detrimental in the current succession of crises in Europe. Without likelihood of a constitutional moment at this juncture, the study identifies a possible way forward through activating adaptive mechanisms for Europe to overcome this obstacle. By doing

[190] See T. Risse, *A Community of Europeans? Transnational Identities and Public Spheres* (Ithaca, NY/London 2010) 107 ff; K. Sarikakis and O. Kolkytha, 'EU Democratic Deficits: The EU Project and a European Public Sphere', in K. Arnold, P Preston and S. Kinnerbrock (eds.), *The Handbook of European Communication History* (Hoboken, NJ 2019).

this, it is possible to advance recommendations for decision-makers, including the judiciaries themselves, to advance the further constitutionalization of Europe as well as to inform future legal and historical research in this field.

1.3.4 Methodological Challenges Addressed

One of the key challenges that this research has faced involved how to illuminate different visions of federalism and constitutionalism in order to form a clearer picture of these concepts and to contextualize the current position of the EU in its constitutional development. A superficial analysis could suggest that the constitutional rhetoric in two particular processes – the American Constitutional debates in the Early Union and the current Constitutional Convention in Europe – are remarkably similar. The reasons given by the Federalists for choosing the original US Constitutional structure do not appear so very different from those advanced by the European Federalists during the Convention debates.[191] This challenge was addressed by looking deeper, presenting a coherent analysis of the ideas and misconceptions behind the European constitutional processes themselves in the context of the decisions of the CJEU and the constitutional courts of key Member States.

A further key challenge was to ensure that the critics did not become the main voice, to avoid being 'captured by the criticism'. This was addressed by taking a composite view that examines three dimensions of similar obstacles identified in the centre and periphery court cases on these issues. Rather than working from a 'laundry list' of individual academic critical objections to constitutionalization, the study adopts a nuanced approach that considers only the key factors debated in the case law with regard to each dimension of constitutionalization. This also allows some consideration of which obstacles are simply due to misconceptions of federalism, which gaps might be shored up with other norms, institutions, processes or actors, and which obstacle remains most essential and unaddressed to date.

[191] Though social expectations have, of course, evolved, and that will be taken into account, this part of the research will be based on legal understandings that can today still be learnt from the Federalist Papers. As Ackerman says: 'I propose to plunge into the Papers at once, searching for commonalities that may remain after we have bracketed the more obvious moral differences that separate us' (*We the People: Vol. 1: Foundations*, 167).

A further challenge involved coherence of proposals. In the end, this book has a central focus on the current absence not of a single homogenous European people or national identity but of a strong and vibrant trans-European public sphere in which transparent, legitimate policy debates can occur, addressing (for instance) the nature of a crisis and the measures needed to resolve them. How could it be possible that an element of my proposed solution was to engage an unelected European judiciary and its Member State counterparts in the work needed to enable such a public sphere? Surely, the elitist nature of the judiciary is even more pronounced than the intergovernmental processes led by Brussels. I addressed this challenge by taking a common law approach to the European jurisprudence and by analytically tracing the interactional dialogues *between* the judicial bodies of Europe, rather than focusing on the personal or political views of one judge or another. In essence, I had to overcome the temptation of abstract analysis by linking the crises challenges – demonstrated in the case law itself – to the very real, concrete problems faced by European citizens attempting to live their lives in the absence of a common European public sphere.

1.4 Structure of the Book

The further sections of this book are presented sequentially. Chapters 2, 3 and 4 address the traditional obstacles to European constitutionalization, presenting the results of the research and considering whether these perceived obstacles remain valid after taking into account other federal experiences and tailored *sui generis* European case law analysis. Here, I examine the *demos*, *civitas* and *ius* dimensions of the further constitutionalization of Europe, explaining the most important obstacle that remains valid after six decades of jurisprudence and treaty-making, and its corollary challenges.

In particular, Chapter 2 examines perceived obstacles related to *demos*, presenting the outcomes of the research on common understanding of a European demos, social and political homogeneity, homogeneity of citizenry, spiritual homogeneity and homogeneity of values, explaining if and how each factor is addressed in the European treaty negotiations and case law, taking into account illustrative examples from the United States and other federal experiences.

Chapter 3 examines perceived obstacles related to *civitas*, presenting the outcomes of the research on unitary elections, European-wide parties, the Presidency, the role of the European Parliament, the role of the

2

Demos Obstacles to European Constitutionalization

2.1 The Importance of *Demos*

One of the most fundamental obstacles to EU constitutionalization is said to be the lack of a European *demos*, which is seen as a precondition for any constitutional system.[1] The term '*demos*' originally referred to the common people of an ancient Greek state. Today, *demos* can describe the populace of a democracy, as a political unit.[2] European Member State courts, such as the GFCC, have raised prominent concerns that further constitutionalization is constrained by the absence, in Europe, of a common attachment as an entity; they emphasize that there is no 'European people' and no future possibility thereof, meaning that the final say in constitutional matters will always rest with each European Member State.[3] In particular, as argued by the GFCC in its *Maastricht* decision, only a State has a people (*Staatsvolk*) and only a people with a certain level of what the judges called 'homogeneity' (*Homogenität*)[4] can form the basis for democratic decision-making. The GFCC found:

[1] Innerarity, *Democracy in Europe*, ch. 5; T. Eijsbouts, 'People and Peoples in EU Law: To Debunk the No-Demos Myth' in Papadopoulou, Pernice and Weiler (eds.), 113. Then there are also works that criticize both! See F. Wolkenstein, 'Demoicracy, Transnational Partisanship and the EU' (2018) 56 *Journal of Common Market Studies* 284; the EU needs to strengthen its *demos*, argues C. Wiesner, *Inventing the EU as a Democratic Polity* (Cham 2018), 297.

See comprehensively Jolly, ch. 3. For a more critical view see A. Moravcsik, 'In Defense of the "Democratic Deficit"', 603. There are, of course, still voices objecting to the characterization of the EU as constitutional, but even if one agrees with P. L. Lindseth's approach in *Power and Legitimacy*, 1, that the EU is best characterized as administrative, it remains a valid question as to whether democratic legitimacy is even possible in the Union as a whole. He later discusses similar questions but with a very contemporary focus in ch. 5 on 'Supranational Delegation and National Parliamentary Scrutiny since the 1970s', 189. See the following for a more political-science-oriented approach: Curtin, *Postnational Democracy*; Jolly; Sbragia, 167; A. D. Smith, 'National Identity', 55.

[2] Stevenson.

[3] *Maastricht Decision*.

[4] It references H. Heller, 421, 427ff, in *Maastricht Decision*.

> If the peoples of the individual States (as is true at present) convey democratic legitimation via the national parliaments, then limits are imposed, by the principle of democracy, on an extension of the functions and powers of the European Communities. State power in each of the States emanates from the people of that State. The States require sufficient areas of significant responsibility of their own, areas in which the people of the State concerned may develop and express itself within a process of forming political will which it legitimates and controls, in order to give legal expression to those matters which concern that people on a relatively homogenous basis spiritually, socially, and politically.[5]

These criteria are hardly well delineated and could rest upon nothing more than an impoverished understanding of the nature of a federal polity. The GFCC's emphasis on broad notions of spiritual, social and political homogeneity raised questions about the actual contours of such a requirement. In its *Lisbon* decision, the GFCC further explained:

> Even if due to the great successes of European integration, a joint European public that engages in an issue-related cooperation in the rooms of resonance of their respective states is evidently growing (see on this already BVerfGE 89, 155 185; Trenz, *Europa in den Medien, Die europäische Integration im Spiegel nationaler Öffentlichkeit*, 2005), it cannot be overlooked, however, that the public perception of factual issues and of political leaders remains connected to a considerable extent to patterns of identification which are related to the nation-state, language, history and culture.[6]

The GFCC's standard is therefore high. *Demos* alone is insufficient. Even if a European *demos* could be shown to exist, it would not be enough due to perceptions held by the publics of the European Member States. This perspective arguably reveals more about the GFCC than about the status of European integration and demonstrates, especially when compared to the constitutional reality in federal states, that, during a certain period, the GFCC did not conceive of or really contemplate the possibility of the European Union developing into a federal polity. In the eyes of such courts, it thus follows that the European Union cannot become more than a confederation of states (*Staatenverbund*). This concept was defined by the GFCC not in its *Maastricht* decision but in its *Lisbon* decision, where it further explained: 'The concept of "Verbund" covers a close long-term association of states which remain sovereign, a treaty-based association which exercises public authority, but whose

[5] *Maastricht Decision*, para. 100.
[6] GFCC, *Lisbon Decision*, para. [251].

fundamental order is subject to the decision-making power of the Member States and in which the peoples, i.e. the citizens, of the Member States, remain the subjects of democratic legitimation.'[7] Indeed, perhaps this question was deliberately raised by the GFCC in order to underline its deeply held conviction – shared even by liberal constitutional lawyers in Germany – that the Member States of the EU alone have been, are and will continue to be the only ultimate source of democratic legitimacy.[8] The GFCC, it appears, was convinced that only a people can engage in democratic decision-making. From this view, only nation states can have *demos* and, therefore, the European Union cannot be democratic or further constitutionalized.

This chapter analyses this obstacle to European constitutionalization, exploring the contours of the *demos* debate through a consideration of related EU jurisprudence and in light of the experiences of other federal polities. I ask whether the absence of a true European *demos* prevents the European Union from becoming a constitutional polity and whether there is a common understanding, in Europe, of the potential character or contours of a European *demos*.

It is not surprising that *demos*-related critiques have, so far, filled much of the European constitutionalization debate. In many theories of democratic development, whether in political science or in law, the existence of *demos* occupies a crucial place: without *demos*, many posit, no democratic form of governance is possible.[9] In various EU Member States, the 'no *demos*' objection appears widely shared among national jurists[10] and for some has not fundamentally changed over the last twenty years.

The actual characteristics of a common attachment or *demos* present a useful starting point for analysis, as certain preconditions can be

[7] GFCC *Lisbon Decision*, para. 229.

[8] Constitutional scholars such as Böckenförde and Grimm have argued in this vein. See also the GFCC in *Lisbon Decision*, at [249]: 'European unification on the basis of a union of sovereign states under the Treaties may, however, not be realised in such a way that the Member States do not retain sufficient space for the political formation of the economic, cultural and social circumstances of life.'

[9] See D. Held, *Models of Democracy*, 3rd ed. (Cambridge 2006).

[10] Most recently the GFCC in *Lisbon Decision*, and the Czech Constitutional Court is openly defiant of the CJEU (against Case C-399/09, *Marie Landtová* v. *Česká správa socialního zabezpečení* [2011] ECR I-05573) in Pl. ÚS 5/12 of 31 January 2012, *Slovak Pensions*); see the very critical review by J. Komárek, 'Czech Constitutional Court Playing with Matches: the Czech Constitutional Court Declares a Judgment of the Court of Justice of the EU Ultra Vires; Judgment of 31 January 2012, Pl. ÚS 5/12, Slovak Pensions XVII' (2012) 8 *European Constitutional Law Review* 323.

easily grouped into three categories: language, history and ancestry.[11] Essentially, the concerns are that there exists (1) no single European citizenship, (2) no European spiritual homogeneity, (3) no common or shared European values, (4) no social or linguistic homogeneity at the European level and (5) no common European public space for political debate. The last need for a common European public sphere emerges from the ongoing *demos* debates in the judicial dialogues between periphery and centre courts, but I believe that it is also an overarching obstacle to further constitutionalization, one that touches on all other remaining obstacles.

The illustrative federal examples invoked are derived from an analysis of recent comparative and historical studies. For instance, scholars have noted certain similarities between the US Early Republic, Canada and the European Union.[12] The EU and the United States may even be described as similar compound democracies.[13] This, as supported by Alex Glencross, suggests that democracy is possible at the EU level and is shaping further integration.[14] And, as Robert Calhoon has posited, such experiences may point to continuation in the theory of compact.[15] The experiences of the United States, Switzerland, Canada and Argentina – taking into account the primary constitutional documents, historical accounts, early case decisions and reports, and related legal treatises and scholarly analysis from each jurisdiction – provide useful illustrative examples here.

My primary source of analysis, however, is the jurisprudence of the European Courts. I analyse cases that refer directly and indirectly to key obstacles to the construction of a European *demos* and select key cases from a wide range to focus on in detail to highlight the prevailing understanding. These include cases such as *Stauder*[16] and *Nold*,[17] which are relevant to common European values; *Martinez Sala*[18] and

[11] Ibid.

[12] D. Mann, *'We, the People' vs. 'We, the Peoples': The Debate over the Nature of the Union in the USA and Canada and Its Lessons for European Integration* (Florence 2012), 16.

[13] S. Fabbrini, *Compound Democracies: Why the United States and Europe Are Becoming Similar* (New York 2007).

[14] A. Glencross, *E Pluribus Europa? Assessing the Viability of the EU Compound Polity by Analogy with the Early US Republic* (Florence 2007), http://cadmus.eui.eu/bitstream/handle/1814/7766/2007_05_Glencross.pdf?sequence=3; Glencross, *What Makes the EU Viable?*.

[15] R. M. Calhoon, *The Loyalists in Revolutionary America, 1760–1781* (New York 1973).

[16] Case 29/69, *Erich Stauder* v. *City of Ulm – Sozialamt* [1969] ECR 00419.

[17] Case 4/73, *J. Nold, Kohlen- und Baustoffgroßhandlung* v. *Commission of the European Communities* [1974] ECR 00491.

[18] Case C-85/96, *María Martínez Sala* v. *Freistaat Bayern* [1998] ECR I-02691.

Rottmann,[19] which concern European citizenship and homogeneity; and *Grzelczyk*,[20] *Chen*[21] and *Ruiz Zambrano*,[22] which concern European solidarity.[23] Debating these elements, I also select key national cases from EU Member States, again based on legal analysis and surveys of the scholarly literature, compilations of the decisions, case materials and reports. These range from the GFCC's *Maastricht* decision,[24] which raises the question as to whether a European *demos* exists; the *Lisbon Treaty* judgment[25] also of the GFCC; *Landtová* in the Czech Constitutional Court,[26] which concerns European homogeneity; *Wallonia* v. *Flanders* in the Belgian Constitutional Court;[27] the *European Stability Mechanism [ESM] Treaty* in the GFCC concerning European solidarity;[28] the *Troika Bailout* in the Portuguese Constitutional Court,[29] which concerns shared European values; the *EPT Broadcaster* in the Greek Council of State,[30] on European solidarity; and the *Amsterdam Treaty* in the Polish Constitutional Court,[31] also on shared European values. Many of the cases contain key tensions in the understanding of the concept of *demos* and its elements, and serve to highlight impoverished understandings of how *demos* in a federal entity is defined or can develop. In the dialogue of the courts, I also identify hesitations on the part of the CJEU to embrace federal thinking.

19 Case C-135/08, *Janko Rottmann* v. *Freistaat Bayern* [2010] ECR I-01449.

20 Case C-184/99, *Rudy Grzelczyk* v. *Centre public d'aide sociale d'Ottignies-Louvain-la-Neuve* [2001] ECR I-06193.

21 Case C-200/02, *Kunqian Catherine Zhu and Man Lavette Chen* v. *Secretary of State for the Home Department* [2004] ECR I-09925.

22 Case C-34/09, *Gerardo Ruiz Zambrano* v. *Office national de l'emploi (ONEm)* [2011] ECR I-01177.

23 A. Biondi, E. Dagilytė and E. Küçük, *Solidarity in EU Law: Legal Principle in the Making* (Cheltenham/Northampton, MA 2018).

24 *Maastricht Decision*.

25 *Lisbon Decision*.

26 Czech Constitutional Court, Decision of 31 January 2012, Pl. ÚS 5/12, *Slovak Pensions*.

27 Case C-212/06, *Government of Communauté française and Gouvernement wallon* v. *Gouvernement flamand* [2008] ECR I-01683.

28 *ESM Decision*.

29 Portuguese Constitutional Tribunal, *Judgment No 187/2013* of 6 April 2013, www.tribunalconstitucional.pt/tc/acordaos/20130187.html.

30 *Council of State Committee decision COE No. 236/2013 of 12/06/2013*; the final and full Council of State decision confirmed the constitutionality due to EU commitments: CoE 1901/2014 Constitutionality provision repealing ERT of 01.06.2014 with a very strong dissent; see www.taxheaven.gr/laws/circular/view/id/18919.

31 Polish Constitutional Tribunal, Judgment of 11 May 2005, case *K 18/04* concerning the constitutionality of the ratification of the Accession Treaty.

2.2 No Homogeneity of Citizenship?

2.2.1 Obstacles to Constitutionalization

Constitutional scholars and certain periphery courts have highlighted that most people do not yet identify with 'Europe' in the same way that they identify with their Member States or in the way other peoples identify with their national states.[32] This lack of self-identification as 'citizens of Europe' may be an important obstacle to developing a European *demos*. In particular, the concern is that EU citizenship is currently based on possessing the nationality of a Member State (Art. 9 TEU and Art. 20 TFEU).[33] The perception, fundamentally, is that Member States decide who is granted their nationality and by extension EU citizenship.[34] This calls into question the unifying value of EU citizenship.

2.2.2 Underlying Concepts of Constitutional Development

Any requirement that one homogenous citizenship should exist *de lege* and de facto, simply in order to allow a federal entity to acquire the necessary *demos* for constitutional development, reveals an impoverished understanding of the nature of federalism. There may not be a need for citizens to choose between one layer of citizenship and another – in contemporary constitutional scholarship, several overlapping levels of citizenship are not only recognized but actually celebrated as part of complex modern self-identification.[35] Several contemporary federal entities, as demonstrated in recent comparative studies, offer illustrative

[32] See 'the largest percentage of people declaring that they are European above other identities is observed in Luxembourg (20%), followed by Switzerland (7%)' etc.; Ballas, Dorling and Hennig, 24.

[33] 'Citizenship of the Union is hereby established. Every person holding the nationality of a Member State shall be a citizen of the Union. Citizenship of the Union shall be additional to and not replace national citizenship.' See differing views on the desirability of EU citizenship's derivative nature in: L. Orgad and J. Lepoutre (eds.), *Should EU Citizenship Be Disentangled from Member State Nationality?* EUI Working Paper RSCAS 2019.

[34] This has been expressly recognized and consistently reiterated by the Court: 'Under international law, it is for each Member State, having due regard to Community law, to lay down the conditions for the acquisition and loss of nationality': Case C-369/90, *Micheletti* [1992] EU:C:1992:295, para. 10.

[35] C. Joppke, 'Transformation of Citizenship: Status, Rights, Identity' (2007) 11 *Citizenship Studies* 37.

examples of the potential to overcome similar challenges during key periods of constitutional development.[36]

As an initial example, the US Constitution did not initially subsume the identity of American citizens.[37] Americans were asked by politicians to feel 'American' but felt first and foremost New Yorkers, Virginians and Pennsylvanians.[38] National identity was secondary to home (constituent) state citizenship. Being part of a federal legal and political system did not extinguish the identity of a particular state or city. Rather, the constitutionalization of the United States gave the individual an added sense of political and legal identity that did not exclude original identities, except in times of direct conflict. Indeed, some might say that US debates regarding states' rights inspired the Declaration of Independence, weakened the Articles of Confederation, influenced the US Constitution and, ultimately, sparked a civil war that threatened to permanently divide the constitutional polity.[39] Citizenship questions during this period were similarly fraught with controversy. For instance, after the Revolutionary War but before the ratification of the Constitution, all citizens were citizens only of their own state. This altered with Reconstruction, but there was no unified approach to citizenship, and large parts of entire populations were excluded from citizenship, particularly in states that allowed slavery. As such, '[s]tate citizenship, before the civil war, mattered a great deal',[40] a reality that had harsh consequences, such as white Americans enjoying federal citizenship while black Americans did not. While the infamous *Dred Scott* ruling of the US Supreme Court signalled many problems of the times,[41] the dominance of federal citizenship is a post-Civil War phenomenon and was largely influenced by the Reconstruction Amendments, in particular the

36 P. H. Schuck, 'Citizenship in Federal Systems' (2000) 48 *American Journal of Comparative Law* 195; R. Hansen and P. Weil, *Dual Nationality, Social Rights and Federal Citizenship in the US and Europe: The Reinvention of Citizenship* (New York/Oxford 2002); F. Requejo, 'Cultural Pluralism, Nationalism and Federalism: A Revision of Democratic Citizenship in Plurinational States' (1999) 35 *European Journal of Political Research* 255; J. L. Cohen, 'Changing Paradigms of Citizenship and the Exclusiveness of the Demos' (1999) 14 *International Sociology* 245; S. Choudhry, 'Citizenship and Federations: Some Preliminary Reflections' in Nicolaidis and Howse.

37 R. M. Smith, *Civic Ideals: Conflicting Visions of Citizenship in US History* (New Haven, CT 1997) 87.

38 Ibid., 88.

39 Ibid., 183–5; see, generally, Laursen, The EU and Federalism.

40 D. Lacorne, 'European Citizenship: The Relevance of the American Model' in Nicolaidis and Howse.

41 US Supreme Court, *Dred Scott* v. *Sandford*, 60 U.S. 393 [1857].

Fourteenth.[42] And while federal citizenship has not replaced state citizenship, with the Fourteenth Amendment, and while state citizenship remains relevant for voting rights, it has become less important. In essence, despite the laws that existed to somewhat superficially support the existence of an American *demos* and to enforce its tenets, this *demos* was not fully at the heart of a citizen's identity. State citizenship highlights that in federal entities, a dominant federal citizenship is not required as a matter of principle since conceptions of citizenship can develop over time.

The constitutional development of Canada provides a further example. During the first twenty years after the creation of Canada, the citizenship identity of the people of Quebec remained quintessentially multi-faceted.[43] Further, indigenous peoples – the 'First Nations' – were not truly considered citizens of Canada until the mid-twentieth century. Indeed, most would argue that founders of the Canadian Dominion purposefully excluded the possibility of citizenship for indigenous Canadians.[44] Different classes of citizens thus still existed in the different provinces for a considerable time, with some even disputing the nationality of Inuit Canadians altogether. For constitutional legal thought this is, therefore, an important example of how different models of citizenship can develop over time and do not require a homogeneous notion of citizenship for either their functioning or their existence.

Similarly, the nature of citizenship in the old German Empire also serves as an illustration. All states of the German Empire of 1871, such as Prussia or Bavaria, had their own rules about citizenship. These rules included, to differing degrees, elements of *ius soli* and *ius sanguinis*, that is, citizenship on the basis of birth and ancestry, respectively. Common citizenship principles were adopted only several decades later in 1913 in the Reichs- und Staatsangehörigkeitsgesetz (RuStAG) of 22 July 1913, which ensured that the award of citizenship rights followed similar principles in all federated states.[45]

42 D. B. Heater, *A Brief History of Citizenship* (New York 2004) 72.

43 L. Oakes and J. Warren, *Language, Citizenship, and Identity in Quebec* (London 2007) 34.

44 S. Grammond, *Identity Captured by Law: Membership in Canada's Indigenous Peoples and Linguistic Minorities* (Montreal, QC/Kingston, ON 2009), 71.

45 I. von Münch, *Die deutsche Staatsangehörigkeit: Vergangenheit, Gegenwart, Zukunft* (Berlin 2007), 14; H. Hagedorn, 'Föderalismus und die deutsche Staatsangehörigkeit: die Einbürgerungspolitik der Bundesländer' in L. Akgün and D. Thränhardt (eds.), *Integrationspolitik in föderalistischen Systemen* (Münster 2001).

These examples highlight that the underlying concepts for citizenship are very diverse and can have a federal and a federate dimension without calling into question the foundational character of citizenship.

2.2.3 *Related EU Developments*

This leads us to an interesting question: Is the mere political request to 'feel European' enough to create a *demos*? There is little doubt that politicians at all levels invoke European feelings when convenient,[46] although clearly there is a perceived lack of homogeneity of citizenry in the EU.

Yet this call to feel European is precisely what has occurred. An area where the EU has been fundamentally transformed over the last twenty years is in the area of citizenship. Development in this domain has not at all been confined to the political arena. Leading cases before the CJEU have fundamentally transformed the Union.

When the EU introduced the concept of EU citizenship in the Maastricht Treaty, Member States formulated the relevant provision very carefully in order to avoid creating the impression of a federal project.[47] The Treaty said (and still says) in Art. 17 TEC (now Art. 20 TFEU and Art. 9 TEU): 'Citizenship of the Union is hereby established. Every person holding the nationality of a Member State shall be a citizen of the Union. Citizenship of the Union shall be additional to and not replace national citizenship.' Although the constitutional foundation was laid at this stage for EU citizenship, few expected the elevation of this concept by the European Courts to the position of a foundational status.

The CJEU first pointed out in *Grzelczyk* that EU citizenship was 'destined' to provide the foundational statute for Member State nationals in other Member States.[48] The case concerned the simple question of

[46] See recently Francois Hollande describing the Franco-German Friendship as constituting the 'Heart of Europe'; BBC News, 'Germany and France Vow to Strengthen Ties', 22 September 2012, www.bbc.co.uk/news/world-europe-19684532. Brexit has exacerbated the political manipulation of European feelings, with the 'New Settlement for the United Kingdom within the European Union' agreed in February 2016 containing both strong sentiments of EU federalism and equally strong sentiments of unfettered Member State sovereignty.

[47] See Opinion of AG Sharpston in Case C-34/09, *Gerardo Ruiz Zambrano* v. *Office national de l'emploi (ONEm)* [2011] ECR I-01177.

[48] Case C-184/99, *Rudy Grzelczyk* v. *Centre public d'aide sociale d'Ottignies-Louvain-la-Neuve* [2001] ECR I-06193. This entitlement of EU nationals to also be citizens is strengthened by substantive rights and expectations that every national may have, as

whether a French national would be entitled to social benefits in Belgium when the benefits were reserved for nationals. The Court pointed out that Member States owed a certain level of solidarity to each other and that citizenship of the Union precluded discrimination on the basis of nationality alone. The Court did not establish that Member State citizenship was no longer relevant but rather attributed substantive rights on the basis of EU citizenship in particular, thus setting in motion a line of case law that served to elevate EU citizenship to a right equivalent to that of other federal entities.

Significant advances have now arguably resulted in fundamental changes to this understanding.[49] An important case for our discussion is the case of Mr Rottmann, who had a criminal conviction in Austria before acquiring German citizenship (and automatically losing his original Austrian citizenship). Problematic for him was that the German Citizenship Act expressly provides that undisclosed criminal convictions lead to an automatic loss of citizenship in Germany. The CJEU was asked by a German administrative court if EU citizenship had any impact on this question and the Court answered that the national court was required by EU law to assess whether Mr Rottmann would lose his genuine enjoyment of EU citizenship rights if he were to become stateless.[50] So Member State citizenship remains the main notion of citizenship in the Union, but decision-making as to whom citizenship is conferred upon is no longer an unfettered left with Member States.

apparent in Advocate General Wathelet's Opinion in Case C-115/15 *Secretary of State for the Home Department* v. *NA* [2016] ECR 00000.

[49] Case C-109/01, *Secretary of State for the Home Department* v. *Hacene Akrich* [2003] ECR I-09607; Case C-209/03, *The Queen (on the application of Dany Bidar)* v. *London Borough of Ealing and Secretary of State for Education and Skills* [2005] ECR I-02119, noted by C. Barnard, 'Case C-209/03, R (on the application of Danny Bidar) v London Borough of Ealing, Secretary of State for Education and Skills, Judgment of the Court (Grand Chamber) 15 March 2005, not yet reported' (2005) 42 *Common Market Law Review* 1465; Case C-158/07, *Jacqueline Förster* v. *Hoofddirectie van de Informatie Beheer Groep* [2008] ECR I-08507; Case C-135/08, *Janko Rottmann* v. *Freistaat Bayern* [2010] ECR I-01449; Case C-256/11, *Murat Dereci and Others* v. *Bundesministerium für Inneres* [2011] ECR I-11315: CJEU elaborates on *Zambrano* and 'genuine enjoyment of substance of citizenship rights'; and, more recently, the shifting dynamics in Case C-67/14 *Jobcenter Berlin Neukölln* v. *Alimanovic* [2015] ECR 00000 and Case C-299/14 *Vestische Arbeit Jobcenter Kreis Recklinghausen* v. *García-Nieto* [2016] ECR 00000 where the CJEU has relied on a distinction between federal conferral of Union citizenship and Member State-controlled availability of benefits for the non-economically active. See S. Mantu and P. Minderhoud, 'EU Citizenship and Social Solidarity' (2017) 24 *Maastricht Journal of European and Comparative Law* 703, 710–20.

[50] Case C-135/08, *Janko Rottmann* v. *Freistaat Bayern* [2010] ECR I-01449, at [58].

Rather, federal citizenship has a direct influence on federated citizenship. The Court has thus arguably moved from a mere interpretation of the relevant constitutional text towards a position that changes the nature of the interaction between the Union and the Member States. Their discretion, while significant, can be limited if rights granted to EU citizens are at stake.

This is an important case, demonstrating that even the starting point of this constitutional criticism is under serious challenge. Member States in the EU no longer have unlimited discretion as to when and how citizenship is awarded, particularly if there is a risk of interference with EU citizenship rights. The CJEU thus displays a carefully argued federal understanding of citizenship in this area. It also, to a certain extent, shows us how important is the understanding of the nature and dynamic of certain concepts and how the interpretation by the courts can have profound constitutional effects on the polity.

Several cases have reached the European Court from Member States who are themselves hesitant to award further citizenship benefits. In all these cases, reluctant or cautious Member State courts requested preliminary references to clarify the scope of EU citizenship. From the centre, these cases then received clear federal guidance. Consider *Martinez Sala*.[51] Mrs Martinez Sala, a Spanish national, had been working in Munich for the Spanish Consulate General and had been living legally in Germany for over ten years. However, she then became unemployed and did not fulfil the requirements of the free movement of workers. Nevertheless, the ECJ decided that she was entitled to a child-raising allowance because the only reason why the German authorities turned down her request was due to her nationality, which in turn constituted discrimination on the basis of nationality, prohibited by the EU Treaties. As seen earlier, the Court went one step further in the case of *Grzelczyk*. Mr Grzelczyk was a French national who studied in Belgium and applied for the *minmax*, a social benefit. His application was turned down on the basis of his nationality. The ECJ decided again that Mr Grzelczyk was entitled to non-discrimination and this time relied on the newly introduced EU citizenship chapter in the EU treaties, declaring that it was destined to become the fundamental status according to which the Member States will relate to

[51] Case C-85/96, *María Martínez Sala* v. *Freistaat Bayern* [1998] ECR I-02691, noted by A. Albors-Llorens, 'A Broader Construction of the EC Treaty Provisions on Citizenship?' (1998) 57 *Cambridge Law Journal* 461.

nationals of other Member States.[52] Other cases include *Bidar*, where the Court decided that a French citizen was entitled to a study grant in the UK on the basis of his connectedness with the UK educational system.[53] These cases arguably display a strong federal understanding of two different but interconnected layers of citizenship in the Union. While Member States in all of these cases were hesitant to award benefits to the nationals of other EU Member States, the ECJ, through its interpretation of what is now Art. 20 TFEU, emphasized the rights that are conferred at the federal level and, in doing so, clarified our understanding of the reach of EU citizenship.

The most striking case after *Rottmann* is *Ruiz Zambrano*. Mr Zambrano, a Colombian citizen, had two children born in Belgium who, by virtue of their birth, acquired Belgian citizenship. The Belgian authorities wanted to expel his entire family on the basis that their asylum request had been turned down. The CJEU stepped in and this time followed a passionate plea by AG Sharpston to read EU citizenship rights expansively.[54] It decided that Mr Zambrano and his entire family had a right to stay and work in Belgium because otherwise the parents of EU nationals could not stay in the Union and earn a living, thus inhibiting the genuine enjoyment of citizenship rights. The Court, as in previous cases, decided this case in a way that demonstrates how different layers of citizenship can be interpreted and, in doing so, displayed a good understanding of the federal nature of the Union. Some critics have highlighted that the case caused a stir among EU Member States and Belgium eventually changed its nationality law,[55] arguably undermining the

[52] Case C-184/99, *Rudy Grzelczyk* v. *Centre public d'aide sociale d'Ottignies-Louvain-la-Neuve* [2001] ECR I-06193.

[53] Case C-209/03, *The Queen (on the application of Dany Bidar)* v. *London Borough of Ealing and Secretary of State for Education and Skills* [2005] ECR I-02119, noted by Barnard, 'Case C-209/03', 1465. This trend has been complicated by the recent decision in Case C-333/13 *Dano* v. *Jobcenter Leipzig* [2014] ECR 00000, where the CJEU inadvertently blurred the lines by making sufficient resources a precondition to the right to reside legally in another Member State rather than a precondition to the right to claim benefits once residence as an EU national was established, allowing both broad and narrow readings of the federal rights to movement, as discussed in H. Verschueren, 'Preventing "Benefit Tourism" in the EU: A Narrow or Broad Interpretation of the Possibilities Offered by the ECJ in *Dano*?' (2015) 52 *Common Market Law Review* 363.

[54] Opinion of AG Sharpston in Case C-34/09, *Gerardo Ruiz Zambrano* v. *Office national de l'emploi (ONEm)* [2011] ECR I-01177.

[55] S. Adam and P. van Elsuwege, 'Citizenship Rights and the Federal Balance between the European Union and Its Member States: Comment on Dereci' (2012) 37(2) *European Law Review* 176. For relevant changes in Member State policy, see S. K. Schmidt, *The European Court of Justice and the Policy Process: The Shadow of Case Law* (Oxford 2018) 187.

reach of EU citizenship by installing a more restrictive practice at Member State level. Belgium's actions served to reinforce the elucidated federated rights of the Member States, demonstrating that, in the EU, different levels of citizenship can and do co-exist and that no higher level of homogeneity is required.

This extensive case law shows that there is a significant level of EU citizenship rights that reaches deep into the Member State legal orders. Full homogeneity is a misconception, and an appropriate complex and federated level of homogenous citizenship is already coming to exist at the European Union level.

2.2.4 Conclusion as to the Validity of This Objection

Is homogeneity truly lacking in the European context, then? What lessons can be learnt from the examples above in regard to the possibility of constitutionalizing Europe? The primary answer is that federal polities are rarely, if ever, built on a homogeneous and single citizenship of their people. This refutes the arguments of those who seek to deny the feasibility of a constitutionalized Europe due to the historical, cultural and identity-based differences present among the states that comprise the European Union. From overlapping conceptions of citizenship to quirks of self-identification within each state, constitutional scholars have conclusively demonstrated that the diverse citizenries were respected and melded into a constitutional system in each federal polity that both respects and incorporates them. Further, in an increasingly important series of European jurisprudence, EU citizenship has been interpreted as being of equal or more importance than Member State levels of self-identification.

2.3 No Religious Homogeneity?

2.3.1 Obstacle

A frequently cited obstacle to the development of European constitutional *demos* is a lack of a shared religion or even a sense of common religious values and traditions.[56] Religion is seen as a significant factor in the development of a common *demos*, and Europe appears to have very

[56] A. Liedhegener and D. Gerstenhauer, 'Auf dem Weg zu einem kooperativen Verhaeltnis Religion und die Vertiefung der Europaeischen Union' in O. Leisse (ed.), *Die Europaeische Union nach dem Vertrag von Lissabon* (Wiesbaden 2010).

little in the way of a homogenous approach to religion,[57] even without taking Turkish accession interests into account. Critics argue that peaceful co-existence is possible only if a certain proximity of dominant religions exists in the population.[58]

2.3.2 *Underlying Concepts of Constitutional Development*

Several contemporary federal entities provide insightful examples of similar challenges during key periods of their own constitutional development. In the United States, the mere fact that most Americans were Christians did not bind them together. Indeed, at key times and on key issues, Christianity per se did not unite American society.[59] Rather, varying religious beliefs – and attenuated social beliefs and mores – were frequently in tension with each other, even leading to incidents of physical violence. Thus, although a shared sense of God existed – and still exists – throughout the history of the United States, and this sense was often used to motivate people, there is little in the constitutional history of the United States to suggest that American national identity depended on one common homogenous religious or spiritual belief. Rather, the colonies that would become the United States of America were far from homogenous, and this is particularly true in terms of religion. The Pilgrims themselves were dissenters in England and left to found a new home as a result.[60] The Huguenots – French Protestants who eventually drew the ire of French authorities and were persecuted – fled to several colonies in what would become the United States.[61] Roman Catholics, long persecuted in England, were granted a place of safe-haven in the New World with the charter of Maryland under Lord Baltimore.[62] Similarly, William Penn was given a charter by the British government to found a colony for Quakers, another minority religious group that was not well received in mainstream cosmopolitan circles.[63] Communities of Amish were created within several of the colonies by the time of the

[57] Grimm, *Braucht Europa eine Verfassung?* vol. 60 Siemens Stiftung, 42.

[58] See political science literature, e.g. K. M. Bakke and E. Wibbels, 'Diversity, Disparity, and Civil Conflict in Federal States' (2006) 59 *World Politics* 1.

[59] S. E. Ahlstrom and D. D. Hall, *A Religious History of the American People* (New Haven, CT 2004) 263.

[60] E. Foner and J. A. Garraty (eds.), *The Reader's Companion to American History* (New York 1991) 169.

[61] J. McManners, *The Oxford History of Christianity* (New York 1993) 288.

[62] Foner and Garraty, 161.

[63] Ibid., 169.

Declaration of Independence.[64] This diversity in many ways also prevented the revolutionaries from an easy shedding of their State identities.

Dichotomies of suspicion existed not only between Catholic and Protestant communities but also within many factions of Protestantism, and reflected the prejudices and policies of the European states from which the immigrants that comprised the colonial settlements came. The goal of those who drafted and signed the Declaration of Independence was to create a moment of rupture – legal and societal – that would last far longer than their own lives.[65] Even where the colonies were chartered by the same British sovereign, they were not all chartered for the same purposes. For example, Maryland and Pennsylvania were chartered to give a home to minority religious groups – Catholics[66] and Quakers,[67] respectively. And Georgia was created as a penal colony, although its founders also sought to make it a place of refuge for those of non-mainstream faiths, including Jews and Catholics.[68] The colonies generally were thought of as being a place of freedom and/or protection from the standard persecutions in Europe, and attracted a wide range of nationalities, ethnic groups and religious groups, which in turn shaped the independent character of each colony.[69]

In essence, only very rudimentary requirements of homogeneity can be seen as fulfilled in spiritual terms for the US Early Republic. The 'living together' of individuals from different religious faiths can be a constituting part of creating a federal polity. Differing religious faiths and denominations will not form a relevant consideration for the homogeneity requirement when assessing a federal entity.

64 Ibid., 359.

65 See Laursen, *The EU and Federalism*, 782–3 quoting John Adams' comments to Abigail Adams: 'The second day of July, 1776, will be the most memorable epoch in the history of America. I am apt to believe that it will be celebrated by succeeding generations as the great anniversary festival. It ought to be commemorated as the day of deliverance, by solemn acts of devotion to God Almighty. It ought to be solemnized with pomp and parade, with shows, games, sports, guns, bells, bonfires and illuminations, from one end of this continent to the other, from this time forward, forevermore. You will think me transported with enthusiasm, but I am not. I am well aware of the toil, and blood, and treasure, that it will cost us to maintain this declaration, and support and defend these States. Yet, through all the gloom, I can see the rays of ravishing light and glory. I can see that the end is more than worth all the means, and that posterity will triumph in that day's transaction, even although we should rue it, which I trust in God we shall not.'

66 Ahlstrom and Hall, 166.

67 Ibid., 97.

68 Ibid., 134.

69 Ibid., 4.

Similarly, taking Canada as an additional example, there were two dominant Christian denominations and other religions such as the Jewish faith, as the debate about reasonable accommodations in Quebec shows even today.[70] This dualism of Canada as a Dominion for both English-speaking Protestants and French-speaking Catholics was one of the founding features of the Union. The Constitution Act of 1867 provided important safeguards against influence from either side and allowed separate schooling and strong support for religiously based school systems in the provinces.[71] It is thus not surprising that public funding for Catholic schools in Ontario has withstood all constitutional challenges, even those based on the Charter of Fundamental Rights, which the Supreme Court declared inapplicable to Sec. 93.[72] The Canadian Supreme Court called this provision a 'historical

[70] M. Potvin, 'Social and Media Discourse in the Reasonable Accommodations Debate' (2010) *Immigration and Diversity* 78.

[71] Art. 93 provides:

> In and for each Province the Legislature may exclusively make Laws in relation to Education, subject and according to the following Provisions: (1) Nothing in any such Law shall prejudicially affect any Right or Privilege with respect to Denominational Schools which any Class of Persons have by Law in the Province at the Union; (2) All the Powers, Privileges, and Duties at the Union by Law conferred and imposed in Upper Canada on the Separate Schools and School Trustees of the Queen's Roman Catholic Subjects shall be and the same are hereby extended to the Dissentient Schools of the Queen's Protestant and Roman Catholic Subjects in Quebec; (3) Where in any Province a System of Separate or Dissentient Schools exists by Law at the Union or is thereafter established by the Legislature of the Province, an Appeal shall lie to the Governor General in Council from any Act or Decision of any Provincial Authority affecting any Right or Privilege of the Protestant or Roman Catholic Minority of the Queen's Subjects in relation to Education; (4) In case any such Provincial Law as from Time to Time seems to the Governor General in Council requisite for the due Execution of the Provisions of this Section is not made, or in case any Decision of the Governor General in Council on any Appeal under this Section is not duly executed by the proper Provincial Authority in that Behalf, then and in every such Case, and as far only as the Circumstances of each Case require, the Parliament of Canada may make remedial Laws for the due Execution of the Provisions of this Section and of any Decision of the Governor General in Council under this Section.

[72] In *Adler* v. *Ontario* [1996] 3 SCR 609, the majority ruled:

> Section 93 of the Constitution Act, 1867 is the product of a historicalcompromise crucial to Confederation and forms a comprehensive code with respect to denominational school rights which cannot be enlarged through the operation of s. 2 (a) of the Charter. It does not represent a guarantee of fundamental freedoms. The appellants, given that they cannot bring themselves within the terms of s. 93's guarantees, have no claim to public funding for their schools. To

compromise crucial to Confederation'.[73] So, in other words, a foundational feature, protected by the courts, can be religious freedom, even when this goes so far as to safeguard certain religious rights in the educational system.

Similarly, in Switzerland, when France insisted on free movement of its citizens, including Jewish citizens, there was a constitutional crisis requiring an amendment of the Constitution in 1866, which introduced equal treatment for Jewish citizens but no right to participate in elections for non-residents.[74] So entrenched were the discussions about religious faiths in Switzerland that some feared that the federal union might break over the question.[75] Even to this day, Switzerland battles with questions of religious tolerance, as demonstrated by disputes surrounding the building of minarets.[76] From a theoretical perspective, the existence of several key religious communities might even be a strong reason for the creation of federal polity rather than a unitary state.[77]

From these illustrative examples, it is unlikely that even a minimum level of religious homogeneity is required for the development of common *demos* in European constitutionalization.

2.3.3 Related EU Developments

Even assuming that a certain level of spiritual homogeneity is characteristic of *demos*, the experiences of the United States and Canada make it

> decide otherwise by accepting the appellants' claim that s. 2 (a) requires public funding of their dissentient religion-based schools would be to hold one section of the Constitution violative of another.

[73] Ibid.

[74] H. C. Peyer, *Verfassungsgeschichte der alten Schweiz* (Zurich 1978).

[75] J. Steinberg, *Why Switzerland?*, 2nd ed. (Cambridge 1996) 206.

[76] J.-F. Mayer, 'A Country without Minarets: Analysis of the Background and Meaning of the Swiss Vote of 29 November 2009' (2011) 41(1) *Religion* 11; D. Danaci, 'The Minaret Ban in Switzerland: An Exception to the Rule?' in W. Marxer (ed.), *Direct Democracy and Minorities* (New York/Heidelberg 2012); D. Miller, 'Majorities and Minarets: Religious Freedom and Public Space' (2016) 46 *British Journal of Political Science* 437.

See Conseil fédéral suisse, 'Message relatif à l'initiative populaire «Oui à l'interdiction de se dissimuler le visage» et au contre-projet indirect (loi fédérale sur la dissimulation du visage)' (Federal Gazette, 15 March 2019), www.admin.ch/opc/fr/federal-gazette/2019/2895.pdf. For a more critical piece on the minaret/burqa ban debates, see V. Eskandari and E. Banfi, 'Institutionalising Islamophobia in Switzerland: The Burqa and Minaret Bans' (2017) 4 *Islamophobia Studies Journal* 53.

[77] A. V. Dicey, *Introduction to the Study of the Law of the Constitution*, 8th ed. (London 1915).

clear that the requirements cannot be seen as exceeding the current level of commonality between EU Member States. Among the EU Member States, there is a certain level of religious homogeneity in the sense that freedom of religion is guaranteed as a correlative of dignity of men, for example, in Art. 10 Charter of Fundamental Rights: '1. Everyone has the right to freedom of thought, conscience and religion. This right includes freedom to change religion or belief and freedom, either alone or in community with others and in public or in private, to manifest religion or belief, in worship, teaching, practice and observance.'[78] In terms of *demos*, the United States is notable for its lack of a common religion, which is also a feature of the current EU configuration and membership. Indeed, some argue that the accession negotiations of Turkey – a state that, although secular since its modern-day founding, has a majority Muslim population and lengthy Islamic history as the seat of the Ottoman Empire – negate constitutionalization as a real possibility because they work against a shared sense of religious understanding.[79] Despite the current view of the United States as religiously homogenous, in that the majority of its citizens have been and are adherents to some form of Christian faith, a review of early US history demonstrates that this homogeneity is actually misleading in terms of the required level of unity. From its colonial inception onward, the United States has attracted all forms of Christian faiths. This is similar to the European distribution of a variety of Christian denominations within the jurisdictions of the European Union Member States.

Cases with a religious content are not exogenous to the European Courts and, indeed, the Strasbourg Court earned certain elements of its global reputation through various sweeping judgments in the area of religious matters that are not binding upon the CJEU.[80]

The ECJ has mainly defended the right to religious tolerance.[81] One of the most hotly debated points of the Constitutional Convention process was the question of a reference to God in the preamble of the Treaty establishing a Constitution.[82] Even the Pope intervened briefly in the

[78] Art. 10, Charter of Fundamental Rights of the European Union (OJ 2000 C 364 p.1).

[79] B. Kuniholm, 'Turkey's Accession to the European Union: Differences in European and US Attitudes, and Challenges for Turkey' (2001) 2 *Turkish Studies* 25.

[80] S. Mancini, 'Taking Secularism (Not Too) Seriously: The Italian "Crucifix Case"' (2006) 1 *Religion and Human Rights* 179.

[81] B. M. Awe, 'Religion in the EU: Using Modified Public Reason to Define European Human Rights' (2009) 10 *German Law Journal* 1439.

[82] See 'Proposal of the Polish members of the European Convention – Mr. Edmund Wittbrodt, Mrs. Danuta Huebner, Mr. Jozef Oleksy, Mrs. Genowefa Grabowska,

debate. In the end there was no reference to God included in either the Constitutional Treaty or the Lisbon Treaty.[83] Rather, the current preamble of the TEU states: 'Drawing inspiration from the cultural, religious and humanist inheritance of Europe, from which have developed the universal values of the inviolable and inalienable rights of the human person, freedom, democracy, equality and the rule of law . . .', itself displaying a high degree of tolerance and freedom of religion.

One of the first cases to occupy the ECJ was the case of *Van Duyn*.[84] A Dutch national, Mrs van Duyn, wanted to do clerical work for the Church of Scientology, which was regarded by UK authorities as an organization against public order. The ECJ concluded that the freedom of workers to work in other Member States was a directly effective right and the UK authorities could deny her entry to the UK only where they relied on concrete personal behaviour of Mrs van Duyn that was giving rise to public order concerns. Mere membership of an organization was not sufficient to ban her from the UK.

Another case dealt with the hot topic of abortion, which is often discussed in religious terms. This was the case of *Grogan*.[85] Mr Grogan had campaigned in the Republic of Ireland as a member of a student union to inform students about the possibilities of abortion in England. He asked for a preliminary reference to be made in his case and the ECJ decided that, while it was not competent to rule on religious matters, the mere fact that a service was prohibited in one country and legal in another did not preclude the application of the fundamental freedom to provide services. However, Mr Grogan was not selling his information; thus, his 'information service' was not considered a commercial activity and as such did not benefit from the fundamental EU freedom in question. In many ways, again, we see that the ECJ displayed an understanding of religious homogeneity that does not leave the question solely to the Member States but, rather, strongly affirms religious freedom and tolerance.

Mr. Janusz Trzciński, Mrs. Marta Fogler' – who wanted to include a reference to the Judaeo-Christian values, http://european-convention.europa.eu/docs/Treaty/pdf/1000/Pre%20Wittbrodt-a%20EN.pdf.

[83] H. Goerlich, W. Huber and K. Lehmann, *Verfassung ohne Gottesbezug?: Zu einer aktuellen europäischen Kontroverse* (Leipzig 2004); A. J. Menéndez, 'A Christian or a Laic Europe? Christian Values and European Identity' (2005) 18 *Ratio Juris* 179.

[84] Case 41/74, *Yvonne van Duyn* v. *Home Office* [1974] ECR 01337.

[85] Case C-159/90, *The Society for the Protection of Unborn Children Ireland Ltd* v. *Stephen Grogan and others* [1991] ECR I-04685.

2.3.4 *Conclusion as to the Validity of This Obstacle*

In this section, I have deconstructed the myth of the United States as a religiously homogeneous polity in which the Constitution could easily flourish. In fact, this example demonstrates that homogeneity can be deceptive and that a variety of religions had to come together to create, enforce and protect the Constitution and the Union it formed. Thus, arguments that constitutionalism in the European Union context is a different – and difficult – concept due to the lack of a common religious tradition are undermined by other illustrative experiences. They prove that it is entirely possible for a constitutional system to exist and succeed despite the presence of varying – and sometimes warring – religious traditions. Further, the ECJ has been instrumental in ensuring a tolerant constitutional approach. Its understanding is thus in line with other federal examples.

2.4 No Homogeneity of Values?

2.4.1 *Obstacle*

One of the obstacles raised for constitutionalization is the lack of common values.[86] Homogeneity of values is judged by some national constitutional scholars to be required for further constitutionalization. Similarly, the GFCC, for instance, has argued that it is not possible to have a European *demos* without homogeneity of values. There is no decision that would affirm the existence or possibility of a European *demos*.

2.4.2 *Underlying Concepts of Constitutional Development*

Common values are not generally a precondition for constitutionalization. Some argue that no such common values are *necessary* in a federal polity; others agree that the level of homogeneity of values is already present in Europe.[87] Indeed, in a number of examples of states with

[86] J. Lacroix, 'Does Europe Need Common Values? Habermas vs Habermas' (2009) 8 *European Journal of Political Theory* 141.

[87] See G. F. Mancini, *Democracy and Constitutionalism in the EU* (Oxford 2000) 31; D. N. Chryssochoou, *Democracy in the European Union* (London 1998); E. O. Eriksen and J. E. Fossum (eds.), *Democracy in the European Union: Integration through Deliberation?* (London 2000); Fabbrini (ed.), *Democracy and Federalism*; C. Lord, *Democracy in the European Union* (Sheffield 1998); V. A. Schmidt, *Democracy in*

a written constitutional tradition, there seems to be an understanding that the constitutional document serves as a source for common values.[88] Indeed, as McDougal explained in the context of international law in the 1950s:

> In this contemporary world, people are increasingly demanding common values that transcend the boundaries of nation-states; they are increasingly interdependent in fact, irrespective of nation-state boundaries, for controlling the conditions which affect the securing of their values; and they are becoming ever more realistic in their consciousness of such interdependences, and hence widening their identifications to include in their demands more and more of their fellow men.[89]

Taking again the example of the US Early Republic, a closer analysis reveals a plethora of competing and often conflicting values, the most fundamental of which concerned the question of slavery.[90] While all revolutionaries were united in their revolutionary experience, there were very few values that were shared among the newly independent Americans. Some commentators have highlighted the commitment to democracy as a fundamental shared value, but, among the leading Federalists, there was growing scepticism of unfettered democratic governance, which was seen in some colonies to lead to new injustices.[91] This example shows that it is difficult to argue that a certain homogeneity of values would be necessary for a federal state.

This concern has been similarly raised but also addressed in the constitutional development of Switzerland and Canada. Their experiences can serve as additional examples from which we can draw out underlying constitutional concepts in this area.

In Switzerland, competing values were enshrined in its 1848 Constitution. Some favoured strong Cantons, while others favoured a Swiss nation state. Most fundamental rights were not formally included until the complete revision of the Swiss Constitution in 1999 and only as a codification of the existing case law on the matter. In this sense, it is

Europe: The EU and National Polities (Oxford 2006); F. W. Scharpf, 'Democratic Legitimacy under Conditions of Regulatory Competition: Why Europe Differs from the United States' in Nicolaidis and Howse.

88 P. H. Russell, 'The Political Purposes of the Canadian Charter of Rights and Freedoms' (1983) 61 *Canadian Bar Review* 30.

89 M. S. McDougal, 'The Comparative Study of Law for Policy Purposes: Value Clarification as an Instrument of Democratic World Order' (1952) 1 *American Journal of Comparative Law* 24.

90 See Wood, *Empire of Liberty*, ch. 14, 531.

91 Ibid.

difficult to argue that, given the competing values represented in the original Swiss Constitution, there was a high degree of homogeneity of values in this federal project. Rather, these values became more homogenous over time. One of the most prominent values of the Swiss Federation is the use of direct democracy for important decisions. This instrument, for instance, though used in some Cantons, did not develop until the late nineteenth century.[92]

In Canada, shared values existed in the 1867 Constitution largely because of the colonial heritage of the four original provinces. Quebec only much later insisted on its own values and tried to even codify them, most recently in the *Charte des valeurs québécoises*.[93] This last example shows that even if a federal polity develops with a high degree of common values, this is no guarantee for the continuation of said values. Respect for a diverse range of values can thus be characteristic of a federation.

2.4.3 Related EU Developments

From the very beginning, EU Member States were significantly more homogeneous in terms of their values (and the values of the Community) than the US Early Republic and other such examples noted here.

The main component of homogeneity in a society today – the question of homogeneity of values – was overlooked by the GFCC. Interestingly, the GFCC does not enunciate in its list of homogeneity the question of political and social values. Rather, the Court seems to substitute the question of *demos* with some kind of pre-established perception of existing values within the polity. While the Court acknowledges the notion of change in its decision (i.e. the fact that EU integration can be successful in certain areas), it stops short of acknowledging that, in some areas, EU countries have already reached a significant level of homogeneity and/or that any homogeneity is not simply because of the ongoing integration project. This is seemingly in contradiction with the jurisprudence of the CJEU,[94] and also Art. 10 TEU, which declares the EU Parliament a direct source of representation of EU citizens and the Council an indirect source.[95] The EU has a strong general statement of

[92] Kobach, 12.

[93] For profound and historic criticism, see J. Maclure, 'Le projet d'une charte de la laïcité: les raisons d'un sain scepticisme' (2013) 34 *La Revue Tocqueville* 155.

[94] Case 294/83, *Parti écologiste 'Les Verts'* v. *European Parliament* [1986] ECR 01339.

[95] 'Citizens are directly represented at Union level in the European Parliament. Member States are represented in the European Council by their Heads of State or Government

values in its Art. 2 TEU: 'The Union is founded on the values of respect for human dignity, freedom, democracy, equality, the rule of law and respect for human rights, including the rights of persons belonging to minorities. These values are common to the Member States in a society in which pluralism, non-discrimination, tolerance, justice, solidarity and equality between women and men prevail.'[96]

These values are also relevant in its international affairs,[97] its neighbourhood policy,[98] as well as in the accession process.[99] All candidate countries must comply with the so-called Copenhagen criteria. They must fulfil a political, an economic and an EU law criterion. In political terms, the candidate country must enjoy stability of institutions guaranteeing democracy, the rule of law, human rights and respect for and protection of minorities. In economic terms, it must have a functioning market economy and the capacity to cope with competitive pressure and market forces within the Union. Finally, in EU terms, it must accept the Union *acquis*, i.e. complying with all EU law in force and having the ability to take on the obligations of membership, including adherence to the aims of political, economic and monetary union.[100] It is these criteria, and not simply geographic proximity, that ensure that common values exist in the Union.[101] Any Member State no longer adhering to these values can be suspended according to Art. 7 TEU, which proscribes:

and in the Council by their governments, themselves democratically accountable either to their national Parliaments, or to their citizens'; Art. 10.2, TEU.

[96] See the commentary on Art. 2 by M. Klamert and D. Kochenov, 'Article 2 TEU' in M. Kellerbauer, M. Klamert and J. Tomkin (eds.), *The Treaties and the Charter of Fundamental Rights: A Commentary* (Oxford 2019) 22.

[97] I. Manners, 'The Normative Ethics of the European Union' (2008) 84 *International Affairs* 45.

[98] P. Leino and R. Petrov, 'Between "Common Values" and Competing Universals: The Promotion of the EU's Common Values through the European Neighbourhood Policy' (2009) 15 *European Law Journal* 654. See Part VI, 'The European Neighbourhood Policy and the Promotion of EU Norms and Values' in T. Schumacher, A. Marchetti, and T. Demmelhuber (eds.), *The Routledge Handbook on the European Neighborhood Policy* (Abingdon/New York 2017).

[99] H. Vollard, *European Disintegration* (London 2018), 99.

[100] See analysis by J.-W. Müller, 'Defending Democracy within the EU' (2013) 24 *Journal of Democracy* 138.

[101] Art. 49, TEU:

> Any European State which respects the values referred to in Article 2 and is committed to promoting them may apply to become a member of the Union. The European Parliament and national Parliaments shall be notified of this application. The applicant State shall address its application to the Council, which shall act unanimously after consulting the Commission and after

> On a reasoned proposal by one third of the Member States, by the European Parliament or by the European Commission, the Council, acting by a majority of four fifths of its members after obtaining the consent of the European Parliament, may determine that there is a clear risk of a serious breach by a Member State of the values referred to in Article 2. Before making such a determination, the Council shall hear the Member State in question and may address recommendations to it, acting in accordance with the same procedure.

In other words, there is a constitutional procedure in the Treaty to deal with Member States no longer adhering to identifiable common values.[102]

While even the GFCC did not completely dismiss the possibility in its *Lisbon* decision, it suggested that such a *demos* remains a very distant potential. The CJEU has not answered this question directly; rather, it has simply ruled in a straightforward way that democracy and transparency are constitutional values of Europe.[103] Perceptions of democracy, administration, the role of the State, fundamental rights, social values in the economy and equality between men and women, just to name a few values, were legally considered shared by the Member States. As such, it is not surprising that the CJEU ruled[104] in *Stauder*, and later more explicitly in *Nold* and also in *Internationale Handelsgesellschaft*, that 'the court is bound to draw inspiration from constitutional traditions common to the Member states'. In *Nold*, the CJEU had to answer the difficult question of whether the fundamental rights of the Member States could influence the implementation of EU law. The original 1958 Treaties of the European Economic Community did not contain any reference to public values beyond market values. The reason for this was simply that an attempt to create a European Political Community had failed in 1952 when the

> receiving the consent of the European Parliament, which shall act by a majority of its component members. The conditions of eligibility agreed upon by the European Council shall be taken into account.

[102] For various takes on this mechanism, see C. Closa and D. Kochenov (eds.), *Reinforcing the Rule of Law Oversight in the European Union* (Cambridge 2016). On the EU action taken in this area to date and additional mechanisms that have been proposed or launched to monitor and enforce, see L. Pech and K. L. Scheppele, 'EU Values Illiberalism Within: Rule of Law Backsliding in the EU' (2017) 19 *Cambridge Yearbook of European Legal Studies* 3.

[103] See, most recently, Opinion of AG Cruz Villalón in Case C-280/11 P, *Council of the European Union* v. *Access Info Europe*, Judgment of the Court (First Chamber) of 17 October 2013, not yet reported.

[104] Case 29/69, *Erich Stauder* v. *City of Ulm – Sozialamt* [1969] ECR 00419 and Case 4/73, *J. Nold, Kohlen- und Baustoffgroßhandlung* v. *Commission of the European Communities* [1974] ECR 00491.

French National Assembly refused to ratify the treaty.[105] While this approach was successfully used in fundamental rights cases, it demonstrates a significant and high level of homogeneity with regard to fundamental values of society. Certainly, the emphasis on diversity as an important European value by the courts demonstrates a rather sophisticated understanding of the federal nature of the EU project.

The protection of human rights may be considered a common European value. While much of the attention of human rights protection is on the Council of Europe's European Court of Human Rights (ECHR),[106] the CJEU has developed a sophisticated human and fundamental rights jurisprudence.[107] In the December 2014 ECHR accession opinion, this communality of values was explicitly recognized, leading to the draft accession agreement being found incompatible with EU law:

> This legal structure is based on the fundamental premise that each Member State shares with all the other Member States, and recognises that they share with it, a set of common values on which the EU is founded, as stated in Article 2 TEU. That premise implies and justifies the existence of mutual trust between the Member States that those values will be recognised and, therefore, that the law of the EU that implements them will be respected.[108]

After the Lisbon Treaty, this area is even more defined because of the entry into force of the Charter of Fundamental Rights, which has the same legal value as the Founding Treaties (Art. 5 TEU). The CJEU has recently engaged much more closely with the Charter text and decided in *Volker/Eifert*[109] and *Test Achat*[110] that the Charter serves as a basis to engage in legislative review of EU norms. In *Kadi*,[111] for example, it decided that even UN Security Council Resolutions and the UN Charter cannot trump the priority of fundamental rights in the EU system. All

[105] Craig and de Búrca, *The Evolution of EU Law*, 15.
[106] On the interaction between the Courts, see Douglas-Scott, 629.
[107] See A. von Bogdandy, 'The European Union as a Human Rights Organization? Human Rights and the Core of the European Union' (2000) 37 *Common Market Law Review* 1307; L. Betten and N. Grief, *EU Law and Human Rights* (Harlow 1998).
[108] Opinion 2/2013, (nyr) para. 167.
[109] Joined Cases C-92/09 and C-93/09, *Volker und Markus Schecke GbR (C-92/09) and Hartmut Eifert (C-93/09)* v. *Land Hessen* [2010] ECR I-11063.
[110] Case C-236/09, *Association Belge des Consommateurs Test-Achats ASBL and Others* v. *Conseil des ministres* [2011] ECR I-00773.
[111] Joined Cases C-402/05 P and C-415/05 P, *Yassin Abdullah Kadi and Al Barakaat International Foundation* v. *Council of the European Union and Commission of the European Communities* [2008] ECR I-06351.

these cases show that, at the level of values, Europe is much more homogeneous than many other polities. Again, emphasizing common values such as human rights can be a double-edged sword, and it perhaps puts into question how truly federal the CJEU's understanding is here. Certainly, in a federal entity we would welcome differing interpretations, above a certain minimum standard of fundamental rights protection. Forcing Member States to perhaps accept lower levels of protection would thus go against the shared values of Europe that are already evolving through the case law. The Court often emphasized the autonomy of the EU legal order and thus did not see itself as bound by the level of protection granted by Member States, for example, in the case of *Mannesmann Roehrenwerke*.[112] In this case, the CJEU decided that a level of protection offered under the German Constitution, specifically regarding the right to privacy for businesses, did not amount to an EU right. This was made more explicit recently in *Melloni*:

> It is true that Article 53 of the Charter confirms that, where an EU legal act calls for national implementing measures, national authorities and courts remain free to apply national standards of protection of fundamental rights, provided that the level of protection provided for by the Charter, as interpreted by the Court, and the primacy, unity and effectiveness of EU law are not thereby compromised.[113]

The emphasis was placed on EU rights even when the constitutional rights of the Member State contravene them.

2.4.4 *Conclusion as to the Validity of This Obstacle*

The analysis of common values plays an important part in our discussion of *demos*. A modern conception of *demos*, rather than relying on existing social structures, linguistic, religious or other homogeneity, has to see society as a commonwealth of shared fundamental values, even if just in the form of recognition that people can have several identities.[114] This obstacle has been advanced by Treaty change and through the CJEU

[112] T-112/98, *Mannesmannröhren-Werke* v. *Commission*, 20 February 2001, [2001] ECR II-729.

[113] Case C-399/11, *Melloni*, 26 February 2013, EU:C:2013:107, para 60.

[114] New anthropological research challenges the understanding that societies need shared values at all; see W. Schiffauer, *Parallelgesellschaften: Wie viel Wertekonsens braucht unsere Gesellschaft?: Für eine kluge Politik der Differenz* (Bielefeld 2008), who argues for a recognition of different values and multiple identities.

jurisprudence, and no longer prevents the further constitutionalization of Europe.

2.5 No Social and Linguistic Homogeneity?

2.5.1 Constitutional Obstacle

Constitutional scholars, as well as certain Member State courts, such as the GFCC, insist that the development of a truly European *demos* requires a certain level of social, ethnic or linguistic homogeneity.[115] Concerns about ethnic homogeneity do not need to be taken further, given the last century's progress in constitutional thinking, which recognizes the legitimacy of racial and ethnic diversity in any polity. However, there is a certain pragmatic obstacle for Europe that is not so easy to dismiss. Europe is currently attempting to develop *demos* with twenty-four official languages. To fully participate in the European *demos*, one would need to be an expert linguist. This, according to many scholars and courts, is unworkable in a purely social and practical sense.[116]

2.5.2 Underlying Concepts of Constitutional Development

Several contemporary federal entities provide examples of similar challenges, though none to the extent of the current European formal requirements for twenty-four official languages.[117] Federal constitutional legal scholarship has argued that many languages and diverse social understandings can be accommodated within a single federal polity,[118] but surely there are reasonable limits. It is simply not possible that to participate competently in real-time European public discussions, one must be an expert linguist with command of two dozen languages.

[115] See the work Heller, 421, 427pp referenced by *Maastricht Decision.*

[116] J. Lacey, 'Must Europe Be Swiss? On the Idea of a Voting Space and the Possibility of a Multilingual Demos' 44 *British Journal of Political Science* 61; P. van Parijs, *Linguistic Justice for Europe and for the World* (Oxford 2011); T. de Mauro, *In Europa son già 103. Troppe lingue per una democrazia?* (Laterza 2014). For a criticism of the idea that there should be a single EU lingua franca, see M. Gazzola and R. W. Ronza, 'The Politics and Policy of Multilingualism in the European Union' (2018) 1 *Brown Journal of World Affairs* 55.

[117] R. L. Creech, *Law and Language in the European Union: The Paradox of a Babel 'United in Diversity'* (Groningen 2007); R. Phillipson, 'Lingua Franca or Lingua Frankensteinia? English in European Integration and Globalisation' (2008) 27 *World Englishes* 250.

[118] Bakke and Wibbels, 1.

One of the main reasons for Canadian federalism was the accommodation of two very different social and linguistic communities.[119] The communities of Lower and Upper Canada, that is, Quebec and Ontario, did not actually share the same languages or social identities. There were parts in the original Constitution Act that protected education, but, rather than specifying protection of the language, Art. 93 emphasized Protestant and Catholic schools. Art. 16, however, determined that 'English and French are the official languages of Canada and have equality of status and equal rights and privileges as to their use in all institutions of the Parliament and government of Canada'.

During the early development of Switzerland, different Cantonal communities did not share linguistic or social homogeneity.[120] The German-speaking Cantonal communities, in the late nineteenth century, were oriented towards conversations in German often from Zurich or Basel or even from Germany, whereas Francophone communities engaged in discussions through Geneva or often Paris. Nonetheless, the Constitution of 1848 was seen as instrumental to forging a new federal nation in Switzerland. However, over time, up to four official languages became genuinely accommodated within the Swiss constitutional order.[121] In Switzerland, as in Canada, the creation of a social and linguistic community evolved over time.

Post-apartheid South Africa is sometimes also put forward as a relevant example where twelve official languages are recognized, but this will not be addressed here, given the unique post-racism and social conditions of its constitutional development and the lack of adequate time to assess the success of its linguistic experiment.[122]

2.5.3 *Related EU Developments*

After sixty years of European integration,[123] there may be a certain growing social and linguistic homogeneity among the peoples of Europe. However, besides two devastating world wars, there is rarely

[119] H. B. Small, *Chronicles of Canada, or a Concise History of the Leading Events in the Old Provinces of the New Dominion* (Ottawa 1868).

[120] C. H. Church and H. R. Conrad, *A Concise History of Switzerland* (Cambridge 2013) 165; W. Oechsli, P. Eden and P. Cedar, *History of Switzerland, 1499–1914* (Cambridge 1922).

[121] E. His, *Schweizer Verfassungsgeschichte: Der Bundesstaat von 1848 bis 1914. Register zu Band I–III* (Zurich 1938).

[122] K. Govender, 'Federalism and Legal Unification in South Africa' in Halberstam and Reimann (eds.), *Federalism and Legal Unification*, 391.

[123] On EU integration, see Wiener, Börzel and Risse.

a common social experience that would provide an increased level of homogeneity. While a level of mutual understanding is wanted at the European level, the motto of the EU is 'united in diversity' (*in varietate concordia*)[124] and this was adopted also in opposition to *e pluribus unum*[125] ('one out of many'), with the aim of highlighting that diversity in Europe is treasured and Member States aim to protect it.

Turning to examine the language regime in Europe, we see diversity as a value. Consciously, Member States of the EU did not opt for a common language regime. As Bruno de Witte commented:

> Adopting a common currency among Member States of the European Union instead of using those countries' national currencies has paved the way for economic benefits and reinforced political cohesion within the European Union. As such, the adoption of a common language should also be able to bring about more economic benefits, since this would not only facilitate the implementation of common policies, but would also enable eased operation within the common European market. Strengthening the sense of European identity would also improve the EU's political and social cohesion. However, imposing a common currency is completely different from imposing a common language, as the latter is faced with several difficulties. European federalists never pursued this common language because of the need to preserve cultural distinctiveness and social cohesion among Member States.[126]

The CJEU has played a crucial role in fostering a certain element of pragmatism in regard to the language regime of European institutions. While at the level of treaties and Union institutions, all twenty-four official languages may be used,[127] this becomes more complicated at the level of Union agencies. In the leading case of *Christina Kik v. OHIM,* where Mrs Kik was vigorously defending her right to use Dutch in applications to the European Trade Mark office, the Court of Justice defended a pragmatic approach to languages, finding that a balance could be struck between official languages and economic expense for translation services.[128] In other words, the CJEU embarked

[124] D:\Mr.Mohan\CUP-Jobs\03-May-GEHRING\3

[125] Phrase incorporated in the official seal of the United States of America.

[126] B. de Witte, 'Language Law of the European Union: Protecting or Eroding Linguistic Diversity?' in R. Craufurd-Smith (ed.), *Culture and European Union Law* (Oxford 2004) 205.

[127] Regulation No. 1/1958 determining the languages to be used by the European Economic Community (OJ L 17, 6.10.1958, p.385).

[128] Case C-361/01 P, *Christina Kik* v. *Office for Harmonisation in the Internal Market (Trade Marks and Designs) (OHIM)* [2003] ECR I-08283; see comment by N. Nic Shuibhne,

on a centralizing trend in language policy that was previously known only at the level of nation states. Interestingly, Member States tried to secure the current language regime by introducing Art. 3 TEU, which states that the Union '... shall respect its rich cultural and linguistic diversity, and shall ensure that Europe's cultural heritage is safeguarded and enhanced'. However, the trajectory in the case law towards a slightly more centralized language regime seems to continue in the post-Lisbon area. Recent attempts to make increased use of 'working languages', for example in the case of the EU patent, were challenged by Spain and Italy.[129] The CJEU, against the arguments advanced by those two Member States, could not find any violation when the Council, after years of deadlock, opted for enhanced cooperation (Art. 20 TEU) instead of trying to bring every Member State on board. The Court resoundingly rejected the notion that the exclusion of the last two countries, who were insisting that their languages be included in an EU patent, could constitute a misuse of powers or violation of Art. 20 TEU. As seen in the examples, a certain level of homogeneity is desirable in Europe. Although there is not yet a clear understanding or need to converge into one single language, and the Court stops far short of finding that English should become some sort of *lingua franca*, the Court itself has recognized the need for a practical smaller subset of working languages (German, French and English).[130]

From the centre, other European cases of relevance to this debate include the case of *Angonese* on official language requirements and testing in the German-speaking province of Bolzano in Italy.[131] Mr Angonese had studied in Austria, but the private bank that was planning to employ him required an official bilingualism certificate from him, demonstrating his proficiency in German. The ECJ decided, on the basis that linguistic diversity is a protected right in Europe, that while the requirement to speak German in Bolzano was not an impediment to freedom of movement in itself, the documentation of such competency only via an official language test from the province was hindering

'Case C-361/01 P, Kik v. Office for Harmonization in the Internal Market (Trade Marks and Designs), (Kik IV)' (2004) 41(4) *Common Market Law Review* 1093.

129 Joined Cases C-274/11 and C-295/11, *Kingdom of Spain and Italian Republic* v. *Council of the European Union*, Judgment of the Court (Grand Chamber) of 16 April 2013, not yet reported.

130 For a critique of the dominance of these languages in the EU, see Q. Jin, 'Linguistic Hegemony in the EU' (2017) Proceedings of 3rd International Symposium on Social Science.

131 Case C-281/98, *Roman Angonese* v. *Cassa di Risparmio di Bolzano SpA* [2000] ECR I-04139.

workers in moving from one part of the Union to another. Several other judgments by the European Courts have confirmed that language requirements, such as speaking Irish to teach art in Ireland, are hindering freedom of movement. This line of case law is important because it prevents even private parties from erecting absolute barriers on the basis of language. As such, it is clear that, for the CJEU, linguistic homogeneity is not a requirement for Europe. Indeed, diversity must be respected and discrimination on this basis will not be tolerated. The Court does not see the use of many languages as an obstacle for Europe, but, rather, is willing to handle them in a flexible manner, balancing linguistic practicalities against other principles.[132]

Despite this approach in the centre courts, certain Member State courts are insisting on a very high level of social or linguistic homogeneity. This is the case in many of the GFCC's judgments. The GFCC does not provide an explanation of the requisite level of homogeneity beyond the pointing out that this homogeneity exists in the German Federal Republic and does not exist in the current European Union. The reasons are somewhat difficult to assess, but this conviction seems to be deeply rooted in German constitutional thought. While nineteenth-century scholars employed this argument to support German unification,[133] it has since become common to divide state sovereignty from other forms of governance.[134] From this perspective, the main reason that a certain level of social and political homogeneity is required seems to be an understanding that even the law cannot create the necessary constitutional consensus for a cohesive *demos* if a certain level of homogeneity is lacking.[135]

In contrast, other periphery courts appear quite willing to defer to the European Court on such matters of linguistic politics, as was the case in

[132] On categorizing the linguistic approaches of the CJEU and national courts, see S. Šarčević, *Language and Culture in EU Law: Multidisciplinary Perspectives* (London/New York 2016) 53.

[133] G. Jellinek, *Die Lehre von den Staatenverbindungen* (Vienna 1882) 137, where he discusses 'Staatenstaaten', i.e. federal states, and highlights that at his time the literature on this topic was very sparse and mainly focused on the German Empire, citing Schulze, who, according to Jellinek, was wrong in assuming that a federal state uniquely existed in Germany at the time.

[134] I. von Münch and P. Kunig, *Kommentar zum Grundgesetz*, 6th ed. (Munich 2012), Art. 146, which describes the process of replacing the German Constitution with a completely new constitutional document. This right, however, is reserved for the 'German nation' ('Deutsche Volk').

[135] Ibid.

the Belgian Constitutional Court in the dispute between *Wallonia* and *Flanders.*[136] The case concerned a new long-term illness insurance scheme that the authorities in Flanders had designed in a way so as to benefit only residents of Flanders or other EU citizens but not Wallonia people. The main criterion used for Belgian nationals of the scheme was the place of residence because, especially, schooling in Belgium is left to the linguistic communities; for instance, people living in Flanders will have their children schooled in Dutch. Francophone Belgians who wish their children to be educated in their mother tongue cannot enjoy the scheme while living in Wallonia where the schooling is in French. The whole insurance scheme was arguably designed to further linguistic objectives about which Wallonia complained in the Belgian Constitutional Court. While the Court did not find any reasons in the Belgian Constitution to strike down the measure, it decided to make a preliminary reference and the ECJ, despite a forcefully argued Opinion by AG Sharpston,[137] decided that this was a question of national law that the ECJ was not competent to answer. In other words, while the central Court does defend diversity and language rights at the European level, it continues to leave difficult constitutional decisions to the Member States. This shows that while social and linguistic homogeneity is not, even from the Member States' perspective, a requirement for European integration, there is a certain degree of under-development of this element of constitutionalization in Europe.

2.5.4 Conclusion as to the Validity of This Obstacle

An area where existing diversity is most pronounced is in the EU's very diverse language rules. There remains the question of whether a polity can – on a very practical level – have and respect twenty-four official languages without losing its *demos* quality. This is one of the questions that arises where illustrative examples from other federal entities provide little guidance for the European situation. Too many languages for open policy debates to actually occur in a European public space might well present one of the corollary obstacles that remain to be overcome in the EU. While English may well be unofficially used as a *lingua franca*, the informal recognition is simply not enough to avoid stifling the

[136] Case No 51/2006, 19 April 2006, Belgian Constitutional Court www.const-court.be /public/f/2006/2006-051f.pdf.

[137] Opinion of AG Sharpston in Case C-212/06, *Government of Communauté française and Gouvernement wallon* v. *Gouvernement flamand* [2008] ECR I-01683.

development of a common European public sphere. The unrealistic number of required languages, without a smaller subset of recognized and functional working languages, creates serious obstacles to open policy deliberation by the people in Europe.

2.6 No Common European Public Space for Political Debate?

2.6.1 *Obstacle to European Constitutionalization*

An important obstacle is the perceived lack of a common European public space for political debate. For successful constitutionalization, a common public space for political debate may be extremely crucial,[138] especially with regard to providing for political discourse beyond exchanges of the political elites, such as common debates about important public issues that affect the federation as a whole in the popular media and in common public forums designed for political dialogue.[139]

2.6.2 *Underlying Concepts of Constitutional Development*

Such a demand for a common European space may be based on an overly simplistic view of constitutional development. Indeed, today's 'common space for public debate' might best be described as simply a 'fragmented set of local public political debates' on common issues that affect the polity as a whole.[140] There is quantitative evidence of functioning public spheres at the Member State level and growing public awareness of other Member State perspectives. However, political scientists find only fragmentation and division at the EU level. In essence, there is interconnectedness of public spheres in the EU but little evidence of a trans-European common public space.[141] Based on qualitative examples, others such as Fossum and Koopmans disagree, highlighting seeds of an EU public sphere.[142] I agree that a public sphere may still develop over time, but

[138] On the importance of constitutionalization and the public sphere, see P. Blokker, 'Constitutional Mobilization and Contestation in the Transnational Sphere' (2018) 45 *Journal of Law and Society* S52.

[139] Risse, *European Public Spheres*, 5.

[140] U. Liebert, 'Civil Society, Public Sphere and Democracy in the EU' in E. O. Eriksen and J. E. Fossum (eds.), *Rethinking Democracy and the European Union* (London 2013).

[141] Sarikakis and Kolkytha; Risse, *European Public Spheres*, with further citations to his earlier works.

[142] J. E. Fossum and P. Schlesinger, *The European Union and the Public Sphere: A Communicative Space in the Making?* (Abingdon/New York 2007); R. Koopmans

the pace and scope of its evolution seems dependent on levels of politicalization, that is, increased political debates, in the European Union itself. Where, with the exception of a weak and under-noticed European Parliament, most decision-making is kept in intergovernmental executive or even administrative deliberations, it is not clear how this policy debate can ever flourish in a transparent and dynamic way.[143] The public sphere or communicative space does not simply occur. It can be constructed, and legal actors can make an important contribution to this process. The Regulation implementing the European Citizens' Initiative demonstrates how legal changes can build greater trans-European cooperation and debate.[144] The EU treaties require 1 million signatures from across a significant number of Member States (Art. 11.4 TEU) for a successful initiative. The corresponding implementation regulation further clarifies that this requires signatures from at least one-quarter of the Member States (seven countries) and that, for each of these seven, a minimum number of citizens must be engaged. In the Regulation, there is a formula for this minimum: the number of the MEPs elected in each Member State, multiplied by 750 (Art. 7 Regulation on the Citizen's Initiative), which translates to 3,750 signatures from Malta or 74,250 from Germany.[145]

Several contemporary federal entities offer insightful examples of overcoming such gaps during key periods of their constitutional development.[146]

For instance, one can consider the US experiences of public debates about democracy within each State of the US Early Republic – as opposed to democratic public debate at the Federal level. Early public debates about political issues during what was essentially a feudal post-colonial society in the relevant period were very different from our understanding of democratic public political debates today. Just as it was difficult to transmit information of the public sentiment from one State to another due to lack of media or modern communications in the late eighteenth century, it is actually difficult to interpret and transmit public political

and P. Statham, *The Making of a European Public Sphere: Media Discourse and Political Contention* (New York 2010).

143 Risse, *European Public Spheres*, 143.

144 J. Greenwood, 'The European Citizens' Initiative: Bringing the EU Closer to Its Citizens?' (2018) *Comparative European Politics* 940.

145 Regulation (EU) No 211/2011 of the European Parliament and of the Council of 16 February 2011 on the Citizens' Initiative, http://eur-lex.europa.eu/LexUriServ/LexUriServ.do?uri=OJ:L:2011:065:0001:0022:EN:PDF.

146 Fossum and Schlesinger.

debates across neighbouring European Member States today, due to not so dissimilar barriers.[147]

As an initial example, while it is easy to think of the United States essentially as a monolith in terms of identity and *demos* – especially at the time of its founding and the ratification of the Constitution – this is far from true and does a disservice to the founders' work in creating an umbrella society that opened a trans-American space for further public political debates.[148] In particular, it is important to mention that there were initially no 'national' newspapers or magazines in the United States.[149] These remained local or state-wide publications and had very little continental reach.[150] It may be that the lack of EU-wide media, for instance, is not necessarily an obstacle to constitutionalization as such.[151]

As a second example, constitutional scholars have demonstrated that Canada had a certain level of common public space in the *demos* of its founding, largely because the French language was either prohibited or severely under-represented in public policy.[152] Nonetheless, Canada is a very good example that social or political homogeneity is not necessary for the founding of a federal state. As noted by Henry Small, Canada was created as a composite dominion and more Provinces then joined the Union fairly early, bringing distinct cultural and social backgrounds that generated ample debate as to how such frontier provinces would fit into the new dominion of Canada.[153] This led, as explained by Peter Hogg, to an initially asymmetrical form of federalism where, even today, some parts of the Canadian Union are Territories with many of their affairs still controlled by the federal government. Initially, it was thought that the conquered French Canadian would not fit the Catholic English-speaking Canadian Provinces, which were governed by a common law system. It

[147] A. Koschnik, 'The Democratic Societies of Philadelphia and the Limits of the American Public Sphere, circa 1793–1795' (2001) 58 *The William and Mary Quarterly* 615.

[148] D. J. Siemers, *Ratifying the Republic: Antifederalists and Federalists in Constitutional Time* (Stanford, CA 2004).

[149] Foner and Garraty, 727.

[150] Interestingly, there is growing historical research suggesting that the American Revolution was made possible only by the widespread availability of mail services and newspapers; see for references the E Pluribus Unum Project directed by Dr John McClymer, Professor of History, Assumption College.

[151] M. Machill, M. Beiler and C. Fischer, 'Europe-Topics in Europe's Media: The Debate about the European Public Sphere: A Meta-Analysis of Media Content Analyses' (2006) 21 *European Journal of Communication* 57.

[152] Oakes and Warren, 34.

[153] Small, *Chronicles of Canada.*

was only after careful negotiations that special privileges were granted to the predominantly Catholic Quebecers.[154]

As a third example, scholars have also argued that in Switzerland, the Constitution of 1848 actually created a nation that did not really exist up to that point.[155] While there was a certain level of cultural and geographical homogeneity, there was close to no social or political homogeneity at the beginning of the new Constitutional federation. This, as explained by Franz Lehner, changed dramatically over the following decades through the new instruments of direct democracy, but, to this day, the Francophone and the German-speaking Cantons have very different voting patterns and prioritize very different issues.[156]

However, considering recent studies, it must be noted that constitutional legal scholarship continues to highlight this lack of a common public political debate as a major obstacle to the constitutional development of these federal polities during their initial period. This distinction indicates a real challenge for EU constitutional development and is discussed further in Chapter 5.

2.6.3 *Related EU Developments*

European constitutional law scholars demand a common frame of historical reference and, according to these scholars, there is value in current attempts to prepare a European modern history book for use in schools.[157] Different dimensions of developing European *demos* over time, namely by fostering a transparent European public debate about federal political issues, have been explored in European Courts. As AG Cruz Villalon said in his Opinion in Case C-280/11P *Council* v. *Access Info Europe*:[158]

> 'Legislating' is, by definition, a law-making activity that in a democratic society can only occur through the use of a procedure that is public in nature and, in that sense, 'transparent'. Otherwise, it would not be

[154] Hogg, 42.

[155] Church and Conrad, 63.

[156] F. Lehner, 'Consociational Democracy in Switzerland: A Political-Economic Explanation and Some Empirical Evidence' (1984) 12 *European Journal of Political Research* 25.

[157] D. Henri, G. Le Quintrec, P. Geiss, R. Prass and E. Mursa, *Histoire/Geschichte* (Stuttgart/Leipzig 2008) is the first of these modern history books to have been co-written by French and German historians. The EU Commission is said to be preparing a pan-European history book.

[158] Case C-280/11 P, *Council of the European Union* v. *Access Info Europe*, Judgment of the Court (First Chamber) of 17 October 2013, not yet reported, para. 63.

> possible to ascribe to 'law' the virtue of being the expression of the will of those that must obey it, which is the very foundation of its legitimacy as an indisputable edict. In a representative democracy, and this term must apply to the EU, it must be possible for citizens to find out about the legislative procedure, since if this were not so, citizens would be unable to hold their representatives politically accountable, as they must be by virtue of their electoral mandate.

While it dismissed the request by Access Info Europe, the Court found: 'Openness in that respect contributes to strengthening democracy by enabling citizens to scrutinise all the information which has formed the basis for a legislative act. The possibility for citizens to find out the considerations underpinning legislative action is a precondition for the effective exercise of their democratic rights.'[159] I would describe this as a very participatory, almost Habermasian vision of democracy in the EU. This, it appears, is different from the jurisprudence in certain constitutional courts at the periphery, which are keen to stress more traditional views of democracy.[160] AG Cruz Villalon later suggested, specifically in relation to Member States:

> It is worth stating, once again, that Member States taking part in an EU legislative procedure as members of an institution are more like the common perception of a national legislature than they are like a sovereign body playing a role in relations governed by international law. The mind-set of discretion and even secrecy, which is justified in the context of relations between sovereign players, is out of place in the context of the European Union, which, in this respect, sees itself primarily and increasingly as a community based on the principles of the rule of law and democracy.[161]

In other words, in the federal interplay between the Union and its Member States, Member States are not permitted to argue that they

[159] Ibid., para. 33, citing *Sweden and Turco* v. *Council*, para. 46.

[160] See GFCC, *Lisbon Decision*, para. [215]:

> However, all systems of representative democracy have this in common: a will of the majority that has come about freely and taking due account of equality is formed, either in the constituency or in the assembly which has come into being proportionally, by the act of voting. The decision on political direction which is taken by the majority of voters is to be reflected in Parliament and in the government; the losing part remains visible as a political alternative and active in the sphere of free opinion-forming as well as in formal decision-making procedures, as an opposition that will, in subsequent elections, have an opportunity to become the majority.

[161] Ibid., 69.

should be treated as foreign sovereigns, that they should not be subject to EU rules on transparency.

In the *Lisbon Treaty* case in 2010, the Grand Chamber of the Court decided that Germany had wrongly transposed the Data Protection Directive.[162] Germany argued that the principle of democracy precluded complete independence of a public body without state supervision. The Court, however, corrected this interpretation:

> That principle does not preclude the existence of public authorities outside the classic hierarchical administration and more or less independent of the government. The existence and conditions of operation of such authorities are, in the Member States, regulated by the law or even, in certain States, by the Constitution and those authorities are required to comply with the law subject to the review of the competent courts. Such independent administrative authorities, as exist moreover in the German judicial system, often have regulatory functions or carry out tasks which must be free from political influence, whilst still being required to comply with the law subject to the review of the competent courts. That is precisely the case with regard to the tasks of the supervisory authorities relating to the protection of data.[163]

In other words, the CJEU has a slightly different understanding of democracy than offered in the argument by Germany. In its view, it is sufficient that an institution is bound by law to be considered democratic as long as independent courts can review its decisions. The CJEU thus endorses an understanding of democracy that is not confined to the EU level or Member State level separately but rather imposes federal values on the federated level in the area of application of EU law.

As a further example, AG Bot's Opinion in the case of Case C-300/11 *ZZ* v. *Secretary of State for the Home Department* (2012)[164] states: 'In a democratic society, it is imperative to allow the very people who are fighting the safeguards provided by the rule of law to benefit from those same safeguards in order to ensure the absolute primacy of democratic values, but this cannot result in a kind of suicide of democracy itself.' In other words, the Advocate General, as a judge of the Court, sees the European people as a guarantor of democracy for Europe at the Member

[162] Case C-518/07, *European Commission* v. *Federal Republic of Germany (Personal data processing)* [2010] ECR I-01885.

[163] Ibid., 42.

[164] Opinion of AG Bot in Case C-300/11, *ZZ* v. *Secretary of State for the Home Department*, EU:C:2012:563, para. 43.

State level. Given the federal examples already mentioned, he endorses a federal understanding of democracy in this argument.

From the periphery of EU Member States, numerous European cases are of direct relevance to whether a common European public space is needed. These include *Solange I*[165] and the *Maastricht* case,[166] both in the GFCC. In *Solange I*, the GFCC refused to refrain from reviewing European Community acts using German fundamental rights because it believed that the Luxembourg Court was providing insufficient protection at the Community level. In *Solange I*, it held that 'as long as' the level of fundamental rights protection is not guaranteed at an equivalent level to the one in Germany, it will be for the GFCC to review Community acts. In its *Lisbon Treaty* case,[167] the Polish Constitutional Court approved Polish ratification of the Lisbon Treaty but warned that the Treaty must not undermine the identity of the Polish Constitution. In other words, it did not think the Union was capable of democratic discussions in a common political space. In the *ESM* cases,[168] the GFCC again reiterated its conviction that real democratic legitimacy can stem only from the national legal order and thus again empowered the German Bundestag to control precisely, for example, the transfer of funds to the ESM by prohibiting automatic increases or autonomous decisions detached from the German political process.[169] The recent case in *OMT* was an interesting German decision because, for the first time, the GFCC referred a question about the validity of unlimited state bond purchases by the European Central Bank to the CJEU.[170] With this decision, one of the last hold-outs among highest courts, the GFCC has entered into direct dialogue with Luxembourg. The impression of these judgments

[165] GFCC, *Solange I*, BVerf 37 of 29 May 1974.

[166] *Maastricht Decision*.

[167] Polish Constitutional Tribunal, *Lisbon Treaty*, Case *K 32/09*, http://trybunal.gov.pl/fileadmin/content/omowienia/K_32_09_EN.pdf.

[168] *ESM Decision*. Applications for the issue of a temporary injunction, www.bundesverfassungsgericht.de/SharedDocs/Entscheidungen/EN/2012/09/rs20120912_2bvr139012en.html.

[169] GFCC, *Lisbon Decision*; GFCC, *ESM Treaty*, ibid.

[170] GFCC, *OMT*, 2 BvR 2728/13 of 14 January 2014, www.bverfg.de/entscheidungen/rs20140114_2bvr272813en.html. A. Pliakos and G. Anagnostaras, 'Saving Face? The German Federal Constitutional Court Decides Gauweiler' (2017) 18 *German Law Journal* 213. The latest version of this ongoing dialogue was the decision in *Public Sector Purchase Programme (PSPP)* of 5 May 2020, in which the GFCC ruled that the CJEU decision in *Weiss* (C-493/17, *Weiss and Others*, EU:C:2018:1000) was *ultra vires* opening a new chapter of constitutional dialogue with significant crisis potential. Unfortunately this decision was decided after the main text of this book had been edited.

from the periphery is one of scepticism about the ability of the EU institution to deliver democratic decisions. This is relevant to the development of a European common space for political debate because the further this judicial interaction develops, given the high level of credibility that both Member State courts and the CJEU enjoy, the higher the level of acceptance that any compromise or inter-se agreement between these important centre-periphery actors will enjoy. In essence, even with increased jurisprudence on transparency and certain expressions of democracy, the crucial emergence of a common public sphere remains elusive.

2.6.4 Conclusion as to the Validity of This Obstacle

If one views the EU more as an administrative structure, as does Peter Lindseth, it is perhaps less pertinent to question the democratic legitimacy at the federal level.[171] But where democratic legitimacy develops over the long term in a federal policy, it becomes a major challenge for constitutionalization (see Chapter 2). Further, this concern is under-explored in the case law of the central CJEU. At the same time, more periphery courts view the requirement for a common legitimizing political debate as crucial for the development of a European *demos* and the need to develop a common European public space for political debate thereof as one of their main conceptual arguments for their scepticism about EU constitutionalization. This obstacle is further discussed in Chapter 5.

2.7 Key Factors for the *Demos* Dimension of European Constitutionalization

In this chapter, I have shown that both central and periphery court case law highlights key tensions in the understanding of the concept and elements of *demos*. Key Member State courts have not adequately considered even the possibility of the EU's nature as a federating polity. Instead, they perpetuate an impoverished understanding of EU constitutionalization, one that is revealed by simple illustrations from other federal experiences. Further, the CJEU itself has yet to embrace a firm federal comprehension of the sub-elements of the constitutional obstacle of *demos* considered here.

The constituting elements of *demos* are discussed as questions of homogeneity, as mentioned by the GFCC in *Maastricht* and then explained further in *Lisbon*. This notion is contentious in itself; 'How

[171] Lindseth, *Power and Legitimacy*.

homogenous is homogeneity?' would be a legitimate question. What makes all discussions about the existence/possibility of a European *demos* difficult is the amorphous nature of homogeneity in political, social and spiritual terms. The further thinking required is mainly legal in nature, rather than sociological or even psychological. It asks what minimum level of commonality might be required in order to attain one constitutional *demos*. It further begs the question whether the existence of different nations in one polity in any way undermines or inhibits each nation's own democratic legitimacy. Does a federal state with more than one nation suffer irreparably from the lack of common *demos*? While some separatists might see the matter this way, a closer look returns to the reason for federalism itself, which lies in co-existence of different peoples in historical, social and perhaps also spiritual terms. These issues need not be discussed only in national terms, if a challenge – and *raison d'être* – of the EU remains a need to overcome national and especially nationalistic sentiments. 'Real-world' examples of homogeneity have been most useful to answer this question.

In this chapter, we conclude that, indeed, there is no 'one size fits all' interpretation and application of *demos*. Rather, I believe that a uniquely tailored federal *demos* is already shaping itself in Europe, though not without serious difficulties. Analysis based on this tailored approach to *demos* allows the genuine remaining obstacles to be identified. The key recurring theme of this chapter is that obstacles to the emerging European *demos* must be seen both in a European-specific context and in a more realistic light than the perfectionist vision currently employed in many European courts. This is necessary for the recent history and development of Europe to be taken seriously, and it is certainly not impossible. One of the fundamental approaches by the CJEU is that European integration is not static but rather developing.[172] This is consistent with approaches to interpretation in other jurisdictions, where founding documents are not viewed as frozen in time but are considered 'living constitutions'.

Illustrative examples from other federal experiences demonstrate that certain elements of *demos* also develop over time through open and transparent exchanges of views in the common public sphere, rather

[172] See Advocate General Sharpston in Case C-34/09, *Gerardo Ruiz Zambrano* v. *Office national de l'emploi (ONEm)*, paras. 171–3; see, for a comparison between EU and other constitutionalizing polities, A. Stone Sweet, 'The Structure of Constitutional Pluralism: Review of Nico Krisch, Beyond Constitutionalism: The Pluralist Structure of Post-National Law' (2013) 11 *International Journal of Constitutional Law* 491, 494.

than being founded upon a single pre-existing and homogenous national identity and *demos*. This is particularly true of the development, over time, of a common public sphere for transparent and engaged policy debate. Political scientists such as Thomas Risse have tracked the incidences of trans-European considerations during public debates over the past twenty years, using quantitative methods such as references, in the national media of EU Member States, to the issues and positions of other Member States.[173] His findings, which identify greatly increased interconnectedness of national public spheres but no true common European debates as yet, reveal the limited progress that has been made and the extent of the remaining challenge.

In this chapter, this study analysed citizenship, highlighting different federal experiences such as state-based, rather than federal, citizenships. It demonstrated how key points that appear to raise obstacles to the existence of a European constitutionalization process are hardly fatal; instead, they appear as initial steps in its evolution. However, it also found that the lack of a common European public sphere remains an important obstacle as yet unaddressed by such evolution.[174] It seems absurd that in times of socio-political, environmental and economic crisis, public policy discussions rage only at a national level, even when decisions must quite clearly be taken at the EU or international level. Is the lack of a certain level of accountability necessary, providing an excuse behind which Member State governments will obscure rather than explain their positions? In the recent *ESM* decision of the GFCC,[175] European institutions were accused of being simply 'smoke and mirrors' masking relevant decisions taken out of sight of the public eye. Rather than seeing the lack/impossibility of a common *demos* as an insurmountable obstacle, it is crucial to further explore why the European public space remains still so elusive, to the point of void.

There seems to be an impoverished understanding of the EU in federal terms by the GFCC and, to a lesser extent, by the European Courts. By clarifying the nature and possibilities of federalism, I have shown that

[173] See, for example, Risse, *European Public Spheres*.

[174] Particularly the Canadian experience is instructive here. Quebecers are considered a 'nation' within the Canadian federation: J. Létourneau, '"Silent Revolution": The Transformation of the Québécois Identity' (2017) 32 *London Journal of Canadian Studies* 98, 101; J. Maclure, *Quebec Identity: The Challenge of Pluralism* (Montreal/ Kingston, Ontario 2013) 10–11.

[175] *ESM Decision*. Applications for the issue of a temporary injunction, www.bundesverfassungsgericht.de/SharedDocs/Entscheidungen/EN/2012/09/rs20120912_2bvr139012en.html.

many supposed obstacles are not valid. However, and in conclusion, I have also highlighted that the lack of a European public space remains a significant obstacle to the further constitutionalization of Europe, transcending *demos* concerns to equally affect the *civitas* and also *ius* dimensions of possible advances. This is compounded by the requirement for twenty-four official languages in Europe, without a widespread pragmatic recognition of a more functional number of working languages in which trans-European public debates could take place.

3

Civitas Obstacles to European Constitutionalization

3.1 Introduction

Democracy and the EU have a heated relationship that has been much debated – by legal scholars and the European courts alike.[1] For many, it is inherently difficult – if not impossible – to claim that the EU, as a whole, is reflective of democratic ideas and practices.[2] There are, allegedly, particular areas of deficiency – from the usurping of domestic legislative jurisdiction,[3] to the absence of civic responsibility among the peoples of Europe per se.[4] As this chapter will demonstrate, it is my belief that most of the particular areas of alleged deficiency are not, in fact, serious obstacles to the European constitutionalization process. Rather, many are a natural and predictable occurrence.

The democratic nature of the EU depends on its accountability towards its citizens. One related obstacle, the lack of a European public sphere, also creates challenges for the democratic nature of the EU and as such for the *civitas* dimension of constitutionalization. The process of citizen control within the EU is based on the notion that decision-makers are empowered by those electing them.[5] For many observers, without such accountability, the EU faces deep

[1] See R. Bellamy, *A Republican Europe of States: Cosmopolitanism, Intergovernmentalism and Democracy in the EU* (Cambridge 2019); P. Craig, 'The EU, Democracy and Institutional Structure: Past, Present and Future', in W. Heusel and J.-P. Regeade (eds.), *The Authority of EU Law* (Berlin/Heidelberg 2019) 311; Innerarity, *Democracy in Europe*; Grimm, The Constitution of European Democracy; T. Kostakopoulou; Devuyst; Nettesheim; Zuleeg; GFCC, *Lisbon Decision*.

[2] Zuleeg, 505, 507; Nettesheim, 358.

[3] Zuleeg, 507; see also claims made before the GFCC, *Maastricht Decision*, at para. [105].

[4] Zuleeg, but see generally Kostakopoulou (arguing against the use of such ideas to classify an entity as democratic).

[5] V. Bogdanor, 'Legitimacy, Accountability and Democracy in the European Union' (2007), Federal Trust Report, https://fedtrust.co.uk/wp-content/uploads/2014/12/FedT_LAD.pdf, at 6; see also the opinion of the GFCC, *Lisbon Decision*, at para. [268].

problems of legitimacy.[6] However, in this chapter I aim to show that while concerns of an EU 'democratic deficit' are not entirely unfounded, different federal polities illustrate less harrowing constitutional experiences when they faced similar challenges.

In this chapter, I analyse each of the alleged gaps in a European *civitas*, in turn. I explore the contours of the *civitas* debate with reference to examples of other federal polities and by giving due consideration to related EU jurisprudence. Criticisms surrounding EU representative democracy focus on several key obstacles. They can be summarized and grouped as (1) the lack of unitary elections in the EU, (2) the lack of EU-wide political parties, (3) the lack of one real president, (4) concern that the European Parliament is not the only law-maker and that the Council of the EU cannot substitute for a proper 'Senate' and (5) the absence of any EU constitutional document, owing to the EU's unique treaty structure. For each of the obstacles, recent theories of federalism as well as pertinent historical examples from other federal jurisdictions are used to dismiss most perceived obstacles but also to recognize that two challenges to the *civitas* dimension of EU constitutionalization remain valid today, due mainly to the absence of a truly European common public sphere.

Questioning the *civitas* dimension of the EU constitutionalization process is not merely an academic exercise – recent judgments in various EU Member States suggest that these obstacles resonate with many national jurists.[7] Right at the heart of the ongoing conversation between the central European Court and the periphery Member State highest courts is a raging debate about *civitas*.

In this chapter, I will argue that appreciation of the history of federalist government structures teaches us that, like *demos*, certain elements of *civitas* developed over time in federal systems. Several constitutional polities, once divided, eventually emerged as fully developed federalist systems. As Burgess explains, both the United States and indeed the EU have actually evolved a great deal, and further development in both polities is possible,[8] in similar vein that some constitutional entities develop from dual to cooperative federalism.[9] I It is a common feature of most federal government structures that most federal elections and parties remain primarily state-based for a prolonged period of time, that federal polities do not require one

[6] *Lisbon Decision.*

[7] C. Barnard and O. Odudu, *The Outer Limits of European Union Law* (Oxford/Portland, OR 2009), 8.

[8] Burgess, In Search of the Federal Spirit.

[9] Schütze, *From Dual to Cooperative Federalism.*

single electoral system and that different responsibilities for federal institutions – including the roles of Parliament, a senate or a president – can evolve. Likewise, the form, or indeed the lack, of any constitutional document does not impinge on the constitutionalization process; the obstacle is plainly not an insurmountable one. As such, I aim to show that several of the key obstacles that appear, on the face of it, to challenge the European constitutionalization process are in fact hardly fatal to the overall project. Instead, they are little more than initial steps in the evolution of the constitutionalization process. Through the use of illustrative examples from federal entities at similar stages of their own development, together with a careful examination of recent European jurisprudence, in this chapter I will suggest that there is no fatal lack of *civitas* within the structure of the EU.[10] However, I will identify two key remaining obstacles that, when seen as corollaries to the over-arching absence of a functioning trans-European public sphere, become nonetheless very difficult to resolve through further *civitas* constitutionalization.

In this chapter, as in Chapter 2, for each key factor and related set of obstacles identified, the obstacles are either found invalid or recognized as significant through case analysis, comparison with other constitutionalization processes and analysis of existing legal scholarship. I draw on illustrative examples from the constitutional experiences of the United States, Germany, Switzerland, Canada and Argentina, but I refer especially to decades of relevant decisions by Member State and European courts for my analysis.

3.2 Lack of Unitary Elections?

3.2.1 Obstacle

Critics argue that the EU lacks genuinely European elections.[11] Of the three legislative entities[12] – the Parliament,[13] the Council[14] and the European

[10] J. Habermas, 'Remarks on Dieter Grimm's "Does Europe Need a Constitution?"' (1995) 1 *European Law Journal* 303.

[11] J. Smith, *Reinvigorating European Elections: The Implications of Electing the European Commission* (London 2005); A. Kreppel, *The European Parliament and Supranational Party System: A Study in Institutional Development* (Cambridge 2001); H. Wallace, M. A. Pollack and A. R. Young (eds.), *Policy-Making in the European Union*, 6th ed. (Oxford 2010), 26.

[12] See European Union, 'How Does the EU Work?' https://op.europa.eu/webpub/com/eu-and-me/en/HOW_DOES_THE_EU_WORK.html.

[13] Ibid.

[14] Ibid.

Commission[15] – only the Parliament has any form of direct election[16] – and this step, as some observers argue, was one taken only grudgingly. Despite clear instructions in the Treaty of Rome,[17] it was not until 1979 that Members of the Parliament were directly elected.[18] Elections for the European Parliament have been held every five years since 1979,[19] with each Member State apportioned a certain number of seats to which it may elect representatives (Members of European Parliament or 'MEPs').[20] With European elections governed solely by individual Member State rules, only rudimentary EU legislation in place and no European-wide laws determining conclusively how elections must be conducted, critics seriously doubt, more than ever, the ability of the polity to develop constitutionally.[21] We have seen these concerns raised decisively in the findings of several Member State courts, including in the jurisprudence of the GFCC.[22]

3.2.2 *Underlying Concepts of Constitutional Development*

Unitary elections are the rule in modern federal polities and for this reason they receive much attention. The advancement of unitary elections is such that several pioneering countries, such as Canada and Australia, now have centralized agencies that organize elections.[23]

15 Ibid.

16 Art. 14(3), TEU (OJ 2012 C 326 p.1). However, some argue that the Council as well is directly elected and therefore accountable to the citizens. See view presented in Bogdanor, at 6.

17 Art. 138(3), Treaty establishing the European Economic Community (EEC), 25 March 1957 ['Treaty of Rome'].

18 Act concerning the election of the representatives of the Assembly by direct universal suffrage (OJ 1976 L 278 p.1) as amended by Council Decision of 25 June 2002 and 23 September 2002 amending the Act concerning the election of the representatives of the European Parliament by direct universal suffrage, annexed to Decision 76/787/ECSC, EEC, EURATOM (OJ 2002 L 283 p.1).

19 European Parliament, 'Welcome to the European Parliament', www.europarl.europa.eu/parliament/public/staticDisplay.do?id=146&language=EN.

20 Art. 14(2), TEU (OJ 2012 C 326 p.1).

21 Grimm, *Braucht Europa eine Verfassung?*, vol. 60 Siemens Stiftung, 36.

22 GFCC, *5% Hurdle European Election*, 2 BvC 4/10 of 9 November 2011, www.bverfg.de/entscheidungen/cs20111109_2bvc000410.html.

23 See Elections Canada mission statement:

> Elections Canada is an independent, non-partisan agency that reports directly to Parliament. We must be prepared at all times to conduct a federal general election, by-election or referendum, administer the political financing provisions of the *Canada Elections Act*, monitor compliance and enforce electoral legislation. Elections Canada is also mandated to conduct voter education and

However, in my view it is still important to recognize that unitary elections are not actually a design feature of federal entities. As illustrative examples, in Germany, the United States and Switzerland, elections are organized with great deference to the federated state level.[24]

The example of Germany is particularly interesting. Here, federated state level elections were much more pronounced in the earlier stages of the country's constitutional history. It was only after 1922 that a federal returning officer (traditionally the president of the national statistics office) was introduced to collect results officially from the Länder administrations that were in charge of conducting the elections.[25] In my view, this demonstrates that, in a federal polity, elections can be organized at the federated level first, then, over time, become more federalized as the polity develops.

Contrasting the German experience with that of the US electoral system, we find that a largely state-based system is also adopted. In the pre-Civil War period,[26] the state-based nature of the electoral system was particularly pronounced – states did not even directly elect Senate representatives until 1913,[27] and even today for that matter they still do not directly elect members of the Electoral College.[28] The elements of a more centralized national election system were not set in stone from the start.[29] Even after the Civil War, this early, fragmented system was reformed in only a few, albeit key, respects. The Fifteenth Amendment (Amendment XV) attached non-discrimination to the right to vote. Yet, even though this right was in existence from 1870, it was not fully guaranteed until the

> information programs, and provide support to the independent boundaries commissions in charge of adjusting the boundaries of federal electoral districts following each decennial census. Finally, Elections Canada may carry out studies on alternative voting methods and, with the approval of parliamentarians, test electronic voting processes for future use during electoral events.

www.elections.ca/content.aspx?section=abo&dir=mis&document=index&lang=e.

24 S. Hix, 'Elections, Parties and Institutional Design: A Comparative Perspective on European Union Democracy' (1998) 21 *West European Politics* 19.

25 W. Woyke, 'Geschichte der Wahlen in Deutschland' in W. Woyke (ed.), *Stichwort: Wahlen*, 12th ed. (Heidelberg 2013) 49–84.

26 Indeed, the incongruity between state elections and voting rights practices resulted in extreme variations in citizen access to voting. As a result, the Fifteenth Amendment to the US constitution – providing for voting equality – was enacted in an attempt to create parity, US Const. Amend. 15.

27 US Const. Amend. 17.

28 US Const. Art. II, sec. 1, cl. 2.

29 R. Taagepera and M. S. Shugart, *Seats and Votes: The Effects and Determinants of Electoral Systems* (New Haven, CT 1983) 173–83.

Voting Rights Act of 1965 and states continue to be challenged to this day for erecting obstacles to the unimpeded access to voting rights for all citizens.[30] The same is also true of Switzerland, where, for many years, women lacked the right to vote for a federal candidate in certain cantons, due to different local rules and customs, even though they were all electing one Federal *Bundesrat* (Parliament).[31]

Today, the power to regulate elections in the US electoral process rests with the individual state, except that Congress can regulate the time, place and manner of holding elections for senators[32] and representatives.[33] In practice, the federal government has used these powers only rarely – for example, when it determined that all members must be elected in single-member districts. A multitude of state-level rules are contributing to the regulation of federal elections here and these rules have evolved dramatically over time. Election rules differ in the United States, for election of the President (through the College of Electors) or Congress (the Senate and House of Representatives) or in the nomination and primary election stages, where individual US states exercise complete freedom.[34] This multiplicity of rules demonstrates the real extent of this evolutionary process. In essence, the illustrative examples raise certain questions. While completely centralized elections may not be necessary for further European constitutionalization along federal lines, it remains challenging for Europe that elections continue to be led by Member State laws and decisions, as this risks stifling a broad common European public debate. Such open debates, across the federal polity, are important forces for the further development of a democratic *civitas*.

3.2.3 Related EU Developments

While it is generally true that no common rules govern the EU elections process, minimal conditions are enshrined in the Treaties (Art. 20.2(b) TFEU) and the Charter of Fundamental Rights (Art. 39 CFR).[35] Art. 14.3

30 See discussions about ID and passports during the 2012 presidential election in *The Philadelphia Inquirer*, 'Pa. Court Rules Voters Can Cast Regular Ballots without ID' (3 October 2012), http://articles.philly.com/2012-10-03/news/34219088_1_voter-id-law-commonwealth-secretary-carol-aichele-league-of-women-voters.

31 Fleiner, Misic and Töpperwien, 54.

32 This is a power that has existed since the Seventeenth Amendment in 1913.

33 See Art. 1, sec. 4, US Constitution.

34 Ibid.

35 See generally R. Corbett, F. Jacobs and M. Shackleton, *The European Parliament*, 8th ed. (London 2011).

TEU clarifies that '[t]he members of the European Parliament shall be elected for a term of five years by direct universal suffrage in a free and secret ballot'. I believe that the history of the European Parliament is particularly relevant for this discussion. It is also this history that explains why no single unitary system of elections was expected or created. I therefore turn to this important history.

Originally and very innovatively for an international organization, the Coal and Steel Community established a parliamentary assembly in 1957.[36] Initially, this embryonic parliamentary assembly consisted of members of Member State parliaments who were sent to Strasbourg to discuss relevant questions. Unsurprisingly, assigned delegates were selected according to very different electoral traditions that prevailed in each Member State. This position was explained in the (relatively short) 1976 Election Act,[37] which mandates in Art. 1 that European elections are conducted on the basis of proportional representation:

> 1. In each Member state, members of the European Parliament shall be elected on the basis of proportional representation, using the list system or the single transferable vote. 2. Member States may authorise voting based on a preferential list system in accordance with the procedure they adopt. 3. Elections shall be by direct universal suffrage and shall be free and secret. (Art. 1.1–3)

Member States are also entitled to draw constituency boundaries as they see fit, though, according to Art. 2, they are not allowed to 'generally [affect] the proportional nature of the voting system'. These rules have begun to have a real effect on the laws governing European elections in each individual Member State. Because of these rules, the UK was no longer free to continue its first-past-the-post electoral system, which was subsequently changed to a system of regional lists.[38] Recently, the CJEU has clarified that the European Parliament has no power to challenge the administration of these elections – even where it sincerely believes that

[36] See B. Cocks, *The European Parliament: Structure, Procedure and Practice* (London 1973); Kreppel, 1.

[37] Act concerning the election of the representatives of the Assembly by direct universal suffrage (OJ 1976 L 278 p.1) as amended by Council Decision of 25 June 2002 and 23 September 2002 amending the Act concerning the election of the representatives of the European Parliament by direct universal suffrage, annexed to Decision 76/787/ECSC, EEC, EURATOM (OJ 2002 L 283 p.1).

[38] The original UK first-past-the-post system had been credited for a substantive influence on the overall composition of the EP, which in turn was criticized heavily, leading to the EU-wide requirement of lists. Jolly, 53.

the Member State in question did not follow its own procedures.[39] The Court decided:

> The respective powers of the Parliament and of the national authorities when they verify the credentials of Members of the Parliament are clearly divided between the Community institutions and the national authorities. ... It is apparent from this that, by virtue of Article 12 of the 1976 Act, the Parliament is required to take note of the declaration made by the National Electoral Office and does not have the power to depart from it on account of the alleged irregularities affecting that national measure.[40]

While the strict interpretation of the CJEU might be of surprise to some, it is in keeping with the spirit of the Treaties. This compromise in itself is the result of several attempts to unify the electoral system for the European Union.[41] For some, it was the lack of consensus on these issues that led European Member States to change the mandate in the Treaty of Amsterdam to allow each Member State to maintain its own electoral system.[42] The CJEU could be more accretive in its interpretation here; its understanding of the requirements of federal electoral systems is not reflective of the federal nature of the Union, and more could be done to encourage trans-European elections that build and support the development of a European public space. This will be analysed further in Chapter 5.

The lack of unitary elections and decision-making was one of the main objections by the Irish and other governments in the recent *Pringle* case.[43] What the governments in this case alleged is arguably very much in line with an elite approach to law-making in the EU: 'Ireland, the governments of ..., the European Council and the Commission submit that the jurisdiction of the Court to examine the first question is limited, if not excluded, because the question relates to the interpretation of primary law. They contend that the Court has no power under Article

[39] Joined Cases C-393/07 and C-9/08, *Italian Republic and Beniamino Donnici* v. *European Parliament* [2009] ECR I-03679.

[40] Ibid., para. [57].

[41] There are Commission recommendations that led a British newspaper to conclude that the UK is forced to hold elections on Sundays, which was evidently not true; see EU Representation in the UK in reply to *Daily Telegraph* and *Daily Mail* articles, 13 March 2013, https://web.archive.org/web/20130415063622/http://blogs.ec.europa.eu/ECintheUK/no-forced-elections-on-sundays/.

[42] See Corbett, Jacobs and Shackleton, 36.

[43] Case C-370/12, *Thomas Pringle* v. *Government of Ireland, Ireland and The Attorney General*, Judgment of the Court (Full Court) of 27 November 2012, not yet reported.

267 TFEU to assess the validity of provisions of the Treaties.' The Court of Justice strongly disagreed and reinforced that while the Court is not called upon to review primary law, it has jurisdiction to ensure that the conditions for the simplified Treaty amendment procedure are observed:

> To that end, it is for the Court to verify, first, that the procedural rules laid down in Article 48(6) TEU were followed and, secondly, that the amendments decided upon concern only Part Three of the FEU Treaty, which implies that they do not entail any amendment of provisions of another part of the Treaties on which the European Union is founded, and that they do not increase the competences of the Union.

I believe that this is a clear indication of the post-Lisbon Court being willing to engage with the dilemma of the EU being still largely driven as an elite project where governments still have the final decision-making power.

European elections have featured prominently in the jurisprudence of the CJEU – a particularly notable case being *Le Pen.*[44] In *Le Pen*, upon Mr Le Pen receiving a criminal conviction for a violent attack and being declared ineligible to hold elected office by the French authorities, and after his appeal to the French courts failed, the European Parliament requested that Mr Le Pen leave his position. Mr Le Pen challenged the decision of the President of the European Parliament by applying to the EU General Court for interim relief, which he was granted. The General Court found that Mr Le Pen's case was inadmissible because the European Parliament's declaration had no self-standing legal effect – it merely took note of a decision by France as a Member State. The General Court held: 'It is not in dispute that, at the material time in the present case, no uniform electoral procedure for the election of Members of the European Parliament had been adopted. Accordingly, pursuant to Article 7(2) of the 1976 Act, the electoral procedure for that election continued to be governed by the national provisions in each Member State.' In my view, the General Court was clear that it is the decisions of Member States in election matters that bind the EU institutions. While the Court of Justice heard the appeal of Mr Le Pen, its decision to uphold the findings of the General Court and the interpretation given to the 1976 Act were predictable. According to the ECJ, it is the role of the European Parliament 'merely to take note that the seat is vacant as already established by the national authorities, whereas in the other cases concerning, inter alia, the resignation or death of one of its members, that institution

[44] Case C-208/03 P, *Jean-Marie Le Pen* v. *European Parliament* [2005] ECR I-06051.

has a more active role to play since Parliament itself establishes that there is a vacancy and informs the Member State in question thereof'.[45] This remark from the Court demonstrates a fundamental distinction between the approach of the Court and a federal understanding of elections. Had a more federal approach been adopted here in creating a European public space, the Court would not have taken the Member State's decision as a given. Rather, the Court would have viewed the Member State merely as the implementing agency of the broader federal decision-making process.

Spain v. *UK (Gibraltar Election)* is another important case on this point.[46] It concerned whether Commonwealth citizens (non-UK nationals) based in Gibraltar could participate in European elections. Previously, the UK had lost the case of *Matthews* v. *UK* in the European Court of Human Rights, where it was declared that the lack of European Parliament elections in Gibraltar was a human rights violation.[47] Subsequently, when Spain complained that the UK was giving Commonwealth citizens in Gibraltar the right to vote in European elections, arguing that these elections are reserved for EU citizens only, the Court of Justice disagreed. It came to the powerful conclusion in this case that nothing in the Treaties explicitly reserved the right to vote for EU citizens. In my view, the Court was able to set aside highly political concerns, displaying an understanding of the nature of these elections that transcended Member State preferences and thus adding to laying the foundation for a European public space.

Of further importance was the response given by the Court of Justice in *Eman* – a case concerning European elections in the Netherlands.[48] In this preliminary reference, the Dutch court sought clarity as to whether Dutch nationals in Dutch overseas territories such as Aruba should be given a vote in EU elections. The Grand Chamber of the ECJ answered this question in a diplomatic manner. First, it confirmed that Member State nationals in overseas countries and territories did enjoy full EU citizenship rights. Second, the Court then deferred to the Member State

[45] Ibid., para. [50].

[46] Case C-145/04, *Kingdom of Spain* v. *United Kingdom of Great Britain and Northern Ireland* [2006] ECR I-07917.

[47] ECtHR, *Matthews* v. *United Kingdom* (Application No. 24833/94) (1991) 28 EHRR 361. In sum, the Court concluded that certain EU rules applied to Gibraltar and thus there was no reason to exclude the inhabitants from EU elections.

[48] Case C-300/04, *M. G. Eman and O. B. Sevinger* v. *College van burgemeester en wethouders van Den Haag* [2006] ECR I-08055. The most recent case in C-646/19 P(R) - *Puigdemont i Casamajó and Comín i Oliveres v Parliament* reveals a more nuanced approach by the CJEU.

to decide whether those EU citizens had the right to vote in EU elections, while highlighting the impact of the principle of non-discrimination, which meant that citizens in similar situations would have to be treated in an equal way. I believe that this case is important because it shows that there are significant – and principled – limits to the deference that the Court will show to individual Member States. Over time, this jurisprudence could develop into much greater scrutiny of those electoral decisions.

The CJEU rulings in *Le Pen, Spain* v. *UK* and *Eman* indicate a significant level of deference towards Member States in the arena of EU elections, much higher than if a common European public space existed, given that differences would be more apparent and striking. While the CJEU has criticized the lack of common electoral rules in the EU, it has also upheld Member State competence through cases such as *Le Pen* and has emphasized fundamental principles such as respect for human rights and non-discrimination, finding that these must be observed in the electoral process. The Court's case law is evolving from an approach characterized by full deference to Member States to a situation where a Member State must observe Union law in the EU electoral process. This requirement upon Member States is more in accordance with an understanding of election processes in federal states and aids in establishing an EU public sphere.

One of the most dramatic innovations is currently taking place. In *Junqueras Vies*, the Advocate General argued that while parts of the election are determined by national law, once the election has taken place, the rights of the elected MEP are wholly determined by EU law, meaning that a Spanish law requiring all new MEPs to swear allegiance to the Constitution and to the Crown cannot be applied to MEPs.[49] This Opinion is significant as it directly restricts Member States to the smallest interpretation of what electoral rules Member States can set. It remains to be seen if the CJEU follows this opinion, but restricting Member States in this dramatic fashion highlights the general trend by the central Court to set clear limits for elections and the electoral process leading to European institutions.

On a periphery court level, *Raoul Georges Nicolo* in the French Conseil D'Etat is a significant case concerning European elections that requires

[49] The Advocate General Opinion in the case C-502/19 *Junqueras Vies* of 12 Nov 2019, http://curia.europa.eu/juris/document/document.jsf?text=&docid=220537&pageIndex=0&doclang=EN&mode=req&dir=&occ=first&part=1&cid=7379428.

consideration. The case concerns the right to vote in European elections for French citizens based in overseas departments.[50] The Conseil D'Etat concluded in this brief judgment that international treaties that are equally applied by the treaty partners must take precedence over ordinary national law. In other words, the Conseil recognized supremacy in this award, giving *outre-mer* citizens the right to vote in European elections. In my view, this demonstrates a highly important issue for the question of unitary elections – a periphery court using the EU elections as important enough issue to rule on supremacy, deviating from previous case law and manoeuvring itself closer to the centre. It is perhaps unexpected that the French Court would display a better understanding of the federal nature of EU elections than some of its 'federal' sister courts. However, I believe that this ruling by the Conseil D'Etat demonstrates that federated courts are aware of the pan-European significance of EU elections and as such their dialogue with the CJEU facilitates the establishment of an EU public space.

While in most EU Member States, decisions treating EU elections as real elections prevail, support for this obstacle can be found in a slightly more nuanced form in a recent GFCC decision. This ruling concerned the minimum threshold for the allocation of seats, which is 5 per cent of votes cast in Germany.[51] The Court found there to be no possibility that the German members of the European Parliament might disrupt its constitutional function. This Court emphasized the equal weight of each vote that would be disrupted by having a 5 per cent boundary, concluding that there was a violation of this important German Constitutional principle. Clearly, in the Court's view, the EU elections held a much lesser importance. It decided that the notion that the 'European Parliament's ability to function would be impaired by the abolition of the five per cent barrier clause cannot rely on a sufficient factual basis and does not adequately take account of the European Parliament's specific working conditions and its duties'.[52] It is as though the European Parliament, to the Court, was sufficiently lacking in important or relevant government functions, and, as such, the lack of cohesion engendered by fragmented voting rules should not prevent it from fulfilling its (presently limited) role. In my view, the underlying obstacle in relation to this concern is not simply the weakness of the Parliament

[50] French Conseil d'Etat, Assemblée, 20 October 1989, No. 108243, www.legifrance.gouv.fr/affichJuriAdmin.do?idTexte=CETATEXT000007742504&dateTexte=.
[51] GFCC, *5% Hurdle European Election.*
[52] Ibid.

itself, nor the lack of European-wide and deeply legitimate elections to date. Rather, the courts are struggling with the problematic absence of a truly trans-European public sphere. The Court's position is based on a view of federalism that treats the EU institutions as less important than Member State ones. However, it is clear that without more open and transparent public debates, any attempt to centralize EU elections becomes much more difficult.

The strong dissent in this decision by Judges Di Fabio and Mellinghoff raises particularly important issues. They highlight that the Court misinterprets the role of European elections and the European Parliament, arguing that it is for all EU Member States to ensure that there is no 'splintering' of parliamentary groups in the European Parliament.[53] The GFCC alluded to the fact that the German Bundestag sets the rules for European elections and because of its 5 per cent threshold does not run the risk of becoming ungovernable. This argument might be seen as a bit of a caricature of the European Parliament, but it was brought up in direct response to the German government's argument that factions (splinter parties) could block decision-making in Europe.[54]

> The representatives of these factions are not inserted into the structures of the European Parliament. ... Connecting members of these splinter parties to parliamentary groups would not result in stable groups or collective action because of their political fragmentation. ... Sufficiently secure majorities could not be reached, so that it would very difficult for the European Parliament to fulfill its legislative function. A higher number of factions could jeopardize forging a general majority. In particular, if qualified majorities are required, there could be a slowdown or even blockage of parliamentary activity and thus impair the functions of the European Parliament.[55]

Interestingly, the German government, as a participant in the EU system, strongly supports the notion that the European Parliament has a legislative function that is worth protecting. Regrettably, it failed to convince its own Constitutional Court of this position.

A further interesting case from the periphery courts endorsing and highlighting the principle of unitary elections is that of *ex-parte Chester.*[56] In this case, the High Court – Administrative Court of England and

[53] Ibid., para. [177].
[54] Ibid., para. [70].
[55] Ibid., para. [70].
[56] English High Court, *The Queen on the application of Chester* v. *(1) Secretary of State for Justice and (2) Wakefield Metropolitan District Council* [2009] EWHC 2923 (Admin).

Wales rejected an application by a prisoner with a life sentence to be admitted to vote in the European election. Mindful of the jurisprudence of the ECHR, which had recently rejected a blanket ban on prohibiting prisoners' voting rights, J Burton rejected the invitation to grant the prisoner the right to vote in European elections. Endorsing the findings in the three seminal ECJ cases examined above, J Burton concluded that he had the requisite authority as a Member State judge to decide this matter autonomously. What we see in this case is a Member State court giving full deference to the ECJ. By rejecting the argument that European elections were not as important as national elections, and thus did not have to follow the rules of Parliament, the Member State court here indirectly re-affirmed the importance of European elections. In similar vein to the French Court in *Raoul Georges Nicolo*, the High Court – Administrative Court displayed a more advanced understanding of the EU as a federal polity with federal elections. In my view, through this dialogue between centre and periphery courts, the jurisprudence on this issue is slowly advancing our notion of a European *civitas* and has partially addressed the challenge presented by the lack of centralized elections in Europe. Without a functioning and legitimate trans-European public sphere, it is hard to see how the point could be further advanced.

3.2.4 Conclusion as to the Validity of This Obstacle

As I have demonstrated, many federal entities do not establish centralized elections from their founding; rather, such processes become unified at a later stage in the process of their historical development. It is also clear from the progress in current dialogue between the centre and periphery courts that there are still different levels of engagement that can influence the rules governing the shape and procedures of EU elections. The lack of universal elections is not a problem itself. Rather, the absence of a truly trans-European public sphere makes progress to address these challenges much more difficult, essentially creating a 'corollary challenge' for the *civitas* dimension of EU constitutionalization. Several clear examples of other federal experiences, coupled with analysis based on the emerging jurisprudence, have demonstrated that most federal entities allow for variations in their electoral systems, even when electing central institutions. Alone, perhaps further progress on this obstacle would not be difficult to achieve. However, coupled with a continuing fatal weakness, which is the inability of Europeans to debate public policy and political issues *as they concern Europe as a whole*, in a manner that transcends the boundaries of their respective Member States and mindsets, this particular corollary obstacle becomes extremely challenging to address coherently.

3.3 No European-Wide Parties?

3.3.1 Obstacle

Candidates within a European Member State run in different political parties specific to the particular Member State.[57] Due to these rules, few shared or supranational parties exist today, and again the near-total absence of an active series of political debates taking place in a functioning and dynamic European public sphere may render efforts to address this obstacle much more difficult in law and in practice. Yet, when MEPs are seated, certain ideological blocs form and trends may be observed in the overall character of political leanings of the parties as a whole.[58] Any affiliations that exist are, however, fluid in their nature.[59] This clear lack of political party consistency between Member States is vehemently criticized for militating against democratic legitimacy in the EU. It is argued by many that it reflects a lack of overall European civic engagement in favour of continued nationality-based ideologies.[60] I suspect that while this obstacle may lack significant validity as an independent problem, without a vibrant European public sphere, it may be nonetheless very difficult to resolve.

3.3.2 Underlying Concepts of Constitutional Development

Political parties are a relatively new phenomenon. In federal entities, it is not uncommon to have separate parties for different parts of the federal State. I argue that this in itself poses difficulties for the federal polity, with

57 European Parliament, 'Political Groups, Parliament', www.europarl.europa.eu/parliament/public/staticDisplay.do?id=45&pageRank=4&language=EN.

58 Ibid.

59 Ibid.

60 In other words, European elections 'fail to express the will of the European people on European issues'; P. Mair and J. Thomassen, 'Electoral Democracy and Political Representation in the European Union' (1 April 2008) Paper prepared for the Conference on Representation, Immigration and the 2009 Election to the European Parliament, Indiana University, Bloomington, https://pdfs.semanticscholar.org/bda2/8336c3b8ae2c9f7f30ca9a4b03d1765d4909.pdf, 8.

political parties representing different communities having more centrifugal effects.[61] Several contemporary federal entities provide examples of party federalism during key periods of their constitutional development.[62]

The situation in Canada is most notable for illustrative purposes here. While, theoretically, large political parties exist in both the Provinces and the Federal Parliament, their structure, political positions and even ideologies differ greatly from one level to another.[63] This means that if you know the position of the Liberal Party of Canada, there is little guarantee that the Liberal Party of British Colombia or Manitoba will adopt the same or similar positions. It is therefore unsurprising that the Bloc Quebecois and the Parti Quebecois, while sharing different positions, are not treated as analogous. When the Bloc virtually disappeared in the last federal election, the Parti scored an electoral victory in the following year. However, federated parties in Canada have slowly learnt to collaborate across provincial boundaries, at least coordinating their work for some reasonable degree of consistency in their political messages and positions.[64]

The US Early Republic provides us with a further particularly useful example of the development of political parties at the federated level. The US Constitution itself does not mention political parties. As Ackerman notes in *The Failure of the Founding Fathers*, the Constitution drafters realized that parties might appear but, as explained by Madison in *The Federalist Papers*, they were linked to factions and divisions and considered as leading to weakness against the common foe.[65] Political parties were believed to be counterproductive and even invalid, from a revolutionary perspective. Yet, Ackerman asserts, and I support, that there was an 'original misunderstanding' in the US Early Republic.[66] The Senate and the House had been designed in a way that was thought to hinder the establishment of national parties. Because the powerful Senate

61 M. Verdussen, *La Constitution belge, lignes et entrelignes* (Brussels 2004) 45.

62 T. Bräuninger and T. König, 'The Checks and Balances of Party Federalism: German Federal Government in a Divided Legislature' (1999) 36 *European Journal of Political Research* 207.

63 R. Dyck, 'Links between Federal and Provincial Parties and Party Systems' (1991) 14 *Representation, Integration and Political Parties in Canada* 129.

64 K. Carty and W. Cross, 'Political Parties and the Practice of Brokerage Politics' in J. Courtney and D. Smith (eds.), *The Oxford Handbook of Canadian Politics* (New York 2010).

65 Ackerman, *The Failure of the Founding Fathers*, 16–18.

66 Ibid.

was not initially directly elected, the main power was thought to rest at the individual State level. However, while this remained true, national parties developed as early as February 1801 with the legally questionable election of Thomas Jefferson as President.[67] As James Sundquist explains, the US system only very *gradually* morphed into the two-party system that exists today.[68] In fact, some commentators have argued that, although the antecedents of a party system were established from quite early on, it was not until the presidential campaign of 1896 that a real national party system was founded – and not until long after the New Deal that national parties had enough power to approve or suggest local candidates.[69] What we can learn from the example of the US Early Republic is, I believe, actually twofold: first, that a federal system does not necessarily require a polity-wide party system from its inception and, second, that such a system can, in any case, develop over time.

As previously explained, Switzerland is properly held out by many as an exceptional example of government, where virtually all political parties participate in the law-making process. I believe that the Swiss example is particularly important. The 'magic formula' of government is a consequence of the sheer extent of federalism in Switzerland. What we also see here is a concerted effort by the Swiss society not to let party politics dominate state governance given the real danger of divisions that could arise – particularly along language lines.[70]

Finally, the example of Germany is also necessary to consider when assessing whether a lack of EU-wide political parties is a real obstacle to the EU constitutionalization project. What we see in Germany is the regulation of political parties explicitly in the German Constitution (Art. 21 Grundgesetz). While there are no Länder-specific parties as such, the Christian Social Union in Bavaria is a distinct party that forms an alliance only with the Christian Democratic Union that has no representation in Bavaria.[71] The German law on political parties allows this situation with the perceived benefit that it allows the two Christian

67 Ibid.

68 J. Sundquist, *Dynamics of the Party System: Alignment and Realignment of Political Parties in the United States* (Washington, DC 1983).

69 M. V. Tushnet, *The Constitution of the United States of America: A Contextual Analysis* (Portland, OR 2009) 51.

70 A. Lijphart, *Democracy in Plural Societies: A Comparative Exploration* (New Haven, CT 1977) 80.

71 See G. Hopp, M. Sebaldt and B. Zeitler, *Die CSU Strukturwandel, Modernisierung und Herausforderungen einer Volkspartei* (Wiesbaden 2010).

democratic parties to adopt varying positions on different aspects of the political agenda.

This study has shown here that when we examine the underlying constitutional development of political parties in federal structures at comparatively early stages of their development, the phenomenon that federal and federated levels of government have different party systems is not an uncommon one. Rather, this lack of unifying election parties is characteristic of early phases of federalism. Taking these illustrations into account, concerns about a dearth of pan-European parties require a much more nuanced evaluation.

3.3.3 *Related EU Developments*

Past attempts to establish full-fledged political parties across the entire breadth of the EU have not been extremely successful.[72] I believe that, in many ways, this is entirely unsurprising, as voting and party lists for EU elections occur at the Member State or even regional level. However, it is incorrect to assume that there is no pan-European political development possible. There may be a dearth of overarching EU-wide party structures governed by one leadership, but political parties have long since cooperated in the European Parliament and are strengthening their coordination at EU level.

The Treaty of Lisbon has changed the constitutional basis for political parties. Art. 10.4 TEU now mandates that '[p]olitical parties at European level contribute to forming European political awareness and to expressing the will of citizens of the Union'.[73] For the first time, the constitutional role of political parties is expressly recognized. Similar to the German constitutional context, the Treaty highlights the 'contribution' that parties can make, where political parties are not themselves the will of the people but, rather, are expected to facilitate the formation of awareness and the expression of this will.[74]

[72] Kreppel, 1.

[73] See also under the heading of Freedom of assembly and of association, Art. 12(2), Charter of Fundamental Rights of the European Union (OJ 2000 C 364 p.1): 'Political parties at Union level contribute to expressing the political will of the citizens of the Union.' This means that activities of political parties are protected as fundamental rights in the EU.

[74] Art. 20.4 of the German Grundgesetz contains a very similar formulation: 'Politische Parteien wirken an der politischen Willenbildung mit' [Political parties contribute to the formation of political will].

Party collaboration has become more and more common – perhaps even successful – at the EU level. So much so that the United Kingdom's Conservative Prime Minister Cameron ordered his Conservative Party representatives in the European Parliament to create a new grouping because the European Peoples Party (the 'EPP') was too pro-European for his liking. The European Parliament has even embarked on discussions for the major groupings to establish an EU-wide candidate for the Commission Presidency.[75] The proposal is not seen as the strongest possible option, largely because the Council would have to agree to nominate the successful candidate and candidates would risk not being elected even after a successful electoral campaign. However, the new system may provide the first signal that the European Parliament can rise to meet its potential in the EU constitutional structure.[76] The formal rules in the Lisbon Treaty do specify that the Council is required to take the outcome of the European elections into account (Art. 17.7 TEU),[77] but it is not required to appoint the EU-wide Commission Presidency *Spitzenkandidat*. In the Parliament, major political groupings were mainly positive about the idea, but controversy still ensued. To the surprise of some – and against the wishes of German Chancellor Angela Merkel – the Christian Democrats in the EPP[78] selected Jean-Claude Juncker as their *Spizenkandidat*. Throughout the process, the exposure of different candidates varied between Member States. In the United Kingdom, for example, only the Green and Liberal candidates participated in the campaigning process, after Ed Miliband asked Social Democrat Martin Schulz not to risk a special visit.[79] In my view, profiles of the *Spitzenkandaten* were further increased when all major groups represented in the Parliament (except for the European Conservatives

[75] See European Parliament Press release of 22 February 2013.

[76] S. B. Hobolt, 'A Vote for the President? The Role of Spitzenkandidaten in the 2014 European Parliament Elections' (2014) 21(10) *Journal of European Public Policy* 1528.

[77] Art. 17.7, TEU:

> Taking into account the elections to the European Parliament and after having held the appropriate consultations, the European Council, acting by a qualified majority, shall propose to the European Parliament a candidate for President of the Commission. This candidate shall be elected by the European Parliament by a majority of its component members. If he does not obtain the required majority, the European Council, acting by a qualified majority, shall within one month propose a new candidate who shall be elected by the European Parliament following the same procedure.

[78] Note the integration-friendly placed apostrophe; see EPP, www.epp.eu/.

[79] B. Wright, 'UK Left Out of Campaign for EU's Top Job' (8 May 2014), *BBC News*, www.bbc.co.uk/news/blogs-eu-27322896.

and the Reformists group) sent their lead candidates to two television debates. This gave greater weight to the European Parliament's reading of Art. 17.7 TEU, suggesting that the Parliament might be winning a role in selecting the Commission President candidate in spite of claims vehemently disputed by some EU Member State governments. Even though the von der Leyen Commission was ultimately not based on the Spitzenkandidaten process, it nevertheless heavily influenced its composition choosing two of the competing Spitzenkandidaten as key Commissioners.

After a relative victory at the polls, the EPP, with the support of other parties, made it known that its lead candidate should be chosen for Commission Presidency. At the first meeting of the European Council, a candidate could not unanimously be approved. To the UK's David Cameron, Juncker was representative of the old EU system – a wrong choice at a time when his own constituency in the UK was becoming all the more Euro-sceptical and nationalistic.[80] The German Chancellor also originally resisted Juncker. However, a remarkable PR campaign was waged in Germany, where the need to select Junker and to avoid undermining EU democracy even made headlines. The German tabloid newspaper *Bild Zeitung* likened any decision to appoint a non-elected candidate to tactics known only in the former 'GDR or right-wing nationalistic banana republics' (*DDR oder in rechtsnationalistischen Bananenrepubliken*).[81] In 2014, only the British and Hungarian governments were able to oppose Juncker as Commission President, and he was selected. This was a significant victory of the European Parliament over both the Council and those governments with nationalist leanings. This demonstrates that European-wide elections, as a matter of constitutional practice, might not be impossible in the future.

Despite remaining challenges, the new *Spitzenkandidaten* system represents a significant step in rebalancing the powers between the Parliament and the Council, and in advancing the *civitas* dimension of European constitutionalization. Before the Lisbon Treaty, the Parliament seemed merely able to rubber-stamp the Commission members selected by the Council and to exert political influence through the election process. While the end result of the 2014 election was not necessarily a foreseeable one, it was the first of any European elections where participation rates actually increased vis-à-vis previous elections, sending

[80] Habermas, 'Remarks on Dieter Grimm', 303, 305.

[81] It called democracy in Europe a 'farce' if Juncker was not to be selected: see commentary by Bild CEO M. Döpfner, 'Juncker muss Präsident werden' (30 May 2014), www.bild.de/news/standards/mathias-doepfner/juncker-muss-praesident-werden-36187236.bild.html.

a positive signal to the establishment of a European public space through treaty change and changed constitutional practice. Although it seems premature to declare a 'watershed' in EU constitutional development,[82] the possibility exists to shifts the constitutional balance of the EU and to advance the development of political parties in the EU, opening a greater space for a trans-European public sphere. While it was somewhat undermined in 2019 through the Von der Leyen Commission, several of the *Spitzenkandidaten* were made Commissioners and the largest Party in the European Parliament was allowed to nominate the President.

The ECJ has been more than active in decisions concerning political parties and party groupings in the European Union. It started with *Les Verts*, the case credited with sparking constitutional debates among EU lawyers.[83] *Les Verts* concerned a payment for the French Green Party that was refused at the time by the EU Parliament. In this case, the ECJ recognized the special role of political parties in the European Parliament despite a lack of explicit reference to their work in the original Rome Treaties. I By recognizing the special role that parties play in the EU's political process, the ECJ demonstrated a federal understanding of the role of parties in the Union – not just at the Member State level but also for the Union itself.

Another important case is *Front National*,[84] where the ECJ was requested to review a decision to dissolve a political group in the European Parliament. *Front National* appealed a General Court judgment that declared the decision by the European Parliament to retroactively dissolve the so-called 'mixed group' – a group for all other parties without any form of ideological or other commonality. The European Parliament argued that the mixed group did not constitute a political grouping, as its constitution '. . . permits the various signatory members total political [independence] within the group'. The General Court decided that the Front National's challenge was admissible but unfounded, because

> [s]uch a provision in a rule dealing with the formation of political groups must necessarily be construed as meaning that Members who choose to

[82] A. Glencross, 'The Spitzenkandidaten Process Has "Presidentialised" the Commission, But Only Time Will Tell Whether It Allows for Better Representation of Citizens' Views', LSE EUROPP blog (10 Sep 2014), http://blogs.lse.ac.uk/europpblog/2014/09/10/the-spitzenkandidaten-process-has-presidentialised-the-commission-but-only-time-will-tell-whether-it-allows-for-better-representation-of-citizens-views.

[83] Case 294/83, *Parti écologiste 'Les Verts'* v. *European Parliament* [1986] ECR 01339.

[84] Joined Cases T-222/99, T-327/99 and T-329/99, *Jean-Claude Martinez, Charles de Gaulle, Front National, and Others* v. *Parliament* [2001] ECR II-02823.

> form a group within the Parliament may do so only on the basis of political affinities. The applicants' argument as to the optional nature of the criterion of political affinities referred to in that provision is therefore negated by the very terms of Rule 29(1), in conjunction with the heading of that Rule.[85]

This decision by the Court highlights the importance of political parties in the decision-making process of Parliament. I believe that this demonstrates a strong affirmation by the General Court that political parties in the European Parliament do not just constitute loose collaborations of convenience; they actually need to share some form of political affinity.

In this case, the General Court took a distinctly constitutional tone:

> . . . [T]he dual requirement for the organisation of Members into political groups, namely that the members of a political group must share political affinities and come from more than one Member State, enables local political particularities to be transcended and promotes the European integration sought by the Treaty. Thus the political groups contribute to the attainment of the political objective pursued by Article 191 EC, that is to say the emergence of political parties at European level as a factor for integration within the Union, contributing to forming a European awareness and to expressing the political will of the citizens of the Union. Such a role could not be performed by a technical or mixed group made up of Members abjuring any political affinity amongst themselves.[86]

The Court of Justice did not contradict the General Court on this issue here but rather decided that its standing criteria to bring a case had been applied too generously to the Front National because it was in fact not directly concerned with the dissolution of the mixed group as

> [a]lthough it cannot be denied that no implementing measure is necessary for the act to produce effects, there is also no question that, pursuant to the actual wording of Article 29, the act can produce effects only on the legal situation of Members of the Parliament and not on that of national political parties from whose lists those Members were elected and which, in some cases, have played a part in securing the election of those Members.

This demonstrates that the Court once more is adopting a very federal decision. By indicating that, even though a mixed party grouping was not allowed for the Front National, the party as a national party was not affected, the Court here recognizes the federal nature of the EU.

85 Joined Cases T-222/99, T-327/99 and T-329/99, *Jean-Claude Martinez, Charles de Gaulle, Front National, and Others* v. *Parliament* [2001] ECR II-02823, [81].

86 Ibid., para. [148].

The *SPÖ Landesorganisation Kärnten* case concerned the more technical matter of charging VAT on advertising services carried out by the regional grouping of a political party in a Member State.[87] While regional authorities in Austria wanted to charge VAT on those activities, the Court of Justice concluded that the party was not liable for VAT because of political party privilege:

> By such activities, the SPÖ is therefore carrying out a communication exercise in keeping with attainment of its political objectives and which seeks to spread its ideas as a political organisation. More specifically, the SPÖ's activity, particularly through the intermediary of the Landesorganisation, is the development of informed political opinion with a view to participation in the exercise of political power. In carrying out that activity, the SPÖ does not however participate in any market.[88]

The CJEU demonstrated a federalist understanding. Rather than giving the Member State full discretion as to how to treat political parties, it conferred upon the SPÖ a party privilege that applied equally across the Union.

3.3.4 Conclusion as to the Validity of This Obstacle

The establishment of political parties is important in a modern democratic system and critics do not yet recognize how such parties can develop over time. Their arguments undervalue the concept that federations do not fundamentally require federal political party structures. As we know, the US Founding Fathers themselves thought federal-level political parties to be dangerous, and potentially divisive, assembling too much power at the federal level. The establishment of political parties must be considered as a process – and this is made all the clearer when illustrative examples from other constitutional experiences are taken into account. The lack of a European public sphere has thus far hampered further progress, however, and, as such, existing weaknesses in the development of trans-European political parties remain a corollary challenge for *civitas* in the EU. Again, the courts play an important role in clarifying and strengthening the European party system over time. While

[87] Case C-267/08, *SPÖ Landesorganisation Kärnten* v. *Finanzamt Klagenfurt* [2009] ECR I-09781.

[88] Ibid., para. [24].

much of political party organization still occurs at Member State level, there are already early signs of EU-wide developments. Arguably, it is the value that the EU places on political parties that distinguishes the EU-level and Member State-level polities, rather than a lack of adequate structure for civic engagement. In my view, the political victory by the European Parliament in convincing the Council to follow its own *Spitzenkandaten* process and appoint Junker as the victor and President from the party-based elections demonstrates that the European polity can advance towards such civic engagement and can also support the construction of a meaningful common public sphere. The parties are seen as 'contributing' to the expression of political will at Union level, and, while they do not yet exist as such at the Union level, the legal foundation for their formation is nonetheless in place and could develop further alongside and as part of the greater development of a European public sphere.

3.4 Lack of One Real President?

3.4.1 Obstacle

Critics argue that the EU currently has three competing presidents, presenting a major obstacle for constitutional development. The Lisbon Treaty brought about the position President of the European Council – a position elected by the Heads of State and Government for a period of two and a half years. However, there is also a President of the Council, which rotates from EU Member State to EU Member State and determines the chairmanship for the different Council configurations. Finally, the EU Commission itself has a President, mandated to speak for the entire European Union.[89] This demonstrates that the historical problem described by Henry Kissinger with his question 'Who to Call in Europe?'[90] persists.[91] This dilemma has led critics to argue that the possibility of constitutional development faces serious obstacles.[92] While a duopoly or even a triumvirate of power might have existed in

[89] For research into the three presidencies, see: I. Tömmel and A. Verdun, 'Political Leadership in the European Union: An Introduction' (2017) 39 *Journal of European Integration* 103, 105–7.

[90] Cited in M. Elsig, *The EU's Common Commercial Policy: Institutions, Interests and Ideas* (Abingdon/New York 2017) 2.

[91] See the speech by David Cameron of 23 January 2013 where he criticized the sense of ever-increasing bureaucracy in the Union: www.bbc.co.uk/news/uk-politics-21160684.

[92] Ibid.

ancient Rome, it is clearly incompatible with the modern requirements of constitutionalism.[93]

3.4.2 *Underlying Concepts of Constitutional Development*

While some federations such as the United States or Argentina have very strong presidential systems, this is much less pronounced in federal systems such as Canada, Germany and Switzerland. I believe that these serve as a very useful example of how a federal entity can subsist with varying levels of power invested in a single president, as well as how the power of a president develops over the course of a federal polity's history. Actually, the extreme power currently held by the US President, in stark contrast to the Early Republic, might well lead to greater problems in the American Republic.[94] The Early Presidency in the United States was much weaker in many ways than the current presidency – it competed, for instance, with the power of other federal institutions, including the Army.[95] While modern US Presidents have, over time, been iconized by history as all-powerful politicians and statesman, Early US constitutional times were starkly different. The powerful Presidency arose relatively late in US constitutional development and was, as Ackerman conclusively proves, extraordinarily assisted by the Supreme Court in its early jurisprudence.[96] In the Early US Republic, Presidents found themselves battling with powerful politicians from other institutions, such as the Senate or the House, or indeed State governors. For many early US Americans, their State governor was not just better known but also more important than the President, who sat with limited powers in faraway lands. The different constitutional institutions were not dependent on a strong Presidency and, as I believe, could actually be said to have functioned for quite a while without one.[97]

93 Ibid.

94 B. A. Ackerman, *The Decline and Fall of the American Republic* (Cambridge, MA 2010). This has become more important with the recent presidency of Donald Trump; see C. Amirfar and A. Singh, 'The Trump Administration and the "Unmaking" of International Agreements' (2018) 59 *Harvard International Law Journal* 443; A. Gonzales, 'Presidential Powers, Immunities, and Pardons' (2018–2019) 96 *Washington University Law Review* 905 or M. A. Genovese, *A Presidential Nation: Causes, Consequences, and Cures* (New York/Abingdon 2013); M. A. Genovese, *Presidential Leadership in an Age of Change* (Abingdon/New York 2017).

95 Ackerman, *The Failure of the Founding Fathers*, 111ff.

96 Ibid.

97 J. Ceasar, *Presidential Selection: Theory and Development* (Princeton, NJ 1979).

It is of real significance to this analysis that other federal systems, such as Germany, confine the Head of State – the Federal President – to a ceremonial role, vested with very few formal powers. Only really does the Federal President exercise its reserve powers and such situations are limited to times of constitutional crisis, such as the failure of the government to secure a parliamentary majority or the resignation of the Bundeskanzler (Art. 69 Grundgesetz). The weak role given to the Federal President was a fully intended one given the terrible historical experience of presidential decrees in the Weimar Republic. But when litigants before the Constitutional Court tried to question even these albeit limited powers, the Constitutional Court argued that the Federal President had full powers to exercise his discretion as to whether any party can establish a viable majority: it was not bound by other provisions of the German Constitution on the matter.[98] I believe that here the Court was interfering to safeguard the role of the President. When, in another case, the Federal President declined to sign an act because he believed that it violated the Constitution (*Fluglotsenprivatisierung*[99]), the Constitutional Court concluded that despite being referred to as the notary public of the state, the Federal President could not be forced to sign an Act of Parliament that he believed to be unconstitutional. Again, what we see here is the Court acting to strengthen the role of the President. In my view, judicial tendency by the Court to uphold the President's role was recently affirmed once more when a radical right-wing party recently complained about the absence of any debate around the election of the Bundspraesident in Germany. Responding to this complaint, the GFCC stated that the office of the Federal President was 'shaped in such a way that he or she belongs to none of the three classical powers, but embodies the unity of the state (Repräsentant der Volkseinheit). The authority and the dignity of the office are expressed by the fact that it is largely based on the President's intellectual and moral impact (geistig-moralische Wirkung).'[100] The Court seems to be placing

[98] BVerfG, *Vote of Confidence* Decision of 25 August 2005, ECLI:DE:BVerfG:2005:es20050825.2bve000405.

[99] GFCC, *Fluglotsenprivatisierung* (Privatization of flight controllers). H. Prantl, 'Horst Köhler macht Geschichte', Sueddeutsche Zeitung, 17 May 2010: 'Der Bundespräsident hat das Gesetz zur Privatisierung der Flugsicherheit nicht unterzeichnet. Köhler wendet sich gegen den Ausverkauf der Staatlichkeit' [The Federal President has not signed the law on the privatization of aviation safety. Köhler opposes the sell-out of statehood].

[100] GFCC, *Federal Convention Case*, Judgment of 10 June 2014, No 2 BvE 2/09; 2 BvE 2/10, www.bundesverfassungsgericht.de/SharedDocs/Pressemitteilungen/EN/2014/bvg14-051.html.

the President outside the normal boundaries of the Constitutional structure; the President is, in the Court's assessment, a separate entity from all three branches of government.

By way of illustrating the exception rather than the norm, it will be no surprise that the Swiss system is yet again truly unique in its approach,[101] with the Head of State changing in a rotational manner. While this particularly extreme form of government should not be taken to represent federal systems in general, it is clear that federal systems do have different forms of ultimate representation, with diverse forms of governance that can exist, develop and thrive.

3.4.3 *Related EU Developments*

In a federal system, there are many variations of the President's role, and different institutions can be represented in diverse ways. In many federal polities, the Presidents of each individual chamber of Parliament play a significant role in representing its institutions. Analogous to this, is the competition that undeniably exists between the President of the Commission and the President of the European Council.

The EU foundational agreements established the EU Presidency as a rolling rotating office, passing from one EU Member State to another at set intervals. There are certain visible parallels between the EU Presidency and the executive branch of government that exists in many democratic constitutions. One particularly analogous example is the power of the President/Executive to drive forward the policy agenda of the governmental apparatus as a whole, as well as the identity of the President/Executive as a political and governmental figurehead. Yet, there are also several glaring differences that cannot be ignored. Key amongst those differences is the inability of citizens to elect the President or to have any direct involvement in the selection of the Member State that will assume the Presidency role.[102] In the EU system, the only citizens that have any control over the identity and policy goals (to a more limited extent) of an EU President are those citizens that reside in the Member State that, on that particular occasion, assumes the role of Presidency. This creates a situation in which the citizens of that particular

[101] E. Cashin Ritaine and A.-S. Papeil, 'Federalism and Legal Unification in Switzerland' in Halberstam and Reimann (eds.), *Federalism and Legal Unification*, 439.

[102] Craig and de Búrca, *The Evolution of EU Law*, 12. See also chapters 3 and 5 in D. Hodson and J. Peterson (eds.), *The Institutions of the European Union* (Oxford 2017) 55–79 and 108–37.

Member State are in a privileged position over those of other EU Member States, having had electoral input in the identity of the President through domestic elections.

A further glaring difference between the role of the national Executive and that of the EU Presidency is that the citizens of the Member State holding the EU Presidency are potentially able to destabilize or diminish the power and abilities of the Presidency in times of domestic political instability. This undermines the standing of the Head of Government who holds the EU Presidency. This power inequality must be seen as more than merely theoretical; it has tangible potential for destabilization. During the recent Czech Presidency, for example, such political destabilization resulted in a less successful Presidential term for the EU.[103] Here, democratic legitimacy was diminished on the EU level despite the fact that it may have been strengthened on the domestic level via the use of accepted democratic channels to challenge an unpopular government or leader. Further, another unique aspect of the EU Presidency is the ability of each EU President to present and act upon his/her particular agenda for the period of their particular tenure.[104] While this is, of course, a feature of other democratic regimes, the time frame of the EU Presidency, along with the absence of a direct election mechanism, makes this system distinct from any role played by the executive branch of government.

Fundamentally, the EU has more than one President. It is unsurprising that the EU has more than one President given that its fundamental objective is to avoid capture by Member State interests. If the rotating Presidency were elevated to the only agenda-setting figure, it would not avoid but rather encourage capture by Member State interests. Following the euro crisis, an even greater perceived need has been created for close and efficient cooperation among Member States. In response to this need, several foreign ministers in the EU have formed a 'Future of Europe' discussion group to map out options for how closer cooperation could manifest itself,[105] with other proposals stemming from academics or individual politicians.[106] While it is not yet certain that the EU actually

[103] European Parliament, 'Balance of the Czech Presidency' www.europarl.europa.eu/sides/getDoc.do?pubRef=-//EP//TEXT+CRE+20090114+ITEM-003+DOC+XML+V0//EN&language=EN.

[104] Ibid.

[105] Future of Europe Group, Final Report (17 September 2012), www.cer.eu/sites/default/files/westerwelle_report_sept12.pdf.

[106] See Piris, *The Future of Europe* and D. Cohn-Bendit and G. Verhofstadt, *For Europe! Manifesto for a Postnational Revolution in Europe* (Munich 2012) (the French original makes clear that the authors were both interviewed by Jean Quatremer (Debout

requires constitutional amendments to enable closer cooperation, it is nonetheless useful to review these (currently hypothetical) proposals.[107]

One proposal regarding the Presidency is that EU parliamentary groups nominate an EU Commission President candidate and elect a Head of the EU administration. The Spitzenkandidaten system was successfully tested and adopted in the previous to last EU elections when the Commission President candidate of the largest political grouping was elected. A further proposal has been given by the former Head of the Legal Service for the Council. The compromise suggestion put forward here is a 'two-speed EU' process in a treaty instrument and permits a subgroup of Member States to engage in much closer, more efficient cooperation. This proposal even suggests separate representatives including a Euro-President.[108] The German, Polish and Danish foreign ministers have also put forward competing proposals. These include, inter alia, a directly elected Commission President who would determine his 'European government' autonomously.[109] More radical proposals include the establishment of a European Federal Union, through a new treaty, in which Member States play the role of Federated States and where only one Head of State (perhaps with more representative powers) and a Head of Government, with more political powers, would be elected.[110]

The judicial dialogue is also highly relevant in this area. From the centre, the CJEU has developed a rich jurisprudence in several cases concerning institutional provisions of the Union. In one recent case, for example, the President of the Council complained about the President of the Parliament having signed the 2011 Budget of the Union by himself, even though, in the view of the President of the

l'Europe!: manifeste pour une révolution postnationale en Europe; Suivi d'un entretien avec Jean Quatremer / Daniel Cohn-Bendit, Guy Verhofstadt (Brussels 2012)).

107 See also in the light of Brexit: European Commission, 'White paper on the future of Europe: Reflections and scenarios for the EU27 by 2025' COM(2017)2025; C. E. de Vries, *Euroscepticism and the Future of European Integration* (Oxford 2018) 204–21; S. Fabbrini, 'Alternative Governance Models: "Hard Core" in a Differentiated Europe' (2019) 17 *Comparative European Politics* 278; F. B. Jacobs, *The EU after Brexit: Institutional and Policy Implications* (Cham 2018); M. Cini and A. Verdun, 'The Implications of Brexit for the Future of Europe' in B. Martill and U. Staiger (eds.), *Brexit and Beyond: Rethinking the Futures of Europe* (London 2018) 63–71; S. Hix, 'Decentralised Federalism: A New Model for the EU' in Martill and Staiger (eds.), 72–80; L. van Middelaar, 'Seven Brexit Propositions: Towards a Union the Protects' in Martill and Staiger (eds.), 81–7.

108 Piris, *The Future of Europe*, 121.

109 Future of Europe Group, Final Report.

110 Cohn-Bendit and Verhofstadt, 71.

Council, both Presidents were responsible for signing the Budget on behalf of their institutions. The CJEU did not agree with the President of the Council on this point and could not find any violation.[111] In coming to this decision, the CJEU rejected the argument given by the Council that the duty of loyal cooperation had been violated:

> Moreover, the Council submits that, in adopting the contested measure, the President of the Parliament acted in breach of the duty to cooperate in good faith, which should govern relations between the institutions. It criticises the President of the Parliament in particular on the ground that he did not participate in the steps taken by the Council to seek a solution that complied with the Treaties, was mutually acceptable and had due regard to both the institutions' powers and the powers of the President of the Parliament.[112]

What makes this decision particularly remarkable is that the Court chose not to strengthen the role of the Council President by supporting his position, even though the Council President is still called 'President of the Union' in the Constitutional Treaty. It is clear from Art. 15.6 TEU that, in the Lisbon Treaty, Member States sought to create a counterbalance to the Commission President by instituting an elected Council President to drive the European Council's work. The Court's ruling here did not support the rise of the Council or its President. The Court can be seen as siding with the Commission and its efforts elsewhere to move towards an elected Commission President.

While it is impossible to detect any significant political appetite for a strong President in the European Union, this is hardly fatal to EU constitutionalization. Given the very different presidential models in existing federal polities, however, this ruling represents a solid understanding of federal thought by the Court. It is also worth noting that courts of the periphery in Europe have not yet had the opportunity to express themselves as to the form of governance the EU should proceed with, particularly with regard to the role of any President(s).

3.4.4 *Conclusion as to the Validity of This Obstacle*

The EU does not currently have just one President – indeed, *The Economist* refers to this structure as a 'flawed temple'.[113] However,

[111] Case C-77/11, *Council of the European Union* v. *European Parliament (Budget signature)* Judgment of the Court (Grand Chamber) of 17 September 2013, not yet reported.
[112] Ibid., para. [64].
[113] *The Economist*, 'Charlemagne: A Flawed Temple'.

illustrative examples from other federal polities clearly suggest that the institution of a powerful President is not required for constitutional development. Even in the United States, the evolution of the Presidency was not an automatic development anchored in the constitutional text but rather an organic development over time. The Court of Justice has not actually chosen to endorse this approach, opting instead to strengthen the powers of the Commission President vis-à-vis the perceived rise of the European Council President. The present structure of the EU may still continue to pose challenges for deeper civic engagement and broader leadership legitimacy. While the absence of a powerful President is clearly not a pre-requisite for further constitutionalization, there is certainly enough debate on the need for a clear Presidential voice to merit further consideration. Certainly, European institutions must query whether the system at present is actually hindering the constitutionalization process – what seems to be lacking is much broader civic support for any of the kind of reform projects envisioned.

3.5 The European Parliament Is Not the Only Law-Maker?

3.5.1 Objection

The European Parliament participates in law-making in the EU, but it does not do so alone. For this reason, critics have objected to further European constitutionalization by arguing that the Parliament is hampered both by the absence of a right to initiate law-making and by the fact that it is not the only legislative organ in the structure of the EU. This sentiment resonates in the recent finding of the GFCC that a 5 per cent hurdle for political parties is unconstitutional in EU elections.

The GFCC ruled that the European Parliament does not require the stability provided by a 5 per cent threshold guarantee because it does not function like a Member State Parliament where a government is elected for the purpose of monopolizing other legislative powers within the State.[114] Such critics see the *pouvoir constituant* in the Member State Parliaments and deny that the European Parliament can be truly representative of the will of the people.[115]

[114] GFCC, *5% Hurdle European Election.*

[115] Cameron, 'EU Speech at Bloomberg'. For a different view, see J. Habermas, 'Citizen and State Equality in a Supranational Political Community: Degressive Proportionality and the *Pouvoir Constituant Mixte*' (2017) 55 *Journal of Common Market Studies* 171. For an overview of the various narratives, see M. Patberg, 'Challenging the Masters of the

3.5.2 *Underlying Concepts of Constitutional Development*

Just as the role of the Head of State varies across federal States, so too does the role of the various Parliaments. Most federal countries have bi-cameral systems, but they vary greatly as to their power and influence.[116] Here, I believe there is a significant difference between European and US experiences. The European Union has only one directly elected Parliament, while its Council contains government representatives with a strict mandate from their respective governments. The US Constitution, on the other hand, was designed with a strict separation of powers approach – Congress is, by its inception, a plainly bi-cameral system,[117] where directly elected representatives and State-sent senators together form the legislative branch. Even though it might seem impossible to imagine today, there were still important debates about State-based decisions in the House in the Early Republic.[118] Representatives were expected to vote in state formations, and although the Senate, with two representatives from each state, had that role specifically, few expected politics to become national (unless grandees such as Washington were to be elected).[119]

Germany serves as another strong example of a similar dynamic, with a strong bi-cameral parliamentary system. The Bundesrat, unlike many other Upper Houses of Parliament, is a direct representation of the Länder governments. Somewhat curious for parliamentary systems is the fact (as in the Council of the European Union) that governments of Länder instruct their representatives, and these representatives are bound by those instructions. In *Zuwanderungsgesetz 2002*,[120] a case concerning votes cast differently among the members of the Land Brandenburg, the Constitutional Court held:

> The Bundesrat is a collegiate constitutional body of the Federation which consists of Members of the Land governments (see Article 51.1 sentence 1 of the Basic Law). It is not formed from the Länder. . . . This participation

Treaties: Emerging Narratives of Constituent Power in the European Union' (2018) 7 *Global Constitutionalism* 263.

116 A. Grenon, 'Unification of Laws in Federal Systems: The Canadian Model' in Halberstam and Reimann (eds.), *Federalism and Legal Unification*, 169; Cashin Ritaine and Papeil, 439; J. Adam and C. Möllers, 'Unification of Laws in the Federal System of Germany' in Halberstam and Reimann (eds.), *Federalism and Legal Unification*, 237.

117 G. Tsebelis and J. Money, *Bicameralism* (Cambridge 1997).

118 Ackerman, *The Failure of the Founding Fathers*, 29–30.

119 Ibid.

120 GFCC, *Zuwanderungsgesetz 2002*, 2 BvF 1/02 of 18 December 2002, www.bverfg.de/entscheidungen/fs20021218_2bvf000102en.html. This book uses the official English translation, which has its shortcomings in terms of expression.

> takes place, not directly, but by the agency of the Members of the Bundesrat coming from the midst of the Land governments.[121] The Länder are in each case represented by their Bundesrat Members who are present.[122]

Essentially, the Constitutional Court turned down the argument by several Länder that the Premier of the Land in question had the competency to direct his Ministers (members of the Bundesrat) to direct their vote within the session of the Bundesrat. However, the GFCC decided:

> Ranking within *Land* constitutional law has no role to play at federal level. The holder of a guideline competence under *Land* law has no prominent status under federal constitutional law permitting him or her to overcome a voting dissent of two other Members present solely by announcing his or her will. The instruction under *Land* law to *Bundesrat* Members, which is permitted by the Basic Law in the *Bundesrat* – unlike in the Joint Committee (Article 53a.1 sentence 3 of the Basic Law) or in the conciliation committee (Article 77.2 sentence 3 of the Basic Law) – is that of the *Land* government, not of the holder of the guideline competence. If there is no instruction of the *Land* government, and if a *Land* and the Members representing its *Land* government vote non-uniformly, this is not unconstitutional. Article 51.3 sentence 2 of the Basic Law merely prohibits accommodating a *Land* will that is split in the ballot result of the *Bundesrat* by splitting the votes of the *Land*.[123]

This example of the governments of Länder demonstrates that even in bicameral systems, where members are instructed by their government, the federal institution has a distinct legal status and the law of the federal level does not intrude on the Land level. In other words, federal institutions develop their own characteristics and are not derived from Länder law.

3.5.3 Related EU Developments

The EU Parliament was created as an advisory body with very limited powers. From that vantage point, it has seen exponential growth in its powers and responsibilities. Its constitutional position is now much closer to that of a Federal Parliament than the advisory body of an international organization. This development has been possible due to a series of constitutional amendments, CJEU judgments and demands

[121] See Decisions of the GFCC, Entscheidungen des Bundesverfassungsgerichts – BVerfGE 8, 104 (120).
[122] Ibid., para. [151].
[123] Ibid., para. [164].

from within the Parliament itself. Once seated, the MEPs enact legislation, although ultimately legislation must be introduced by the European Commission[124] and needs the approval of the Parliament and the Council to become effective.[125] However, both the Parliament and the EU Council have some oversight capabilities vis-à-vis the EU Commission, meaning that there is at least some level of monitoring by an elected body.[126]

While Parliament is one of the legislative entities involved in the promulgation of budgetary provisions for the EU,[127] these budgetary provisions are limited by the amount of monies given to the EU by the Member States.[128] Assessments from the Member States are generally based on domestically generated customs duties,[129] agricultural levies,[130] VAT resources[131] and GNP resources.[132] This is essentially the converse of other democratic systems, such as the United States where the federal polity provides monies to the states based on certain programmes and requirements, and the states do not themselves have the same federal payment requirements as in the EU. In addition to this irregularity, the sliding scale of fiscal responsibility for economic support to the EU is also problematic. Based on the wealth of each Member State, the variations in fiscal responsibilities for the EU borne by different Member States can be seen as creating a difference in the vesting of individual Member States in the EU overall. This in turn has a bearing on the democratic legitimacy of the EU as a whole.

However, it is worth noting that, in the context of taxation, EU citizens have the ability to directly petition Parliament and/or an Ombudsman with grievances.[133] Further, citizens may petition the Ombudsman for claims regarding the policies and actions of Member States.[134] These

[124] Art. 17(2), TEU (OJ 2012 C 326 p.1).

[125] Except for the cases in which special legislative procedure applies.

[126] European Parliament, 'Oversight over the Commission and Council', www.europarl.europa.eu/about-parliament/en/powers-and-procedures/supervisory-powers.

[127] Art. 14(1), TEU (OJ 2012 C 326 p.1).

[128] Art. 311, TFEU (OJ 2012 C 326 p.1).

[129] European Parliament, 'The Budget of the European Union', www.europarl.europa.eu/about-parliament/en/powers-and-procedures/budgetary-powers.

[130] Ibid.

[131] Ibid.

[132] Ibid.

[133] Art. 20(2)(d), Art. 228, TFEU; European Parliament, 'Supervisory Power', www.europarl.europa.eu/parliament/public/staticDisplay.do?id=46&pageRank=8&language=EN.

[134] Ibid.

abilities appear to bolster the democratic legitimacy of the EU's governing structures, at least within this particular field.

On a related note, a mechanism exists through which the national Parliament of a Member State may send legislative suggestions directly to the European Parliament and, in effect, bypass the MEPs of that particular Member State.[135] This dynamic allows a national Parliament (which perhaps might have changed in political composition since the past MEP election and thus holds different values and beliefs) to bypass the Member State's own MEPs, further complicating the responsibility between the federal and the federated levels in the EU governance structure.

While it has been argued by some that democratic representation occurs within the EU mainly through the Parliament, it is clear that the bulk of the EU's governance activity is in fact taking place within its other institutions – the Commission and the Council.[136] The lack of effective parliamentary control over these institutions amounts to a form of democratic deficit.[137] One particularly contested area lacking in real democratic legitimacy is the negotiation of international trade and investment agreements and policies by the EU, especially in the WTO.[138] While under the ordinary legislative procedure, both the Parliament and the Council define the framework, the principles and the objectives of the EU's common commercial policy,[139] it is in fact the EU Commission, under the supervision of the Council, that is involved in the negotiation and implementation of EU WTO law and policy.[140] Following the ratification of the Treaty of Lisbon, the field of foreign direct investment (FDI) is now under the competence of the EU's common commercial policy.[141] Parliament is not absent entirely from this

135 Protocol on the Role of National Parliaments in the European Union (OJ 2012 C 326 p.203); see also European Parliament, 'Relations with National Parliaments', www.europarl.europa.eu/webnp/cms/lang/en/pid/1.

136 View presented in Mair and Thomassen, at 4.

137 B. Crum and J. Fossum, 'The Multilevel Parliamentary Field: A Framework for Theorizing Representative Democracy in the EU' (2009) 1(2) *European Political Science Review* 249, 252.

138 See M. Gehring, 'Subnational Participation in International Trade Law: Options for the European Union' (2018) CIGI Papers No. 167, www.cigionline.org/sites/default/files/documents/Paper%20no.167_web_1.pdf; M. Gehring and M. C. Cordonier Segger, *Sustainable Development in World Trade Law* (Alphen aan den Rijn 2005); and M. C. Cordonier Segger, M. Gehring and A. Newcombe, *Sustainable Development in World Investment Law* (Alphen aan den Rijn 2010).

139 Art. 207(2), TFEU.

140 Ibid.

141 Paragraph 158 (replacing Article 133 with Article 188 C), Treaty of Lisbon amending the Treaty on European Union and the Treaty establishing the European Community (OJ 2007 C 306 p.1); Part 5, Title II of the TFEU, ibid.

exercise, however, and the Commission must report regularly to the Parliament on the progress of negotiations.[142] While there is some sense of direct participation – in that the citizen-elected body must approve these measures and agreements – the Parliament does not have the ability to actually lead negotiations on international trade or related topics.[143] The consent of the Parliament is also required to conclude trade agreements[144] and to approve measures taken by the EU at the WTO level, and in any new bilateral investment treaties (BITs).[145] According to the 2012 BIT Regulation, for example,[146] Member States are entitled to keep their existing investment treaties and even negotiate new ones if there is no overarching EU interest in negotiating a BIT with the country in question. Although the EU has started to exercise potentially far-reaching competence in BIT negotiation, there is in fact a long-term transitional arrangement in place with deference to individual EU Member States. Essentially, the EU has opted for a supervised version of dual federalism in this field.

Jurisprudence helps us to see how this balance has evolved over time. From the centre, the leading case on the functions of the Parliament remains the *Les Verts* case.[147] When considering payments withheld from the French Green Party early in its existence, the Court held that the European Parliament had an elevated position within the constitutional order of the European Union. I believe that, by this judgment, the ECJ was instrumental in helping the Parliament to increase its relative weight in the European Union. Parliament was provided with principles, accepted in the case law, that enabled it to litigate on the basis of all questions pertaining to its prerogative. Subsequently, the effect of this judgment was codified in Art. 267 para. 2 TFEU.[148] In my view, this finding shows that on certain questions of *civitas*, the Court is well able to balance the differences between federal and federated institutions,

[142] Art. 207(3), TFEU.

[143] See K. Meissner, 'Democratizing EU External Relations: The European Parliament's Informal Role in SWIFT, ACTA, and TTIP' (2016) 21 *European Foreign Affairs Review* 269; C. Roederer-Rynning, 'Parliamentary Assertion and Deep Integration: The European Parliament in the CETA and TTIP Negotiations' (2017) 30 *Cambridge Review of International Affairs* 507.

[144] Roederer-Rynning; Art. 218(6) TFEU.

[145] Roederer-Rynning; Art. 218(6) TFEU.

[146] Regulation (EU) No 1219/2012 of the European Parliament and of the Council of 12 December 2012 establishing transitional arrangements for bilateral investment agreements between Member states and third countries (OJ 2012 L 351 p.40).

[147] Case 294/83, *Parti écologiste 'Les Verts'* v. *European Parliament* [1986] ECR 01339.

[148] Craig and de Búrca, *The Evolution of EU Law*, 18.

and the democratic legitimacy derived by them from the Union. Indeed, I see a general trend in which the Parliament has, over the years, increased its relative weight in the decision-making process, greatly aided by the ECJ.

As previously explained, the role of the Parliament has also been altered through treaty changes. The most important of these has been the changes in the Maastricht Treaty from cooperation to co-decision procedure and again in the Lisbon Treaty, turning this procedure into the default procedure. These changes were often accompanied by leading judgments from the Court underlining the rights of the Parliament and strengthening its competences. In the *Environmental Crimes* case,[149] for example, the Court strengthened the Parliament significantly. It decided that Member States had an obligation to adopt a measure under the Community Pillar of core competences, if possible. When it opted for the competence of criminal law cooperation with no Parliamentary involvement, the Council was found to be violating the Treaties. Instead, the Court found that environmental crimes fall under the environmental law core competence and that, as such, Directives on environmental crimes must be adopted together with the European Parliament.[150] The Court has, in essence, decided jurisdictional cases in a way that strengthens the engagement of the European Parliament in law-making vis-à-vis the Member States and the Council.

However, because of the financial crisis and the necessary rescue efforts by the Member States, the institutional balance that has been developed over the decades shifted back in favour of the Council.[151] The Council assumed responsibilities for balancing budget provisions and even passed the Stability Pact and the ESM Treaty.

So, the question is this: Have we witnessed a reversal in the function of the Parliament and the Commission, for the benefit of the Council? Many decisions during the financial crisis were taken by the Council – often only in fact by the Euro Ministers Council and with minimal oversight or input from either the Commission or the Parliament. Political science literature readily accredits decision-making in this form with the rise of

[149] Case C-176/03, *Commission of the European Communities* v. *Council of the European Union (Environmental Crimes)* [2005] ECR I-07879.

[150] Ibid., para. [43].

[151] Supported e.g. by S. B. Hobolt, 'The Crisis of Legitimacy of European Institutions' in M. Castells and others (eds.), *Europe's Crises* (Cambridge, UK/Medford, MA 2018) 249.

the Council.[152] Yet, in many ways, what we see is not a rise but, rather, a re-assertion of old ways of policy-making in the EU where the Council determines all major decisions without any shared decision-making. The Court of Justice has – with the exception of the *Pringle* judgment – been generally less sympathetic to the rise of the Council. In several further decisions, it has emphasized the role of the Parliament and the role of the Commission in decision-making.[153] In several cases, most prominently in the *Philippines* case, the Council had sought to add legal basis to its decision to endorse the Framework Agreement. This clearly demonstrates that the European Union did not have exclusive competence to conclude the Agreement. The Court of Justice sided with the Commission, which was supported by the Parliament. It ruled that the Framework Agreement, although containing provisions related to immigration, social and environmental protection, fell under the common commercial and development cooperation competences. In the *Philippines* case, the Court seems to deliberately take a balancing approach against the re-rise of the Council as the central decision-making organ, providing a constitutional counterweight to the central role that the Council played in the financial crisis. Especially in external relations, the Court of Justice has expressed its clear opinion that the Union should speak with one voice, which shifts the power from the Council back to the Commission, with Parliament having a strong voice.

I believe that this analysis demonstrates a crucial, even instrumental role played by the Court in shaping the constitutional position of the Parliament as a whole. This is in real contrast to some Member State national court decisions, which have, as demonstrated by the GFCC's *5% Hurdle* decision, largely dismissed the role of the European Parliament.[154] The GFCC's finding was that

> a similar interest [to create a stable government through stable majorities in Parliament] does not exist at the European level as determined by the European Treaties. The European Parliament does not elect a Union Government, which would be dependent on its continued support. Nor

[152] U. Puetter, 'Europe's Deliberative Intergovernmentalism: The Role of the Council and European Council in EU Economic Governance' (2011) 19 *Journal of European Public Policy* 161, 171.

[153] Case C-377/12, *European Commission* v. *Council of the European Union (Philippines)*, Judgment of the Court (Grand Chamber) of 11 June 2014 and case C-137/12, *European Commission* v. *Council of the European Union (European Convention to protect services)*, Judgment of the Court (Grand Chamber) of 22 October 2013, not yet reported.

[154] GFCC, *5% Hurdle European Election.*

> is the legislation of the Union dependent on a consistent majority in the European Parliament, which would be formed by a stable coalition of certain political groups and being opposed by an opposition.[155]

In other words, the Court appears to believe that the European Parliament has little real role in the law-making of the EU and therefore does not require a stable majority. On this issue as well, the GFCC displays an impoverished understanding of the constitutional role of the Parliament. If the Court had been able to give due consideration to the constitutional function actually performed, particularly with regard to the Parliament's interaction with the Council and the bi-cameral relationship that exists, its findings may have differed. As Judges Di Fabio and Mellinghoff highlighted, despite the Member State tendency to experiment with different parties, the twofold objective in the EU election law to create stable majorities and not to overemphasize the fringes was a legitimate one that should not be undermined. This dissent may be a better reflection of the growing constitutional functions of the European Parliament since the Treaty of Lisbon.[156] As the judges concluded,

> [the] preservation of the functionality of a composite Parliament is not a question of either-or, but a question of more or less ability to act. In this respect, the Court should not draw analogies to the case law developed for the federal election concerning the ability to form a government with a parliamentary majority, but rather, the functional specificities of the European Parliament shall be adequately appreciated. An objective reason to justify the five-percent electoral threshold is here already the reduction of possible functional impairments.[157]

Regarding the role of Parliament, certain Member State court decisions are already beginning to re-align towards the centre. As one example, in the English High Court – Administrative Court in *ex parte Chester*, it was found that the European Parliament could not be treated as a lesser institution, and its elections were recognized as being of high importance.[158] In similar vein, in *Redmond* v. *Minister for the Environment*, the Irish High Court decided that a deposit of 1,000 EUR to stand in both the Irish and the European elections was

[155] Ibid., para. [118].
[156] Ibid., para. [158].
[157] Ibid.
[158] English High Court, *The Queen on the application of Chester* v. *(1) Secretary of State for Justice and (2) Wakefield Metropolitan District Council* [2009] EWHC 2923 (Admin).

entities and that these entities do not lose their identity by acting within the federal institutions.

3.6.3 *Related EU Developments*

The Council of the European Union comprises ministers of relevant portfolios from the individual Member States. These ministers act in various committees and address a variety of important topics to the EU and its Member states, ranging from agriculture to defence.[175] This structure is explained as an optimal one because it allows ministers with particular areas of expertise and knowledge to use their skills to benefit the community as a whole, as well as their home constituencies.[176] Some commentators also add that, with respect to democratic representation, the Council can be seen as a 'second channel' of representation (the first being Parliament), as EU citizens are represented in their Parliaments, which in turn control the governments and thus also the Member State's representatives to the Council.[177]

However, it is important to recognize that the Council structure and composition can also be seen in a more negative light, as severely undermining the democratic legitimacy of the EU and its governing institutions. Typically, a Minister is elected in his/her home Member State, from a particular constituency. However, he/she must then be given a Ministerial appointment by the ruling party(ies). Only after this appointment is a Minister qualified to represent the interests of his/her home state at the Council level.[178] There are various problems raised by the evident juxtaposition between how the system for appointing Ministers at the Council level operates and our understanding of democratic legitimacy. I submit that first, and perhaps most obvious, is the existence of several layers between direct election to a particular seat in a national parliament and participation at the European Council. At each successive layer, interests change and become less clear. Rather than being elected to a seat and representing its members, the Minister must also carry with him/her the concerns of the party he/she represents, the

175 Art. 15, TEU (OJ 2012 C 326 p.1); see also Council of the European Union, 'The Council', https://europa.eu/european-union/about-eu/institutions-bodies/council-eu_en.

176 Ibid.

177 Crum and Fossum; D. Jančić, 'TTIP and Legislative-Executive Relations in EU Trade Policy' (2016) 40 *West European Politics* 202.

178 Council of the European Union, 'Council Configurations', www.consilium.europa.eu/showPage.aspx?id=427&lang=EN.

concerns of the particular portfolio (such as farmers in an agricultural portfolio) and the overall concerns of the Member State he/she represents. Not only does this raise significant questions of transparent representation of interests and constituencies; it also raises the issue of accountability on the part of the Minister and his/her government. Second, I believe, is the issue of overall representation. Ultimately, the fate of a Minister lies in the hands of his/her home constituencies and national party. Thus, the issue becomes whether the interests of the whole home State related to the particular portfolio are given primacy, as opposed to the primacy of those responsible for re-electing the Minister.[179] Third, as mentioned by Vernon Bogdanor,[180] is the concern that, where majority voting applies, a Minister cannot be held accountable to the Council's decisions by his national parliament when he has been outvoted. The Council decision, in such a case, is simply not his own.

With these issues of democratic legitimacy in mind, I believe that just a cursory glance at the areas of Council competence raises significant questions about the connection between the Council and standard democratic tenets. Each of the policy areas within the Council's competence has its own meeting structure and agenda system, in essence creating a multiplicity of specialized entities that act in their own realms and remove themselves from the general context of the needs of EU citizens. There are certain areas of policy in which Member States are allowed to remove themselves – and have removed themselves – from the jurisdiction of the Council.[181] The primary example of this is the removal of the UK and Ireland from the Council's jurisdiction in matters of visas and other areas related to the Justice and Home Affairs Council.[182] In my view, this step implies that there are some areas of policy that relate to national sovereignty and consequentially are still Member State focused. Although this is attractive from the viewpoint of preserving sovereignty, it is still a decision that is made at the Member State level, and thus another step removed from the citizens that will be affected.

[179] As argued before the GFCC, the views of opposition parties are not receiving any representation in the Council; see *Maastricht Treaty* at para. 106.

[180] Bogdanor, at 6; similar argument was made before the GFCC, *Maastricht Treaty* at para. [109].

[181] Council of the European Union, 'Cooperation in the Fields of Justice and Home Affairs', www.consilium.europa.eu/en/council-eu/configurations/jha/.

[182] Ibid.

From the central courts, other European cases that are important to this debate include the *PFOS* case[183] and the *Pringle* case.[184] In *PFOS*, Sweden, as an EU Member State, was barred from participating actively in an international environmental negotiation because the Council had already started to discuss its international position. According to the ECJ, the EU principle of loyalty mandated that Sweden must refrain from making a submission without support in the Council, given that the EU and all its Member States were already participating in the international instrument. Counterintuitive as this may seem, the decision actually reflects a federalist understanding – the institution at Union level is found to be separate from (and more than) a meeting of individual Member States. In *Pringle*, the CJEU highlighted that Member States were free to conclude international agreements among themselves in Council in areas outside of EU competences. They were even entitled to use EU institutions to facilitate the implementation of such inter-se agreements. In other words, the Court sought to uphold the idea that Member States are free to attribute further functions to the EU institutions if they so decide. The federalizing nature of these decisions by the CJEU is only, in my view, becoming understood over the next couple of years.

However, from the periphery, the GFCC in *OMT*[185] displayed a different understanding of the function of a federated state-level institution. In this case, the Constitutional Court criticized the open-ended nature of Council mandates, requiring increased involvement not just of the government but also of the German Bundestag with regard to financial expenditure issues originating in Council decisions. This was decided by the Court, even though mandates for Council Members should be treated as deriving from the government without further diffusion of responsibility down to individual members in federated parliaments. A similar attempt by the Greek government to have a referendum on the financial bailout was rejected by the Council and subsequently abandoned. While there might be different levels of mandates and legal constraints in the different Member States, this hardly undermines the nature of the Council as an institution. In essence, it appears that while dialogues among Courts are still ongoing, it is far from clear that these

183 Case C-246/07, *European Commission* v. *Kingdom of Sweden (PFOS)* [2010] ECR I-03317.

184 Case C-370/12, *Thomas Pringle* v. *Government of Ireland, Ireland and The Attorney General*, Judgment of the Court (Full Court) of 27 November 2012, not yet reported.

185 GFCC, *OMT*.

elements of European *civitas* are required for a federal constitutional order. For this reason, I believe that the gaps that have been noted by critics simply cannot constitute valid obstacles to further constitutionalization.

3.6.4 *Conclusion as to the Validity of This Obstacle*

The argument that a second chamber of Parliament can function as such only if it is completely free of any Member State mandate is powerfully disproven by the existing constitutional set-ups explored in the comparative examples in this chapter. Many federated representations in federal constitutions either were not originally directly elected or, as in the case of the Canadian Senate, are still appointed today. Others still have representational responsibilities, and some even function on the basis of a direct mandate. The Council has arguably regained some of its lost territory in the Lisbon Treaty, and some have observed that the rise of the Council in the EU underlines a potentially challenging trend towards increased inter-governmentalism. This perception is somewhat in contrast with the increased role of the EU Parliament after the Lisbon Treaty. When the Council exerts greater influence in practice, it still has to convince the Parliament to adopt legislation, taking on a more democratic role than was previously the case. As such, this objection does not need to be considered further.

3.7 The Foundational Documents of the Union Are International Treaties, Not a Constitution?

3.7.1 *Obstacle*

One of the criticisms of the constitutionalization of the EU is often its lack of a written constitution and, instead, its reliance on an international treaty. Concerns have been raised that the 'format' of the *charte constitutionelle* of the EU, that is, the TEU, the TFEU and the Fundamental Rights Charter, is simply the format of international treaties. As Grimm explains, these documents were concluded between the Heads of State of the EU's Member States, and this prevents their interpretation as constitutional documents that are given by the people.[186] The obstacle goes deeper than the mere form, however. It is suggested that an international

[186] Grimm, *Braucht Europa eine Verfassung?*, vol. 60 Siemens Stiftung, 34.

treaty that is, after all, concluded by States cannot serve as a valid constitutional basis due to its inception. From this critical perspective, a constitution must be developed and approved by the people, not just their representatives, and thus, due to the very manner and form of its conclusion, a treaty on this basis lacks the constitutional legitimacy necessary for constitutional development.

3.7.2 *Underlying Concepts of Constitutional Development*

It is important to start with the recognition, as noted originally in Chapter 1, that very few constitutional lawyers take the form of their constitution into account. This is especially true in the United Kingdom; its Constitution consists of many different documents, such as the unilateral declaration by the King in the form of the Magna Carta and the Act of Union between Scotland and England, an international treaty. I believe that a similar system can also exist in a federal system and there are in fact numerous examples of this today. In Canada, for instance, the Constitution consists of a colonial act and treaties between provinces.

Further, as recent comparisons with the early US constitutional experience have pointed out,[187] the Articles of Confederation, as the first US Constitution after independence, can be seen more as a treaty among the thirteen original founding states than as a 'real' constitution.[188] Although the legislative basis for the US Constitution has subsequently been changed, it took the living Constitution of the United States almost a century to develop into its current constitutional form and shape. However bold, the assertion of the Founding Father to be speaking on behalf of 'We, the People' nevertheless required ratification by the States and, in this sense, was not unlike a treaty. What this particular example teaches us is that, regardless of its format or adoption, a constitution has to 'earn' its status as a constitution. Even the best words and the clearest constitutional texts adopted by vast majorities sometimes fall victim to post-revolutionary developments that bring back old autocratic structures and regimes.[189] In a similar fashion, another early federation – the German Federation (Deutscher Bund) of 1832 – also relied on international treaties for its constitutional order. The format of the

[187] Glencross, *What Makes the EU Viable?*, 38.
[188] Ibid.
[189] B. A. Ackerman, *The Future of Liberal Revolution* (New Haven, CT 1992).

constitutional document is thus not important when change over time is taken into the equation.

3.7.3 *Related EU Developments*

Looking closely at the EU's constitutional development in this regard, the Maastricht Treaty – considered to be the foundation of the modern European Union – was silent on issues relating to grievances between Member States.[190] However, in the 1997 Treaty of Amsterdam, this issue was addressed by provisions requiring a combination of the Parliament and the European Council to decide on whether to sanction a Member by suspending, amongst other rights, its voting rights within the European Union structure.[191] These provisions were supplemented in the Treaty of Nice where the procedure was extended to include powers of investigation into a potentially serious breach of EU laws and policies by a Member State, as well as an overall punitive element.[192] This practice most certainly calls into question the democratic legitimacy of the EU structure. By allowing a Member State to suffer what amounts to a severe penalty implemented by the unelected Council, with only minimal involvement by the Parliament, I believe that this system is in direct contrast to the goals of forming a democratic system encompassing the interests of all EU citizens, as stated in the Maastricht Treaty and the additional foundational documents.[193] This system is also in contrast with other systems in which democratic legitimacy has been established. For example, in the United States, a State cannot be suspended from the Union by virtue of its actions.

As mentioned, EU Member States are acutely aware of criticisms related to the EU's democratic deficit. Following the Treaty of Lisbon, several changes were made in the EU's foundational documents, including changes to the EU's decision-making procedures. Most notably, these changes were the adoption of the Co-Decision mechanism meaning that consent from the Parliament is now required for the majority of the EU's decisions,[194] as well as the more 'declarative' Art. 10 TEU.

[190] See generally Treaty of Maastricht on European Union (OJ 1992 C 191 p.1).

[191] See Title I section 9 (amending Title I), Treaty of Amsterdam amending the Treaty on European Union, the Treaties establishing the European Communities and certain related acts (OJ 1997 C 340 p.1); Title VII Article 3(10).

[192] Article 1(1), Treaty of Nice Amending the Treaty on European Union (OJ 2001 C 80 p.1).

[193] See generally Treaty of Maastricht on European Union (OJ 1992 C 191 p.1).

[194] J.-C. Piris, *The Lisbon Treaty: A Legal and Political Analysis* (Cambridge 2010) 118.

Despite bringing about such changes, the Treaty of Lisbon can be seen as aggravating the EU's democratic deficit by extending the EU's supranational powers. For example, the role of EU High Representative of the Union for Foreign Affairs and Security Policy (a post that was originally initiated by the Treaty of Amsterdam) is appointed by the Council (with the President of the Commission's consent) and represents the EU in its external relations.[195] The High Representative's appointment does not require the Parliament's consent, and, furthermore, her/his appointment requires only a qualified majority within the Council. It could therefore pass without the consent of some Member States.[196]

The Court of Justice has shown little interest in the form of the founding treaties and has rightly concluded, in seminal cases such as *Van Duyn* and *Defrenne*, both that citizens can rely directly on the treaties before national and EU courts and that these provisions also apply horizontally between private citizens. I submit that the CJEU therefore recognizes the importance of the treaty and applies it as a Constitutional Court would apply a constitution.[197]

The GFCC, on the other hand, as demonstrated in the *Lisbon* and *ESM Treaty* cases, still considers the EU Treaties as special international treaties requiring special democratic legitimacy that is granted by an informed and consulted German Parliament.[198] This became particularly evident when the Constitutional Court in its ESM interim decision required that Germany request a formal clarification from all other ESM Member states in the form of a diplomatic note (which read like an interpretative declaration but was a veiled reservation[199]). While the special character of pooled sovereignty does not go unnoticed by the Constitutional Court, it firmly adopts a formal assessment of the Treaty and does not regard it as a constitution. It went further in the May 2020 decision in *PSPP* to instruct German governmental institutions not to participate in related ECB actions.

By way of further example, a similar formal position has been adopted by the Czech Constitutional Court, which regards itself as the final arbiter on constitutional matters and sees the EU and the CJEU as institutions

195 Ibid., 229.

196 Ibid.

197 Case 41/74, *Yvonne van Duyn* v. *Home Office* [1974] ECR 01337; Case 149/77, *Gabrielle Defrenne* v. *Société anonyme belge de navigation aérienne Sabena* [1978] ECR 01365.

198 GFCC, *Lisbon Decision*; GFCC, *ESM Treaty*, 2 BvR 1390/12, 2 BvR 1421/12, 2 BvR 1438/12, 2 BvR 1439/12, 2 BvR 1440/12, 2 BvE 6/12, etc. of 12 September 2012.

199 M. Waibel, 'Karlsruhe gives Green Light for ESM Treaty Ratification' (12 September 2012), EJIL:Talk!, www.ejiltalk.org/karlsruhe-gives-green-light-for-german-esm-ratification.

created by and governed by an international treaty (albeit a special one).[200]

In some ways, the failure of the EU Constitutional Treaty (considered by some an oxymoron) can be seen as an important example here. While some argued that the common ratification on the same day in all Member States should have been considered, the fact that ratification was attempted in different Member States at different times contributed to the lack of a pan-European discussion about the document and meant that Euro-sceptical publics could focus on individual Member States' interests rather than on forms of pan-European public interest.

3.7.4 *Conclusion as to the Validity of This Obstacle*

While there are important factors that justify the format of the treaty being considered as an object to constitutionalization, there are equally important factors that support not attaching too much weight to the form of the constitutional principles contained with the documents. Certainly, in the example of the United States, the Articles of Confederation were relatively quickly overcome through the Philadelphia Convention, which led to a Constitutional document that has since become the model for modern constitutionalism. This obstacle – even after a comparison with early US history – requires careful consideration. While the format of a constitutional document does not seem to be important, the fact that one chosen format can raise perceptions of constitutionalization as an elite project, while another suggests broader popular support, should mean that this obstacle is taken seriously. In this way, while not an obstacle to constitutionalization,[201] the form of the constitutional

[200] Czech Constitutional Court, Decision of 31 January 2012, Pl. ÚS 5/12, *Slovak Pensions*.

[201] See, for a strong pro-Constitution claim ('there is no plausible sense in which the Treaties of the European Union are not a constitution properly so called'), M. Kumm, 'Beyond Golf Clubs and the Judicialization of Politics: Why Europe Has a Constitution Properly So Called' (2006) 54 *American Journal of Comparative Law* 505, 506. There's also this claim that the EU does not have 'a constitution in a Kelsenian sense' – A. Somek, 'Postconstitutional Treaty' in R. A. Miller and P. C. Zumbansen (eds.), *Comparative Law as Transnational Law: A Decade of the German Law Journal* (Oxford 2011) 448; see also P. B. Griffin, 'The European Union and Its Issue with Democracy: A Closer Look at the Irish Rejection of the Lisbon Treaty' (2018) https://ssrn.com/abstract=3205274 who argues that the Treaties are just treaties (based on Aristotle's idea of a constitution as the arrangement of state offices and that EU ≠ state – note 43) ('So the Lisbon Treaty is to all intents and purposes the draft Constitution, now correctly identified not as a constitution but as the treaty it always was') p.10 and ('The original draft constitutional document was not a constitution') p.17.

document is related to the lack of a European public sphere where the form of the EU constitution could be debated publicly.

3.8 Key Factors for the *Civitas* Dimension of European Constitutionalization

After employing a comparative federalist approach, this study demonstrated that very few fundamental 'civic' objections to EU constitutionalization remain valid today. Indeed, all of those still valid have an intrinsic connection with the identified lack of a common public sphere in Europe. At several stages of this analysis, I have used illustrations from other federal constitutional experiences. I believe that this demonstrates the ability of a federal polity to subsist and thrive without many of the elements that some critics deem fundamental. America has no real direct national election governed by common rules (only Congress and Senate), no single US Presidential Parties (state-by-state primaries), no common, deliberate space and no direct Presidential elections (electoral college and super-delegates). While we should not forget that the Early Republic in the United States suffered from a very weak form of federalism that eventually ended in Civil War, it nevertheless demonstrates the potential for further constitutionalization in Europe. I also believe, however, that there are also clear lessons to be learnt from the German and Swiss experiences where the organization of elections at the federated State level has not visibly precluded a constitutional polity from developing in either case.

The EU and its Member States are aware that there are 'civic' obstacles to federalism – reflected not only by recent changes to the EU's foundational documents but also in its structure. These changes are reflected in some new decision-making procedures that are aimed at increasing the EU Parliament's power (such as the adoption of the ordinary legislative procedure, for example). However, these changes can also be observed on the declarative level. For example, the Member States have found it necessary to include in the preamble of the Treaty of Lisbon the need for 'enhancing the efficiency and democratic legitimacy of the Union'.[202] Furthermore, following the entering into force of the Treaty of Lisbon, Art. 10 TEU now emphasizes[203] that 'the functioning of the Union shall

[202] Preamble, Treaty of Lisbon amending the Treaty on European Union and the Treaty establishing the European Community (OJ 2007 C 306 p.1).

[203] Article 10, TEU (OJ 2012 C 326 p.1).

be founded on representative democracy . . .. Citizens are directly represented at Union level in the European Parliament . . .. Every citizen shall have the right to participate in the democratic life of the Union. Decisions shall be taken as openly and as closely as possible to the citizen.' In my view, these changes may reflect a concerted effort to overcome existing obstacles. As in the case of most multilateral international institutions, the existence of a certain democratic deficit is inevitable and not specifically an EU problem. Moreover, in my view, as it is an international institution, it is wrong to compare the EU with 'regular' States, and with this it is wrong to expect similar representative democracy from its institutions. The GFCC explicitly recognized this when it stated: 'Even as an association with its own legal personality, the European Union remains the creation of sovereign democratic states. In the present state of integration, it is therefore not required to democratically develop the system of the European institutions in analogy to that of a state.'[204] Democracy is not perfect, nor can it be absolute. And in a federal system, democracies can be shared and tiered and may manifest themselves on many levels simultaneously. Participation and the emergence of a sense of citizenship are important, but these can be achieved through many methods and continue to be hampered by the lack of a common public sphere in the EU. Courts throughout Europe must grasp that there is not one single route to a well-functioning federal entity.

All is not lost, however. Because of the highly integrative nature of the EU, such as that in present times, this international institution cannot be realistically compared with any other. The path of constitutionalization in Europe must evolve to respond to concerns surrounding democratic legitimacy, and I believe that the critics and the European Courts alike must remember that this endeavour will remain a unique and European one.

As this chapter demonstrates, the majority of 'civic' obstacles examined here are based on the fundamental conflict that while the EU is becoming closer in shape and character to a state entity, it continues to act as a supranational institution. Decisions by the European Courts display an impoverished understanding of the federal nature of the Union in this regard. Likewise, neither the GFCC nor any of its sister Member State courts has been able to answer this problem and display an equally impoverished understanding of the federal nature of the Union. Critically, dismissing these concerns, the national courts of individual

[204] GFCC, *Lisbon Decision* at para. [278].

Member States are also ignoring deep-rooted 'Euro-scepticism' – a state of mind that many of the EU's citizens share and that, thus, directly affects the EU's own legitimacy.

As I have illustrated, EU constitutionalization is a process. Even measured against the demanding yardstick of the US 'role model', the development of the EU as a constitutional polity has been remarkable in recent years and should not be underestimated. In many important ways, the institutional structure of the EU today is not dissimilar from other federal structures at equal points in their formative history. Yet, there are also still significant limitations to the advancements that have been made, including in the various areas related to the development of a common European public sphere, especially concerning European elections and cross-European political parties. I will examine these aspects more closely in Chapter 5, proposing recommendations to address the major obstacle and its corollary *demos* and *civitas* challenges.

4

Ius Obstacles to European Constitutionalization

4.1 Introduction

The absence of a single legal system, according to critics, is one of the three most important dimensions in which further European constitutionalization finds itself stymied.[1] For critics, a constitutional polity must be founded with one common legal system.[2] From this view, if the European Union has no common understanding of the rule of law,[3] it is doomed. Concerns include (1) an unclear role for a Federal Court and its appellate powers, (2) a lack of uniform trans-European procedures for selection of justices, (3) a lack of clear rules for constitutional review, (4) indeterminate jurisdiction vis-à-vis the (Member) States[4] and (5) the unresolved matter of ultimate legal authority itself (*Kompetenz-Kompetenz*).[5] Not only scholars raise these concerns but also the

[1] See the GFCC repeatedly in *Solange I*, BVerf 37 of 29 May 1974, *Solange II*, BVerfGE 73 of 22 October 1986, *Maastricht*, BVerfGE 89, 155 and *Lisbon Decision*.

[2] With an emphasis on fundamental rights (similar to *Solange I*), see Grimm, *Braucht Europa eine Verfassung?*, vol. 60 Siemens Stiftung.

[3] The alleged lack of a common rule of law definition has also been used in states characterized by rule of law backsliding to justify such tactics: K. Miklóssy, 'Lacking Rule of Law in the Lawyers' Regime: Hungary' (2018) 26 *Journal of Contemporary European Studies* 270, 276.

[4] For a very long time it was usual for constitutional courts to engage with the Court of Justice of the EU through the preliminary reference procedure, but after the Italian Constitutional Court referred to the CJEU most recently, it is now mainly the GFCC that does not engage in a direct dialogue with the European Court. However, of late the GFCC is considering a reference to the European Court for the very first time with regard to the main proceedings concerning the constitutional challenge for the ESM; see decision of the GFCC of 12 September 2012 in 2 BvR 1390/12, 2 BvR 1421/12, 2 BvR 1438/12, 2 BvR 1439/12, 2 BvR 1440/12, 2 BvE 6/12.

[5] On the notion of Kompetenz-kompetenz in EU law, see J. Lindeboom, 'Why EU Law Claims Supremacy' (2018) 38 *Oxford Journal of Legal Studies* 328, 344–5. See e.g. a criticism of the Court's claim to Kompetenz-kompetenz in G. Davies, 'Interpretative Pluralism within EU Law' in G. Davies and M. Avbelj (eds.), *Research Handbook on Legal Pluralism and EU Law* (Cheltenham/Northampton, MA 2018), 323. The GFCC in its *Lisbon Decision* highlighted its own competence to review the transfer of competence to

Courts of Europe. There is a lack of willingness, at least on behalf of some Member State judicial bodies, to relinquish control over jurisdictional decisions – at least not until requested to do so by a self-determined 'European People'.[6] Related obstacles include the concern that (6) Europe cannot rely on one unitary body of criminal law, (7) nor can Europe call on a single police force with powers of enforcement.[7] A further concern along this vein is that (8) the EU lacks a seamless and reliable system of human rights protection.[8]

This chapter examines each of the *ius* obstacles to EU constitutionalization in turn, seeking to explore which (if any) of these concerns are fundamentally incompatible with the movement towards a federal union, in the light of analysis. As in earlier chapters, careful attention is given to the related jurisprudence of centre and periphery Member State courts, and illustrative examples are drawn from other early federal polities, with a view to better understanding options that may lie ahead for the EU. The

the EU while the Court of Justice has repeatedly exercised its own exclusive competence to interpret the EU Treaties, including the competence provisions. See also at para. [193] ('The Basic Law not only prohibits the transfer of competence to decide on its own competence (*Kompetenz-Kompetenz*) to the European Union or to institutions created in connection with the European Union (see BVerfGE 89, 155 <187–188, 192, 199>; see also BVerfGE 58, 1 <37>; 104, 151 <210>; 123, 267 <349>). Blanket empowerments for the exercise of public authority may also not be granted by the German constitutional bodies (see BVerfGE 58, 1 <37>; 89, 155 <183–184, 187>; 123, 267 <351>). It is therefore constitutionally required not to agree dynamic treaty provisions with a blanket character, or if they can still be interpreted in a manner that respects the responsibility for integration, to establish, at any rate, suitable safeguards for the effective exercise of such responsibility. Accordingly, the Act of assent and the national accompanying laws must therefore be capable of permitting European integration continuing to take place according to the principle of conferral without the possibility for the European Union, or for institutions created in connection with the European Union, of taking possession of *Kompetenz-Kompetenz* or of otherwise violating the Basic Law's constitutional identity, which is not open to integration. For borderline cases of what is still constitutionally admissible, the German legislature must, where necessary, make effective arrangements in its legislation accompanying the Act of assent to ensure that the responsibility for integration of the legislative bodies can sufficiently develop (BVerfGE 123, 267 <353>)'); on this, see G. Beck, 'Judicial Activism in the Court of Justice of the EU' (2017) 36 *University of Queensland Law Journal* 333, 336; and R. D. Kelemen, 'The Dangers of Constitutional Pluralism' in G. Davies and M. Avbelj (eds.), *Research Handbook on Legal Pluralism and EU Law* (Cheltenham/Northampton, MA 2018) 392.

[6] GFCC, *Lisbon Decision*, at para. [233].

[7] Grimm, *Braucht Europa eine Verfassung?*, vol. 60 Siemens Stiftung.

[8] Ref to Czech Constitutional Court ruling that the right to a fair trial was not guaranteed in the Court of Justice, rendering its decision in Case C-399/09, *Marie Landtová* v. *Česká správa socialního zabezpečení* [2011] ECR I-05573 *ultra vires*. The early *Solange* jurisprudence by the GFCC was based on this criticism.

chapter refers especially to the early experiences of the United States and other constitutional polities where it is clear that the lack of 'a single law' was in fact a defining feature of federal construction, yet this neither prevented nor arguably even hindered constitutionalization. It assesses the validity of each objection, commenting on whether it can be considered valid today, taking into account recent developments in EU constitutionalization. Further discussion of the most valid obstacles, particularly those linked to the absence of a European public sphere and its corollary challenges, is then provided in Chapter 5.

In this chapter, it is argued that in many federal systems, rule of law principles have developed over time, rather than appearing *ab initio* as part of a 'ready-made' constitutional order, and that key gaps that raise strident objections to further European constitutionalization are actually in no way fatal. Instead, it is suggested that many obstacles can be seen as initial steps in the evolution of the European constitutional order. Further, it shows that many aspects of the European *ius* are highly context-specific, developing differently in the EU with distinct potentialities. Taking various illustrative examples into account, several Court decisions will be highlighted, displaying an impoverished understanding of federalism in the current jurisprudence related to *ius*. However, through a judicial dialogue between centre and periphery courts of Europe, we are also advancing the *ius* dimension of constitutionalization.

4.2 No Single Rule of Law?

4.2.1 Obstacles

Critics argue that the EU is unable to develop beyond its current constitutional order simply because it is 'based on' Member State law rather than a single, independent legal system; a concern raised by different constitutional courts of the EU Member States.[9] From this view, a federal entity cannot derive its legal system entirely from its federated entities – a genuine source of law is required for its existence and further development. In essence, the EU's lack of a single, unified rule of law presents an obstacle that is insurmountable for further constitutionalization.[10]

[9] Czech Constitutional Court, *Landtová*.

[10] See A. Wiener and V. della Sala, 'Constitution-Making and Citizenship Practice: Bridging the Democracy Gap in the EU?' (1997) 35 *Journal of Common Market Strategies* 595; A. Moravcsik, 'What Can We Learn from the Collapse of the European Constitutional Project?' (2006) 47 *Politische Vierteljahresschrift* 219.

4.2.2 *Underlying Concepts of Constitutional Development*

It is a fundamental aspect of most federal polities that different levels of governance exist within the polity itself. In federal systems, such as Germany, Switzerland or Canada, where the federated levels of government enjoy state sovereignty and/or have default forms of competence, multi-level governance is common and expected.[11] Such developments have been tracked and compared across several federal systems, and multi-level responsibility for law and governance is very much the norm.[12]

Whether a single, consistent approach to rule of law issues must be established can be illustrated with examples of other constitutional experience. For instance, while US law was considered to exist as *law*, and was not subject to questions about its validity in the way that international law continues to be questioned to this day,[13] the United States was initially not very clear about how the two spheres of state law and federal law would co-exist. At first, it was argued that only the states are sovereign – the federation's authority was derived solely through the state. Only later did the United States and, in particular, 'We, the People' come to be viewed as a sovereign power and an important level of authority.[14] In my view, these potentially divisive debates can eventually be resolved through recognition of dual sovereignty.[15] The US Early Republic provides an illustration of a case in which development of the rule of law was greatly aided by an explicit Supremacy Clause in the American Constitution.[16] The way that US federal supremacy was

[11] G. Bermann, 'The Role of Law in the Functioning of Federal Systems' in Nicolaidis and Howse; Glencross, *What Makes the EU Viable?*, ch. 5; L. F. Goldstein, *Constituting Federal Sovereignty*; Nolte, part V, 195; Fossum and Menéndez, ch. 6, 177.

[12] See Fossum and Menéndez.

[13] H. L. A. Hart, *The Concept of Law*, 3rd ed. (Oxford 2010) 210.

[14] There is no explicit reference in the US Constitution to the sovereignty of the Federation, although there is a mention of the powers that were granted explicitly to the federal government and an explanation that the remainder of legal powers were to be devolved to the states.

[15] Schütze, *From Dual to Cooperative Federalism*, 77; D. Halberstam, '"A People for Certain Purposes": On the History and Philosophy of Federalism(S) in the United States And Europe' (2018) University of Michigan Public Law Research Paper No. 619, 25, https://ssrn.com/abstract=3241597. Some argue that 'dual sovereignty is already operative' in the Union, e.g. M. Fichera, *The Foundations of the EU as a Polity* (Cheltenham/Northampton, MA 2018), preface.

[16] V. C. Jackson, 'US Constitutional Law and History' in R. Masterman and R. Schütze (eds.), *The Cambridge Companion to Comparative Constitutional Law* (Cambridge 2019) 122.

shaped by intellectual and open legal and policy debates in the public sphere is particularly instructive for the EU's development. As Alexander Hamilton has argued, '. . . the laws of the Union are to be the supreme law of the land. But what inference can be drawn from this, or what would they amount to, if they were not to be supreme? It is evident they would amount to nothing. A LAW, by the very meaning of the term, includes supremacy.'[17] Indeed, in defence of Supremacy in the US Constitution, James Madison wrote that without it,

> . . . as the constitutions of the States differ much from each other, it might happen that a treaty or national law, of great and equal importance to the States, would interfere with some and not with other constitutions, and would consequently be valid in some of the States at the same time that it would have no effect in others. In fine, the world would have seen, for the first time, a system of government founded on an inversion of the fundamental principles of all government; it would have seen the authority of the whole society everywhere subordinate to the authority of the parts; it would have seen a monster, in which the head was under the direction of the members.[18]

The United States has not necessarily resolved this debate even today and US legal systems have, across the centuries, continued a dialogue on the interrelationships between state law and federal law.[19] The United States recognized the supremacy of federal law early in its existence by way of an explicit Supremacy Clause. In this instance, I find the US experience instructive. The explicit Supremacy Clause did not just have a semantic function; it gave real power to the US Supreme Court to overturn state laws.[20] This power became one of the most controversial aspects of the new US Constitution, featuring prominently in the Anti-Federalist Papers that sought to underline state constitutions and powers.[21]

What is most pertinent about the US example, in my view, is the way that a 'single' rule of law emerged gradually and continues to evolve into

[17] A. Hamilton, 'The Federalist No. 33' in *The Federalist Papers* (1787–1788).

[18] J. Madison, 'The Federalist No. 44' in *The Federalist Papers* (1787–1788).

[19] More recently on the US Supremacy Clause, see US Supreme Court, *James* v. *City of Boise*. R. H. Seamon, 'Supreme Court Supremacy in a Time of Turmoil: James v. City of Boise' (2017) 50 *Loyola of Los Angeles Law Review* 175.

[20] US Supreme Court, *Ware* v. *Hylton*, 3 US (3 Dall) 199 (1796); US Supreme Court, *McCulloch* v. *Maryland*, 17 US (4 Wheat) 316 (1819); US Supreme Court, *Martin* v. *Hunter's Lessee*, 14 US 304 (1816); US Supreme Court, *Cohens* v. *Virginia*, 19 US 264 (1821); or the unfortunate decision in US Supreme Court, *Ableman* v. *Booth*, 62 US 506 (1859).

[21] See generally *Anti-Federalist Papers* (1787) as edited by R. Ketcham, *The Anti-Federalist Papers and the Constitutional Convention Debates* (New York 2003).

being over time. Whereas, on the one hand, early dissent centred on whether, in the English tradition, with its strong notion of sovereignty of Parliament, there was really no specific necessity for a rule of law, on the other hand, a more Augustinian approach argues that unjust laws could never enjoy legal force.[22] For the United States, the question was settled by the Supreme Court in *Marbury* v. *Madison*,[23] where it was determined that constitutional review by the judiciary against the will of a legislature was possible.[24]

Not unlike in the EU today, it was recognized by the US Supreme Court in *Martin* v. *Hunter's Lessee* that: 'States have always jealously guarded their rights. The Tenth Amendment (1791) gave them the right to govern all aspects within their state not specifically given to the federal government under the Constitution.'[25] In this case, the State of Virginia, via its highest court, proclaimed that state governments and the federal government were equal and therefore the Supreme Court had no jurisdiction over the highest court of a state.[26] However, the US Supreme Court found that every state had lost part of its sovereignty when it accepted the Constitution and therefore all states were subject to the rulings of the Supreme Court.[27] Further, in *McCulloch* v. *Maryland*, to avoid a tax, it was argued that the 'federal status of the bank meant that it must be allowed to carry out the duties required of it' with the US Supreme Court declaring the tax unconstitutional, and establishing the Supreme Court's right to review state governmental acts.[28] As noted by legal scholars of the period, '[s]ince the era of Marshall, the principle of judicial review within America has largely gone unquestioned'.[29] Concerns were only resolved – to a certain extent – by the Civil War and Reconstruction.[30]

22 Ibid.

23 US Supreme Court, *Marbury* v. *Madison*, 5 US (1 Cranch) 137 (1803).

24 For the history, see C. F. Hobson, *The Great Chief Justice: John Marshall and the Rule of Law* (Lawrence, KS 1996).

25 US Supreme Court, *Martin* v. *Hunter's Lessee*, 14 US 304 (1816).

26 Ibid.

27 Ibid.

28 US Supreme Court, *McCulloch* v. *Maryland*, 17 US (4 Wheat) 316 (1819). On the influential nature of this decision, see D. S. Schwartz, *The Spirit of the Constitution: John Marshall and the 200-Year Odyssey of McCulloch v. Maryland* (Oxford 2019).

29 Wood, *Empire of Liberty*.

30 Ibid. See also L. H. Rosenthal and G. P. Joseph, 'Foundations of U.S. Federalism' (2017) 101 *Judicature* 39, 43–5.

There are other examples that can aid our understanding of federal legal systems. For instance, in Germany, sovereignty is also vested in the federated level. Article 70 of the Grundgesetz determines: 'The Länder shall have the right to legislate insofar as this Basic Law does not confer legislative power on the Federation.' The Constitutional Court has interpreted this provision as giving reserve powers to the state level, that is, Länder, while constitutional jurisprudence has guarded against federal encroachment of their competences. For example, it determined in a case concerning university education that Art. 70 GG requires that a 'separate area of policy making of substantial weight' is reserved for the Länder level.[31]

The Canadian experience offers similar illustrations. Interestingly, although the provinces of Canada have many specific, limited powers, the Privy Council and the Canadian Supreme Court have been keen to emphasize their competences, perhaps even more generously than in Australia.[32] The most significant developments have occurred through the interpretations of courts under the common law, in particular, the *ILO Labour Conventions Case*[33] in which the Privy Council established that a certain level of respect for the jurisdiction of the provincial governments and their right to be consulted is required – even in international affairs, when negotiations concern their constitutional competences.[34] Prior to this case, it was possible for the Canadian government, by negotiating an international treaty on a particular issue of provincial competence, including rule of law and human rights, such as labour rights, to argue that it had gained an important role in ensuring treaty compliance, taking jurisdiction over this competence. After this case, it became evident that, beyond the authorities and competences of the federal government of Canada, the Canadian provinces each hold important sovereignty and the ability to govern in relation to rule of law and human rights concerns, even as this extends to international affairs.[35]

[31] GFCC, *Hochschulrahmengesetz* 2 BvF 2/02 of 27 July 2004, www.bverfg.de/entscheidungen/fs20040727_2bvf000202.html [author's own translation].

[32] Hogg, 23.

[33] Canada, Privy Council, *The Attorney General of Canada* v. *The Attorney General of Ontario and Others* [1937] UKPC 6. A. Blackett, '"This Is Hallowed Ground": Canada and International Labour Law' (2018) CIGI Papers No. 22, www.cigionline.org/sites/default/files/documents/Reflections%20Series%20Paper%20no.22%20Blackett.pdf, 5–10.

[34] Hogg, 64.

[35] S. Pacquin, 'Multilevel Governance and International Trade Negotiations: The Case of Canada's Trade Agreements' in G. Lachapelle and P. Oñate (eds.), *Borders and Margins: Federalism, Devolution and Multi-Level Governance* (Opladen/Berlin/Toronto 2018) 153.

These examples provide clear evidence that in a federal polity, the rule of law develops over time and at different levels of governance.[36] What we see in each of these examples is that, traditionally, the courts will balance competing levels of legislative jurisdiction to interpret the text of the federal constitution. For Europe, this is particularly relevant because the European Union relies on the Member States for implementation of its rules and thus the competing levels of legislative jurisdiction continue to exist and be reinforced,[37] exacerbated by the lack of a common European space for legal or political debates to take place.

4.2.3 *Related EU Developments*

Supremacy has been firmly enshrined at the heart of the EU legal order since the seminal judgment of *Costa* v. *ENEL.*[38] In this case, we hear a certain resonance of the language used by Hamilton in justifying the existence of the Supremacy clause.[39] In this decision, the Court found:

> [I]t follows from all these observations that the law stemming from the treaty, an independent source of law, could not, because of its special and original nature, be overridden by domestic legal provisions, however framed, without being deprived of its character as community law and without the legal basis of the community itself being called into question.[40]

Madison's argument justifying the existence of the Supremacy clause is echoed in *Costa* v. *ENEL*, when the Court states that 'the executive force of community law cannot vary from one State to another in deference to

[36] On the rule of law as an evolving concept in the EU, see A. Magen and L. Pech, 'The Rule of Law and the European Union' in C. May and A. Winchester (eds.), *Handbook on the Rule of Law* (Cheltenham/Northampton, MA 2018), 235.

[37] J. Maśnicki, 'From Integration to Fragmentation? The Late and Incorrect Transposition of the EU Directives' in R. Grzeszczak (ed.), *Renationalisation of the Integration Process in the Internal Market of the European Union* (Baden-Baden 2018); V. Perju, 'On the (De-) Fragmentation of Statehood in Europe: Reflections on Ernst-Wolfgang Böckenförde's Work on European Integration' (2018) 19 *German Law Journal* 403, 414.

[38] S. M. Carbone, 'The Principle of the Primacy of EU Law over the National Legal Systems of Member States' in G. Amato, E. Moavero-Milanesi, G. Pasquino and L. Reichlin (eds.), *The History of the European Union: Constructing Utopia* (Oxford 2018) 187; Lindeboom, 328.

[39] Hamilton, 'The Federalist No. 33': 'But what inference can be drawn from this, or what would they amount to, if they were not to be supreme? It is evident they would amount to nothing. A law, by the very meaning of the term, includes supremacy. It is a rule which those to whom it is prescribed are bound to observe.'

[40] Ibid.

subsequent domestic laws, without jeopardizing the attainment of the objectives of the treaty . . .'.[41]

The EU Constitutional Treaty proposed the following formulation of the Supremacy principle in Art. I-6 [Union law]: 'The Constitution and law adopted by the institutions of the Union in exercising competences conferred on it shall have primacy over the law of the Member States.' Interestingly, this formulation was not included in the Reform Treaty project because it was considered too politically complex to explain to the general population in a climate where both French and Dutch nationalistic referenda actors had engaged strong arguments against extending the reach of EU law. At the time, the explicit Supremacy clause was seen as controversial for many reasons, including that different Constitutional Courts in the Member States either had not accepted EU law supremacy or had considered EU law supremacy only with restrictions. Given these differences, it was felt that no single formulation was able to capture the essence of supremacy.[42]

Actually, the drafters of the Lisbon Treaty did seem willing to explain the different forms of competence in the Union, including exclusive competence, in Art. 2 TFEU. This article determines: 'When the Treaties confer on the Union exclusive competence in a specific area, only the Union may legislate and adopt legally binding acts, the Member States being able to do so themselves only if so empowered by the Union or for the implementation of Union acts.' The provision is in essence very close to an explicit supremacy clause. Nonetheless, the constitutional position remains unaffected, and supremacy of the EU from an EU law perspective remains deeply enshrined within its own institutional order.[43] In fact, in a commentary on seminal European cases such as *Costa* v. *ENEL*, Justice Breyer of the US Supreme Court noted that the European Court had demonstrated its role as interpreter of the 'constitutional' text of the EU Treaties, finding that the CJEU 'seemed far more familiar than foreign'.[44]

[41] Case 6/64, *Flaminio Costa* v. *E.N.E.L.* [1964] ECR 00585. See also M. G. Puder, 'Supremacy of the Law and Judicial Review in the European Union: Celebrating Marbury v. Madison with Costa v. Enel' (2005) 36 *George Washington International Law Review* 567.

[42] Interview with UK Advocate General, 7 November 2014 in Cambridge; M. Claes, 'The Primacy of EU Law in European and National Law' in A. Arnull and D. Chalmers (eds.), *The Oxford Handbook of European Union Law* (Oxford 2015) 178, 200.

[43] R. Schütze, *European Constitutional Law* (Cambridge 2012) ch. 10.

[44] S. Breyer, 'Changing Relationships among European Constitutional Courts' (1999–2000) 21 *Cardozo Law Review* 1045, 1051.

The question of the supremacy of EU law over constitutional law was, on the view of the CJEU, settled by the case of *Simmenthal*.[45] Here, the Court decided that it did not matter which part of Member State law was in conflict with an aspect of EU law – be it an administrative decision, a local ordinance, a regional law or in fact a national constitution, the fact remained that the Member State was deviating from the autonomous legal order.[46] There was considerable debate in academic scholarship on whether the ruling in *Simmenthal* would also be valid in circumstances of conflict between secondary EU law and a constitutional provision. However, in my view, the CJEU's decision on this was a relatively easy one, and in the case of *Tanja Kreil*, the Court found the non-discrimination Directive to trump the German constitutional prohibition that women could not serve in the armed forces with weapons.[47] The German constitutional legislator was forced to rectify this situation by amending the German Constitution itself. Without the level of supremacy demonstrated in this case, of course, EU law would have ceased to function, and rule of law would have simply become impossible in the Union. But this alternative outcome, supported by a broader public debate on Europe's vision of equality and the dialogues between the GFCC and the CJEU itself, demonstrates the possible benefits of a dialogue between centre and periphery courts of Europe on the nature and effects of federalism for citizens themselves.

Despite the necessity for supremacy, there remains a space for constitutional pluralism that should not be ignored.[48] While supremacy is fundamentally indispensable to maintaining EU law as an 'autonomous legal order', some of the more radical consequences that flow from this are arguably difficult to explain. Were a more explicit federal approach adopted by the CJEU, the CJEU in turn could position itself to be more respectful of Member State laws and more able to combine the principles of conferral and

[45] Case 106/77, *Amministrazione delle Finanze dello Stato* v. *Simmenthal SpA*. [1978] ECR 00629. For early comments, see e.g. L. Condorelli, 'Il caso Simmenthal e il primato del diritto comunitario: due corti a confronto' (1978) I *Giurisprudenza costituzionale* 669; D. Carreau, 'Droit communautaire et droits nationaux: concurrence ou primauté? La contribution de l'arrêt Simmenthal' (1978) *Revue trimestrielle de droit européen* 381; P. W. Schroth, 'Marbury and Simmenthal: Reflections on the Adoption of Decentralized Judicial Review by the Court of Justice of the European Community' (1978–1979) 12 *Loyola of Los Angeles Law Review* 869. For a more recent work, see D. Piqani, 'The Simmenthal Revolution Revisited: What Role for Constitutional Courts?' in B. de Witte and others (eds.) *National Courts and EU Law: New Issues, Theories and Methods* (Cheltenham/Northampton, MA 2016) 26.

[46] Piqani, 26.

[47] Case C-285/98, *Tanja Kreil* v. *Bundesrepublik Deutschland* [2000] I-00069.

[48] Craig and de Búrca, *EU Law*, 297.

supremacy. By adopting such an approach, the CJEU could live up to the Member State priority of cooperation rather than domination.[49]

More recently, the Court has expanded on its rule of law jurisprudence. The Courts of the Member States are important for the European Union because when they apply EU law they effectively act as EU courts. The crisis arose when the conservative government of Poland decided to reform its judiciary and dismiss many of the longest serving (and arguably politically not sympathetic) judges. The Court has an extensive case law on enforcement of EU law by Member State courts, ensuring that the effectiveness of EU law and the non-discrimination of EU law claimants are not undermined while ensuring national procedural autonomy.[50] While the organizational autonomy for the justice sector was guaranteed and no new remedies were required,[51] there had been cases where the CJEU had criticized a Member State, making it more difficult for litigants to enforce their rights by, for example, assigning all subsidies cases to just one local court.[52] For the Polish situation, the CJEU relied extensively on the decision in *Portuguese Judges*.[53] The Court ruled:

> The guarantee of independence, which is inherent in the task of adjudication (see, C-506/04, *Wilson*, EU:C:2006:587, paragraph 49; C-685/15, *Online Games and Others*, EU:C:2017:452, paragraph 60; C-403/16, *El Hassani*, EU:C:2017:960, paragraph 40), is required not only at EU level as regards the Judges of the Union and the Advocates-General of the Court of Justice, as provided for in the third subparagraph of Article 19(2) TEU, but also at the level of the Member States as regards national court . . .. The second subparagraph of Article 19(1) TEU must be interpreted as meaning that the principle of judicial independence does not preclude general salary-reduction measures, such as those at issue in the main proceedings, linked to requirements to eliminate an excessive budget deficit and to an EU financial assistance programme, from being applied to the members of the Tribunal de Contas (Court of Auditors, Portugal).[54]

In other words, the Court in this case signaled that there could be situations in which the judicial independence and thus the rule of

[49] P. Kirchhof, 'The Balance of Powers between National and European Institutions' (1999) 5 *European Law Journal* 225.

[50] Case 33/76 *Rewe Zentralfinanz* v. *Lanwirtschaftskammer für das Saarland* (inspections) [1976] ECR 1989. See also Case 106/77 *Simmenthal* [1978] ECR 629; Case 14/83 *Von Colson* [1984] ECR 1891; or the case law concerning the repayment of charges levied in breach of EU law (Case 199/82 *San Giorgio* [1983] ECR 3595).

[51] Case C-437/13 *Unitrading Ltd* v. *Staatssecretaris van Financiën*, Judgment of 23 October 2014.

[52] Case C-93/12, *ET Agrokonsulting-04-Velko Stoyanov*, Judgment of 27 June 2013.

[53] Case C-64/16 *Associação Sindical dos Juízes Portugueses* (GS) ECLI:EU:C:2018:117.

[54] Ibid., para 42.

law would be undermined by the structure adopted by the Member States.

In *Commission* v. *Poland (Independence of the Supreme Court)*, the Grand Chamber of the CJEU went one step further.[55] The Court ruled that Poland violated EU law by trying to remove the judges from its Supreme Court. It said:

> As is apparent from Article 49 TEU, which provides the possibility for any European State to apply to become a member of the European Union, the European Union is composed of States which have freely and voluntarily committed themselves to the common values referred to in Article 2 TEU, which respect those values and which undertake to promote them, EU law being based on the fundamental premiss that each Member State shares with all the other Member States, and recognises that those Member States share with it, those same values (see, to that effect, judgment of 10 December 2018, *Wightman and Others*, C-621/18, EU:C:2018:999, paragraph 63 and the case-law cited). That premiss both entails and justifies the existence of mutual trust between the Member States and, in particular, their courts that those values upon which the European Union is founded, including the rule of law, will be recognised, and therefore that the EU law that implements those values will be respected (see, to that effect, judgments of 27 February 2018, *Associação Sindical dos Juízes Portugueses*, C-64/16, EU:C:2018:117, paragraph 30, and of 25 July 2018, *Minister for Justice and Equality (Deficiencies in the system of justice)*, C-216/18 PPU, EU:C:2018:586, paragraph 35).[56]

In other words, the centre court will go to great lengths to ensure that the rule of law in the Member States is not undermined by Member State actions. The Court in this case further explained:

> Furthermore, although, as the Republic of Poland and Hungary point out, the organisation of justice in the Member States falls within the competence of those Member States, the fact remains that, when exercising that competence, the Member States are required to comply with their obligations deriving from EU law (see, by analogy, judgments of 13 November 2018, *Raugevicius*, C-247/17, EU:C:2018:898, paragraph 45, and of 26 February 2019, *Rimšēvičs and ECB* v. *Latvia*, C-202/18 and C-238/18, EU:C:2019:139, paragraph 57) and, in particular, from the second subparagraph of Article 19(1) TEU (see, to that effect, judgment of 27 February 2018, *Associação Sindical dos Juízes Portugueses*, C-64/16, EU:C:2018:117, paragraph 40). Moreover, by requiring the Member States thus to comply with those obligations, the European Union is not in any way

[55] Cass C-619/18, *Commission* v. *Poland* (Indépendance de la Cour suprême) (GS), ECLI: EU:C:2019:531.

[56] Ibid., para. 43.

> claiming to exercise that competence itself nor is it, therefore, contrary to what is alleged by the Republic of Poland, arrogating that competence.[57]

In other words, even though the Polish law was struck down by the Court of Justice, it underlined that, while there are substantive obligations on ensuring the rule of law, the competence of Member States to organize their judiciary is not abrogated, that is, the Court ensures a common rule of law but does not dictate the concrete decisions to be taken by the Member States.

Further, one of the more obvious acts of defiance from the periphery was launched by the Czech Constitutional Court against the decision of the CJEU in *Landtová*, a case involving pension payments.[58] After the CJEU found that the Czech Republic was under an EU obligation to consider the disputed pension payments, in effect asking the referring court to set aside important decisions of the Czech Constitutional Court, the Czech Court made a dramatic decision to declare the CJEU's decision *ultra vires*. For the Constitutional Court, it was difficult to accept that not only was EU law applicable and supreme, but that, added to this, its own decisions could be found to violate this supreme EU law. The Czech Court ruled:

> Not to distinguish legal arrangements following from the dissolution of a State with a single social security system from the arrangements concerning the consequences for social security systems of the free movement of persons in the European Communities, or the European Union, amounts to the failure to respect the European history, it means to compare the incomparable. For this reason, it is not possible to apply European law, ie. the Regulation, to the Czech citizens' claims stemming from social security. Following the principle explicitly stated in its judgment [of 26. 11. 2008, Pl. ÚS 19/08, Lisbon Treaty I], it is not possible to do otherwise than to find in relation to the consequences of the [CJEU's judgment in the Landtová Case] for similar cases that in its [the CJEU's] case the situation where an act of an institution of the EU exceeded the competences transferred to the EU by virtue of Article 10a of the Czech Constitution occurred, that an act ultra vires was occurred.[59]

57 Ibid., para. 52.

58 Czech Constitutional Court, Decision of 31 January 2012, Pl. ÚS 5/12, *Slovak Pensions*. See, further, K. Kovács, 'Ethnocultural Identity in East Central European Courts' (2017) 18 *German Law Journal* 1703, 1711; Z. Kühn, 'Ultra Vires Review and the Demise of Constitutional Pluralism: The Czecho-Slovak Pension Saga, and the Dangers of State Courts' Defiance of EU Law' (2016) 23 *Maastricht Journal of European and Comparative Law* 185; J. Přibáň, 'Constitutional Sovereignty in Post-Sovereign Jurisprudence of the Czech Constitutional Court: From the Lisbon Judgments to the Landtová Ultra Vires Controversy' in M. Bobek (ed.), *Central European Judges under the European Influence: The Transformative Power of the EU Revisited* (Oxford 2015) 323.

59 See also Komárek, 323.

A more recent case in Denmark came to a similar conclusion arguing that the EU had acted *ultra vires* in *Ajos.*[60] As illustrated in this chapter, even in important cases, the rule of law would be undermined if federated entities could each individually determine the interpretation or application of federal law. However, this decision did not take the nature of the EU as a federal polity into account. It is important because it reveals that on the issue of supremacy, a public debate continues to rage in the European Union. Not all courts agree with the absolute standard set out by the CJEU.

In general, the experience of other European periphery courts demonstrates that a much closer and more amenable dialogue with the CJEU is possible. Taking the example of the Constitutional Courts of Italy and Spain, resistance has slowly given way to active use of the preliminary reference jurisdiction of the Court of Justice. A trend began with the French Conseil d'Etat, when it referred the very difficult issue of the scope of the European Carbon Emission Trading Scheme to the ECJ in *Arcelor*. Both the Court and the Advocate General acknowledged the historic occasion of having the highest French public law court refer a case before resorting to a straightforward answer of the European Emission Trading System (ETS) question at hand.[61] More recently, the Court found that France had violated EU law because its Conseil d'Etat had not asked a preliminary reference question.[62] Meanwhile, the Spanish Constitutional Court requested its very first preliminary reference in *Melloni*, a case concerning the European Arrest Warrant and the interplay of national and EU fundamental rights. Again, the Advocate General acknowledged this ground-breaking occasion while

[60] *Ajos* in respect to a Member State court declaring EU is acting ultra vires: ECJ ruling: Case C-441/14, *Dansk Industri* v. *Rasmussen* [2016] ECLI:EU:C:2016:27 and Danish response: Case no. 15/2014 *Dansk Industri (DI) acting for Ajos A/S* v. *The estate left by A.* See Madsen, Olsen and Šadl, and Holdgaard, Elkan and Schaldemose,.

[61] Case C-127/07, *Société Arcelor Atlantique et Lorraine and Others* v. *Premier ministre, Ministre de l'Écologie et du Développement durable and Ministre de l'Économie, des Finances et de l'Industrie* [2008] ECR I–09895. See, further, O. Pollicino, 'The Conseil d'Etat and the Relationship between French Internal Law after Arcelor: Has Something Really Changed?' (2008) 45 *Common Market Law Review* 1519.

[62] See Case C-416/17 *Commission* v. *France* [2018] EU:C:2018:811; A. Turmo, 'A Dialogue of Unequals: The European Court of Justice Reasserts National Courts' Obligations under Article 267(3) TFEU: ECJ 4 October 2018, Case C-416/17, Commission v France' (2019) 15 *European Constitutional Law Review* 340. The most recent GFCC case in *Public Sector Purchase Programme (PSPP)* comes to a similar conclusion but by finding a CJEU decision to be *ultra vires*. This seems to indicate a new quality of dissent and conversation and has even in its initial reception generated great controversy, see M. Maduro, "Some Preliminary Remarks on the PSPP Decision of the German Constitutional Court" VerfBlog, 2020/5/06, https://verfassungsblog.de/some-preliminary-remarks-on-the-pspp-decision-of-the-german-constitutional-court/.

politely not noticing that a Constitutional Court was asking the question. Perhaps oddly, the CJEU decided that ultimately it was for Spanish constitutional law to decide the issue at hand.[63] The progress and growing understanding of federalism in Italian and Spanish Courts, facilitated through a dialogue with the centre European Court, enables a more informed and constructive public debate on the complex questions of rule of law and supremacy, with the potential for greater levels of engagement and acceptance among citizens.

Today, we see more Constitutional Courts engaging in direct conversation with the CJEU than ever. It is, in my view, a clear sign of the advancing maturity of the EU legal system; however, it remains to be seen whether the participation in preliminary referencing acknowledges the supremacy of EU law over constitutional law in all cases.

4.2.4 *Conclusion as to the Validity of This Obstacle*

This chapter has illustrated that complete homogeneity is not the goal of any federal system, let alone the goal of a federal system that strives to promote regulatory competition as the EU does.[64] Further, by drawing upon examples of other federal entities, it demonstrated that most tensions between federal and local/state laws are entirely supportable within a federal constitutional system, with the contours of this tension being inevitably smoothed over time. Indeed, this process of resolving tensions allows for the development of a well-reasoned body of jurisprudence – one that is informed by the practicalities of the system that emerge after the initial constitutionalization process.

4.3 No Powerful Unitary Federal Court System?

4.3.1 *No Single Constitutional Court with Appellate Powers?*

4.3.1.1 Obstacle

Most constitutional entities have one highest federal court. From its inception, it has been argued that the European Union lacks an adequate

[63] Case C-399/11, *Stefano Melloni* v. *Ministerio Fiscal*, Judgment of the Court (Grand Chamber) of 26 February 2013, not yet reported.

[64] See D. C. Esty and D. Geradin (eds.), *Regulatory Competition and Economic Integration: Comparative Perspectives* (New York 2001); J. P. Trachtman, 'International Regulatory Competition, Externalization, and Jurisdiction' (1993) 34 *Harvard International Law Journal* 47.

federal court because the Court of Justice was created as a specialized court,[65] or even, as others critics argue, an international court.[66] In the EU, there is no practical choice between a Member State Court and the European Court; the CJEU and the General Court were created to adjudicate a very specialized area of law.[67] Critics might point to the historically important constitutional system used at the founding of the Court of the German Empire in 1879, when the German Reich as a whole was integrated in a legal fashion and provincialism was significantly abolished.[68] Arguably, it was only after this process that the rule of law was established in its entirety, and from this viewpoint, the strength and power of a Constitutional Court for federal matters are crucial for successful constitutionalization. The criticism that emerges in this area is rooted in a special perspective on the importance of the role of the Constitutional Court within a federal entity, striking at the heart of constitutional development.[69] The lack of a powerful federal court without direct appellate powers can be seen as an important obstacle. While some constitutional critics are aware of the 'judicial construction of Europe'[70] and understand that the most striking advances of EU integration have been achieved through sweeping judgments and judicial developments by the Court of Justice, this concern is important to examine.

4.3.1.2 Underlying Concepts of Constitutional Development

Many federal structures thrive on unitary courts. Indeed, for many, a solid and stable court system is at the centre of a successful federal project.[71] Taking the US example, the Supreme Court was originally mandated with very few powers and it was not entirely clear from the outset whether it would even hear many cases. Under the Articles of

65 Craig and de Búrca, *EU Law: Text, Cases, and Materials*, 27.

66 R. Higgins, 'The ICJ, the CJEU, and the Integrity of International Law' (2003) 52 *International and Comparative Law Quarterly* 1.

67 Brown and Kennedy.

68 See M. Payandeh, 'Constitutional Review of EU Law after Honeywell: Contextualizing the Relationship between the German Constitutional Court and the EU Court of Justice' (2011) 48 *Common Market Law Review* 9.

69 S. Breyer, *America's Supreme Court: Making Democracy Work* (Oxford 2010) 4.

70 Stone Sweet, *The Judicial Construction of Europe*; S. K. Schmidt, *The European Court of Justice*; M. A. Longo, *Constitutionalising Europe: Processes and Practices* (Farnham/Burlington, VT 2006) 58. See e.g. the literature discussed in M. de Somer, *Precedents and Judicial Politics in EU Immigration Law* (Cham 2019) 10–16.

71 Halberstam and Reimann, 'Federalism and Legal Unification: Comparing Methods, Results, and Explanations across Twenty Systems' in Halberstam and Reimann (eds.), *Federalism and Legal Unification*, 3–67.

Confederation, no real central court was envisaged at all.[72] Instead, the Congress of the Confederation had the power to mediate disputes between two states with arbitrators or judges from different states.

Article III of the US Constitution contains only very general language about the judiciary and the Supreme Court: 'The judicial Power of the United States shall be vested in one Supreme Court, and in such inferior

[72] US Const. Art. IX contained an elaborate procedure under which conflicts between two states could be submitted to arbitration under the guidance of Congress:

> [T]he United States in Congress assembled shall also be the last resort on appeal in all disputes and differences now subsisting or that hereafter may arise between two or more States concerning boundary, jurisdiction or any other causes whatever; which authority shall always be exercised in the manner following. Whenever the legislative or executive authority or lawful agent of any State in controversy with another shall present a petition to Congress stating the matter in question and praying for a hearing, notice thereof shall be given by order of Congress to the legislative or executive authority of the other State in controversy, and a day assigned for the appearance of the parties by their lawful agents, who shall then be directed to appoint by joint consent, commissioners or judges to constitute a court for hearing and determining the matter in question: but if they cannot agree, Congress shall name three persons out of each of the United States, and from the list of such persons each party shall alternately strike out one, the petitioners beginning, until the number shall be reduced to thirteen; and from that number not less than seven, nor more than nine names as Congress shall direct, shall in the presence of Congress be drawn out by lot, and the persons whose names shall be so drawn or any five of them, shall be commissioners or judges, to hear and finally determine the controversy, so always as a major part of the judges who shall hear the cause shall agree in the determination: and if either party shall neglect to attend at the day appointed, without showing reasons, which Congress shall judge sufficient, or being present shall refuse to strike, the Congress shall proceed to nominate three persons out of each State, and the secretary of Congress shall strike in behalf of such party absent or refusing; and the judgment and sentence of the court to be appointed, in the manner before prescribed, shall be final and conclusive; and if any of the parties shall refuse to submit to the authority of such court, or to appear or defend their claim or cause, the court shall nevertheless proceed to pronounce sentence, or judgment, which shall in like manner be final and decisive, the judgment or sentence and other proceedings being in either case transmitted to Congress, and lodged among the acts of Congress for the security of the parties concerned: provided that every commissioner, before he sits in judgement, shall take an oath to be administered by one of the judges of the supreme or superior court of the State, where the cause shall be tried, 'well and truly to hear and determine the matter in question, according to the best of his judgement, without favoured, affection or hope of reward': provided also, that no State shall be deprived of territory for the benefit of the United States.

Courts as the Congress may from time to time ordain and establish.' Initially, the Federalists and the Anti-Federalists debated how broadly this Article should be interpreted. While staunch Anti-Federalists wanted a much-reduced Supreme Court, and perhaps federal admiralty courts,[73] Federalists sided with Hamilton:

> It seems scarcely to admit of controversy, that the judiciary authority of the Union ought to extend to these several descriptions of cases: 1st, to all those which arise out of the laws of the United States, passed in pursuance of their just and constitutional powers of legislation; 2d, to all those which concern the execution of the provisions expressly contained in the articles of Union; 3d, to all those in which the United States are a party; 4th, to all those which involve the PEACE of the CONFEDERACY, whether they relate to the intercourse between the United States and foreign nations, or to that between the States themselves; 5th, to all those which originate on the high seas, and are of admiralty or maritime jurisdiction; and, lastly, to all those in which the State tribunals cannot be supposed to be impartial and unbiased.[74]

In the Judiciary Act of 1789, US legislators followed a more encompassing vision, creating not just Courts of Admiralty but also Federal Courts of almost general jurisdiction across (originally) thirteen judicial districts. These districts were later to be organized into three circuits (today nine).[75] It was all the more frequent for a case to start its judicial life in the Federal Court directly during this period. For example, during the 12-month period ending 30 September 2009, 30,161 cases were removed from the State to Federal Court, compared with 185,900 cases filed as an original matter in the Federal Courts.[76] This is, of course, quite a different arrangement than the one that characterizes the EU judicial system. At this stage in the EU's constitutional development, by far the greatest numbers of cases reaching the EU Courts are preliminary reference questions forwarded by Member State courts, rather than cases logged directly with the EU Courts.[77]

[73] See R. Yates [Brutus], 'Anti-Federalist No. XI' (1788), who warns of a 'subversion' of the states' powers to the federal judiciary.

[74] A. Hamilton, 'The Federalist No. 80' in *The Federalist Papers* (1787–1788).

[75] R. Wheeler and C. Harrison, *Creating the Federal Judicial System*, 3rd ed. (Washington, DC 2005) 4.

[76] J. Duff, 'Annual Report of the Director of the Administrative Office of the United States Courts' (2009); C. Wright and A. Miller, *Federal Practice and Procedure, Jurisdiction and Related Matters*, 4th ed., Vol. 14B (Minneapolis, MN 2013) table S-7, p.46, sec. 3721.

[77] In 2009, 302 references for preliminary ruling were made, in comparison to 143 direct actions. See UK Parliament, European Union Committee, 'The Workload of the European Court of Justice of the European Union', www.publications.parliament.uk /pa/ld201011/ldselect/ldeucom/128/12806.htm#a12, ch. 3, at figure 1.

While US State Supreme Courts are formally bound to follow Supreme Court decisions in the area of federal competence, *ultra vires* decisions are not in fact binding upon them. It was not until the now-infamous decision in *Bush* v. *Gore*[78] that the Supreme Court majority decided that a State Supreme Court cannot arrogate to itself power that violates the equal protection clause. It ruled:

> Where, as here, a court orders a statewide remedy, there must be at least some assurance that the rudimentary requirements of equal treatment and fundamental fairness are satisfied. The State has not shown that its procedures include the necessary safeguards. Upon due consideration of the difficulties identified to this point, it is obvious that the recount cannot be conducted in compliance with the requirements of equal protection and due process without substantial additional work. The court below has said that the legislature intended the State's electors to participate fully in the federal electoral process, as provided in 3 U. S. C. § 5, which requires that any controversy or contest that is designed to lead to a conclusive selection of electors be completed by December 12. That date is here, but there is no recount procedure in place under the state court's order that comports with minimal constitutional standards.[79]

Of particular interest in this case was the concurring opinion of Rehnquist, Scalia and Thomas who sought to justify their overturning of the Florida Supreme Court decision not purely on national law but rather out of respect for the 'State legislator'. In their view, this figure required defending against the decision in Florida to order a recount in several counties.

Turning now to examine other important examples of federal structures, even today, the GFCC has no jurisdiction to decide on questions of Länder constitutional law. This is a domain reserved for Länder Constitutional Courts.[80] In essence, this shows, to my mind, that while court structures are important, they do develop over time and it is not clear at the starting point of constitutionalization that a federal court system is even needed. In Germany, to this day, the administration of justice is a question of Länder competences and only the highest courts

[78] US Supreme Court, *Bush* v. *Gore*, 531 US 98 (2000).

[79] Ibid.

[80] C. Bumke and A. Voßkuhle, *German Constitutional Law: Introduction, Cases, and Principles* (Oxford 2019) 461; R. Grote, 'Constitutional Courts in Federal States: The Case of Germany' (2017) 17 *Fédéralisme Régionalisme*, https://popups.uliege.be/1374-3864/index.php?id=1691. In 2008, the last of the Länder, Schleswig-Holstein, established its own constitutional court because individual constitutional complaints were not possible based on Land constitutional law – all other cases were redirected to the GFCC.

are federal courts. A lack of a federal court system thus does not present a significant obstacle to constitutionalization.[81]

In Argentina, which has a unitary court structure, the power of the Supreme Court is consistently put to the test within the constitutional system. This challenge stems less from the provincial level and more from central government authorities who feel uneasy about the long-established tradition of constitutional review in Argentina. Here we have an example of the constitution of even a strong federal institution being tested and developing over time.[82]

4.3.1.3 Related EU Developments

The objection to EU constitutionalization based on the lack of a unitary federal system seems particularly apposite if we analyse the EU courts simply in the context of the foundational treaties of the European Union. As I have explained, the original intention of the Rome Treaty drafters when introducing the Preliminary Reference procedure (now Art. 267 TFEU (ex Art. 234 TEC)) was precisely not to create a federal court.[83] The primary intention was in fact to create a horizontal relationship between the CJEU and the Member State Systems of Courts[84] in the hope that this procedure could ensure harmonious interpretation of a highly specialized area of law. In this way, EU judges were to be most appropriately regarded as friends of the national courts, rather than appellate or, in an even more extreme view, constitutional judges.[85]

I believe that in a similar way to which the original Articles of Confederation envisioned a dispute settlement function for Congress, the ECJ maintains the power to hear disputes between different Member States on the interpretation of the EU Treaties. This jurisdiction for State-to-State infringement proceedings is regarded as exclusive and Member States of the EU are now barred from engaging one another for a purpose that would circumvent the role of the Court of Justice. This was strongly affirmed in *Commission* v. *Ireland (Mox Plant)*,[86] which involved

[81] Adam and Möllers, 237–54.
[82] A. M. Vítolo, 'The Argentine Federal Legislative System' in Halberstam and Reimann (eds.), *Federalism and Legal Unification*, 71–85.
[83] Craig and de Búrca, *EU Law: Text, Cases, and Materials*, 24.
[84] M. Broberg and N. Fenger, *Preliminary References to the European Court* (New York 2010) 5.
[85] Slaughter, Stone Sweet and Weiler.
[86] See Case C-459/03, *Commission of the European Communities* v. *Ireland* [2006] ECR I-04635; see also P. J. Cardwell and D. French, 'Who Decides? The CJEU's Judgment on Jurisdiction in the MOX Plant Dispute' (2007) 19(1) *Journal of Environmental Law* 121.

a complaint by Ireland before the International Tribunal on the Law of the Seas (ITLOS) against the UK's nuclear enrichment plant. The Court has further clarified this view by restricting the discretion of Member State courts to decide whether a preliminary reference is required. In *CILFIT* v. *Ministry of Health*, it was found that EU Member States and their courts have a general obligation to refer cases involving interpretation of the EEC Treaty or aspects of EU Community law to the European Court.[87] The CJEU qualified this obligation by affirming that where the issue at hand is either (1) irrelevant to the scope of EU Community law, (2) has already been addressed by the European Court or (3) involves such an obvious conclusion that further pursuance of the matter would not be appropriate, no such referral is required.[88]

The case law on the preliminary reference procedure is striking and has clear characteristics of a central(izing) court. The Court has, against the explicit wording of Art. 267 TFEU, claimed power to review the admissibility of all cases that are referred to it.[89] In the case of *Foglia* v. *Novello*,[90] for example, the ECJ declined the admissibility of a preliminary reference from an Italian court because the court had not provided enough information for the ECJ to decide the case conclusively.[91] Otherwise, and I submit, quite unlike the US Supreme Court, the CJEU has no discretion as to whether it will hear a case.[92] The court at the centre thus forced the courts at the periphery to facilitate its

This was further reiterated by the Court in regards to the ECHR Draft Accession Agreement: Case Opinion 2/13 [2014] EU:C:2014:2454 paras. [201]–[214].

87 Case 283/81, *Srl CILFIT and Lanificio di Gavardo SpA* v. *Ministry of Health* [1982] ECR 03415.

88 Ibid., paras [10]–[11], [16]. For a recent analysis of these conditions, see J. van Dorp and P. Phoa, 'How to Continue a Meaningful Judicial Dialogue about EU Law? From the Conditions in the CILFIT Judgment to the Creation of a New European Legal Culture' (2018) 34 *Utrecht Journal of International and European Law* 73.

89 A. Rosas, 'The Interaction between the European Court of Justice and National Courts in Preliminary Ruling Proceedings: Some Institutional and Procedural Observations' in H. Ruiz Fabri (ed.), *International Law and Litigation: A Look into Procedure* (Luxembourg 2019) 603, 615.

90 Case 244/80, *Pasquale Foglia* v. *Mariella Novello* [1981] ECR 03045.

91 The Court has become increasingly willing to reject referrals on admissibility grounds: N. Wahl and L. Prete, 'The Gatekeepers of Article 267 TFEU: On Jurisdiction and Admissibility of References for Preliminary Rulings' (2018) 55 *Common Market Law Review* 511, 538.

92 See Case 283/81, *Srl CILFIT and Lanificio di Gavardo SpA* v. *Ministry of Health* [1982] ECR 03415, where the Court extensively discusses the question of discretion both on the side of the Member State court and by the Court of Justice.

central role. This is the type of decision, as a federal court, that can lead to further constitutionalization.

4.3.1.4 Conclusion as to the Validity of This Obstacle

In conclusion, this chapter has made my claim that, taking into account illustrative examples of other federal constitutional experiences, this obstacle to constitutionalization becomes unconvincing. The federal courts in the United States, particularly the Supreme Court, have clarified the centrality of their positions over time and in turn have developed into the strong institutions that are known today. EU federal institutions were not originally structured as strong, centralized authorities. While the EU court may still lack firm appellate powers, through its jurisprudence and interaction with Member State courts, it has begun to acquire a de facto appellate function over the years. Now, only in very few circumstances do Member State courts retain the flexibility to decide whether or not to refer cases that are relevant to EU law to the CJEU itself. In my view, over time, this discretion has been significantly reduced. As such, this obstacle has to a great extent been overcome in practice by CJEU jurisprudence.

4.3.2 *No Clear Procedures for Selection of Justices?*

4.3.2.1 Obstacle

Critics suggest that no common rule of law exists in Europe because the CJEU lacks clear rules and procedures for the selection of justices – an important task in any constitutional polity. This criticism is often used as the main argument against non-democratic, and indeed dictatorial, regimes.[93] In the European Union context, it has been argued that CJEU justices are still Member State appointees who represent their Member States, rather than the most able jurists who are selected from across Europe by a constitutional process.[94] Indeed for some, this selection process should be entirely removed from the Member States' jurisdiction and conducted by an independent panel, which would select justices according to a preset, published list of qualities.[95] Thus, a radical departure from current practices would probably require a broader

[93] L. Hilbink, *Judges beyond Politics in Democracy and Dictatorship: Lessons from Chile* (New York 2007).

[94] L. F. Goldstein, *Constituting Federal Sovereignty*, ch. 5.

[95] A. Arnull, 'A Constitutional Court for Europe?' (2003–2004) 6 *Cambridge Yearbook of European Legal Studies* 24.

public discussion. This, in turn, requires a more developed European public sphere.

4.3.2.2 Underlying Concepts of Constitutional Development

A key question for every constitutional order is how judges should be selected. The importance of this task cannot be undervalued; it is the judiciary who, in any democratic society, enjoy a great degree of independence. This is particularly important in federal structures where disputes between various levels of government have to be either negotiated in the democratic institutions or litigated in the courts.[96]

In most federal systems, great emphasis is placed on the selection of justices and, as I believe, it is fundamental to any analysis here to appreciate that this selection is one that develops over time. In Canada, for example, a rule exists whereby at least four of all Supreme Court justices must originate from the Civil Law part of Canada or be at least familiar with civil law. This has created controversy in recent years because of its tendency to be interpreted as a requirement for francophone Supreme Court justices. The previous Harper administration adopted a different approach, making efforts to nominate justices who are arguably not adequately qualified. This decision not only offended constituents in Quebec but also provoked open dispute between the government and the Supreme Court.[97] Certainly, this issue has to do with language and, to a lesser degree, with cultural politics, but I believe that there is also a distinctly federal element in the debate, whereby Quebec sees itself as a very special province whose rights and requirements have to be respected in important matters such as the selection of Supreme Court justices.

Perhaps a more controversial example is that of the United States, where the selection of Supreme Court justices has developed into a highly contentious and politicized issue.[98] While initially the state origin of the nominees was critical, later courts were largely selected from the most successful judges and, much later, academics in the country.[99] The

[96] M. H. Redish, 'Federal Judicial Independence: Constitutional and Political Perspectives' (1994) 46 *Mercer Law Review* 697.

[97] J.-F. Gaudreault-DesBiens and N. Karazivan, 'Canada: Upcoming Appointment of Supreme Court Judges' (October 2011) *Canada Public Law* 827, 830.

[98] R. Davis, *Electing Justice: Fixing the Supreme Court Nomination Process* (New York 2005).

[99] For a review of the US Judges selection process, see D. S. Rutkus, 'CRS Report for Congress: Supreme Court Appointment Process: Roles of President, Judiciary Committee, and Senate' (2005) US Department of State, http://fpc.state.gov/documents/organization/50146.pdf; N. Dorsen, 'The Selection of U.S. Supreme Court Justices' (2006) 4 *International Journal of Constitutional Law* 652.

selection of Supreme Court justices is not codified in any particular statute but rather follows the same procedure as the appointment of other high-level civil servants, with the additional requirement that the President's nominee for the position also faces the Senate judicial committee in a manner generally used for high-level Presidential nominees. The effect has been that, at least after the New Deal constitutional moment where Roosevelt 'packed the Court', presidential politics have heavily influenced Supreme Court selections.[100] The lack of any real merit-based process for the nomination or appointment of Supreme Court justices[101] leads some commentators to believe that this appointment process is much more political than legal in nature.[102]

To understand the US example fully, I believe that it is necessary to briefly consider the history behind it. Traditionally, justices have been elected with political considerations in mind rather than concerns about particular legal expertise. However, today almost all justices[103] are former federal judges and, therefore, more frequently than not can be considered to have passed a merit-based appointment process in some form.[104] Quite surprisingly, modern justices are no longer selected on the basis of which state they are from.[105] Of the current Supreme Court justices, for example, four were born in New York, two are from California and New Jersey, respectively, and one originates from Georgia.[106] Here we see a striking departure from the historic precedent of choosing justices from different states. Moreover, it must also be mentioned that, historically, the connection of Supreme Court justices with those particular states was much closer. For the first 121 years of the US federal system, Supreme Court justices had to 'ride circuit', holding court in specified cities in the thirteen judicial districts.[107] This was, of course, partly the result of very different logistical and communicative structures in the early United

[100] B. A. Ackerman, *We the People: Vol. 2: Transformations* (Cambridge, MA 2000).

[101] D. L. Bassett, 'Recusal and the Supreme Court' (2005) 56 *Hastings Law Journal* 657.

[102] H. P. Monaghan, 'The Confirmation Process: Law or Politics?' (1988) 101 *Harvard Law Review* 1202, 1204.

[103] With the notable exception of Elena Kagan. See C. Cushman, *Supreme Court Decisions and Women's Rights: Milestones to Equality*, 2nd ed. (Washington, DC 2011).

[104] See interesting analysis by R. Alleman and J. Mazzone, 'The Case for Returning Politicians to the Supreme Court' (2010) 61 *Hastings Law Journal* 1353.

[105] Rutkus; Dorsen.

[106] See the biographies of the current justices of the Supreme Court, www.supremecourt.gov /about/biographies.aspx.

[107] D. Stras, 'Why Supreme Court Justices Should Ride Circuit Again' (2006–2007) 91 *Minnesota Law Review* 1710; J. Glick, 'On the Road: The Supreme Court and the History of Circuit Riding' (2002–2003) 24 *Cardozo Law Review* 1753.

States, but I believe that it explains why the federally centralized selection of justices would not have created greater concern; the goal was not in fact to create a Supreme Court of justices who were removed from the general population of the United States and its legal concerns.[108] It is my belief that the ritual of riding circuit ensured a close connection between the justices themselves and the individual states. In this way, this process acted to balance out any impulses that were to be swayed by obscure decision-making bodies located far away in the swampy environs of Washington. On this basis, it is my claim that the increased political nature of US Supreme Court appointments grew greatly over the first decades. It would be a number of years before Supreme Court justices were divorced from exposure to the greater interests of the states and their citizens.

4.3.2.3 Related EU Developments

The CJEU is similar to a federal court in the way that, despite the fact that it was originally designed to interact in a horizontal fashion with Member State courts, it has a vertical relationship with these periphery courts. On this basis, it has been argued that the selection of justices for the CJEU does not reflect their increasingly important role within the constitutional structure and demonstrates the inherent limits to any attempt by the EU to become a constitutional polity.[109]

The procedure for the selection of judges remains unchanged from the early days of the European Communities. As Art. 19.2 TEU sets out, echoing earlier versions of the Treaties:

> The Judges and the Advocates-General of the Court of Justice and the Judges of the General Court shall be chosen from persons whose independence is beyond doubt and who satisfy the conditions set out in Articles 253 and 254 of the Treaty on the Functioning of the European

[108] The reasons mentioned for the ride circuit were: 1. Costs; 2. Exposing judges to viewpoints and customs from all over the country; 3. Ensuring that justices remained connected to local/state laws; 4. Education of local citizens about the new constitutional system and the centralized federal government; 5. Enhancing the legitimacy of the circuit courts; 6. Enhancing the uniformity of federal law. See Stras, at 1716–17. Glick adds: 7. Ruling on questions of federal law; 8. Keeping in touch with state courts. See Glick, at 1760–1.

[109] E. Böckenförde, 'Die Nation: Identität in Differenz' (1995) *Politische Wissenschaft* 974. See also M. Bobek, *Selecting Europe's Judges: A Critical Review of the Appointment Procedures to the European Courts* (Oxford 2015) especially A. von Bogdandy and C. Krenn, 'On the Democratic Legitimacy of Europe's Judges' and R. D. Kelemen, 'Selection, Appointment, and Legitimacy'.

> Union. They shall be appointed by common accord of the governments of the Member States for six years. Retiring Judges and Advocates-General may be reappointed."[110] Then Art. 253 TFEU stipulates that CJEU judges or advocates-general need to 'possess the qualifications required for appointment to the highest judicial offices in their respective countries or who are jurisconsults of recognised competence'.[111]

By this provision, decisions on the appointment of judges have been left largely to Member States, with little room for a real selection across the Union. Moreover, the unwritten convention that no Member State would question the proposal made by a fellow government makes the reality of a pan-Union selection process all the more unachievable.[112]

An element of constitutional reform was attempted with the Lisbon Treaty. Negotiations here tried to address, to some degree, earlier criticism that the selection of judges was not in accordance with their actual role within the Union. Under Art. 255 TFEU, there is now, not unlike the selection of judges in national systems, a committee established in accordance for the selection of judges. A panel was established to

> give an opinion on candidates' suitability to perform the duties of Judge and Advocate-General of the Court of Justice and the General Court before the governments of the Member States make the appointments referred to in Articles 253 and 254. The panel shall comprise seven persons chosen from among former members of the Court of Justice and the General Court, members of national supreme courts and lawyers of recognised competence, one of whom shall be proposed by the European Parliament. The Council shall adopt a decision establishing the panel's operating rules and a decision appointing its members. It shall act on the initiative of the President of the Court of Justice.

The mandate of this committee, as I believe, clearly corrects the impression that the selection of judges is left to political priorities and Member State discretion.[113]

[110] TEU (OJ 2012 C 326 p.1).

[111] Treaty on the Functioning of the European Union ['TFEU'] (OJ 2012 C 326 p.1).

[112] J. Bell, 'The Role of European Judges in an Era of Uncertainty' in P. Birkinshaw and M. Varney (eds.), *The European Union Legal Order after Lisbon* (Alphen Aan Den Rijn 2010).

[113] See for the selection of AGs, L. Clement-Wilz, 'Advocate General: A Key Actor of the Court of Justice of the European Union' (2011–2012) 14 *Cambridge Yearbook of European Legal Studies* 587, 610. See now T. Dumbrovský, B. Petkova and M. van der Sluis, 'Judicial Appointments: The Article 255 TFEU Advisory Panel and Selection Procedures in the Member States' (2014) 51 *Common Market Law Review* 455, 456 and O. Shalaby and others, 'Transparent Selection of Judges for EU Courts: Complaint to

There are no central cases that deal with the selection of judges as such in the EU. Most individual staff cases concern administrative or linguistic staff of the Court of Justice, but even those cases concern only between 5.04 per cent and 1.26 per cent of all Staff Tribunal Cases in the years 2009–2011.[114] Typical Court of Justice cases mainly concern non-retention after an initial stage period for juri-linguists, that is, legally trained translators for the Court. One such example is that of *Mrs Krcova* who, after an initial trial period, was not retained because her translations were found to be 'trop littérale, les erreurs et omissions qu'elle commet et une mauvaise exploitation des fonds documentaires et de recherche rendent nécessaire une révision approfondie de ses traductions' [too literal, the errors and omissions she makes and a poor use of the documentary and research collections make it necessary to significantly revise her translations].[115] However, neither the function of the Court nor the appointment of judges has yet to form part of a Court proceeding and other European Courts have tended to respect the selection of judges, which itself is analogous to many European constitutional orders.

4.3.2.4 Conclusion as to the Validity of This Obstacle

The selection of judges in any constitutional polity is undeniably problematic. But, as demonstrated by the US experience, it can develop over time and become more relevant as the constitutional influence of the court grows and, albeit in the particular example of the United States, the political influence manifests. While it is much less possible to develop a 'judge personality' in a court with no signed opinion, many observers of the EU now know and can detect from the language of an opinion what has been likely proposed by particular judges. While state origin is no longer an important factor in the US context, it remains politically important in the EU context for now; the rule regarding anonymous judgments is unlikely to change in the near future and it is preferable to have one European decision on the matter. This rule could be changed only if

the European Ombudsman' (2017) HEC Research Paper Series 1239, https://ideas.repec.org/p/ebg/heccah/1239.html.

[114] See Court of Justice of the European Union, *Annual Report 2012* (Luxembourg 2013) 232 An interesting new 2020 case could be the case by AG Sharpston against her dismissal following Brexit in the Court of First Instance, T-184/20 - *Sharpston v Court of Justice of the European Union.*

[115] Case F-112/06, *Erika Krcova* v. *Court of Justice of the European Communities* [2007] ECR FP-I-A-1–00305; FP-II-A-1–01723, at [5]. Also see its appeal, which was equally rejected: Case T-498/07 P, *Erika Krcova* v. *Court of Justice of the European Communities* [2009] ECR FP-I-B-1–00035; FP-II-B-1–00197.

a greater European public sphere were developed, providing a space for debate and trans-European deliberation leading to identification of judicial candidates from among a pool of pan-European applicants. In essence, in my view, the selection of justices remains a challenge, and the lack of a public sphere does hamper further constitutionalization in this respect.

4.3.3 *No Federal Court Powers of Constitutional Review?*

4.3.3.1 Introduction to the Obstacle

Another obstacle to the constitutionalization of the European Union is the perceived lack of constitutional review at the European level. There is, as several critics comment upon, no provision in the treaties mandating the CJEU to engage in a constitutional review as such.[116]

4.3.3.2 Underlying Concepts of Constitutional Development

Constitutional review, and even the power to review federated legislation for compatibility with the Constitution, is a power claimed by most federal constitutional courts around the world.

In Germany, for example, the GFCC can review the actions of Länder institutions only in accordance with federal constitutional law and not by using the Länder constitutions. The GFCC simply has no jurisdiction to hear constitutional complaints based on Länder law.[117] As discussed, this was one of the reasons leading Schleswig-Holstein to create its own Constitutional Court in 2008.

In the United States, after constitutional review was found to be a 'natural' consequence of a written constitution in *Marbury*,[118] it was many years before it was established that highest courts do hold this power. For fifty years following *Marbury*, the Court struck down state

[116] Art. 93 of the German Grundgesetz, for example, vests the Constitutional Court with constitutional review power and even gives citizens direct access to the court. See also M. Rosenfeld, 'Comparing Constitutional Review by the European Court of Justice and the U.S. Supreme Court' (2006) 4 *International Journal of Constitutional Law* 618.

[117] M. Dombert, 'Landesverfassungen und Landesverfassungsgerichte in ihrer Bedeutung für den Föderalismus' in I. Härtel (ed.), *Handbuch Föderalismus – Föderalismus als demokratische Rechtsordnung und Rechtskultur in Deutschland, Europa und der Welt* (Berlin/Heidelberg 2012).

[118] US Supreme Court, *Marbury* v. *Madison*, 5 US (1 Cranch) 137 (1803) ['*Marbury* v. *Madison*']. See, further, E. Chemerinsky, *Constitutional Law: Principles and Policies*, 6th ed. (New York 2019) 47; W. E. Nelson, *Marbury v. Madison: The Origins and Legacy of Judicial Review*, 2nd ed. (Kansas 2018); G. E. White, 'The Constitutional Journey of "Marbury v. Madison"' (2003) 89 *Virginia Law Review* 1463.

statutes and other acts but refrained from striking down a federal statute until 1857 in the infamous decision of *Dred Scott* v. *Sandford.*[119]. What we clearly see here is legislative judicial review taking hold slowly and developing over time. In fact, judicial review, even today, is not without its limits. Since the seminal ruling in *Murdock,*[120] the Supreme Court has consistently declined jurisdiction to review a finding of a State Supreme Court[121] based on an 'adequate and independent State ground'.[122] This position was clarified by the Supreme Court in *Cooper* v. *Aaron,*[123] to mean that state action involving any violation of fundamental rights would be reviewable.

The timing of the initiation of a constitutional review process in the United States remains hotly debated.[124] Some claim that it was invented in the state courts before the revolution, while others see the origins in English law, particularly the repugnancy of judicial review.[125] However, putting aside these historical discussions, I note that while legislative judicial review remains controversial at all levels of constitutional law, it has nonetheless gained international popularity following the decision in *Marbury* and subsequent US practice.[126]

In *Marbury* v. *Madison,*[127] the Supreme Court declared:

> It is emphatically the province and duty of the Judicial Department to say what the law is. Those who apply the rule to particular cases must, of necessity, expound and interpret that rule. If two laws conflict with each other, the Courts must decide on the operation of each. So, if a law be in opposition to the Constitution, if both the law and the Constitution apply to a particular case, so that the Court must either decide that case conformably to the law, disregarding the Constitution, or conformably to the Constitution, disregarding the law, the Court must determine which of these conflicting rules governs the case. This is of the very essence of

[119] 60 US (19 How) 393 (1857).

[120] *Murdock* v. *Memphis*, 87 US 590 (1875).

[121] The role of State Courts was highlighted by Justice W. J. Brennan, Jr., 'State Constitutions and the Protection of Individual Rights' (1977) 90 *Harvard Law Review* 489, 502.

[122] J. F. Mitchell, 'Reconsidering Murdock: State-Law Reversals as Constitutional Avoidance' (2010) 77 *University of Chicago Law Review* 1335.

[123] 358 US 1 (1958).

[124] S. B. Prakash and J. C. Yoo, 'The Origins of Judicial Review' (2003) 70 *University of Chicago Law Review* 887 and P. Hamburger, 'Law and Judicial Duty' (2003) 72 *George Washington Law Review* 1.

[125] M. S. Bilder, 'The Corporate Origins of Judicial Review' (2006) 116 *Yale Law Journal* 502.

[126] C. Landfried, *Constitutional Review and Legislation: An International Comparison* (Baden-Baden 1988).

[127] Ibid.

> judicial duty. If, then, the Courts are to regard the Constitution, and the Constitution is superior to any ordinary act of the Legislature, the Constitution, and not such ordinary act, must govern the case to which they both apply. Those, then, who controvert the principle that the Constitution is to be considered in court as a paramount law are reduced to the necessity of maintaining that courts must close their eyes on the Constitution, and see only the law. This doctrine would subvert the very foundation of all written constitutions.[128]

In essence, the Supreme Court was claiming, in this very early decision, a right in principle to strike down laws adopted by democratic institutions. Initially, this was to take place only in theory, however, with judicial review not becoming the norm until the early twentieth century, when the Supreme Court became active in striking down statutes adopted by Congress.[129]

But, I believe, as *Marbury* rightly lays out, it would not make sense to have a constitutional document if Parliament could just unilaterally amend its meaning through the adoption of a simple law.[130] It was this particular ability of non-elected judges to overturn statutes that led commentators to question whether the judiciary really was the least dangerous branch of government to which proper checks and balances need not apply.[131]

A similar concern has been seen to exist in Switzerland. In my view, the Swiss experience is a particularly pertinent example of successful federal polity functioning well without judicial review.[132] Although a process of judicial review is in place, there exists no formal coordination between the different Cantons and their respective judiciaries.[133] This is combined with a historical distrust of courts in Switzerland, which has prevented the courts from having the power to review parliamentary legislation except in the Canton of Geneva.[134] Even today, this competence is severely

[128] Ibid.

[129] For a list of Congress Acts held unconstitutional by the Supreme Court, see Justia, 'Acts of Congress Held Unconstitutional in Whole or in Part by the Supreme Court of the United States', http://law.justia.com/constitution/us/046-acts-of-congress-held-unconstitutional.html.

[130] See *Marbury* v. *Madison*.

[131] A. M. Bickel, *The Least Dangerous Branch: The Supreme Court at the Bar of Politics*, 2nd ed. (New Haven, CT 1986).

[132] A. Lienhard and others, 'The Federal Supreme Court of Switzerland: Judicial Balancing of federalism without Judicial Review' in N. Aroney and J. Kincaid (eds.), *Courts in Federal Countries: Federalists or Unitarists?* (Toronto 2017) 404.

[133] Cashin Ritaine and Papeil, 439, 450.

[134] F. W. O'Brien, 'Baker v. Carr Abroad: The Swiss Federal Tribunal and Cantonal Elections' (1962) 72 *Yale Law Journal* 46.

restricted and recent attempts to allow for full judicial review of federal legislation have failed.

Regarding cantonal laws, Federal courts have intervened only in very restrictive cases.[135] As Ritaine and Papeil explain:

> Surprisingly, Article 95 of the Federal Supreme Court Act (LTF), which defines the types of actions brought before the Federal Supreme Court, does not mention cantonal legislation. As a result, the application and judicial control of cantonal law are cantonal competences. This competence follows from Articles 3 and 47 of the Constitution, which obliges the Confederation to respect cantonal autonomy. In exceptional cases, however, the Federal Supreme Court may examine the application and the interpretation of cantonal law. Such is the case, for example, when there are serious restrictions of liberty. The Federal Supreme Court also judges the compatibility of cantonal acts with superior federal norms.[136]

4.3.3.3 Related EU Developments

In the earliest days of the EU, the CJEU was seen and acted as a specialist court, but, over the course of the last three decades, it has evolved to become the ultimate defender of the treaties, upholding the founding treaty as a basic constitutional charter. However, the question, I believe, still remains: Does the CJEU engage in constitutional review? And the answer is not quite as straightforward as it might seem. Normally, particular judges in civil law systems are not mandated to engage in constitutional review. They cannot, as unelected public officials, strike down laws made by parliament. This power is reserved for constitutional judges. As the constitutionalization process of EU law plays out, it becomes much more straightforward to argue that EU judges are actually constitutional judges.[137] However, certainly the concept that non-elected European judges can strike down EU laws has raised questions and debates.[138] Interestingly, the replies to these questions are almost constitutional in their nature. The CJEU will review the legality of acts against the treaties and, equally importantly, it reviews such acts against general principles such as proportionality, legal certainty and

135 Lienhard, 405.

136 Cashin-Ritaine and Papeil, 439, 453. See also M. Hottelier, 'La justice constitutionnelle en Suisse' (2017) 17 *Fédéralisme Régionalisme* 5–6, http://archive-ouverte.unige.ch/unige:102293.

137 See Stone Sweet, *Governing with Judges* and *The Judicial Construction of Europe*.

138 See discussion in M. Thatcher and A. Stone Sweet, 'Theory and Practice of Delegation to Non-majoritarian Institutions' (2002) 25(1) *West European Politics* 1.

predictability.[139] Moreover, the fact that the CJEU gives European institutions a much larger margin of discretion in comparison to similar rules adopted by individual Member States demonstrates that it clearly favours a federal (here Union) approach to problem-solving and will not lightly strike down EU rules.[140] This approach is particularly prominent in the field of free movement of goods.[141]

Open questions remain as to why successive treaty reforms have not recognized these most fundamental principles and have failed to grant explicit recognition of the CJEU's ability to engage in constitutional review.[142] To say it with Doreen Lustig and Joseph Weiler: 'A democracy without some form of judicial review is considered deficient. This has certainly been the case in Europe with hardly any exception.'[143] Even though Member States cited lack of support by the public for supremacy as the main reason for limited advances in the Lisbon Treaty, actually the inclusion of explicit provisions recognizing constitutional review powers remains rare in the world.

Further, while the CJEU has yet to fully exert these same powers over Member State courts and their decisions, the CJEU has not shied away from finding that the highest Member State courts have violated EU law, even, for example, where no preliminary reference was made as in the case of *Koebler*.[144] Nonetheless, the Court has yet to affirm that it has the power to review Member State decisions in areas outside the scope of EU law, with *Melloni* restricting the application of Charter rights to

[139] Case 240/78, *Atalanta Amsterdam BV* v. *Produktschap voor Vee en Vlees* [1979] ECR 02137; Case 114/76, *Bela-Mühle Josef Bergmann KG* v. *Grows-Farm GmbH & CO. KG* [1977] ECR 01211; Case C-375/96, *Galileo Zaninotto* v. *Ispettorato Centrale Repressione Frodi – Ufficio di Conegliano – Ministero delle risorse agricole, alimentari e forestali* [1998] ECR I-06629, at [57]–[67]. For varying views on ECJ judicial review, see e.g. G. Davies, 'The European Union Legislature as an Agent of the European Court of Justice' (2016) 54 *Journal of Common Market Studies* 846; R. Widdershoven, 'The European Court of Justice and the Standard of Judicial Review' in S. Lavrijssen, E. H. Ballin and J. de Poorter (eds.), *Judicial Review of Administrative Discretion in the Administrative State* (The Hague 2019) 39.

[140] See also J. Öberg, 'The Rise of the Procedural Paradigm: Judicial Review of EU Legislation in Vertical Competence Disputes' (2017) 13 *European Constitutional Law Review* 248, 249.

[141] Barnard, *The Substantive Law of the EU*.

[142] It should be noted that the Treaty on the Constitution for Europe contained an explicit recognition of supremacy in its text but this reference was dropped for the Lisbon Treaty.

[143] D. Lustig and J. H. H. Weiler, 'Judicial Review in the Contemporary World: Retrospective and Prospective' (2018) 16 *International Journal of Constitutional Law* 315.

[144] Case C-224/01 [2003] ECR I-10239.

situations where EU law applies or where Member States are acting in the sphere of EU law.

The question of constitutional review by the CJEU as such has not played a major role in periphery Member State courts. However, two decisions are perhaps pointing in a different direction and are important to note. First, the *Landova* decision[145] of the Czech Constitutional Court, discussed already with regard to supremacy of Union law, indicates that this particular Member State court was unhappy with the way the CJEU exercised its power of review. The Czech Court was particularly critical that its own determination was set aside by the Court; an act it considered to be *ultra vires* because, in the eyes of the Czech Court, the CJEU had no competence to review Member State constitutional court decisions. The Czech Court was unwilling, in the absence of an open, public, trans-European debate on these matters, to accept the authority of the CJEU. Even though, in most federal structures (with the exception of Switzerland), the judicial review of State acts, regardless of their nature, is accepted as a legitimate process, the Czech Court was unwilling to cede this space to the centre.[146] Second, a similar decision stems from the GFCC. In *Mobilcom*,[147] the German Court had to review whether the *Mangold* line of jurisprudence by the ECJ was an *ultra vires* act of the EU. *Mangold* remains a controversial judgment whereby the ECJ held that a Directive did in fact have direct effect in a horizontal relationship between an employer and an employee because the Directive in question codified a general principle of EU law (here the principle prohibiting age discrimination).[148] The GFCC decided in *Mobilcom* that this decision was not *ultra vires* because it followed normal standards of interpretation. However, the ruling was strongly criticized by a dissenting opinion, strongly criticizing the CJEU for overstepping its boundaries and arguing that Germany should not follow this case because it violated the transfer of sovereignty outlined by the GFCC in its *Maastricht* decision. Although these particular cases demonstrate a challenge to the power

[145] Czech Constitutional Court, Decision of 31 January 2012, Pl. ÚS 5/12, *Slovak Pensions*.

[146] See also A. Hofmann, 'Resistance against the Court of Justice of the European Union' (2018) 14 *International Journal of Law in Context* 258, 265–6.

[147] GFCC, *Mobilcom*, 2 BvR 2661/06 of 6 July 2010, www.bverfg.de/entscheidungen/rs20100706_2bvr266106en.html.

[148] Case C-144/04, *Werner Mangold* v. *Rüdiger Helm* [2005] ECR I-09981. See also D. Petric, 'Game of Courts: A Tale of Principles and Institutions' (2019) 25 *European Law Journal* 273.

of the CJEU by the periphery courts and a continuing concern with regard to the application of federal judicial review in general, the CJEU has nonetheless managed to develop a solid jurisprudence on judicial review.

4.3.3.4 Conclusion as to the Validity of This Obstacle

In conclusion, it is my fundamental claim that, even without explicit reference to formal review powers in the Treaty, the CJEU has long maintained its ability to review legislative decisions of the Union organs and thus engage in constitutional review. While the Court has yet to act fully like a federal court in reviewing Member States' judicial actions, it has greatly advanced the discussion in this field. This said, more often than not, the Court returns important evaluations and decisions to Member State courts to make, in keeping with the preliminary reference jurisdiction of the Court, as distinct from an appellate decision.[149] While a clearer expression of federal review powers would be helpful, the remaining gaps do not actually undermine the general ability of the EU to further constitutionalize. This obstacle has, essentially, been nearly overcome through an informed dialogue between the central European Court and the periphery Member State courts.

4.3.4 Court Jurisdiction vis-à-vis the (Member) States Is Undetermined?

4.3.4.1 Obstacle

An important objection to any constitutionalization process pertains to the perceived lack of any clear definition of jurisdiction between the federal and the federated levels of government.[150] As in any federal polity, this is an important question because it defines the degree and form of federalism. While there are various models that can be followed, each one has more or less a precisely prescribed jurisdiction for the exercise of specific federal powers. The concern of critics, therefore, is that without such precisely defined divisions between the powers of the Union and those of Member States, further constitutional development within the EU would be impossible.

[149] See with further comparisons J. C. Cohen, 'The European Preliminary Reference and U. S. Supreme Court Review of State Court Judgments: A Study in Comparative Judicial Federalism' (1996) 44 *American Journal of Comparative Law* 421.

[150] See discussion in L. F. Goldstein, *Constituting Federal Sovereignty*, ch. 5.

4.3.4.2 Underlying Concepts of Constitutional Development

In many federal systems, the power of the federal court to review acts of federated States is not precisely defined. Some federations have strong unitary courts and thus do not distinguish between different cases, but most federal States also have a separate federated judicial system for the State/provincial level.[151]

As one useful example of a federal State where federal powers were limited, the United States was ultimately founded as a union with limited powers.[152] From the Federalist viewpoint, there were only certain issues over which federal level should have jurisdiction. As James Madison explained:

> They will see, therefore, that in all cases where power is to be conferred, the point first to be decided is, whether such a power be necessary to the public good; as the next will be, in case of an affirmative decision, to guard as effectually as possible against a perversion of the power to the public detriment. That we may form a correct judgment on this subject, it will be proper to review the several powers conferred on the government of the Union; and that this may be the more conveniently done they may be reduced into different classes as they relate to the following different objects: 1. Security against foreign danger; 2. Regulation of the intercourse with foreign nations; 3. Maintenance of harmony and proper intercourse among the States; 4. Certain miscellaneous objects of general utility; 5. Restraint of the States from certain injurious acts; 6. Provisions for giving due efficacy to all these powers.[153]

As the country continued to develop, states found it important to underline in the Tenth Amendment, the so-called 'States' Rights Amendment', that all residual power lies with the states.[154] While it initially served to defend against federal encroachment of state powers, even long after the New Deal, the Tenth Amendment was considered to be stating a truism of any federal state.[155] The central concept was that where and when the

[151] See further N. Aroney and J. Kincaid (eds.), *Federal Countries: Federalists or Unitarists* (Toronto 2017) 524–5.

[152] P. W. Low and J. C. Jeffries, *Federal Courts and the Law of Federal-State Relations*, 4th ed. (New York 1998).

[153] J. Madison, 'The Federalist No. 41' in *The Federalist Papers* (1787–1788).

[154] Ibid. See further H. Murray, *Limiting Federal Powers: The Tenth Amendment* (New York 2019); L. Ackerman, 'Tenth Amendment: The United States' Defining Compromise' (2019) 20(1) *Federalism-E* 44; K. Abrams, 'On Reading and Using the Tenth Amendment' (1984) 93 *Yale Law Journal* 723.

[155] G. Lawson, 'A Truism with Attitude: The Tenth Amendment in Constitutional Context' (2007–2008) 83 *Notre Dame Law Review* 469; S. E. Rush, 'Oh, What a Truism the Tenth

federal level does not have the power to act, it is for the state to have jurisdiction.

That said, it was in only one case prior to the 1990s – *National League of Cities* v. *Usery*[156] – that the US Supreme Court chose to strike down a federal statute because it was seen to violate the state's right to regulate – and even this one case was expressly overturned in *Garcia* v. *San Antonio*.[157] However, since these isolated instances, a Supreme Court of conservative justices has rediscovered the 'meaning' of the Tenth Amendment. As Justice Rehnquist predicted in his dissent in *Garcia*, the Tenth Amendment took on greater importance for cases such as *New York* v. *United States*[158] and *Printz* v. *United States*.[159] In the case of *Reno*, for example, the Supreme Court upheld the federal statute, but only because it did not compel state authorities to act.[160]

It is thus fair, at present, to conclude that 'at least five Justices viewed federalism and the Tenth Amendment as a judicially enforceable limit on Congress's power. The debate continues to be whether the Amendment should be subjected to interpretation by the judiciary or whether its meaning should be determined politically, namely by the legislative branch.'[161]

German experience, in my view, provides another illustrative example of a federal state where federal jurisdiction is regulated explicitly by the Constitution. As noted by Jürgen Adam and Christoph Möllers:

The FCC is explicitly appointed to resolve conflicts between the Federation and the *Länder* (*Bund-Länder-Streit*), or among the *Länder* in the case of alleged breaches of constitutional obligations (Art. 93 section 1 no. 3, 4). The German Constitutional Court also has competence to decide upon the compatibility of state law with federal law or the constitution, as well as the compatibility of federal law with the constitution (see explicitly Article 93 section 1 number 2 GG; this power can become relevant in other kinds of procedures as well). The latter competence includes the power to police whether federal legislation has exceeded the lawmaking power allocated to the federal government. A 'compatibility' decision of the German Constitutional Court can be requested by state governments, by

Amendment Is: State Sovereignty, Sovereign Immunity, and Individual Liberties' (2019) 71 *Florida Law Review*, https://ssrn.com/abstract=3259988.

156 US Supreme Court, *National League of Cities* v. *Usery*, 426 US 833 (1976).

157 US Supreme Court, *Garcia* v. *San Antonio Metropolitan Transit Authority*, 469 US 528 (1985).

158 US Supreme Court, *New York* v. *United States*, 505 US 144, 157 (1992).

159 US Supreme Court, *Mack and Printz* v. *United States*, 521 US 898 (1997).

160 US Supreme Court, *Reno* v. *Condon*, 528 US 149 (2000).

161 Bassett.

one third of the *Bundestag*, or by the federal government. There is also a special procedure of federal character affecting the compatibility of federal statutes with Article 72 section 2 GG.[162]

In my view, this example shows that jurisdiction is frequently less well defined vis-à-vis Member States in a federal polity. Such jurisdiction often requires further translation or definition by relevant courts.

Further, in Switzerland, as Ritaine and Papeil have observed:

> Surprisingly, Article 95 of the Federal Supreme Court Act (LTF), which defines the types of actions brought before the Federal Supreme Court, does not mention cantonal legislation. As a result, the application and judicial control of cantonal law are cantonal competences. This competence follows from Articles 3 and 47 of the Constitution, which obliges the Confederation to respect cantonal autonomy.[163]

In essence, it is only in exceptional cases – where fundamental human rights are threatened – that the Swiss Federal Supreme Court will step in and exercise its power to review cantonal legislation. The Swiss federal polity involves a compromise by which the jurisdiction of federal courts vis-à-vis the Cantons can be exercised only in exceptional circumstances. This is very far from a clearly determined federal court with often-exercised jurisdiction; however, it was clearly not a serious barrier to Swiss constitutionalization.

While different federal systems recognize varying forms and degrees of supremacy of the federal institutions over federated legislation, very few federal systems actually allow detailed review of State/provincial legislation.

4.3.4.3 Related EU Developments

The European Union, at its foundation, was not perceived as an entity of shared competence. Rather, EU Member States were seen as pooling resources and engaging in close cooperation. Few concerns were raised as to Union jurisdiction over Member States, as this was seen as inconceivable – indeed, some of the most eminent EU scholars still describe the EU as a 'constitutional order of States', precluding any such discussion of federal jurisdiction.[164] This obstacle to EU constitutionalization

162 Adam and Möllers, 237, 249.

163 Cashin Ritaine and Papeil, 439, 450.

164 Arnull, Barnard, Dougan and Spaventa; A. von Bogdandy and J. Bast (eds.), *Principles of European Constitutional Law* (Oxford/Portland, OR 2006); K. Lenaerts and J. A. Gutierrez-Fons, 'A Constitutional Perspective' in R. Schütze and T. Tridimas

has triggered lengthy debates in the EU Constitutional Convention itself.[165]

The competence catalogue of the first part of the TFEU has been of assistance in addressing certain aspects of the problem of competing jurisdictions,[166] just as it has helped to clarify matters concerning human rights. Indeed, in other federal structures with competence catalogues, such as Germany and South Africa, the mere existence of such a catalogue has led to an increase in federal decision-making.

Briefly considering this history of the European Union, it is important to remember that prior to the Lisbon Treaty, there was a distinct level of uncertainty about the scope of Union versus Member State competences. The Union was, upon its formation, a community granted with only limited powers,[167] even if the way the CJEU has interpreted these powers has been considered by some to be very expansive.[168] Taking as one example the ground-breaking *ERTA* case,[169] the Court confirmed the Commission's opinion that the exercise of an internal competence had to be mirrored by an external competence so as not prevent Member States from undermining internal Union rules through international treaties. In other words, the Court of Justice assigned jurisdiction here without explicit references in the Treaty text. The Union relied heavily on these competences until the early 1990s.

The impact of the *ERTA* case was clarified and corrected in Opinion 1/94,[170] where the Court found that there could be mixed agreements

(eds.), *Oxford Principles of European Union Law: Volume 1: The European Union Legal Order* (Oxford 2018) 104, 105.

165 The European Convention, Secretariat, Final Report of Working Group V, Brussels, 4 November 2002, CONV 375/1/02.

166 The catalogue distinguishes among exclusive, shared, supportive and CFSP competence. Art. 2(6), TFEU concretizes that the 'scope of and arrangements for exercising the Union's competences shall be determined by the provisions of the Treaties relating to each area'.

167 A. Dashwood, 'The Relationship between the Member States and the European Union/European Community' (2004) 41 *Common Market Law Review* 355.

168 Weiler, for example, described the CJEU ruling on human rights as 'bold judicial activism': J. H. H. Weiler, 'Eurocracy and Distrust: Some Questions Concerning the Role of the European Court of Justice in the Protection of Fundamental Human Rights within the Legal Order of the European Communities' (1986) 61 *Washington Law Review* 1003, 1105.

169 Case 22/70, *Commission of the European Communities* v. *Council of the European Communities (European Agreement on Road Transport (ERTA)* [1971] ECR 00263.

170 Opinion 1/94, Opinion of the Court of 15 November 1994 on the Competence of the Community to conclude international agreements concerning services and the protection of intellectual property [1994] ECR I-05267.

where both the Union and the Member States shared competences and which had to be negotiated and ratified by both. Yet, even with this caveat, the Court ensured that an expansive reading of Union competences was taken right from the outset. Support for this proposition is found by the fact that there are very few cases where the Court has struck down a legislative act for complete lack of competence, as opposed to wrong choice, which is something that occurs all the more frequently. One example is the case of *Tobacco Advertising*,[171] in which Germany prevailed in its arguments that a ban on advertising cannot be based on internal market competence since the Directive does not facilitate but rather prohibits economic activity.

Without naming a principle of conferral, the EEC Treaty in its original version agreed, in Art. 4.1 second paragraph, to a requirement that each European institution would 'act [only] within the limits of the powers conferred upon it by this Treaty'.[172] A more general formulation can be found also in Art. 3b of the Maastricht Treaty, in which the parties agreed that '[t]he Community shall act within the limits of the powers conferred upon it by this Treaty and of the objectives assigned to it therein'.[173] In the Lisbon Treaty, this was finally named and recognized as a principle of conferral, integrated in Art. 5 TEU:

1. The limits of Union competences are governed by the principle of conferral. The use of Union competences is governed by the principles of subsidiarity and proportionality.
2. Under the principle of conferral, the Union shall act only within the limits of the competences conferred upon it by the Member States in the Treaties to attain the objectives set out therein. Competences not conferred upon the Union in the Treaties remain with the Member States.[174]

A second way in which the EU Member States and institutions have tried to address the federal encroachment problem is with reference to the principle of subsidiarity. Subsidiarity (Art. 5.3 TEU) means that

> in areas which do not fall within its exclusive competence, the Union shall act only if and in so far as the objectives of the proposed action cannot be

[171] Case C-376/98, *Federal Republic of Germany* v. *European Parliament and Council of the European Union (Tobacco Advertising)* [2000] ECR I-08419; but see also the failure to convince the court in Case C-380/03, *Germany* v. *European Parliament and Council (Tobacco Advertising II)* [2006] ECR I-11573.

[172] Art. 4(1), Treaty of Rome.

[173] Art. 3b, Treaty of Maastricht on European Union (OJ 1992 C 191 p.1).

[174] Art. 5, TEU.

> sufficiently achieved by the Member States, either at central level or at regional and local level, but can rather, by reason of the scale or effects of the proposed action, be better achieved at Union level.[175]

This provision was included in the Maastricht Treaty at the insistence of the German Chancellor, Kohl, who expressed concern at a perceived 'competence encroachment' by EU institutions. Subsidiarity, prior to Lisbon, had been paid little more than lip service, as the CJEU decided, in a constitutionally significant judgment on the *Working Time Directive*, that if the Council came to the political conclusion that the objectives of the particular action could not be sufficiently achieved by Member States, it was not for the Court to second guess this assessment.[176] Through the Additional Protocol annexed to the Lisbon Treaty on Proportionality and Subsidiarity, it can now be expected that the Court will at least hear arguments based on this principle rather than rejecting them outright.[177]

Similarly, in Europe, prior to Lisbon, the CJEU did not shy away from reading powers into the Treaties.[178] This was the tendency that the Lisbon Treaty drafters tried to curtail through a 'German-style' competence catalogue.[179]

Interestingly, the introduction of a fundamental rights catalogue has revived the debate about Member State competences. The Court of Justice made headlines in the cases of *Melloni* and *Akerberg Franson*, where it decided that Charter rights were applicable whenever Member States were acting in the sphere of EU law.[180] In reality, this

[175] Art. 5, TEU.

[176] Case C-84/94, *United Kingdom of Great Britain and Northern Ireland* v. *Council of the European Union (Working Time)* [1996] ECR I-05755.

[177] One of the first cases in this vein seems to be 'has not stated its third plea in law in detail sufficient as to permit review by the Court of the extent to which national rules could be sufficient to achieve the objective pursued by Directive 2009/12 in a Member State in which the main airport does not reach the minimum size laid down in Article 1(2) of that directive'; ibid., at para. [80]. For an overview of the subsidiarity-related cases to date, see F. Fabbrini, 'The Principle of Subsidiarity' in Schütze and Tridimas, 14–18, https://ssrn.com/abstract=2781845.

[178] F. Wasserfallen, 'The Judiciary as Legislator? How the European Court of Justice Shapes Policy-Making in the European Union' (2010) 17(8) *Journal of European Public Policy* 1128.

[179] Even though it should be mentioned that, for the most part, until the *Environmental Code Case* [1999], the Constitutional Court adopted a very wide reading of the existing catalogue provisions and rarely struck down federal statutes for violation of Länder competences.

[180] Case C-399/11, *Stefano Melloni* v. *Ministerio Fiscal*, Judgment of the Court (Grand Chamber) of 26 February 2013, not yet reported, and Case C-617/10, *Åklagaren* v. *Hans Åkerberg Fransson*, Order of the Court (Grand Chamber) of 7 May 2013, not

means that EU fundamental rights are no longer confined at the Member State level to mere implementation of EU law but rather are also valid when Member States act in the field of applying EU law. This interesting 'federalizing' jurisprudence has its source in the Charter of Fundamental Rights and the fact that, with the Treaty of Lisbon, this document is now legally binding.

In *Opinion 1/09*[181] concerning the possibility of setting up an independent EU patent court with no direct link to the legal order of the Member States or the CJEU, the CJEU, I believe, went one step further here. It declared the proposal to be invalid on the basis that Member State courts have to be regarded as EU courts when they apply EU law and thus the creation of the proposed patent court undermined the role that Member State courts play in the system of judicial protection. The Court held:

> The national court, in collaboration with the Court of Justice, fulfils a duty entrusted to them both of ensuring that in the interpretation and application of the Treaties the law is observed (see Case 244/80 Foglia [1981] ECR 3045, paragraph 16, and Joined Cases C-422/93 to C-424/93 *Zabala Erasun and Others* [1995] ECR I-1567, paragraph 15).

This finding brings the CJEU very close to proclaiming Member State courts as ordinary EU courts.[182] It is important case law, demonstrating that in the instances when Member States act within the sphere of EU competences, they are required to observe EU rules. One of the

yet reported; see also D. Sarmiento, 'Who's Afraid of the Charter? The Court of Justice, National Courts and the New Framework of Fundamental Rights Protection in Europe' (2013) 50 *Common Market Law Review* 1267 and P. Eeckhout 'The EU Charter of Fundamental Rights and the Federal Question' (2002) 39 *Common Market Law Review* 945. This has been widened further by the potential for Charter rights to have horizontal direct effect (provided they pass the three justiciability criteria) in Case C-176/12 *Association de médiation sociale* v. *Union locale des syndicats CGT and Others* January 15, 2014; see also A. Albors-Llorens, 'The Direct Effect of EU Directives: Fresh Controversy or a Storm in a Teacup? Comment on Portgas' (2014) 39(6) *European Law Review* 851.

[181] Opinion 1/09, Opinion of the Court (Full Court) of 8 March 2011 on the draft agreement for the creation of a unified patent litigation system – European and Community Patents Court [2011] ECR I-01137.

[182] R. Baratta 'National Courts as "Guardians" and "Ordinary Courts" of EU Law: Opinion 1/09 of the ECJ' (2011) 38(4) *Legal Issues of Economic Integration* 297, 302. Indeed, such is the political and legal influence of the CJEU that it has led to the establishment of international courts that model themselves operationally on it, providing further centripetal force to Member States' national courts modelling themselves on the CJEU: K. J. Alter, 'The Global Spread of European Style International Courts' (2012) 35(1) *West European Politics* 135.

objections by the CJEU to the accession of the EU to the ECHR[183] concerned the level of review possible for the CJEU versus the potential of review of the European Court of Human Rights (ECtHR). The CJEU defended the view that only in the instances where it holds actual review powers could these powers be exercised by other courts. This demonstrates that the CJEU has continued to be very careful in reviewing the scope of its own powers, remaining fully cognizant of its own jurisdictional limits vis-à-vis Member State legislation.

4.3.4.4 Conclusion as to the Validity of This Obstacle

A constitutional polity does not require clearly defined competences or division thereof at the moment of founding. These competences can develop over time and can be part of a living constitution,[184] and indeed, in some cases, may never be required yet still do not pose a barrier to constitutionalization. The lack of initial clarity is therefore not, in principle, a valid objection to further constitutional development. While rule of law may have different features in different Member States, there is nonetheless a common core. When the CJEU decided in *Van Gend and Loos* that the treaties had formed an autonomous legal order with direct effect for the citizens,[185] it created the common ground for EU Member States to apply and thus rely on EU law directly, rather than merely

[183] Opinion 2/13 of the Court (Full Court) of 18 December 2014 on the draft agreement providing for the accession of the European Union to the Convention for the Protection of Human Rights and Fundamental Freedoms (ECHR).

[184] See US Supreme Court, *State of Missouri* v. *Holland*, 252 US 416 (1920). In this decision, Justice Holmes stated:

> With regard to that we may add that when we are dealing with words that also are a constituent act, like the Constitution of the United States, we must realize that they have called into life a being the development of which could not have been foreseen completely by the most gifted of its begetters. It was enough for them to realize or to hope that they had created an organism; it has taken a century and has cost their successors much sweat and blood to prove that they created a nation. The case before us must be considered in the light of our whole experience and not merely in that of what was said a hundred years ago. The treaty in question does not contravene any prohibitory words to be found in the Constitution. The only question is whether it is forbidden by some invisible radiation from the general terms of the Tenth Amendment. We must consider what this country has become in deciding what that amendment has reserved.

State of Missouri v. *Holland*, at 434.

[185] ECJ, *Van Gend en Loos*.

through implementation of EU legal norms into their own legal order. In *Costa* v. *ENEL*, the Court further strengthened a core of European rule of law by assigning supremacy to these European rules where they existed.[186]

This obstacle to further constitutionalization in terms of *ius*, or the development of a truly common rule of law, stems from the way that current jurisprudence has led to a rather complex 'mixture'. Parts of a subset of some EU rules are, in fact, mainly enforced by EU Member States, while other competences, such as competition and state aid, owe their existence to the European Courts. While it remains to be seen how this catalogue will be interpreted by the European Courts, I find that the suggestion that a federal court must possess clear and uncontested jurisdiction vis-à-vis its own federated authorities, and exercise this jurisdiction often, lacks validity as it is based on a misconception of federalism.

4.3.5 *No Federal Court Kompetenz-Kompetenz?*

4.3.5.1 Obstacle

One of the most challenging obstacles to constitutionalization concerns the question of ultimate jurisdiction over determining jurisdiction, or *Kompetenz-Kompetenz.*[187] In this regard, the German Basic Law declares the Länder to be the bearers of residual legislative power (Art. 30 GG).[188] The question that occupied the GFCC late in 2010 in *Mobilcom* was whether the main source of concern, that is, CJEU jurisprudence, could be a violation of this very important principle. As discussed, the German Court decided that the '*Mangold* judgment of the European Court of Justice does not transgress Community competence in a constitutionally objectionable manner'.[189] The complainants had argued that the wide interpretation of general principles of EU law effectively created an *ultra vires* decision in this case. In other words, the CJEU was assigning itself jurisdiction by relying on general principles.[190] Such an exercise of *Kompetenz-Kompetenz* had been explicitly excluded in the *Maastricht*

[186] ECJ, *Costa*.

[187] See critique by Höreth.

[188] Art. 30 [Division of authority between the Federation and the Länder] reads: 'Except as otherwise provided or permitted by this Basic Law, the exercise of state powers and the discharge of state functions is a matter for the Länder.'

[189] GFCC, *Mobilcom*.

[190] K. Tuori, 'The Pluralism of European Fundamental Rights Law' in S. Douglass-Scott and N. Hatzis (eds.), *Research Handbook on EU Law and Human Rights* (Cheltenham/ Northampton, MA 2017) 35, 41.

decision in 1992. Greater competences for the Court in this sense might require public discourse and debate and thus a greater European public sphere.

4.3.5.2 Underlying Concepts of Constitutional Development

The question of *Kompetenz-Kompetenz* can be considered at the heart of any federal debate. Are federal courts the final arbiter on these matters, with the power to delineate their own powers, or do institutions at the federated level play a significant role?

The Swiss situation provides one interesting and illustrative example. Art. 3 of the new constitution clarifies what had been recognized as the situation in the case law, namely that '[t]he Cantons are sovereign insofar as their sovereignty is not limited by the Federal Constitution; they shall exercise all rights which are not transferred to the Confederation'. In the interpretation of constitutional scholars, Cantons do not have *Kompetenz-Kompetenz*, that is, 'the right to define in their constitutions the distribution of tasks between federal government and themselves. Cantons therefore only have a subsidiary or indirect competence'.[191]

Further, the constitutional experience of the United States provides another interesting example of how the relevance of the *Kompetenz-Kompetenz* question can shift over time. In early US constitutional history, it appears that this matter was initially of grave concern to individual states. However, in the last important constitutional moment of the New Deal, new directions were agreed and, through important decisions concerning the Court, along with significant levels of popular support, the Federal Court gained important constitutional competences.[192] There is no doubt, in my view, that the US Supreme Court has the ability to determine the limits of federal jurisdiction.[193] It is

[191] Cashin Ritaine and Papeil, 439, 449; T. Fleiner-Gerster, 'Problèmes de la souveraineté intérieure et extérieure' in T. Fleiner-Gerster and S. Hutter (eds.), *Federalism and Decentralization* (Fribourg 1987) 64; T. Fleiner-Gerster and A. Misic, 'Föderalismus als Ordnungssprizip der Verfassung' in D. Thürer, J.-F. Aubert and J.-P. Müller (eds.), *Verfassungsrecht der Schweiz* (Zürich 2001) 436.

[192] Ackerman, *We the People: Vol. 2: Transformations.*

[193] On this topic, see E. Delaney, 'Managing in a Federal System without an "Ultimate Arbiter": Kompetenz-Kompetenz in the EU and the Ante-Bellum United States' (2005) 15(2) *Regional and Federal Studies* 225, 227; D. Moull, 'Lessons the EU Should Learn from the Formative Years of the US: Challenges to EU Authority in the Areas of Legitimacy and Interpretive Competence and the Implications for the Conceptualization of the EU' (2004) 51 *Jean Monet Working Papers in Comparative and International Politics*, www.fscpo.unict.it/EuroMed/jmwp51.pdf.

clearly in possession of *Kompetenz-Kompetenz*. Yet, as seminal as this may seem, there was certainly nothing automatic about this development. In the history of the creation and evolution of the US Supreme Court, the jurisdiction over jurisdiction was not one that was easily granted.[194] Rather, it was the outcome of a very difficult series of legal and constitutional struggles.[195] It was not clear in the original discussions whether the state courts and legislatures would defer to the US Supreme Court when it took a role in determining its own federal powers.[196] In many ways, the later introduction of the Tenth Amendment and its chequered constitutional history illustrates this development quite well.[197]

In Germany during the relevant period of constitutionalization, only the federal level possessed *Kompetenz-Kompetenz*, and this has not changed. The federal level has the ability to extend its own competences via formal constitutional amendments, but only if the character of the current constitution is not altered (*Ewigkeitsgarantie* in Art. 79 para. 3 GG). This includes its character as a federal State.

These examples demonstrate that decisions about federal competences are often closely intertwined with questions of supremacy.

4.3.5.3 Related EU Developments

Similar to the German Grundgesetz, the Lisbon Treaty adopted seemingly clear language for the European Union (Art. 5.2 second sentence): 'Competences not conferred upon the Union in the Treaties remain with the Member States.' This clear indication was thought to clarify the position as to whether the Union or the Member States have the competence to determine their competences. So, the starting point for discussions is that this provision allocates, at least in theory, the competence to the Member States. However, in practice and through the development in the case law, the institutions of the Union are responsible for determining the exact limits of Union competences.[198] This is an interesting proposition –

194 Höreth.
195 Delaney; Moull.
196 Moull.
197 Delaney.
198 P. Craig, 'Competence and Member State Autonomy: Causality, Consequences and Legitimacy' (2009) Oxford Legal Studies Research Paper No. 57/2009, http://papers.ssrn.com/soL3/papers.cfm?abstract_id=1474325.

despite the somewhat formalistic affirmation in the Treaties, this area is also, in reality, heavily influenced by the Court of Justice.

The current position by the European Union can be contrasted with the position of those litigants in the *Lisbon* case before the GFCC who argued that '[t]he European Union is provided with the competence to decide on its own competence (*Kompetenz-Kompetenz*) (Art. 48.6 and 48.7 TEU Lisbon; Art. 311, Art. 352 TFEU)'[199] whereas the German Parliament argued:

> The Treaty of Lisbon does not grant the European Union '*Kompetenz-Kompetenz.* The flexibility clause under Article 352 TFEU cannot be understood as an unrestricted competence to extend competences; Article 311 TFEU does not go beyond the current provision on the procurement of own resources. The provisions on the simplified Treaty revision procedure and the provisions that concern the passing over to majority decisions in the Council [Articles 48.6 and 48.7] also do not establish a *Kompetenz-Kompetenz* of the European Union. Rather, the provisions anticipate the respective Treaty amendments. Content and modalities of the decision-making procedures are laid down in a sufficiently determined manner. ... The Member States are said to remain the 'masters of the Treaties' and are said not to have granted the European Union *Kompetenz-Kompetenz.* The principle of conferral is said to continue to apply. The use of the flexibility clause is said to be subjected to substantive requirements and procedural safeguarding mechanisms by the Treaty of Lisbon.[200]

It is clear that through this *Lisbon* judgment, the German Court is laying down further important markers, albeit markers founded upon a particular interpretation of its own country's constitutional experience. In the *Maastricht* judgment, the GFCC had given prior indication that it would not accept a European Union with the power to unilaterally determine and expand its own competence.[201] As such, later in the *Lisbon* judgment, the GFCC underlined that assigning *Kompetenz-Kompetenz* to the EU is incompatible with its country's constitution and, as such, should be considered an insurmountable obstacle to the further constitutionalization of Europe. It recounted:

> The Basic Law does not grant the German state bodies powers to transfer sovereign powers in such a way that their exercise can independently establish other competences for the European Union. It prohibits the

[199] *Lisbon Decision*, at para. [112].
[200] Ibid., para. [142].
[201] Grimm, 'The European Court of Justice and National Courts'.

> transfer of competence to decide on its own competence (*Kompetenz-Kompetenz*) (see BVerfGE 89, 155 <187–188, 192, 199>; see also BVerfGE 58, 1 <37>; 104, 151 <210>). Also a far-reaching process of independence of political rule for the European Union brought about by granting it steadily increased competences and by gradually overcoming existing unanimity requirements or rules of state equality that have been decisive so far can, from the perspective of German constitutional law, only take place as a result of the freedom of action of the self-determined people.[202]

Fundamentally, this demonstrates that, distinct from most federal polities, the German Court outright rejects the possibility that the Union might ever acquire *Kompetenz-Kompetenz.* However, I believe that an important question remains whether this finding is really to be described as accurate. Given Germany's own constitutional development, which experienced a shift from the *Kompetenz-Kompetenz* of the Länder to the federal level, this finding appears doubtful. It simply cannot be ignored that the ruling seems to rest on a technical distinction. Whereas Member States acting collectively have the power to add powers to the European Union, they remain the 'masters of the Treaties'[203] while the European Council and the Council are European institutions. In other words, while currently there is ample provision in the Treaties for even a simplified procedure to amend the Treaties (requiring only ratification by the Member State parliaments as non-EU institutions), the ordinary procedure rests on constitutional conventions and intergovernmental conference as the decisive forum. I believe that it is thus a mere jurisprudence of concepts (*Begriffsjurisprudenz*) question, to dwell upon whether the intergovernmental conference that is tasked with constitutional duties in Art. 48 is actually an EU institution or not.

There is a strong argument that this finding by the German Court could be seen as a major obstacle to further constitutionalization, but I believe that this cannot be the case for two compelling reasons. First, there already exists a multitude of powers conferred on the Union, the contours of which are determined by the CJEU. Second, the Member States acting collectively have the power to award more powers to the Union and even to task Union institutions with further duties, as confirmed in the *Pringle* case. In constitutional practice, it is therefore

[202] GFCC, *Lisbon Decision*, at para. 233.

[203] See K. J. Alter, 'Who Are the "Masters of the Treaty"? European Governments and the European Court of Justice' (1998) 52 *International Organization* 121; K. Sowery, 'The Nature and Scope of the Primary Law-Making Powers of the European Union: The Member States as the "Masters of the Treaties"' (2018) 2 *European Law Review* 205.

possible for the Union to add further powers, when the Council so decides.[204]

4.3.5.4 Conclusion as to the Validity of This Obstacle

My conclusion is that, just as in any federal polity, the EU has the ability to determine the reach and breadth of its own competences. As long as these do not depart from the accepted methods of interpretation that one might prefer to characterize as *Kompetenz-Kompetenz*,[205] in essence, the EU determines the precise limits of its own competence and, thus, this is no real obstacle to further constitutionalization. That Member States, under the ordinary revision procedure, do have the final say does not undermine the Union's *Kompetenz-Kompetenz*. We can be satisfied on this point because, in many federal constitutions, there is a role for the constituent parts to ratify the amendments. This said, the CJEU could insist more explicitly that the power to determine its own competences must be recognized. However, the CJEU is limited in that it cannot review the validity of the Treaties themselves and, in turn, the Union has to rely on the Member States to amend its constitution via an IGC. This does curtail the exercise of the CJEU's *Kompetenz-Kompet*enz and has led some observers to conclude that, in the end, the Union is still firmly Member State driven.[206] The lack of a European public sphere creates a further obstacle for this field. Rather than relying on pan-European debates, such debates of the Court's powers would remain at Member State level without much realistic prospect of change.

However, given the influence and standing of the Court, its influence should not be underestimated. As Stone Sweet concludes:

In some areas, including free movement of goods and sex equality, judges – not governments or legislatures or the Member States – have broadly determined the paths along which institutions evolved. Judicial supremacy partly inheres in the ECJ's status as trustee, partly in the

[204] Uninhibited by a written constitution, the UK government embarked on a Balance of Competences review that tried to analyse which competences should be transferred, taken back or left with the European Union; see www.gov.uk/review-of-the-balance-of-competences. Somewhat surprisingly, and in apparent contradiction of the political nature of the exercise, government officials concluded that, in several areas, more competences for the Union would be helpful.

[205] N. Brando and H. de Schutter, 'Federal Commons' in S. Cogolati and J. Wouters (eds.), *The Commons and a New Global Governance* (Cheltenham/Northampton, MA 2018), 41–4.

[206] Moravcsik, 'Negotiating the Single European Act'; Moravcsik, 'Preferences and Power in the European Community'.

dynamics of the constitutionalization process provoked by the ECJ in the mid-1960s, and partly by the propagation and diffusion of specific techniques of judicial governance, such as those associated with precedent-based balancing standards.[207]

4.4 No Common Criminal Law or Police Force?

4.4.1 Obstacle

Critics argue that the existence of State is defined by its ability to command effective control over its territory and, for this, a police force is indispensable.[208] Should the European Union command its own police force? Should effective governance of a territory not include a common criminal law? The GFCC drew the connection between criminal law and democracy when it ruled that '[w]hat has always been deemed especially sensitive for the ability of a constitutional state to democratically shape itself are decisions on substantive and formal criminal law (1), on the disposition of the police monopoly on the use of force towards the interior and of the military monopoly on the use of force towards the exterior . . .'.[209] It is not clear, as the Court notes, whether the EU has a common criminal law.[210] Significant doubts exist as to whether the EU is even competent to adopt criminal sanctions as part of its First Pillar competences, rather than such decisions being the exclusive domain of the Third Pillar (Justice and Home Affairs), prior to these issues being integrated into the EU Treaties.

[207] Stone Sweet, *The Judicial Construction of Europe*, 235.

[208] S. Puntscher Riekmann, M. Mokre and M. Latzer (eds.), *The State of Europe: Transformations of Statehood from a European Perspective* (Frankfurt 2004). An EU police force was called, for example, by former French Prime Minister Lionel Jospin: K. M. Torbiorn, *Destination Europe* (Manchester 2018) 203–4.

[209] The *Lisbon Decision*, para. [252] continued:

> [T]he fundamental fiscal decisions on public revenue and public expenditure, with the latter being particularly motivated, inter alia, by social-policy considerations (3), decisions on the shaping of circumstances of life in a social state (4) and decisions which are of particular importance culturally, for instance as regards family law, the school and education system and dealing with religious communities (5).

[210] On the current state of EU cooperation police matters, see K. Ambos, *European Criminal Law* (Cambridge 2018) 411–14. On the current forms of EU police cooperation, see M. Joutsen, 'The European Union and Cooperation in Criminal Matters' in M. Natarajan (ed.), *International and Transnational Crime and Justice*, 2nd ed. (Cambridge 2019) 287, 288.

4.4.2 *Underlying Concepts of Constitutional Development*

In many federal polities, police powers are devolved. Argentina's constitutional experience provides one illustrative example. A relatively centralized federal system exists, where provinces have the power to organize their own police systems. Its constitution determines, in sec. 121, that 'Provinces retain for themselves all powers not delegated by this Constitution to the federal Government.' This, in theory, should give Argentinian Provinces a broad sway of exclusive right. Yet, over the decades, only 'matters pertaining to the structure of their respective provincial governments, police and municipal matters, as well as the power to lay and collect direct taxes' have been retained.[211] Thus, to claim that there must be a federal police force is not a convincing argument.

In addition, it is important to stress that these particular powers can and do develop over time. For instance, while the EU still struggles with criticisms that it has no common criminal law or police force, it is almost natural for the United States to accept that there is only ever going to be a very limited federal criminal law. In the United States, most of the recognized crimes are 'state' as opposed to 'federal' crimes, and most police forces are local in nature and quite distinctively not federal.[212] In terms of a federal police force, even the FBI was not founded until 1908 and needed strong political support of 'Progressives' in federal politics, such as Teddy Roosevelt.[213] A central intelligence agency was not founded until 1947, although aspects of this agency existed as somewhat nebulous entities during wartime.[214] From the inception of the United States onwards, there was huge resistance against a federal police force, rooted in the assurance that police powers were local in nature. Indeed, in *The Federalist Papers*, No. 17, Hamilton wrote:

> There is one transcendent advantage belonging to the province of the State governments, which alone suffices to place the matter in a clear and satisfactory light,—I mean the ordinary administration of criminal and civil justice. This, of all others, is the most powerful, most universal,

211 Vítolo, 71, 76.

212 Out of almost 900,000 police officers in 2009, 79 per cent are employed by local government and about 35,000 are working for the FBI. For data on general police officers, see United States Department of Labor, Bureau of Labor Statistics, www.bls.gov/ooh/protective-service/police-and-detectives.htm; for data on the FBI, see www.fbi.gov/about-us/quick-facts.

213 FBI, *The FBI: A Centennial History, 1908–2008* (Washington, DC 2008).

214 National Security Act of 1947, PL 80–235, 61 Stat 496 (1947) (establishing the CIA).

> and most attractive source of popular obedience and attachment. It is that which, being the immediate and visible guardian of life and property, having its benefits and its terrors in constant activity before the public eye, regulating all those personal interests and familiar concerns to which the sensibility of individuals is more immediately awake, contributes, more than any other circumstance, to impressing upon the minds of the people, affection, esteem, and reverence towards the government.[215]

It is thus not surprising that any federal police force was, and to some degree still is, viewed with suspicion by individual states. As is often dramatized, when the Federal Agents arrive, their jurisdiction is frequently questioned and needs to be specifically asserted.

Though many federal countries, such as Germany and Switzerland, now also have federal police forces, these too developed over the decades and only a fraction of the members of the force exist at the Cantonal or Länder levels.[216] In fact, it does not only seem to be that a federal police force is not necessary; as this analysis has shown, a limited enforcement potential is actually standard practice in many federal polities.

4.4.3 Related EU Developments

The CJEU did not remain silent as to whether the Union could adopt criminal law under its Community pillar. In a surprising decision, the Court sided with the Commission against no fewer than sixteen Member States, addressing the case of environmental crimes by deciding that a legislative act under consideration should have been adopted under the Environmental competence, not the Justice and Home Affairs competence.[217]

It is worth asking ourselves: Does the European Union even need a common police force? Under the EU founding treaties, critics pay attention to the fact that there is very little reference to police powers. In fact, from the very beginning, matters such as government services ('exercise of official authority' Art. 51 TFEU) and employment in the public service (Art. 45.4 TFEU) were entirely excluded to allow for, amongst other freedoms, the free movement of workers. Even with the

[215] A. Hamilton, 'The Federalist No. 17' in *The Federalist Papers* (1787–1788).

[216] See description of Swiss Federal Police, International Relations and Security Network, www.isn.ethz.ch/Digital-Library/Organizations/Detail/?ots591=cab359a3-9328-19cc-a1d2-8023e646b22c&lng=en&id=14849.

[217] Case C-176/03, *Commission of the European Communities* v. *Council of the European Union (Environmental Crimes)* [2005] ECR I-07879.

introduction of the Third Pillar (what has come to be called Justice and Home Affairs) in the Maastricht Treaty,[218] the process of erosion is embryonic at best.[219] While Member States may cooperate in these matters, adopting recommendations and even agreeing that Europol will serve as an institution to coordinate inter-Member State police actions, I do not perceive that it is yet possible to argue that Europe's diverse police forces fall under one rule of law. As a side note, however, it is recognized that in matters of exclusive EU competence such as competition law, the Commission has the power to enlist Member State forces in order to support its activities.[220]

The most seminal of all EU developments in this field, however, is the European Arrest Warrant. By prohibiting a substantive review of the matter by the holding State, in my view, Europe can be seen to have embarked on a project in favour of criminal law integration. While some fundamental rights objections do perhaps remain[221] to be tested before the Court of Justice, even the UK, the Member State with the largest Euro-sceptical contingent in its national parliament, did not opt out of the European Arrest Warrant.[222] Further, the Court of Justice, with the entry into force of Lisbon, has added an urgent procedure (PPU) that allows Member State courts to request preliminary references in cases where the defendant is imprisoned.

4.4.4 Conclusion as to the Validity of This Obstacle

While a common criminal law and a common police force are often elements of the composition of a single unitary State,[223] they are by no

218 See Art. 88, TFEU: 'Europol's mission shall be to support and strengthen action by the Member States' police authorities and other law enforcement services and their mutual cooperation in preventing and combating serious crime affecting two or more Member States, terrorism and forms of crime which affect a common interest covered by a Union policy.'

219 M. Bergström and A. J. Cornell, *European Police and Criminal Law Co-operation* (Oxford 2014) 2.

220 B. Perrin, 'Challenges Facing the EU Network of Competition Authorities: Insights from a Comparative Criminal Law Perspective' (2006) 31(4) *European Law Review* 540.

221 O. Pollicino, 'European Arrest Warrant and Constitutional Principles of the Member States: A Case Law-Based Outline in the Attempt to Strike the Right Balance between Interacting Legal Systems' (2008) 9 *German Law Journal* 1313.

222 BBC News, 'MPs Back EU Arrest Warrant in Commons Motion Brought by Labour', 19 November 2014, www.bbc.co.uk/news/uk-politics-30118664.

223 Otherwise the UK, which has two different criminal law systems and no national police force besides Scotland Yard, would not even be considered a State. See Open University,

means conditions *sine qua non* for the existence of a constitutional polity, especially a federal body. Over time, these entities might well develop and become key actors in the federal/State dichotomy and, as the US example proves, this development can safely occur within a constitutional system that provides oversight of the growth of these police agencies. Illustrative examples from Argentina and the United States show that the absence of a unified police force is really no obstacle to constitutionalization. On the contrary, these examples provide proof of the varying ways in which federal entities can develop enforcement powers and/or integrated criminal sanctions that, over time, can become effective tools within the framework of the constitution.

4.5 Lack of a Common and Effective System to Protect Human Rights?

4.5.1 Obstacle

The lack of protection for fundamental rights has often been cited as an obstacle to the constitutional polity of the EU.[224] The apparent lack of human rights protection was in fact part of the early dialogue of the highest courts of the Member States with the CJEU.[225] Further, the absence of clear human rights language distinguishes the European Union from all post-war constitutional entities in continental Europe.[226] Without explicit inclusion of human rights in the European structures, European constitutional development has, for many years, seemed blocked.[227] Indeed, prior to the Lisbon Treaty, it seemed to most observers that reliance on general principles alone made it near impossible to know which human rights could be enforced or defended in the European Courts.

Origins of the Metropolitan Police, 2009, www.open.ac.uk/Arts/history-from-police-archives/Met6Kt/MetHistory/mhFormMetPol.html. It's also been stated, for instance, that 'the EU's lack of coercive power – for example, the absence of an EU police force and the lack of a full set of enforcement powers comparable to those possessed by member states – is often highlighted as one of the criteria distinguishing it from a fully formed nation state': E. Herlin-Karnell, 'The Domination of Security and the Promise of Justice: On Justification and Proportionality in Europe's "Area of Freedom, Security and Justice"' (2017) 8 *Transnational Legal Theory* 79, 81–2.

224 See overview in A. Williams, *EU Human Rights Policies: A Study in Irony* (Oxford 2004).

225 Stone Sweet, *The Judicial Construction of Europe*, 124.

226 R. L. Maddex, *Constitutions of the World* (New York 1996).

227 For a review of the 'constitutional coming-of age' of human rights under the EU framework, see de Búrca, 'The Evolution of EU Human Rights Law'.

4.5.2 Underlying Concepts of Constitutional Development

Many federal polities did not recognize very detailed fundamental rights in their early days.[228] As one illustrative example, in Switzerland, only very few fundamental rights were included in the original Constitution. The level of fundamental rights protection needed to be developed over time by the Federal Court, taking until 1999 for this extensive case law to be codified into the new Constitution.[229]

While, like the oft-critiqued EU founding treaties, many other constitutions have not actually included any explicit human rights protections, the US Declaration of Independence did name certain human rights objectives[230] and the Canadian Charter of Rights and Freedoms was an addition to the constitutional documents of Canada.[231] In the United States, human rights objectives were introduced by way of a Bill of Rights, in the form of amendments to the Constitution very soon after its adoption by the first Congress. Initially, as has been well documented in US Constitutional literature, twelve amendments were adopted, though only the last ten of these were ratified at that time.[232] What is interesting for the purposes of this study is that there was significant debate as to whether to include a Bill of Rights for the United States. Federalists did not see this as being necessary because they did not see the federal government as being in a position to make laws restricting individuals' freedoms.[233] It was further argued that a catalogue of rights might be too limiting, as some rights might be forgotten. Finally, they argued that all states had constitutions in which to protect individual rights in a much more direct and state-specific way. These debates mirror, to an extent, discussions taking place in the EU. Considering

228 'Even in states like Italy or West Germany where constitutional courts were technically empowered to review national legislation in light of constitutional human rights, a study of the case law of the courts discloses that in the 1950s and 1960s high courts were anything but aggressive in protecting fundamental rights': G. Delledonne and F. Fabbrini, 'The Founding Myth of European Human Rights Law: Revisiting the Role of National Courts in the Rise of EU Human Rights Jurisprudence' (2019) 2 *European Law Review* 178.

229 W. Haller, 'The New Swiss Constitution: Foreign and International Influences' (2002) 30 *International Journal of Legal Information* 256.

230 M. P. Zuckert, *Natural Rights and the New Republicanism* (Princeton, NJ 1994) 12.

231 R. A. Sedler, 'Constitutional Protection of Individual Rights in Canada: The Impact of the New Canadian Charter of Rights and Freedoms' (1983) 59 *Notre Dame Law Review* 1191.

232 The original Second Amendment later became the Twenty-Seventh Amendment when a modern ratification movement rediscovered this old rule.

233 A. Hamilton, 'The Federalist No. 84' in *The Federalist Papers* (1787–1788).

that it was founded as an economic integration project and in opposition to a political community that had failed in 1952, the drafters perhaps understandably avoided all human rights language in the original treaties.

Going back to the US example, it was after demands from several states and a successful campaign by James Madison that the Bill of Rights was adopted by the House and the Senate and sent to the states for ratification.[234] While, ultimately, the Bill of Rights was adopted and incorporated into the US constitutional structure, this historical example demonstrates that an expressed Bill of Rights is not the defining factor for human rights protection within a constitutional system and that it can, in fact, be successfully introduced at a later stage.

4.5.3 Related EU Developments

To consider related EU developments in this area, we must look first at one of the initial cases on these issues, that of *Internationale Handelsgesellschaft*, in which the CJEU denied reliance on the fundamental rights of a Member State.[235] In this case, a German company argued that its fundamental rights, protected under the German Constitution, had been violated by an EU act that forfeited a deposit for an export licence. In response, the same case was taken to the GFCC, which rendered the *Solange I* decision.[236] The GFCC, in *Solange I*, found that 'the guarantee of fundamental rights in the Constitution prevails as long as the competent organs of the Community have not removed the conflict of norms in accordance with the Treaty mechanism'.[237] These two contradicting decisions created what commentators have since referred to as a 'dialogue between Member State courts and the European Court'.[238] While, to some extent, the Lisbon Treaty provides a significant end point to this particular objection, as will be discussed in Chapter 5, it is important to examine this concern.

[234] P. Finkelman, 'James Madison and the Bill of Rights: A Reluctant Paternity' (1990) 9 *Supreme Court Review* 301.

[235] Case 11/70, *Internationale Handelsgesellschaft mbH* v. *Einfuhr- und Vorratsstelle fur Getreide und Futtermittel* [1970] ECR 01125.

[236] *Solange I.*

[237] Ibid.

[238] M. A. Pollack, *The Engines of European Integration: Delegation, Agency, and Agenda Setting in the EU* (New York 2003) 177.

The decision in *Solange II*[239] partly laid to rest this matter, when the GFCC held that the Union, through the jurisprudence of the CJEU, had now reached such a level of human rights protection that the GFCC would refrain from reviewing EU acts as to their human rights compatibility.[240] Thus, even though there was no explicit recognition of human rights language in the founding treaties,[241] the CJEU has very little difficulty in reading human rights protection into the treaties by way of general principles 'as they result from the constitutional traditions common to the Member States'.[242] We see this decision now enshrined in Art. 6.3 TEU.[243]

In constitutional terms, human rights were not an explicit part of the legal texts until the Maastricht Treaty of 1992,[244] and, even in Maastricht, the Treaty simply included recognition that human rights form part of the constitutional fabric of the European polity.[245] As such, a crucial gap existed in the protection of common human rights. The lack of a human rights charter even led some commentators to question the value and strength of the CJEU's case law.[246] Interestingly, the Court had also decided itself that the diversity of Member State constitutions could not provide one adequate baseline for the Union's human rights protection. Although many different human rights are protected in the constitutions of Member States, the CJEU found that it could recognize only those rights that were truly 'common' among the Member States.[247] In fact, a recent claim by *Mannesmann Roehrenwerke* was actually denied by the Court with

239 *Solange II.*

240 Ibid.

241 Although, as mentioned by de Búrca, human rights were discussed and considered in the early 1950s by the founding Members of the evolving European Community; see G. de Búrca, 'The Road Not Taken: The EU as a Global Human Rights Actor' (2011) 105 *American Journal of International Law* 649.

242 Case 29/69, *Erich Stauder* v. *City of Ulm – Sozialamt* [1969] ECR 00419.

243 For detailed review, see de Búrca, 'The Road Not Taken'. On the fundamental rights dialogue between the ECJ and the German court, see further C. Rauchegger, 'The Bundesverfassungsgericht's Human Dignity Review: *Solange III* and Its Application in Subsequent Case Law' in L. Violini and A. Baraggia (eds.), *The Fragmented Landscape of Fundamental Rights Protection in Europe* (Cheltenham/Northampton, MA 2018) 94.

244 See Preamble, Treaty of Maastricht on European Union (OJ 1992 C 191 p.1).

245 Ibid.

246 Grimm, *Braucht Europa eine Verfassung?* vol. 60 Siemens Stiftung.

247 Case 29/69, *Erich Stauder* v. *City of Ulm – Sozialamt* [1969] ECR 00419; Case 11/70, *Internationale Handelsgesellschaft mbH* v. *Einfuhr- und Vorratsstelle fur Getreide und Futtermittel* [1970] ECR 01125; Case 4/73, *J. Nold, Kohlen- und Baustoffgroßhandlung* v. *Commission of the European Communities* [1974] ECR 00491.

the reasoning that, although companies enjoy the right to privacy in the German Constitution, it is not clear that such a right should be protected across the entirety of the EU.[248]

Criticism of the EU's ability to protect human rights is arguably now outdated since the declaration of the Charter of Fundamental Rights of the European Union as of 7 December 2000, and as adapted at Strasbourg on 12 December 2007 to have the same legal value as the founding treaties. It is clear that the Charter is now part of the constitutional fabric of the European Union,[249] yet I believe that the role that it will play remains unclear now that it is of legally binding force. While litigants and institutions previously had to prove the existence of a human right in order to appeal for its protection, this need appears to have disappeared – or at least has been confined to extreme cases in which neither the Charter nor the European Convention allows for fundamental rights protection granted by the legal traditions of the Member States.

We are now in a position to observe how the CJEU will apply the Charter. For the first time, in the case of *Volker and Eifert*, the CJEU struck down an EU legislative act for breach of the Charter.[250] This was even more pronounced in *Digital Rights Ireland*.[251] The fact that the CJEU did not hesitate to use Charter rights to strike down EU laws, in my view, suggests that the door has been opened for full constitutional review. Most recently, in *Melloni*[252] and *Ackerberg Fransson*,[253] the CJEU strongly confirmed the impression that fundamental rights are valid and applicable when Member States act in the sphere of EU law. This jurisprudence is unlikely to go unnoticed by the Member State courts and it would be unsurprising if a periphery court objected to this jurisprudence on the basis that it extends the reach of the Charter beyond mere EU acts.[254]

[248] Case T-112/98, *Mannesmannröhren-Werke AG* v. *Commission of the European Communities* [2001] ECR II-00729.

[249] TEU (OJ 2012 C 326 p.1).

[250] Joined Cases C-92/09 and C-93/09, *Volker und Markus Schecke GbR (C-92/09) and Hartmut Eifert (C-93/09)* v. *Land Hessen* [2010] ECR I-11063.

[251] Joined Cases C-293/12 and C-594/12, *Digital Rights Ireland* [2014] EU:C:2014:238.

[252] Case C-399/11, *Stefano Melloni* v. *Ministerio Fiscal*, Judgment of the Court (Grand Chamber) of 26 February 2013, not yet reported.

[253] Case C-617/10, *Åklagaren* v. *Hans Åkerberg Fransson*, Order of the Court (Grand Chamber) of 7 May 2013, not yet reported.

[254] Sarmiento.

It remains open for debate as to whether the critics on this point are now completely disproven. On the basis of the Protocol on the Application of the Charter in the United Kingdom and Poland,[255] some have argued that this provides a direct carve-out for the UK and Poland.[256] However, in my view there is a stronger argument. In essence, the Protocol provides not necessarily for a carve-out but rather, simply, a clarification, as it reiterates provisions already contained in the Charter itself that confine the Charter to the application of EU law. This reading of the Protocol has been recently confirmed by the CJEU in the case of *Saeedi*.[257] Following this case, it appears that we can be satisfied with some certainty that the EU benefits from a common human rights protection. For this reason, in my view there is very little basis for considering this as a continuing obstacle to constitutionalization since the turn of this century.

4.5.4 *Conclusion as to the Validity of This Obstacle*

In conclusion, I have demonstrated how the initial lack of human rights protection might have been considered to have hampered early EU constitutional development. However, as the US example demonstrates, it is feasible for constitutionalization to continue even where human rights protections are a later addendum to an existing constitutional structure. In my view, the later addition of a human rights charter has served this precise function and has put the EU firmly on track – and perhaps even accelerated it further – towards constitutionalization.[258]

[255] Protocol on the Application of the Charter of Fundamental Rights of the European Union to Poland and to the United Kingdom (OJ 2012 C 326 p.313).

[256] E. Defeis, 'The Treaty of Lisbon and Human Rights' (2009–2010) 16 *ILSA Journal of International and Comparative Law* 413, 417; M. Hall, 'Mixed Reaction to "Opt-Out" from EU Charter of Fundamental Rights' (2007) 7 European Industrial Relations Observatory Online, www.eurofound.europa.eu/eiro/2007/07/articles/uk0707049i.htm.

[257] Joined Cases C411/10 and C493/10, *N.S. (C-411/10)* v. *Secretary of State for the Home Department* and *M.E. and Others (C-493/10)* v. *Refugee Applications Commissioner and Minister for Justice, Equality and Law Reform* [2011] ECR I-13905.

[258] Further on EU constitutionalism and fundamental rights, see S. P. Fernandes, 'Fundamental Rights at the Crossroads of EU Constitutionalism: Decoding the Member States' Key(s) to the Charter' (2018) 60 *Revista de Derecho Comunitario Europeo* 677. For a comparative federalism analysis in the field of EU human rights, also see C. I. Nagy, *The EU Bill of Rights' Diagonal Application to Member States Comparative Perspectives of Europe's Human Rights Deficit* (The Hague 2018).

4.6 No Foreign Relations According to the Rule of Law?

4.6.1 *Obstacle*

A further alleged concern is that the new Common Foreign and Security Policy (CFSP) does not follow the rule of law because the Treaties have not vested the CJEU with competency to review decisions in this field.[259] Ensuring compliance with democratic principles in this area is particularly important. As the GFCC declared in the case of *Lisbon*, decision-making in this area had an inextricable link to the realization of democracy.[260] In other words, foreign policy, in the eyes of the German Court, required some form of judicial review.

4.6.2 *Underlying Concepts of Constitutional Development*

How valid is this particular obstacle? Reference to the US federal system provides us with useful illustrative insights. As we have seen in recent US Supreme Court cases on the Guantanamo prison and *habeas corpus*, when it comes to foreign relations, which at their core have an executive function, any type of judicial review is hard fought and even harder won.[261] Foreign relations are firmly within the preserve of the executive in the United States.[262] The judiciary and even the legislature have comparatively fewer competences in this field, while the President can act with broad powers and has wide discretion.[263] The President relies on the Senate to ratify international treaties, though modern American executives have circumvented this obstacle by adopting executive agreements that are based on prior statutory authorizations.[264] This state of affairs is perfectly normal at the federation level.[265] It could even be

[259] L. Bonfield, 'The Foreign Affairs' Power of the European Union: All Hat and No Cattle?' (2011) 20 *Tulane Journal of International and Comparative Law* 123; F. Nicola, 'The European Union 20 Years after Maastricht: Transatlantic Perspectives' (2011) 20 *Tulane Journal of International and Comparative Law* 65.

[260] See GFCC, *Lisbon Treaty*, para. [252].

[261] For example, exceptionally in the US Supreme Court, *Rasul* v. *Bush,* 542 US 466, 487 (2004). See also US Supreme Court, *Boumediene* v. *Bush,* 128 S Ct 2229, 2248 (2008).

[262] US Const. Art. II.

[263] For a review, see L. Henkin, 'The Constitution for Its Third Century: Foreign Affairs' (1989) 83(4) *American Journal of International Law* 713 and E. L. Richardson, 'Checks and Balances in Foreign Relations' (1989) 83(4) *American Journal of International Law* 736.

[264] K. Hall (ed.), *The Oxford Companion to the Supreme Court of the United States*, 2nd ed. (New York 2005) 308.

[265] Ibid.

argued that, at least in part, the US Constitution was adopted because, at the time, conducting foreign relations, despite being mandated under the Articles of Confederation, was not an easy feat.[266] And in comparison to procedure in other countries, the understanding that the US Constitution requires Senate approval to ratify treaties was seen as revolutionary. As Hamilton explained:

> The President is to have power, with the advice and consent of the Senate, to make treaties, provided two thirds of the senators present concur. The King of Great Britain is the sole and absolute representative of the nation in all foreign transactions. He can of his own accord make treaties of peace, commerce, alliance, and of every other description. It has been insinuated that his authority in this respect is not conclusive, and that his conventions with foreign powers are subject to the revision, and stand in need of the ratification, of Parliament. But I believe this doctrine was never heard of, until it was broached upon the present occasion.[267]

These original developments are significant given the recent court cases noted already concerning the exact extent of this presidential power. Experiences from other federal states provide us with similar examples. Provinces in Canada participate in the implementation of international norms and maintain jurisdiction over their areas of competence, although they do not always have a direct say in international negotiations, with the recent exception of an invited seat from the EU at the trade negotiations for the Canada–EU Trade Agreement (CETA). While there is an obligation to consult, it is difficult to challenge federal actions in this regard. Germany, as we have seen, has long adopted the so-called Landau Agreement under which German Länder refrain from using their external relations powers in fields of their competence under the condition that the Bundesrat (their representative organ at the federal level) is consulted early and is given a say in the ratification process of the new international treaty.[268] This demonstrates that, in many federal polities, external relations are not exclusive to the government alone but take place with the participation of Member States in the area of their jurisdiction.

[266] Richardson.
[267] A. Hamilton, 'The Federalist No. 69' in *The Federalist Papers* (1787–1788).
[268] On the interesting ramifications and for their interaction with the EU, see C. Panara, 'In the Name of Cooperation: The External Relations of the German Länder and Their Participation in the EU Decision-Making' 2010 6(1) *European Constitutional Law Review* 59.

4.6.3 *Related EU Developments*

The CJEU has competence to determine only whether a CFSP decision violates Union competences in other fields in accordance with Art. 40 TEU. This provision appears to be somewhat cryptic in fashion. It states:

> The implementation of the common foreign and security policy shall not affect the application of the procedures and the extent of the powers of the institutions laid down by the Treaties for the exercise of the Union competences referred to in Articles 3 to 6 of the Treaty on the Functioning of the European Union. Similarly, the implementation of the policies listed in those Articles shall not affect the application of the procedures and the extent of the powers of the institutions laid down by the Treaties for the exercise of the Union competences under this Chapter [on CFSP].[269]

The CJEU (or, as it was then, the ECJ) had occasion under the old law to interpret this provision and did so with significant attention in the *ECOWAS* decision. Of course, this case did not mean that the Court would suddenly gain competence over external relations; instead, it decided that it had the power to review compliance with Art. 40 TEU. In other words, the CJEU plays the role of guardian against encroachment of the Union competences against CSFP measures adopted exclusively by the Member States in Council. Interestingly, the CJEU struck down a CFSP for the collection of small arms and light weapons in the ECOWAS region because part of the mission could also be achieved under development cooperation.[270] Even though the Court concluded in *Rosneft* that the exclusion of the Court's jurisdiction in the field of CFSP should be interpreted strictly,[271] it is still fair to conclude that repeated attempts by litigants to ask for a review of foreign policy have not been successful, as would be the case in most countries.[272]

The GFCC, however, would be very wary of this line of case law because it considers foreign relations, such as deployment of the military,

[269] Art. 40, TEU.

[270] Case C-91/05, *Commission of the European Communities* v. *Council of the European Union (ECOWAS)* [2008] ECR I-03651.

[271] Case C-72/15, *PJSC Rosneft Oil Company* v. *Her Majesty's Treasury and Others.* M. Kuisma, 'Jurisdiction, Rule of Law, and Unity of EU Law in Rosneft' (2018) 37 *Yearbook of European Law* 3; S. Poli, 'The Common Foreign Security Policy after Rosneft: Still imperfect but Gradually Subject to the Rule of Law' (2017) 54 *Common Market Law Review* 1799.

[272] M. Cremona, 'The Position of CFSP/CSDP in the EU's Constitutional Architecture in S. Blockmans and P Koutrakos (eds.), *Research Handbook on the EU's Common Foreign and Security Policy* (Cheltenham/Northampton, MA 2018) 5, 11.

to be one of the core elements of a sovereign state. This approach by the Court can be gleaned from the *Lisbon* decision.[273] In my view, while federal polities often concentrate competence for foreign relations at the federal level, many do allow the federated level to participate. It remains troubling that the German Court does not see that such participation is pertinent for the European Union, but ultimately this concern is not particularly valid.

4.6.4 *Conclusion as to the Validity of This Obstacle*

Fundamentally, this criticism cannot stand. From the discussions, it is clear that within the EU judicial review of foreign policy, decisions are a constitutional rarity – if they even exist at all.[274] This is a general practice in any federal entity and therefore clearly cannot be a requirement for European constitutionalization. Rather, it is a misconception that foreign relations must be entirely governed by the federal level to be legitimate.

4.7 Key Factors for the *Ius* Dimension of European Constitutionalization

As we have seen, decisions that point to the existence of a common rule of law in Europe are becoming increasingly evident. Through my analysis of federal constitutional history, it has become clear that a single rule of law is not a necessary condition to begin the process of constitutionalization. By reflecting on the US experience, federated systems can function even in the absence of a common rule of law. In the early US Republic, the US Supreme Court itself was a weak establishment located within a weaker federal system.[275] During this time, states had their own criminal laws, which reflected their unique histories and societal concerns.[276] States – and localities within their territory – had police forces that were all charged with enforcing criminal laws without any reference to the federal

[273] GFCC, *Lisbon Treaty*.

[274] See in greater detail G. Butler, *Constitutional Law of the EU's Common Foreign and Security Policy: Competence and Institutions in External Relations* (Oxford 2019).

[275] G. Haskins and H. Johnson, *History of the Supreme Court of the United States: Foundations of Power, John Marshall 1801–15* (New York 1981).

[276] See, for example, A. Goldstein, 'History, Homosexuality, and Political Values: Searching for the Hidden Determination of Bowers v. Hardwick' (1987) 97 *Yale Law Journal* 1073; C. Mooney and M.-H. Lee, 'The Influence of Values on Consensus and Contentious Morality Policy: U.S. Death Penalty Reform 1956–82' (2000) 62(1) *Journal of Politics* 223.

government.[277] Indeed, from the time of the American Revolution onward, we see states with their own militias[278] and in some cases even their own navy, which in peacetime served the interests and commands of State officials.[279] It was not until the Civil War that state militias were largely replaced by the US Army, Navy and National Guard, and the term itself was re-interpreted as referring to all arm-bearing citizens.[280] Similarly, the US Bill of Rights, which is now regarded as a fundamental component of US constitutional law, was added later as a series of amendments to the US Constitution.[281] The debates surrounding its adoption revealed a deep chasm in concepts of federal governmental function between representatives of the original founding states.[282] Indeed, the frequent invocation of the dualist nature of federal sovereignty can serve as exemplar for understanding the complex evolution of the rule of law in the European Union.

4.7.1 Obstacles Overcome Early in Comparative Constitutional Development and Early in EU Constitutional Development

Several of the fundamental constitutional obstacles discussed early in this chapter have already been addressed in early EU constitutional

277 For a review of the US police structure, see A. Reiss, 'Police Organization in the Twentieth Century' (1992) 15 *Crime and Justice* 51.

278 One of the most important debates at the US Constitutional Convention concerned the existence of these state militias. While it was clear that they would not be abolished, their exact relationship with the US Army was unclear. This debate was ultimately settled in Art. 1, sec. 8 of the US Constitution, which provides that Congress has the power:

> To provide for calling forth the Militia to execute the Laws of the Union, suppress Insurrections and repel Invasions; To provide for organizing, arming, and disciplining, the Militia, and for governing such Part of them as may be employed in the Service of the United States, reserving to the States respectively, the Appointment of the Officers, and the Authority of training the Militia according to the discipline prescribed by Congress.In other words, States maintained the right to appoint officers and train their militias in accordance with a federal standard for their operation. For a review of the evolution of the US Militia's legal status with respect to the Federal State, see J. N. Heath, 'Exposing the Second Amendment: Federal Preemption of State Militia Legislation' (2001–2002) 79 *University of Detroit Mercy Law Review* 39.

279 R. A. Epstein 'Executive Power, the Commander in Chief, and the Militia Clause' (2005–2006) 34 *Hofstra Law Review* 317, 323.

280 S. T. Ansell, *Legal and Historical Aspects of the Militia* (New Haven, CT 1917) 479.

281 B. Schwartz, *The Great Rights of Mankind: A History of the American Bill of Rights* (New York 1977).

282 Ibid.

development. The main example here is supremacy. While the US Constitution contains a supremacy clause, this needed to be exerted over time in the courts. On the other hand, while the EU founding treaties did not contain any hint of supremacy, this notion was found early in the case law of the CJEU. We have seen EU judges move from a specialist legal review to a functionally better constitutional review of Member State laws and EU legislative acts. This ability of courts to review democratically adopted laws is a confirmation of a constitutional structure rather than an argument against the rule of law – or, worse, the constitutional nature of the polity. But while recognizing the difficulties this inevitably brings, the principle that a 'new legal order' such as the EU should evaluate democratic decisions against its own founding documents has been affirmed strongly over the decades of EU integration. However, in my view, the central criticism of European constitutionalization is the question of who is the final arbitrator for determining competences. While the GFCC in its *Lisbon Decision* reiterated its claim to that power,[283] it is clear from our analysis that in both the United States and the EU the mere existence of an independent court is a de facto answer to the question. Both the US Supreme Court and the CJEU have claimed to establish the right to determine the limits of their own respective powers.

4.7.2 Obstacles Overcome through Evolution of Federal Polities, which Are Evolving over Time in the EU

Several of the fundamental objections to EU constitutionalization, such as the lack of human rights provisions, evolved in the United States and other countries over time and have also now evolved in the EU. In my view, federal institutions can and do develop and become increasingly more centralized over time.[284] The role of the US Supreme Court has matured from an early, limited use of constitutional review to a powerful force of constitutional change. The development of the CJEU may be more gradual but, in the end, it may be similar. It used certain minor issues to express itself on more fundamental, 'constitutional' issues.[285] It slowly increased its jurisdiction and, in this incremental manner,

283 *Lisbon Decision*, para. [233].

284 For instance, with the exception of Canada, this was found in the study by P. Dardanelli and others, 'Dynamic De/Centralization in Federations: Comparative Conclusions' (2019) 49 *Publius: The Journal of Federalism* 194.

285 See analysis of Weiler, 'The Transformation of Europe'.

achieved 'constitutional' changes, especially with respect to the role of the Member States and their courts. Every federal project struggles to define the competences of different levels of government. The United States has shown, through the different constitutional moments in US history,[286] that this balance can shift away from the federated entities towards the federal level and, perhaps equally disconcerting, it can also shift back. A key issue for the concept of federalism is the jurisdiction of the Federal Court vis-à-vis the (Member) State. This has been heavily examined in the jurisprudence and analysis of the legal and political academic literature. While the CJEU has been cautious about Member States' actions, it has proceeded to strike down cases of community action in violation of the treaty. Partly at least, this is due to the processes involved. The way to enforce EU law vis-à-vis a Member State was the infringement procedure by other Member States (now Art. 259 TFEU, former Art. 227 TEC)[287] or the infringement procedure initiated by the Commission (now Art. 258 TFEU, former Art. 226 TEC).[288] Finding this to be a rather limiting approach to enforcement of EU law, twice the CJEU expanded its jurisdiction. First, it decided on the question of EC law supremacy, that is, the fact that EC law trumps conflicting national law, even if the national parliament has expressed itself on the issue. Second, it decided that EC law is directly applicable, that is, that preliminary reference procedures by national courts can be based on the sole fact of national noncompliance with EC law. The Court later enhanced this decision but confirmed that even a conflicting national constitutional law is required to comply with EU law. The incremental influences of two Court systems leading to strikingly similar outcomes is, as I see, an interesting result.

286 Ackerman, *The Future of Liberal Revolution*; Ackerman, *The Decline and Fall of the American Republic.*

287 A Member State which considers that another Member State has failed to fulfill an obligation under this Treaty may bring the matter before the Court of Justice. Before a Member State brings an action against another Member State for an alleged infringement of an obligation under this Treaty, it shall bring the matter before the Commission. The Commission shall deliver a reasoned opinion after each of the States concerned has been given the opportunity to submit its own case and its observations on the other party's case both orally and in writing. If the Commission has not delivered an opinion within three months of the date on which the matter was brought before it, the absence of such opinion shall not prevent the matter from being brought before the Court of Justice.

288 If the Commission considers that a Member State has failed to fulfill an obligation under this Treaty, it shall deliver a reasoned opinion on the matter after giving the State concerned the opportunity to submit its observations. If the State concerned does not comply with the opinion within the period laid down by the Commission, the latter may bring the matter before the Court of Justice.

We have seen that the selection process of justices influences the constitutional position of the respective court. A more detailed examination of the constitutional function of the selection process and the CJEU as a political actor[289] has provided the background for understanding the current European constitutional process, as well as the strengths and weaknesses of the new European constitution. Selection of justices is very different in the United States and in Europe, and current constitutional debates are not likely to result in a change to the currently inconsistent procedure. Interestingly, I believe that it might be the EU situation on this point that has advantages; it does not become incredibly political to the point where appointments become close to impossible. Because justices of the CJEU are selected from each Member State for a term of six years with a partial replacement every three years,[290] this dynamic is wholly different from the selection process of the US Supreme Court. To take but one example, there is almost no opportunity to nominate politically radical justices to the CJEU because no majority decision exists within the Council and the aim is in fact to establish a climate of consensus. Different again from the procedure of the US Supreme Court is the fact that not only are there no dissents by the CJEU but the writers of the judgment are unknown except for the Advocate General's opinion. This makes many judgments, and in particular those that constitute compromises among the European judges, very difficult to read and understand, even creating incentives for litigation that were not intended. However, it also contributes to the development of a unique jurisprudence, founded on greater coherence in constitutional interpretations.

No constitution deserves its name without provisions to secure the protection of human rights. However, the level of comfort with potential

[289] See Stone Sweet, *Governing with Judges*, ch. 6.

[290] Art. 253 TFEU (former Art. 223 TEC):

> The Judges and Advocates-General of the Court of Justice shall be chosen from persons whose independence is beyond doubt and who possess the qualifications required for appointment to the highest judicial offices in their respective countries or who are jurisconsults of recognised competence; they shall be appointed by common accord of the governments of the Member States for a term of six years.
>
> Every three years there shall be a partial replacement of the Judges and Advocates-General, in accordance with the conditions laid down in the Statute of the Court of Justice.
>
> The Judges shall elect the President of the Court of Justice from among their number for a term of three years. He may be re-elected.

interference by the polity is a matter that develops over time, as the US constitutional experience illustrates. The eventual introduction of human rights protections in the form of a US Bill of Rights is understandable, especially in circumstances where the founders were convinced that this new entity would not be empowered to violate individual citizens' rights. The EU has employed a very similar argument to that of the United States for the omission of human rights protections in the original treaties. It was only after constitutional dialogues in the courts of several Member States, such as the *Solange I* decision[291] in Germany, that human rights concerns were taken seriously at the EU level. In the United States, the precise protection of human rights still varies today due to differences between states; a defining feature of a federal structure.

An interesting feature – again more in line with other constitutional entities – is the new role that the law plays in the foreign relations of both the European Union and the United States. Given that foreign relations served as one of the very reasons for the formation of the US Constitution in the first place, as it did for the European Union,[292] this is an interesting tendency and arguably confirms that constitutionalization is occurring rather than disproving its existence.

[291] GFCC, *Solange I*.

[292] It was one of the explicit objectives in the Laeken Declaration on the Future of the European Union (2001) for the EU Constitutional Convention to strengthen its international role:

> Europe's new role in a globalised world – Beyond its borders, in turn, the European Union is confronted with a fast-changing, globalised world. Following the fall of the Berlin Wall, it looked briefly as though we would for a long while be living in a stable world order, free from conflict, founded upon human rights. Just a few years later, however, there is no such certainty. The eleventh of September has brought a rude awakening. The opposing forces have not gone away: religious fanaticism, ethnic nationalism, racism and terrorism are on the increase, and regional conflicts, poverty and underdevelopment still provide a constant seedbed for them. What is Europe's role in this changed world? Does Europe not, now that it is finally unified, have a leading role to play in a new world order, that of a power able both to play a stabilising role worldwide and to point the way ahead for many countries and peoples? Europe as the continent of humane values, the Magna Carta, the Bill of Rights, the French Revolution and the fall of the Berlin Wall; the continent of liberty, solidarity and above all diversity, meaning respect for others' languages, cultures and traditions. The European Union's one boundary is democracy and human rights. The Union is open only to countries which uphold basic values such as free elections, respect for minorities and respect for the rule of law.

In this chapter, and the two chapters preceding this, I have been able to dispel several fundamental objections to EU constitutionalization on the basis of 'no single rule of law', by examining early and some more recent comparative constitutional experiences. While we have seen similarities in the areas of supremacy of federal law, there are significant differences in the areas of enforcement and the ability to mandate the action of federal institutions. In the EU, as my analysis shows, this area remains underdeveloped. Further, the origin of members still plays an important role in the appointment decision to EU institutions (here the new 'EU' judge for the ECtHR will play an integrating role, since only one judge will represent the entire Union). While there remain limitations in these two areas, I think that a common EU public space would help to overcome these. The appointment of judges could be debated on an EU-wide scale (as is currently the case only with regard to Commissioners) and the usefulness of supremacy and *Komptenz-Kompetnez* could be debated involving the European public.

An important outstanding question remains, however, and this is the interaction of different elements of the constitution. But the real question to ask is whether the lack of certain elements can really mount a persuasive argument against further constitutionalization or whether it simply suggests the need for further constitutional reform of the European Union as a 'constitutionalizing' polity? In essence, the lack of adaptive mechanisms at the European level hampers any higher-level law-making that relies on the federated level of the EU.

5

Addressing the Legal Obstacles to EU Constitutionalization

5.1 Introduction

In Chapter 1, by way of brief reminder, I introduced the European Union's historical development, highlighting the constitutional underpinnings of the current successive economic, social and political crises in Europe. After summarizing relevant literature, my goal was to outline and analyse an increasingly constructive series of judicial dialogues in Europe, which I believe has brought to light a number of perceived obstacles to three key *demos*, *civitas* and *ius* dimensions of European constitutionalization.

Having identified these obstacles, in Chapters 2, 3 and 4, I went on to determine which of these obstacles remained valid once the underlying misconceptions found in the jurisprudence had been examined and the invalid (or 'already addressed') concerns had been discounted. Europe's current fundamental constitutional weakness is the gaping absence of a truly European public space for debate, political discussion and legitimate pan-European policy compromise. Its corollary key challenges are, inter alia, the lack of acceptance of a more pragmatic number of 'working' languages, which continues to block European *demos*; the lack of effective and democratic unitary elections and truly trans-European political parties, which continues to inhibit the development of European *civitas*; and continuing weaknesses in the selection of judges and the recognition and defence of *Kompetenz-Kompetenz* by the central courts, which continue to stymie European *ius*.

In this chapter, not only will I discuss and build upon the analysis presented in the preceding three chapters but I will also turn to analyse the one major remaining obstacle and critical continuing deficiency in the EU constitutionalization process and its corollaries. I conclude this chapter with solid proposals for constitutional strategies based on adaptive mechanisms to overcome this last remaining issue.

First, what is the key remaining chink in Europe's constitutional armour? Fundamentally, Europe's most important remaining constitutional weakness is the lack of a common European public sphere and that this is as a result of the elite-driven nature of Europe's origins. Here, I aim to demonstrate how this deficiency is compounded by, and continues to confound, the ability of Europe to overcome the remaining related minor obstacles to the constitutional development of a more cohesive European *demos*, *civitas* and *ius*.[1] While the existence of this remaining fundamental obstacle and its corollaries may appear to suggest that further constitutionalization of Europe is impossible, my findings and conclusions are much more nuanced, building on the detailed analysis of more than a decade of European jurisprudential developments, tracking and analysing over 240 decisions of the CJEU and the Member State courts, and taking into account illustrative examples from the early transitions of other federal polities. Indeed, there is a strong relationship between overcoming this major obstacle and its corollaries, showing that to address this issue in a manner that can endure will make a difference in resolving the continuing succession of EU constitutional crises.

Adopting this deeply nuanced understanding of the judicial construction of Europe, which builds on recent legal scholarship,[2] I find that the most recent case law in Luxembourg (the 'centre') and in key Member States (the 'periphery') has led to new developments in the constitutional dialogue since the Lisbon Treaty entered into force in 2009. In light of this dialogue, I believe that although constitutionalization through incremental constitutional change is currently occurring, this last major persistent and systemic obstacle of a lack of a common European public sphere continues to confound and frustrate attempts to overcome other related challenges. Specifically, it is my claim that the absence of a European common public space is not a question of misinterpretation and cannot simply be overcome by minor tweaks or even constitutional design. Something more is required. What role, then, can Europe's courts and jurisprudence play in addressing this remaining obstacle as we move steadily forward towards Europe's Second Constitution? In particular, I will consider what more needs to be done, including possible test cases that could be brought, to overcome this obstacle.

[1] See Chapters 2, 3 and 4.
[2] Stone Sweet, *The Judicial Construction of Europe*, xiii, 279.

One of the key questions addressed in this chapter is whether, despite case law and treaty design, the remaining identified obstacle could be overcome by constitutional practice.[3]

Linking the more abstract discussions in Chapter 1 with the research outcomes presented in Chapters 2, 3 and 4, in this chapter I bring the elements of the book together, focusing on what I believe the research findings and analysis can contribute to a more nuanced understanding of Europe's constitutional development and recommendations for future directions. Specifically, in this chapter, I will:

1. evaluate the different dimensions of European crises;
2. summarize the analysis of key constitutional obstacles, analyse the major remaining obstacle of lack of a common European public space and its corollary challenges, and consider the inter-connections between these various obstacles;
3. highlight the crucial contributions that the lack of a EU public space has made to the current series of European crises;
4. analyse the need for a constitutional moment in Europe and also consider possible adaptive mechanisms, highlighting a constitutionally transformative role of the dialogue between courts;
5. consider the way forward, advancing specific steps, including test cases, that could be brought to strengthen the EU public sphere, through European case law; and
6. summarize key findings from the research and analysis, laying foundations for the conclusions presented in Chapter 6.

5.2 Dimensions of European Crises

5.2.1 Europe's Economic and Financial Crises

The most recent 'Euro crisis'[4] began as a financial crisis among banks invested in the US markets. When it became clear that eurobonds issued by different euro Member States did not benefit from a joint financing mechanism, levels of risk were higher than expected and the crisis was

[3] I am especially grateful to Professor Bruce Ackerman for raising this question.

[4] Beblavý, Cobham and Ódor; Arestis and Sawyer; G. Moro, *The Single Currency and European Citizenship: Unveiling the Other Side of the Coin* (London 2013); A. Mody, *Eurotragedy: A Drama in Nine Acts* (Oxford 2018); W. R. Cline, *Managing the Euro Area Debt Crisis* (New York 2014); Hinarejos, *The Euro Area Crisis in Constitutional Perspective.*

compounded.[5] The consequences for Europe were dramatic. As Miroslav Beblavy noted, '[p]olicymakers on both sides of the Atlantic found themselves in a difficult situation after hitting the effective lower bound for nominal interest rates. They had to chart unknown waters using non-standard monetary policy measures, including quantitative and credit easing'.[6] As Thorvardur Tjörvi Olafsson and Thórarinn G. Petursson explain: 'Our results suggest that the macro channel played a prominent role [in triggering the Euro Crisis], as domestic macroeconomic imbalances and vulnerabilities are found to be crucial in determining the incidence and severity of the crisis.'[7] Once it was clear in the financial markets that different euro Member States had very diverse economic conditions and prospects of delivering on euro debt, concerns began to circulate.[8] Suddenly, according to Adrian Blundell-Wignall and Silvia Merler/Jean Pisani-Ferry, individual euro members came under increased scrutiny, affecting the value of the common currency.[9] The Council of Euro Finance Ministers offered a bail-out package to Ireland and another to Greece.[10] This euro rescue package, while of doubtful legality,[11] was provided and later converted into a European Stability Mechanism (ESM), a permanent euro rescue fund, through the ESM Treaty, which in turn was part of the European Growth and Stability Pact.[12]

For some, the crisis resembled a dark constitutional moment for the European Union.[13] The mere fact that an economic solution was impossible under the existing framework demonstrates that underlying issues

[5] Lane, 'The European Sovereign Debt Crisis', 52; D. Hodson and U. Puetter, 'The Euro Crisis and European Integration' in M. Cini and N. Pérez-Solórzano Borragán, *European Union Politics*, 5th ed. (Oxford 2016) 365, 367.

[6] Beblavý, Cobham and Ódor, 6.

[7] T. T. Olafsson and T. G. Petursson, 'Weathering the Financial Storm: The Importance of Fundamentals and Flexibility' in Beblavý, Cobham and Ódor, 23, 24.

[8] Arestis and Sawyer.

[9] Blundell-Wignall, 201–2 and S. Merler and J. Pisani-Ferry, 'Sudden Stops in the Euro Area' (2012) 3(3)*Review of Economics and Institutions* 23.

[10] See P. R. Lane, 'The Irish Crisis' in Beblavý, Cobham and Ódor, 59, 61.

[11] Hofmeister, 103, 104.

[12] C. Calliess, 'From Fiscal Compact to Fiscal Union? New Rules for the Eurozone' (2011–2012) 14 *Cambridge Yearbook of European Legal Studies* 101, 103; J. Atik, 'From No Bailout to the European Stability Mechanism' (2015–2016) 39 *Fordham International Law Journal* 1201.

[13] G. Teubner, 'A Constitutional Moment? The Logics of 'Hitting the Bottom' in P. F. Kjaer, G. Teubner and A. Febbrajo (eds.), *The Financial Crisis in Constitutional Perspective: The Dark Side of Functional Differentiation* (Oxford 2011). See review by Georgosouli; K. Tuori, 'The Eurozone Crisis as a Constitutional Crisis' in M. Fichera, S. Hänninen

of a constitutional nature were also at play. More significantly, the pragmatic nature of Member States' responses to the financial crisis exemplifies a wider approach to Europe's constitutional dilemmas.

There are strong arguments to say that the Court of Justice in *Pringle* endorsed this crisis management approach, to the detriment of further democratic and other legitimacy in the Union.[14] As Callies and Hinarejos explain, both of these financial stabilization instruments, that is, the Stability Pact and the ESM, were adopted as intergovernmental agreements, as the UK Prime Minister had vetoed the package because euro Member States had refused his request to safeguard the UK financial industry from future common European banking regulations.[15] Again, legal uncertainties arose, which were finally resolved in the *Pringle* judgment by the Grand Chamber of the CJEU[16] and the interim *ESM* judgment of the GFCC.[17] With a somewhat flexible approach to legal interpretation, the Courts were able to sustain the ESM measures, but commentators note that this may have come at some cost. The constitutional dimensions of the arrangements remain problematic, impacting the legitimacy of both the measures and the institutions that have affirmed their constitutionality. The ESM has also been criticized from an accountability perspective.[18] As Mark Dawson and Floris de Witte explain, the problem lies in the fact that the decisions of the ESM are not taken in accordance with accepted Council or Commission voting standards; rather, they are taken, not unlike in the World Bank, according to contribution.[19] This creates a situation where, for example, Germany holds 27.15 per cent of the overall vote in the ESM. The ESM, though

and K. Tuori (eds.), *Polity and Crisis: Reflections on the European Odyssey* (London/New York 2016) 3; P. Schlosser, *Europe's New Fiscal Union* (Cham 2019) 16, 186.

[14] G. Beck, 'The Legal Reasoning of the Court of Justice and the Euro Crisis: The Flexibility of the Court's Cumulative Approach and the Pringle Case' (2012) 20 *Maastricht Journal of European and Comparative Law* 635.

[15] Calliess, 101, 102 and A. Hinarejos, 'Fiscal Federalism in the European Union: Evolution and Future Choices for EMU' (2013) 50(6) *Common Market Law Review* 1621, 1632.

[16] Case C-370/12, *Thomas Pringle* v. *Government of Ireland, Ireland and the Attorney General*, Judgment of the Court (Full Court) of 27 November 2012 [*Pringle*]. On this case, see P. Craig, 'Pringle: Legal Reasoning, Text, Purpose and Teleology' (2013) 20 *Maastricht Journal of European and Comparative Law* 3; V. Borger, 'The ESM and the European Court's Predicament in Pringle' (2013) 14 *German Law Journal* 113.

[17] GFCC, *ESM Treaty*, 2 BvR 1390/12, 2 BvR 1421/12, 2 BvR 1438/12, 2 BvR 1439/12, 2 BvR 1440/12, 2 BvE 6/12, etc. of 12 September 2012.

[18] D. Howart and A. Spendzharova, 'Accountability in Post-Crisis Eurozone Governance: The Tricky Case of the European Stability Mechanism' (2019) 57 *Journal of Common Market Studies* 894.

[19] Dawson and de Witte.

advised by the European Central Bank (ECB), is not bound by its unanimity requirements and can thus set bail-out conditions that could violate other EU norms.[20] The Commission denies such dangers since all ESM conditions are just recommendations to the Member States who would like to rely on the fund. This is constitutionally questionable, since Member States would rely on the fund only if they experience a grave financial crisis and thus would not have alternative forms of financing. This form of crisis management seems to suggest that sweeping treaty changes, or even setting up new arrangements to achieve European integration objectives, are the proper and only ways forward.

The lack of certainty in European financial markets has not assisted with related economic and structural challenges, such as continued high unemployment in the European Union.[21] While the European economic crisis has lost some of its severity,[22] largely due to external factors such as a bi-partisan budget in the United States and growth in China, unemployment across the Union remains stubbornly high.[23] In some Member States, such as Greece and Spain, youth unemployment has reached levels of over 60 per cent, which means that more than one in two Spaniards or Greeks under twenty-five has no paid employment. The European dimension to this problem is clear; according to the Treaty of Lisbon, access to free placement services, fair access to work and protection of youth in work are protected as fundamental rights.[24] However, a failure to address constitutional questions has meant that the EU has been unable to fully address problems of unemployment in a bid to uphold these fundamental rights. Competence for the European Union in social matters is restricted to trans-border movement of workers and service providers[25] and, as such, the Union adopts recommendations but cannot actively intervene in social or labour matters of the Member States. To

[20] Calliess, 101, 105.

[21] P. M. Larkin, 'Incapacity, the Labour Market and Social Security: Coercion into "Positive" Citizenship' (2011) 74 *Modern Law Review* 385, 392; S. Deakin and J. Browne, 'Social Rights and Market Order' in T. K. Hervey and J. Kenner (eds.), *Economic and Social Rights under the EU Charter of Fundamental Rights: A Legal Perspective* (Portland, OR 2003); C. Joerges, 'What Is Left of the European Economic Constitution? A Melancholic Eulogy' (2005) 30 *European Law Review* 461–89.

[22] V. K. Fouskas and C. Dimoulas, 'The Greek Workshop of Debt and the Failure of the European Project' (2012) 14 *Journal of Balkan and Near Eastern Studies* 1, 14.

[23] E. L. Mourelo, S. Khatiwada and M. Corley-Coulibaly, 'Overview of Employment Trends and Projections' (2013) World of Work Report 1, 12.

[24] Arts. 29–32, Charter of Fundamental Rights of the European Union (OJ 2000 C 364 p.1).

[25] C. Barnard, *EU Employment Law* (Oxford 2012) 47.

tackle this dimension of the crisis, as recommended by Catherine Barnard, decision-making and a different kind of review by the Court would be necessary. Some commentators have highlighted that, given the fundamental nature of the four economic freedoms, the Court might accord Member States large margins of discretion. Indeed, when the Court recently ruled on workers' rights in *Viking/Laval*, it was criticized for having overemphasized the economic rather than the human rights dimensions of labour disputes.[26] The social dimension of the crisis is also linked to the discussion of citizenship and *demos* more generally. While the vision of EU rights as exclusively economic has significantly changed to include more political and participatory rights, there remain serious questions.

5.2.2 *Europe's Socio-political Crisis*

The economic crisis is mirrored by a continuing political brinkmanship. One aspect of this, as noted by Mai'a D. Cross, is the widespread and growing popular support for Eurosceptical parties and the growing momentum of exit movements.[27] This is also where the impoverished understanding by the GFCC, seeing the European Parliament as not worthy of constitutional protection through the electoral system, becomes highly relevant.[28] It is not entirely clear whether support for

[26] Case C-341/05, *Laval un Partneri Ltd* v. *Svenska Byggnadsarbetareförbundet, Svenska Byggnadsarbetareförbundets avdelning 1, Byggettan and Svenska Elektrikerförbundet* [2007] ECR I-11767 and Case C-438/05, *International Transport Workers' Federation and Finnish Seamen's Union* v. *Viking Line ABP and OÜ Viking Line Eesti* [2007] ECR I-10779; C. Barnard, 'Viking and Laval: An Introduction' (2007–2008) 10 *Cambridge Yearbook of European Legal Studies* 463; C. Joerges and F. Roedl, 'Informal Politics, Formalised Law and the "Social Deficit" of European Integration: Reflections after the Judgments of the ECJ in Viking and Laval' (2009) 15 *European Law Journal* 1; C. Barnard and S. de Vires, 'The "Social Market Economy" in a (Heterogeneous) Social Europe: Does It Make a Difference?' (2019) 15 *Utrecht Law Review* 47, 50. See also M. Doherty, 'W(h)ither Social Europe? Labour Rights in a Social Market Economy' in D. Ferri and F. Cortese (eds.), *The EU Social Market Economy and the Law: Theoretical Perspectives and Challenges for the EU* (Abingdon/New York 2019) and G. Grekousis, 'Further Widening or Bridging the Gap? A Cross-Regional Study of Unemployment across the EU Amid Economic Crisis' (2018) 10 *Sustainability*, www.mdpi.com/2071-1050/10/6/1702.

[27] M.D. Cross, 'Identity Politics and European Integration' (2012) 44 *Comparative Politics* 229. See also de Vries, *Euroscepticism and the Future of European Integration*; A. L. P. Pirro, P. Taggart and S. van Kessel, 'The Populist Politics of Euroscepticism in Times of Crisis: Comparative Conclusions' (2018) 38 *Politics* 378.

[28] GFCC, *5% Hurdle European Election.*

Eurosceptical parties – or provincial or nationalist – stems directly from the economic elements of the crisis. As Nicolò Conti explains, there are clear political factors related to the financial crisis, mixed with a fear of all things foreign and different, which have led to soaring rates of support for staunchly Eurosceptical parties such as the Alternative fuer Deutschland (AfD), the UK Independence Party (UKIP), the Dutch Party of Freedom, the French Front National (FN), Italian Lega Nord, the Sweden Democrats and the True Finns. All share an unappetizing level of fear of 'the other', as is now well documented by the new field of 'Euroscepticism studies'.[29] The rise of these parties, which paradoxically did very well in the 2014 European elections, has converted the topic of exit from the European Union into a serious agenda item, even in some of the larger EU Member States such as the UK.[30] While the Treaty of Lisbon does open the possibility of leaving the Union, it remains a negotiated process (Art. 50 TEU). As Pieter De Wilde, Asimina Michailidou, Hans-Jörg Trenzhave explained, deeper underlying reasons appear to be triggering feelings of detachment from Europe. There are constitutional dimensions to these challenges, indicating that certain constituencies remain under-represented in the EU, including by their respective governments. This may indicate certain shortcomings in the area of representation, particularly in the constitutional design of EU institutions where certain types of concern are not represented.[31] The participation and decision-making by the European people are at the centre of the necessary analysis, as a central role for the People of Europe and, to an extent, their Courts may be required to move away from the current focus upon actions and reform by elite institutions.

As Wolfgang Streeck has noted, Europe today is characterized by low participation levels in European elections, as well as a lack of European parties that allow these interests to be represented.[32] Levels of political

[29] N. Conti (ed.), *Party Attitudes towards the EU in the Member States: Parties for Europe, Parties against Europe* (Abingdon/New York 2014); A. Szczerbiak and P. A. Taggart, *Opposing Europe? The Comparative Party Politics of Euroscepticism*, Vols. 1 and 2 (Oxford 2008); UACES Collaborative Research Network on Euroscepticism, https://sites.google.com/site/uaceseuroscepticismcrn.

[30] The Economist, 'Great Britain or Little England? Fingers Crossed that the Country Will Choose Wisely', Special Report (9 November 2013), www.economist.com/special-report/2013/11/07/great-britain-or-little-england, 25.

[31] P. de Wilde, A. Michailidou and H.-J. Trenz, *Contesting Europe: Exploring Euroscepticism in Online Media Coverage* (Colchester 2013).

[32] W. Streeck, 'The Crisis in Context: Democratic Capitalism and Its Contradictions' in W. Streeck and A. Schaefer (eds.), *Politics in the Age of Austerity* (Chichester 2011) 165.

representation for those in the lowest income brackets remain particularly low. Especially populations with lower levels of education find it difficult to have their views represented in formal politics and even more so in European politics. The elite character of parts of the European constitutional structure makes it more difficult to understand the European Union, and thus such representation becomes more unlikely.[33]

Even fifteen years after the failed ratifications by France and the Netherlands of the TCE, the region remains in a political crisis.[34] Rather than using the period of reflection to review the concerns raised in the campaigns during the two Member State referenda, Member States chose to embark on a treaty reform process through the Treaty of Lisbon. Further, rather than reviewing whether the Constitutional Convention process and the decisions of the IGC, followed by individual Member State ratification, would be the best option for a Constitutional transformation, Member States preferred to agree to a Treaty of Lisbon, which was not even available during the debates as a consolidated official version (instead being proposed as a long list of textual amendments).[35] As Jean-Claude Piris observes, the Treaty constituted a compromise between integrationist and co-operationist forces.[36] Indeed, some see the Lisbon Treaty as a good example of how the EU has moved away from constitutional patriotism, away from its own form of rhetorical constitutionalism and symbolism.[37] But to minimize dissent, the official consolidated version was not published until after it entered into force on 1 December 2009.[38] Some considered these developments a scandal of constitutional proportions, while others argued that it simply displayed deep levels of mistrust of 'We, the European People'.[39] The TCE, although in the end ratified in the majority of EU Member States in accordance with their constitutional requirements, remains the

[33] K.-O. Lingren and T. Persson, 'Participatory Governance in the European Union' in H. Heinelt (ed.), *Handbook on Participatory Governance* (Cheltenham/Northampton, MA 2018) 225, 230.

[34] Laursen, *The EU and the Eurozone Crisis*, 3, 199, 201.

[35] M. Dougan, 'The Treaty of Lisbon 2007: Winning Minds, Not Hearts' (2008) 45 *Common Market Law Review* 617, 618.

[36] Piris, *The Lisbon Treaty*, 49.

[37] Scicluna, 441, 442.

[38] J. Monar, 'Eurojust and the European Public Prosecutor Perspective: From Cooperation to Integration in EU Criminal Justice?' (2013) 14 *Perspectives on European Politics and Society* 339.

[39] K. Oppermann, 'The Politics of Avoiding Referendums on the Treaty of Lisbon' (2013) 35 *Journal of European Integration* 73.

main political argument as to the difficulty of sweeping reforms in Europe, among those who argue that only incrementalism can be successful.[40] Given the limited mandate of the Constitutional Convention and the backstop by the IGC, this is not necessarily conclusive evidence.[41] This EU incrementalism and minimal treaty change might well be part of the broader constitutional problem. In essence, the mechanisms to change the Treaties are not reflective of the federal nature of the Union, unable to address the most important obstacles to constitutionalization.

5.2.3 *Europe's Legitimacy Crisis*

Europe's socio-political and economic crises are compounded by a growing crisis of legitimacy, especially among the diverse and fragmented publics of the European Member States.[42] This crisis of legitimacy can be linked with the rise of global terrorism and transnational crime. Since 9/11, the rise of global terrorism and transnational crime has moved to the forefront of all political agendas and, unfortunately, both the measures adopted and the governments adopting them have raised significant questions of constitutional legitimacy.[43] This was arguably exacerbated by the migrant crisis in which refugees fleeing war in Syria and Libya were rejected by some of the Member States.[44] It is still not

[40] D. G. Dimitrakopoulos, 'Incrementalism and Path Dependence: European Integration and Institutional Change in National Parliaments' (2001) 39 *Journal of Common Market Studies* 405.

[41] Pfersmann.

[42] F. W. Scharpf, 'Legitimacy Intermediation in the Multilevel European Polity and Its Collapse in the Euro Crisis' in K. Armingeon (ed.), *Staatstätigkeiten, Parteien und Demokratie* (Heidelberg 2013) 567; Y. Papdopoulos, 'Eurozone Crisis Management and the Changing Nature of the Democratic Deficit in the European Union' in R. Careja, P. Emmenegger and N. Giger (eds.), *The European Social Model under Pressure* (Wiesbaden 2020) 567; C. Schweiger, 'The Legitimacy Challenge' in D. Dinan, N. Nugent and W. E. Paterson (eds.), *The European Union in Crisis* (London 2017) 188.

[43] B. A. Ackerman, 'The Emergency Constitution' (2004) 113 *Yale Law Journal* 1029; F. de Londras, 'Convergence Gaps in EU Counter-Terrorism' in F. de Londras and J. Doddy (eds.), *The Impact, Legitimacy and Effectiveness of EU Counter-Terrorism* (London/New York 2015) 204, 208 ff; J. Jansson, 'Building Resilience, Demolishing Accountability? The Role of Europol in Counter-Terrorism' (2018) 28(4) *Policing and Society* 432.

[44] See P. Nedergaard, 'Borders and the EU Legitimacy Problem: The 2015–16 European Refugee Crisis' (2019) 40 *Policy Studies* 80 and P. Murray and M. Longo, 'Europe's Wicked Legitimacy Crisis: The Case of Refugees' (2018) 40 *Journal of European Integration* 411.

entirely clear how the EU should react to global terrorism and this context of crisis compounds existing problems with the issue of forming a cohesive European response. On the one hand, the CJEU in its *Kadi* line of jurisprudence strongly defended fundamental rights, even in the face of UN resolutions to freeze someone's assets.[45] On the other hand, Member States have not yet agreed on common strategies or enforcement actions by a European police force that would have investigative and enforcement powers across the Union.[46] This evidence of incrementalism raises questions of the legitimacy of the Union, according to Daniel Cohn-Bendit and Guy Verhofstadt, who argue that the EU cannot effectively respond to the most pressing problems of today in this manner.[47] Others have suggested that, since the Treaty of Lisbon, the police powers of the Union have been greatly enhanced and the groundwork has been done to form an effective response to the global threat of terrorism; many believe this to be true in spite of the decisions of certain governments, such as the UK's, to opt out from the process.

Terrorism and transnational crime are not the only areas presenting legitimacy issues for the EU. Many further legitimacy concerns are raised in addressing environmental degradation, such as overfishing and GHG emissions causing climate change.[48] Each environmental crisis, globally and regionally, is raised as another example of the lack of significant success by the EU in securing effective resources management or enforcement of regional standards. As argued by Maria Lee, while the EU clearly does has competence over environmental issues and has adopted very progressive legislation in the area, enforcement at the national level remains weak and the lack of direct federal enforcement authority hampers the very rule of law in this area.[49] The situation has, in some instances, become so dire that several Member States have been taken to the CJEU to ensure that they agree to comply with EU environmental legislation. The European institutions, while given a strong competence mandate in the area, appear to lack certain basic tools to ensure direct enforcement of commonly accepted rules. It is this continued lack of

[45] Joined Cases C-402/05 P and C-415/05 P, *Yassin Abdullah Kadi and Al Barakaat International Foundation* v. *Council of the European Union and Commission of the European Communities* [2008] ECR I-06351.

[46] Ackerman, 'The Emergency Constitution'.

[47] Cohn-Bendit and Verhofstadt.

[48] L. Krämer, *EC Environmental Law*, 7th ed. (London 2011).

[49] M. Lee, 'The Ambiguity of Multi-Level Governance and (De-)Harmonisation in EU Environmental Law' (2012–2013) 15 *Cambridge Yearbook of European Legal Studies* 357.

effectiveness that leads to lack of legitimacy of EU institutions, with severe doubt cast upon governance capabilities.

These interrelated strands of European crises are being reflected in European legal scholarship,[50] jurisprudence and political debates, and at the heart of these crises are a series of constitutional questions that 'the peoples of Europe' have yet to resolve. These constitutionally relevant debates rage within each of Europe's Member States, in the Union as a whole and perhaps even on a global level. Their conclusions will be vital in the years to come, for everyone involved.

5.3 The UK's Brexit as a Special European Crisis

For some, the Brexit crisis is the most important constitutional challenge for the EU since its founding in 1957.[51] Others see the potential for a 'constitutional moment' given that the UK was always a 'reluctant Member State'.[52] For the purposes of this volume, it is helpful to review the Brexit experience with a focus on how the Courts have guided many elements of the situation.

One of the first formal indications of a potential British 'exit' from the EU was raised by then-Prime Minister James Cameron, during his speech at Bloomberg's offices in London in January 2013.[53] Commenting on the future of the European Union, in response to long-standing internal debates, he fatefully offered to hold an 'in-or-out' referendum on the UK's membership in the EU after some form of re-negotiation. He

[50] G. Falkner, 'The EU's Problem-Solving Capacity and Legitimacy in a Crisis Context: A Virtuous or Vicious Circle?' (2016) 39 *West European Politics* 953; M. Castells and others (eds.), *Europe's Crises* (Cambridge, UK/Medford, MA 2018); T. A. Börzel and T. Risse, 'A Litmus Test for European Integration Theories: Explaining Crises and Comparing Regionalisms' (2018) KFG Working Paper 85, www.ssoar.info/ssoar/handle/document/57753#; F. Schimmelfennig, 'Liberal Intergovernmentalism and the Crises of the European Union' (2018) 56 *Journal of Common Market Studies* 1578; P. Márton, 'Europe's Crises: Preparing to Study Disintegration' (2018) 14 *Journal of Contemporary European Research* 274; I. Goldner Lang, 'The EU Financial and Migration Crises: Two Crises – Many Facets of EU Solidarity' in A. Biondi, E. Dagilyte and E. Kucuk (eds.), *Solidarity in EU Law: Legal Principle in the Making* (Cheltenham/Northampton, MA 2018) 161.

[51] See Jacobs, but also, with the opposite conclusion, N. Huhe, D. Naurin and R. Thomson, 'Don't Cry for Me Britannia: The Resilience of the European Union to Brexit' (2019) *European Union Politics* 1.

[52] See K. Nicolaidis, 'Braving the Waves? Europe's Constitutional Settlement at Twenty' (2018) 56(7) *Journal of Common Market Studies* 1614, https://doi.org/10.1111/jcms.12791.

[53] Cameron, 'EU Speech at Bloomberg'.

promised: 'It is time for the British people to have their say. It is time to settle this European question in British politics. I say to the British people: this will be your decision. And when that choice comes, you will have an important choice to make about our country's destiny.'[54] His framing of both the options and the ultimate decision-maker (as the people, but only those people of the UK) highlights the constitutional difficulty of this approach. On the one hand, Mr Cameron was attempting to convince the EU to fundamentally change its ways by, for example, objecting to the treaty purpose and slogans encouraging an 'ever closer union'. On the other hand, the British referendum was conceived as an opportunity for the citizens of just one EU national Member State to express their own views on the Union as a whole, with no say for the citizens of the rest of the European Union.

This promise was possible only because the Lisbon Treaty introduced a new Art. 50 TEU, which allowed all Member States to leave the European Union:

> 1. Any Member State may decide to withdraw from the Union in accordance with its own constitutional requirements. 2. A Member State which decides to withdraw shall notify the European Council of its intention. In the light of the guidelines provided by the European Council, the Union shall negotiate and conclude an agreement with that State, setting out the arrangements for its withdrawal, taking account of the framework for its future relationship with the Union. That agreement shall be negotiated in accordance with Article 218(3) of the Treaty on the Functioning of the European Union. It shall be concluded on behalf of the Union by the Council, acting by a qualified majority, after obtaining the consent of the European Parliament.[55]

This provision is somewhat unusual for a federal structure. Indeed, some federations, such as that of the United States, fought a civil war to keep the Union together.[56] By entering the debate on these terms, Prime Minister Cameron was actually 'playing with fire' from an EU perspective. All recognized that Mr Cameron's hands were – to a certain extent – politically tied by many Eurosceptic MPs on the UK backbenches. Most hoped that he would forget his promise to let the British people decide

54 Ibid.

55 Art. 50, TEU.

56 I am grateful to Professor Jed Rubenfeld, who asked me at the very beginning of this research project if I was predicting a civil war in Europe. I was horrified at the time, but I can see more clearly now how federal development can take very different twists and turns.

about their EU membership, once he had won an outright majority in 2015. However, in the end it was the opposite – the electoral victory meant that Mr Cameron had to start a good faith re-negotiation attempt. His priorities were outlined, and arguably the EU made fairly significant concessions, including the agreement that

> [i]t is recognised that the United Kingdom, in the light of the specific situation it has under the Treaties, is not committed to further political integration into the European Union. The substance of this will be incorporated into the Treaties at the time of their next revision in accordance with the relevant provisions of the Treaties and the respective constitutional requirements of the Member States, so as to make it clear that the references to ever closer union do not apply to the United Kingdom.

He also won concessions allowing the UK (and all other Member States) to institute an emergency brake on in-work benefits if they become a burden for the State, a quasi-veto on Eurozone legislation and a political commitment to competitiveness and cutting of red-tape.[57] These special arrangements were adopted under the condition that the UK voted to remain in a referendum, and, indeed, several parties ostensibly campaigned to remain in the EU during the 23 June 2016 referendum.[58] The European Union Referendum Act 2015 did not contain any provisions concerning the result of the vote or its implementation. Unlike the previous referendum on the Alternative Vote in 2011, which specifically stated that the outcome had the force of law, the EU referendum was silent on the issue.[59] The legal value became less important when the referendum participation had one of the highest turnouts of any general election with over 72 per cent of voters. At this point, it became politically impossible to ignore the result, which has since divided the country into 48.1 per cent voting to remain and 51.9 per cent voting to leave the EU. The somewhat odd formulation of the question ('Should the United Kingdom remain a member of the European Union or leave the European Union?') was necessary because informal polling had revealed that not enough people were aware that the UK was at the time already a Member State of the EU.

[57] A New Settlement for the United Kingdom within the European Union, OJ C 69I, 23.2.2016, pp.1–16.

[58] Ibid.

[59] Full Fact, 'Was the EU Referendum "Advisory"?' (8 November 2016), https://fullfact.org/europe/was-eu-referendum-advisory.

The result was followed by a political earthquake. Mr Cameron, who as Prime Minister had campaigned to remain in the EU, resigned the next morning. After a short period, Mrs Teresa May became leader of the Conservatives and Prime Minister. She insisted that only the government, without any parliamentary involvement, could trigger Art. 50 and submit the relevant declaration. This was met with a dissenting commentary by leading constitutional law scholars in the UK writing arguably the most influential blog post in a long time.[60] At this point, the Courts were involved because Gina Miller, who campaigned for the UK to remain in the EU, challenged the government's position on triggering Art. 50. She won her case in the High Court and this judgment generated the most odious headlines declaring the judges 'enemies of the people' because, somehow, they were 'stopping Brexit'. The High Court had merely decided that a fundamental decision such as Brexit had to be taken by Parliament, not by the government alone.

The government appealed and two months later the UK Supreme Court decided that the referendum was strictly advisory and, for legal reasons, an act of the UK Parliament was required to trigger Art. 50 TEU.[61] The European Union (Notification of Withdrawal) Act 2017 was passed quickly and allowed the government to trigger Art. 50 on 31 March 2017 starting a two-year withdrawal period. The government, buoyant from its perceived success, then called a general election in May 2017, which the Tories nearly lost, also because many believed that the Labour Party would generally support remain, which turned out to be only partially true. The reduced majority made it necessary to enter into a confidence and supply agreement with the Northern Irish Democratic Unionist Party, a right-wing Protestant party.

The EU did not make the leaving process easy for the UK. It insisted on a staggered timetable whereby the 'divorce issues' of citizens' rights, the Irish border and the financial settlement had to be agreed first, followed by a negotiation on the future relationship. The May Withdrawal Agreement opted for a ten-year guarantee for citizenship rights, a backstop that included the entire UK and a financial settlement in the order of 50 billion euros (subject to further determinations). The May political declaration left all options, including a customs union and near complete single market access with the EU, on the table. However, this

[60] N. Barber, T. Hickman and J. King, 'Pulling the Article 50 "Trigger": Parliament's Indispensable Role', UK Constitution Law blog (27 June 2016), https://ukconstitutionallaw.org.

[61] *R (on the application of Miller and another)* v. *Secretary of State for Exiting the European Union* [2017] UKSC 5.

Withdrawal version of the Agreement proved unacceptable to UK Parliamentarians largely because the Tory European Research Group and its anti-EU wing ('Spartans') rejected it three times. After the third defeat, Mrs May resigned and Boris Johnson was elected Tory leader with the promise to crash the UK out of the EU if a deal could not be reached that Parliament would accept. In a dramatic move, the Prime Minster then attempted to prorogue Parliament to facilitate negotiations and in order to stop Parliament from legislating against a no-deal Brexit. This prorogation was later deemed null and void by the UK Supreme Court.[62] Parliament, however, had stopped a no-deal Brexit in an amendment to the European Union (Withdrawal) (No. 2) Act 2019 (c. 26), which it had done on 9 September 2019. This forced the Prime Minister to ask for an extension until 31 January 2020 to allow for a second referendum or a general election. As part of the constitutional theatre, Mr Johnson did not actually sign the letter that the Act forced him to send, but his Ambassador signed an accompanying letter claiming that the Prime Minster rejected an extension. This letter was necessary because even though he had reached an amended deal with the EU, Parliament did not agree the necessary implementation legislation before 31 October 2019. The Johnson Deal both rejected the UK-wide backstop, effectively creating a customs border in the Irish Sea, and changed the political declaration to refer only to a free trade agreement rather than leaving all options of a future relationship on the table. This very significant constitutional agreement between the EU and its former constituent Member State was reached on 19 October 2019.[63] It contains a transition period in which all EU obligations apply to the UK. At the same time, the UK will have left the EU and thus will not participate in the decision-making of the Union. This transition was included to facilitate the negotiation of a future trade agreement, which the UK cannot do prior to its exit from the EU (which in turn has the exclusive competence for foreign trade).[64] On

[62] *R (on the application of Miller)* v. *The Prime Minister and Cherry and Others* v. *Advocate General for Scotland*, decided 24 September 2019 [2019] UKSC 41.

[63] Agreement on the withdrawal of the United Kingdom of Great Britain and Northern Ireland from the European Union and the European Atomic Energy Community, 19 October 2019, https://assets.publishing.service.gov.uk/government/uploads/system/uploads/attachment_data/file/840655/Agreement_on_the_withdrawal_of_the_United_Kingdom_of_Great_Britain_and_Northern_Ireland_from_the_European_Union_and_the_European_Atomic_Energy_Community.pdf.

[64] See M. Gehring, 'Brexit and EU–UK Trade Relations with Third States' EU Law Analysis (6 March 2016), http://eulawanalysis.blogspot.com/2016/03/brexit-and-eu-uk-trade-relations-with.html.

12 December 2019, Mr Johnson then won a decisive electoral victory largely based on the promise to 'get Brexit done', allowing him to adopt his Withdrawal Agreement, which required a 'meaningful vote' and the implementation legislation quickly and without much delay.

The EU Courts shaped the Brexit discussions through the *Wightman* case.[65] In this preliminary reference case, the Scottish Court asked if the Art. 50 notification could be unilaterally revoked. The UK and the Commission argued that this would be impossible. The Commission submitted that the UK would need to seek permission from the EU and its Member States to revoke the notification in order to avoid an abuse of right. Both the Advocate General and the CJEU disagreed. It ruled:

> [W]hen a Member State has notified the European Council of its intention to withdraw from the European Union, as the UK has done, that Member State is free to revoke unilaterally that notification. That possibility exists for as long as a withdrawal agreement concluded between the EU and that Member State has not entered into force or, if no such agreement has been concluded, for as long as the two-year period from the date of the notification of the intention to withdraw from the EU, and any possible extension, has not expired. The revocation must be decided following a democratic process in accordance with national constitutional requirements. This unequivocal and unconditional decision must be communicated in writing to the European Council. Such a revocation confirms the EU membership of the Member State concerned under terms that are unchanged as regards its status as a Member State and brings the withdrawal procedure to an end.[66]

This spurred constitutional activities on both sides of the leave–remain discussion. For remain supporters, it opened a new, radical avenue to end the Brexit process and for leave supporters, it was seen as another example of meddling by the European Courts in domestic UK affairs. The CJEU draws a fine line between EU law requirements and the constitutional and democratic requirements on the EU-withdrawing Member State side. It did not, contrary to the accusation, take any side. It defended the federal institutions but without overstepping the boundaries of Member State competence in taking the constitutionally most radical decision of leaving the Union.

Paradoxically, Brexit had politically a galvanizing effect on the EU. Even Eurosceptics in larger Member States have now changed their political programmes and are no longer arguing for an exit from the Union. The domestic political problems created inside the UK are a powerful reminder

[65] Case C-621/18, *Wightman and Others* v. *Secretary of State for Exiting the European Union*, 10 December 2018.

[66] Ibid.

of how difficult the question of EU membership is. The simple in–out referendum did not, in fact, answer the question of how the UK wanted to leave or what the future relationship should look like. These questions largely remain to be answered by the future free trade agreement that the Political Declaration aims to facilitate.

What does Brexit as a crisis mean for EU constitutionalization? It first highlights that legal constraints are also constitutional constraints for the EU and its Member States. Suggestions by some Tory politicians that the EU should just ignore the law fell on deaf ears. While faster, deeper integration is not currently on the EU's agenda, the Brexit negotiations were so jarring that currently no other EU Member State is hoping to leave the Union. In that sense, it had the opposite effect of constitutional corrosion. It galvanized the Union[67] and thus turned it arguably into a closer Union in the short term. Having a former Member State right at the doorstep could be problematic in the long term, but the Withdrawal Agreement tries to prevent the worst excesses.

With regard to another *demos* topic, there was a short discussion as to whether English would cease to be an official language, as one Commissioner suggested. However, the Junker Commission answered the question affirmatively:

> According to article 342 of the Treaty on the Functioning of the European Union, it is for the Council, acting unanimously, to determine the rules governing the languages of the institutions of the Union. Today, English is one of the 24 official and working languages of the European Union institutions. The Commission notes that, besides the United Kingdom, Ireland and Malta have English as an official language.[68]

A much more important lesson can be drawn from Brexit. The discussions were very public and antagonized from the beginning; cast as us against them. No common deliberative space existed between British and other EU Member State peoples. Both the EU and the UK debated the issues surrounding Brexit in their own echo chamber, but while hearing, though perhaps not listening to, the other side. This highlights a constitutionalization problem for the EU. The fact that the exit from the Union is largely a unilateral decision (albeit at a very high price) makes

[67] European Parliament News, 'Eurobarometer Survey Shows Highest Support for the EU in 35 Years', 23 May 2018, www.europarl.europa.eu/news/en/headlines/eu-affairs/20180522STO04020/eurobarometer-survey-highest-support-for-the-eu-in-35-years.

[68] Parliamentary question of 21 May 2017; Answer given by President Juncker on behalf of the Commission on 9 August 2017, Reference: E-003658/2017.

a common deliberative space even more important. Brexit might thus be a crisis that would also benefit from Europe's Second Constitution.

5.4 The Remaining Obstacle to European Constitutionalization and Its Corollary Challenges

In spite of certain civil law scholarly claims to the contrary,[69] constitution-making is less a question of negotiating the one 'correct' constitutional document and more a matter of progressive constitutional development, built on increasingly widespread popular support that renders the transition legitimate.[70] This 'common law' style development focuses on judicial writings and case law, offering a more fulsome picture of constitutional development in any entity, providing insights and understanding into how the constitutionalization process should progress.[71] Indeed, jurisprudence can play an important part in the progressive development of a constitutional entity. As Ackerman explains with regard to the 'judicial' constitutional moment in US constitutional history,

> [t]here is anxiety here, but also a certain confidence in organic judicial development, nurtured by a scholarly tradition that now stretched back for more than half a century (and a common law tradition rooted in centuries of practice). Organism had triumphed over mechanism: if the Constitution were to survive, judges had no real choice but to use their judgment to determine which constitutional traditions would survive the 'transplant' onto modern American 'soil'.[72]

This legitimacy built on popular support that Ackerman refers to is a key missing ingredient in each of the *demos*, *civitas* and *ius* dimensions of European constitutionalization analysed already, as a matter both of design and of organic development. As Ackerman has identified, the most important foundations of any constitutional arrangement are the people within that entity. In the following section, my focus becomes the areas where careful organic extension of the jurisprudence itself has the potential to contribute to a stronger constitutionalization.

The periphery courts and scholars have argued against the evolution of a European *demos*, finding that Europe lacks social and political homogeneity, homogeneity of citizenship, spiritual homogeneity or any kind of

[69] C. Möllers, *Das Grundgesetz : Geschichte und Inhalt* (Munich 2009) 5.
[70] See Ackerman, *We the People: Vol. 1: Foundations*.
[71] M. Elliott and R. Thomas, *Public Law*, 2nd ed. (Oxford 2014) 11.
[72] Ackerman, 'The Holmes Lectures'.

homogenous values. In essence, they claim that there is not even a common understanding of what *demos* means in the European context.[73] As demonstrated in Chapter 2, the majority of these objections are neither relevant nor valid. Judicial findings, as well as scholarly and legal debates on the possibility of a European *demos*, remain relevant, albeit difficult, due to the lack of a European public space for deliberation, which in turn is linked to a related challenge of the lack of acceptance of a pragmatic number of common working languages for public debates.

Periphery judgments also suggest that there is no European *civitas*, as evinced, they submit, by the lack of unitary elections; the lack of EU-wide parties; the non-existence of a real EU President; the absence of a powerful parliament; the lack of functional senate; and the dearth of a single constitutional charter. As explained in Chapter 3, while many of these objections are invalid ones, certain aspects of civic legitimacy do remain problematic. In particular, the EU institutions themselves, as well as the treaties, are still perceived as an elite project, due to the absence of an EU public space to debate and consider European policy issues adequately and transparently. This problem, as I espouse in this work, remains particularly pronounced with regard to the lack of unitary European elections and cross-European political parties.

Finally, certain periphery judgments argue that there is actually no European *ius*, finding that in Europe there exists no single rule of law; no federal court system with clear selection of judges; no constitutional review powers; no jurisdiction vis-à-vis Member State courts or judicial *Kompetenz-Kompetenz*; no common criminal law or EU police force; no effective system of human rights and environmental protection; and no foreign relations provisions in line with the rule of law. However, as shown in Chapter 4, many of these obstacles have been overcome. This said, clear procedures for the selection of trans-European judges and the ability to mandate and enforce federal action in the areas where EU law enjoys supremacy (*Kompetenz-Kompetenz*) will be critical to future successful constitutionalization and are linked to gaps in a truly European public sphere. This is especially true given that Member States remain the most important actors in the appointment of EU constitutional actors, as this hinders both popular knowledge of the law and the possibility of open debates on European law in a common European public space.

[73] J. L. Martí, 'European Democracy and the No-Demos Thesis' in D. Innerarity and others (eds.), *A New Narrative for a New Europe* (2018) 9–10.

In essence, the research and analysis from this research, based on the existing case law and treaties, and taking into account illustrative comparisons with other federal systems, have shown that while most of the main obstacles to European constitutionalization raised by Member State courts and scholars across Europe are not valid, there is one (and its corollaries) which remains fatal and must be overcome for further constitutionalization to proceed.

Table of Obstacles: Demos, Civitas, Ius

Dimensions/Obstacles	Research Findings
Demos	
No homogeneity of values	Advanced by CJEU
No homogeneity of citizenship	Misconception
No spiritual homogeneity	Misconception
No linguistic homogeneity	Advanced by CJEU, *remains a challenge without a European public space*
No common European public space	*Main remaining obstacle*
Civitas	
Lack of unitary elections	Advanced by CJEU, *remains a challenge without a European public space*
No European-wide parties	Advanced by CJEU, *remains a challenge without a European public space*
Lack of one real president	Misconception
The European Parliament is not the only law-maker	Misconception
The Council of the European Union cannot serve as a Senate	Misconception
The foundational documents of the Union are international treaties, not a constitution	Misconception
Ius	
No single rule of law	Advanced by the CJEU
No powerful unitary federal court system	Advanced by the CJEU
	Advanced, *remains a challenge without European public space*

(*cont.*)

Dimensions/Obstacles	Research Findings
– No single Constitutional Court with appellate powers	Advanced by the CJEU Misconception
– No clear procedures for selection of justices	Advanced, *remains challenge without European public space*
– No Federal Court powers of constitutional review	
– Undetermined Court jurisdiction vis-à-vis the Member States	
– No Federal Court *Kompetenz-Kompetenz*	
No common criminal law or police force	Misconception
Lack of a common and effective system to protect human rights and the environment	Advanced by the CJEU
No foreign relations according to the rule of law	Misconception

As demonstrated in the table, the jurisprudential analysis reveals that certain obstacles represent misconceptions in the understanding of numerous courts and that many advances have been made by the Courts – often the CJEU – in overcoming the obstacles. It also reveals that a major important obstacle to further EU constitutionalization does, in fact, remain. This key remaining obstacle – the lack of a truly European public space for political and constitutional debates – transcends the dimension of *demos* and has effects on constitutionalization discussions across the dimensions of *civitas* and *ius*.

The continuing problem of this fatal obstacle begs the question of whether the existence of different nations in one polity creates insurmountable obstacles to their democratic legitimacy. Does a federal State with more than one nation always lack a common *demos*? Certainly, this is how some separatists would see the matter, but a closer examination simply returns to the reason for federalism itself, which lies in the creation of a common polity among different peoples in historical, social and perhaps also spiritual terms. Rather than seeing the lack or impossibility of a common European *demos* as an insurmountable obstacle, this study advocates a more nuanced analysis. The definition of a European public sphere, as initially discussed in Chapters 1 and 2 and expanded here, is founded upon this nuanced view.

According to Habermasian theory, a public sphere is distinguished by a clear communicative structure[74] that is kept intact by the existence of an 'energetic' civil society.[75] As explained in Chapter 2, without the existence of such a public space defined in these terms, constitutional development will face significant obstacles.[76] One such example is Switzerland at the beginning of its new constitutional federation. While cultural and geographical linkages were in existence on the eve of the federalist State, social and political conversations were seriously lacking. The development towards greater social and political public debate and engagement across the various federated linguistic and other communities came hand-in-hand with new instruments of direct democracy being developed.

On one level, the Swiss example is a clear demonstration of the importance of a public sphere in the constitutionalization process. However, in my view, there is another level to the Swiss example; it illustrates the importance of establishing a public sphere from early on in the constitutionalization project. In essence, the lack of any real public space at the time of the Constitution of 1848 led to the cementing of disparate political agendas and voting patterns across the Francophone and German Cantons of Switzerland. Arguably, had a forum existed in which to transfer information, opinions and ideas at an earlier stage, there may be greater political engagement in Switzerland today.

Engaged and active social and political dialogue across countries is crucial in the context of a federated European Union. The existence of a European public space that exists for the fostering and sharing of social and political norms is, however, vital. Such a space could help to overcome disparate political priorities and create a common civil discourse, addressing the key corollary weaknesses along the *demos*, *civitas* and *ius* dimensions of European constitutionalization.

In my view, the real question is 'Why?'. Why does the European public space remain still so premature or void of content? How is it possible that in times of financial and economic crisis, discussions remain at a national level, even regarding decisions that are clearly being taken at the EU or international level? Is the lack of a certain level of accountability perhaps even convenient, allowing

[74] J. Habermans, *Between Facts and Norms: Contributions to a Discourse Theory of Law and Democracy*, translated by William Rehg (Cambridge 1996) 360.
[75] Ibid. 369.
[76] See Section 2.6.

for ever-decreasing levels of democratic accountability among the Member States and concentration of decision-making powers among a tightening circle of technocratic elite and their national liaisons? In relation to the recent *ESM* decision of the GFCC,[77] for example, it was suggested that European institutions were simply 'smoke and mirrors' masking that all relevant decisions are taken out of sight of the public eye. In times of political instability, the convenience of a scapegoat cannot be underestimated.

The lack of a European public space is the remaining constitutional obstacle that is most problematic for even a very loose federal constitutional system,[78] as seen by Brexit, where the lack of a trans-European discussion was most obvious. It makes informed policy debates about matters of common heritage or public concern impossible and undermines the very foundations of democratic, civil and legal legitimacy. As Thomas Risse, a political theorist, has suggested, the opening of one European public sphere remains elusive. Rather, many public spheres continue to exist at mainly national levels because, as he suggests, a 'European-wide communicative space' is much more difficult to achieve.[79] The emergence of such a space requires, alongside simply administrative and executive choices, further actual politicization of European Union decision-making, as well as higher levels of interconnectedness of the different public spheres of the Member States.[80] At present, Europe is still fundamentally best characterized as a conglomeration of national public spheres. It is my claim that although these spheres can and do occasionally speak 'at' or 'past' each other, it must also be recognized that these conversations are not always conducive to mutual understandings or compromises.

As explained in Chapter 2, discussions about the existence or possibility of a European *demos* are difficult, due to the amorphous nature of homogeneity in the European Union in political, social or spiritual terms. As seen through the developments in European jurisprudence and the prism of other federal systems, however, homogeneity is not – at least not

[77] GFCC *ESM Treaty*. Applications for the issue of a temporary injunction, www.bverfg.de /en/decisions/rs20120912_2bvr139012en.html.

[78] Risse, *European Public Spheres*; see also J. Wouters, H. Cuyckens and T. Ramopoulos, 'The European Union: A Federation in All but Name' in D. Halberstam and M. Reimann (eds.), *Federalism and Legal Unification* (Heidelberg/Berlin 2013), 191–235.

[79] Fossum and Schlesinger, and Koopmans and Statham.

[80] See Risse, *European Public Spheres*, 141, 142.

during the relevant periods of constitutional development – necessarily strong or even present in many federal entities. Thus, it should be unsurprising that a discussion on the possibility of *demos* is still, to this day, viewed in national terms, even though the EU challenges national and especially nationalistic sentiments.[81] There is, however, a real and concerning risk that such nationalism will reign supreme when there is no real forum for common policy debates or informed discussions among the citizens of the federal constitutional entity, where debates and positions that represent the public interests of all can be expressed, understood and (when necessary) compromised rather than demonized.[82] My research findings argue that this obstacle, along with all of its related challenges, must be overcome in order for Europe's Second Constitution to become a reality.

What are the connections between this remaining obstacle and other remaining challenges for European constitutional development, and how are they interrelated? The absence of a truly European public space is fundamentally linked to other EU constitutional challenges and underlies the ones that have been found, in Chapters 2, 3 and 4, to be least advanced by the Courts in fundamental and important ways.

The absence of a European public space has been at the heart of the objection raised by critics and periphery Member State courts; indeed the GFCC has found that such a forum is 'not yet' in existence.[83] The possibilities of public debate and scrutiny of political decisions by an informed citizenry are two crucial elements of any constitutional polity.[84] Yet, in the European Union, much of the debate about lack of EU democratic legitimacy focuses on the lack of public debate and scrutiny of political decisions.[85]

In my view, while the absence of public debate and the lack of scrutiny of political decisions form the basis of the European debate, these two fundamental tenets of democracy rely on the existence of a European public sphere. By acting as an independent space, where *European polity*

[81] See J. M. Barroso, 'State of the Union 2012 Address', Plenary Session of the European Parliament, Strasbourg, vol. 12 (2012).

[82] R. K. Herrmann and others, *Transnational Identities: Becoming European in the EU* (Oxford 2004) 7, 32.

[83] *Lisbon Decision.*

[84] J. Habermas, 'Religion in the Public Sphere' (2006) 14 *European Journal of Philosophy* 7.

[85] C. Meyer, 'Political Legitimacy and the Invisibility of Politics: Exploring the European Union's Communication Deficit' (1999) 37 *Journal of Common Market Studies* 617.

is the point of reference, the European public sphere enables *European* opinions to be formed.[86] It is for this reason that several commentators regard the existence of an established public sphere as a crucial tenet of democracy.[87] The GFCC, for example, has acknowledged the necessity of a public sphere on several occasions. Notably, in the *Euro* case,[88] it acknowledged that democracy is premised on free debate among social forces, interests and ideas, out of which public opinion is derived and from which political will is formed. What is particularly interesting in the *Euro* case is the GFCC's recognition that free debate in a democracy should be '*ongoing*' in nature – that is, continual and evolving. Here, the GFCC is clearly moving the discussion around a common public space towards an emphasis upon its necessity within the context of any democratically legitimate European Union.

The lack of recognition or acceptance of fewer – perhaps five rather than twenty-four – EU working languages is one of the most closely related challenges to the absence of a lack of European public sphere. A subset of practical working languages would facilitate the possibility for public and informed discussions among all citizens at the EU level,[89] influencing in turn both the understanding of a common history in the past and the education of a common citizenry in the future. Further and in grim irony, the very deficiencies in a trans-European public space mean that the absence of a reasonable number of common working languages can be discussed only in Member State terms, rather than on a trans-European basis. This inevitably gives ultimate priority to the cultural attachments, unwillingness to compromise or find pragmatic solutions, and even the very definition of perceived political interests of many Member States. Without a European public space for an informed debate, it will be very difficult to come to a working solution to this challenge.

[86] J.-H. Meyer, *The European Public Sphere: Media and Transnational Communication in European Integration 1969–1991* (Stuttgart: Franz Steiner Verlag 2010) 26.

[87] J. Gerhards and F. Neidhart, 'Strukturen und Funtionen moderner Offentlichkeit. Fragestellungen und Ansatze' in S. Muller-Dohm and K. Neumann-Braun (eds.), *Oeffentlichkeit, Kultur, Massenkommunikation. Beitrage zur Medienkommunikationssoziologie* (Oldenburg 1991) 39–41.

[88] Bundesverfassungsgericht [BVerfG – Federal Constitutional Court], Case No. 2 BvR 1877/97, 31 March 1998, 97; BVerfGE 350, 369 (Ger.).

[89] M. Gazzola and F. Grin, 'Is English as Lingua Franca More Effective and Fair than Translation? An Evaluation of the EU's Multilingual Regime' (2013) 23 *International Journal of Applied Linguistics* 93.

The lack of a common European public space is also problematic for the establishment of truly EU-wide parties, which, in turn, renders the goal of having genuine EU-wide elections currently impossible. If such a common public space existed, debates could take place at a European level and thus facilitate the creation and development of EU-wide parties that exist to exert influence and advance policy proposals in, and specifically for, the common space.[90] The televising of the *Spitzenkandaten* process for EU Commission candidacy was initially an important step by the European Parliament that has enabled greater conceptualization about the form that an EU-wide election process could take. However, the televised debates on the *Spitzenkandaten* were no more than a momentary common use of the public sphere for European Union purposes. In order to foster continued debate to a sufficient level for EU-wide elections to take place, a new, permanent and specifically designated European public sphere must exist. This is further evidenced by the fact that, in 2019, the Member States could not agree to appoint Mr Weber, who was the *Spitzenkandidate* of the largest party in the European Parliament.

Vice versa, the current differences and potential injustices in the way that Member States administer and regulate EU elections[91] could be debated in a more open and comparative fashion. Strikingly, while Finland and Sweden appear to be very similar Nordic welfare state countries sharing many common cultural elements, European Parliament campaign regulations vary dramatically even between these two Member States.[92] In Finland, for example, there are no legal restrictions on campaign expenses and elected candidates bear the burden of financing their campaigns.[93] This differs entirely from the position in Sweden where campaign financing is entirely within the public domain and individual candidates are heavily dependent on the party organization.[94] In a common European public sphere, such discrepancies could be more readily highlighted and notable inconsistencies addressed through public pressure. Thus, the existence of a European public sphere

90 Koopmans and Statham, 25.

91 J. Fortin-Rittberger and B. Rittberger, 'Do Electoral Rules Matter? Explaining National Differences in Women's Representation in the European Parliament' (2014) *European Union Politics* 1.

92 M. Maier, J. Strömbäck and L. Lee Kaid, *Political Communication in European Parliamentary Elections* (Farnham 2011) 49.

93 Ibid., 50.

94 Ibid., 50.

could assist in identifying potential paths to strengthen and improve levels of political equality for EU citizens and, in turn, increase democratic legitimacy across the entirety of the Union.

Finally, the absence of a European common public space hampers the re-alignment of competences and separation of powers. At present, such redefinitions and institutional changes are wholly in the hands of the Member States, represented only by their governments each with its perceived and vested interest in retaining national-level powers, with little direct voice for the European population at large.[95] The CJEU has repeatedly, and most recently in the *UPA* case,[96] hesitated to trigger constitutional re-alignments without explicit Member State support. Without a European public space in which to build understanding and support, the CJEU is unlikely to garner support for redefined competences from the European people directly. Meanwhile, a similar challenge exists for the selection of judges. A common European public space could provide the ideal proving ground for candidates, at clerkship and judicial ranks, to gain deeper understanding of the tensions and rule of law concerns that are important for Europe as a whole. Without such a sphere for trans-European debate, and with a selection process that is centred on and in the end determined by the Member States, it remains difficult (though not impossible) for the composition of the Court truly to reflect European legal knowledge, based on understandings that transcend expertise in specific Member State common or civil law systems. Indeed, a European public space can facilitate rule of law debates at a European level, not just at the level of Member States, each of which is subject to its own particularities of legal historical development and systemic bias.

5.5 Lack of a European Public Space and Its Contribution to the European Crises

As mentioned, the recent successive European crises have shaken the foundations of the European project, bringing democratic disillusionment, economic crisis, environmental concerns and social problems. It is my view that certain key dimensions of these European crises are directly linked to the main European constitutionalization obstacle analysed, namely the absence of a common

95 Piris, *The Lisbon Treaty*, 361.

96 Case C-50/00 P, *Unión de Pequeños Agricultores* v. *Council* [2002] ECR I-6677.

European public space.[97] In particular, Europe's continuing series of crises have three basic underlying constitutional dimensions, each of which could be addressed by the opening of a truly European public sphere.

In the absence of such a European public sphere, discourse in light of Europe's many crises inevitably fails to accurately identify causes or solutions. This issue is rooted in the disjuncture between where the public believe that national decisions are or should be made – namely at the Member State level – which is also where the only public discourse can occur, and where, in reality, the responsibility for addressing many of the crises rests – namely at the European level. In my view, this has been an extremely important revelation in the context of the European euro crisis, which spread and broadened into a financial crisis that, in turn, revealed important political fault-lines in the European Union, particularly among its poorest and most indebted Member States. For instance, during the recent European financial crisis bail-out, in a clear protest against the established parties of Greece,[98] the electorate turned to a fascist party in Greek elections, responding in particular to the withdrawal of a promised referendum on the bail-out package and its conditions. Similarly, the Italian electorate turned to Pepe Grillo's extra-parliamentary Five Star Movement, having lost trust in conventional Italian political promises made by the accepted parties. Such public loss of confidence, and political reactions, took place against a background of bail-outs and austerity decisions that were recommended by the so-called 'troika' of the ECB, the International Monetary Fund (IMF) and the EU Commission. Countries were faced with significant problems in selling their public debt and issuing bonds at reasonable rates unless they agreed to follow ECB recommendations. While the crisis response decisions were being made by Europe, the publics of the affected countries expected their national governments to be able to influence the outcomes and held them accountable when it became clear that such influence had become marginal in the face of crisis.

Member State governments, on the other hand, have also begun to point to such non-democratic and under-debated decision-making at the European or even international levels as justifications for their own weak

[97] On the consequences of the financial and refugee crises for the development of a European public sphere, see H. G. Sicakkan, 'The Role of EU Policies in the Making of the European Public Sphere' in H. G. Sicakkan (ed.), *Integration, Diversity and the Making of a European Public Sphere* (Cheltenham/Northampton, MA 2016) 209, 223 ff.

[98] See Chapter 1.

and ineffectual response. Greek politicians and public discourse, including the media, called vocally for an end to austerity, blaming harsh bail-out decisions on Germany's Chancellor Merkel.[99] Meanwhile, Spain's political elite strongly rejected calls for a bail-out, citing their own impressions of overly harsh bail-out conditions for Greece and Ireland as their principal concern.[100] Finally, the public in Cyprus lost complete faith in the EU when the bail-out included the condition that clients would be required to rescue their own collapsing banks.[101] While these conditions were perceived to be illegitimate in the eyes of the affected publics, at the same time they formed hot debate in the publics of countries who contributed to the bail-out.[102] In the context of the euro crisis, Thomas Risse argues that it was not necessarily the lack of a European public sphere that created the crisis; rather, the crisis highlighted that politics in EU Member States have become Europeanized and that the EU has become politicized. This, in turn, led to higher visibility of EU issues in the media and contributed to higher levels of interconnectedness of the different public spheres.[103]

In my view, this public outrage points to gaps in the emergence of a pan-European sense of community. The characteristics of such a community have been identified as a 'political community which identifies itself as such and which has the regulatory wherewithal, the resources and the sense of common attachment necessary to make decisions which are . . . capable of addressing matters of common interest and are broadly perceived as so doing'[104] (*demos*). A major factor contributing to the gap in a pan-European sense of community is the continuing lack of a trusted and stable European public space in which the crisis and its response could be discussed and which, in turn, would build the sense of common attachment necessary to make accountable decisions.

A second factor that calls into question the pan-European sense of common attachment is, in my opinion, the continuing proliferation of very real language barriers between key groups across Europe. The EU

[99] See Chapter 1.
[100] See Chapter 1.
[101] See Chapter 1.
[102] See Chapter 1.
[103] Risse, *European Public Spheres*, 141, 142.
[104] N. Walker, 'After the Constitutional Moment' in I. Pernice and M. Maduro (eds.), *A Constitution for the European Union: First Comments on the 2003 Draft of the European Convention* (Baden-Baden 2004); also inFederal Trust Constitutional Online Paper Series No. 32/03. p 26.

itself has twenty-four official languages, leading some to conclude that meaningful public discourse across so many formal linguistic boundaries is at best difficult and at worst impossible. While it is not impossible to have many official languages in a country – South Africa as a rather special case does have twelve – many countries work practically with no more than two or three functional working languages. A sense of community requires mutual understanding and, even though technological advances have helped, a direct European exchange of political views and decision-making is still hampered by having different languages, which, in turn, proliferates existing barriers to the development of a widespread popular media that is a trusted and viable outlet for political debate.

The key concern with this second factor is not a lack of recognition and respect for diverse languages but, rather, a lack of recognized, workable, parallel solutions to communication barriers.[105] While the Court has been pragmatic in this regard, there are further steps that could be taken by the Court and by the institutions, particularly in the area of competition law. For instance, Europe seeks to attract and retain important investors and commercial retailers. However, many investors have signalled that prohibitive costs of translation hamper their ability to ensure truly trans-European establishment and marketing in the most marginalized areas. Certain investors may even choose to establish themselves only in certain European countries – not necessarily the zones where investments are most needed – in order to avoid the challenge of engaging with uncommon languages.[106]

The final factor hindering the pan-European community is the lack of trans-border media transmission on EU issues. For example, during the financial crisis, it is quite possible that the Greek media completely misunderstood and in part misrepresented policy statements by German politicians at the time.[107] These media reports received high levels of attention in Germany but were not debated in most other EU Member States. Once such a dynamic leads to journals such as the *Frankfurter Allgemeine Zeitung* disseminating the idea that Germany, which heavily contributed to the bail-out, was being blamed by bail-out countries for the crisis itself or was being blamed for the bail-out conditions,[108] rational political exchange and decision-making becomes more difficult.

[105] See Section 2.5.3.
[106] See Chapter 1.
[107] See Chapter 1.
[108] See Chapter 1.

In my view, the corollary to this understanding is that successive crises in Europe engage important questions of legitimacy at the European level itself. Many have highlighted growing inequalities and rising costs of living for socially and economically excluded groups in European Member States.[109] If these marginalized communities had a better voice in the governance of Europe, these issues could be properly debated in a common public sphere, and decreases in living conditions and rising poverty levels could be taken into account more directly, rather than being addressed simply through agricultural subsidies or structural funds. Without mechanisms for such inclusion, these groups turn to Eurosceptical parties, as evidenced by the dangerously low approval rating of EU decision-making in the polls of many European countries.[110]

Eurosceptic parties are on the rise in all Member States – mainly on the right of the political spectrum. For example, the German AfD achieved 4.5 per cent in the German general election in 2013[111] and the UK Prime Minister was forced to calm Eurosceptic backbenchers in his own Conservative Party, as well as members of the UK Independence Party, who had made sweeping gains in local elections in England, with the promise of an in–out referendum.[112] Meanwhile, extreme parties such as the Dutch Freedom Party and the French Front National appear poised to achieve double-digit results in the next European election.[113] Increases in Euroscepticism are linked to a public perception that Europe is not representative and, indeed, as discussed in Chapter 4, that there is a lack of pan-European political parties in which political ideas and European answers are debated at the EU level.

A further sign of the political crisis in Europe is indicated by the firm rejection of the European Constitutional Treaty in key Member States.[114] In my view, the fact that these referenda were held in different EU Member States at different times made it easy for critics to recast them as votes on EU integration in general, rather than debating the finer points of constitutional change proposed.[115] As noted in Chapter 1,

[109] See C. Joerges, 'Europe's Economic Constitution in Crisis', ZenTra Working Papers in Transnational Studies 6/2012 (Bremen 2013), http://ssrn.com/abstract=2179595. See Chapter 2.

[110] See Chapter 1.

[111] See Chapter 1.

[112] See Chapter 1.

[113] See Chapter 1.

[114] See Chapter 1.

[115] See proposals by the German Green Party and comment by Weiler. It has also been dubbed an 'integration referendum': F. Schimmelfennig, 'Getting Around No: How

popular sentiment from media outlets, including *The Economist* after the 2005 referenda in France and the Netherlands, focused on the need for the EU to 'decentralize' and 'loosen' its structure, rather than more nuanced aspects of this debate. The fact that each of the referendum States focused on its own national interest, rather than a common European one, has, in part, been identified as one of the problems of the EU constitutional process. This, some have argued, points to deeper levels of discomfort and concern with regard to the degree and pace of EU integration and potentially the sustainability of the European electoral processes more broadly. The organization of these elements is still carried out at the Member State level, which in turn undermines its constitutional relevance for the European Union as a whole and, as seen by Member State court decisions such as in the GFCC, it allows Member States to declare the functioning of the European Parliament as irrelevant from a national perspective. This undermines legitimacy and a sense of civic duty in the EU.

Crucially, a further corollary series of challenges remains in the essential problems related to a pan-European public sphere perception of law. Key sustainable development commitments at the European level include efforts to halt serious environmental degradation and to promote widespread respect for basic human rights; however, these problems continue and are in fact growing across Europe. In particular, the EU is grappling with a lack of effective enforcement mechanisms, both in terms of environment and human rights directives and regulations that are consistently not respected and in terms of a lack of access to justice for those whose rights have been violated. One such example is the lack of access to justice for victims of trans-boundary environmental harms in collective situations such as climate change or species loss, or the lack of control over illegal degradation of fisheries, forests, water or ecosystem services.

It is my understanding and analysis that these elements of continuing European crises relate particularly to the lack of any EU public sphere. At the moment, global concerns that require a Europe-wide response, such as climate change, environmental decisions and human rights enforcement, are largely subject only to administrative or executive European decision-making and implementation. The political debates about such

Governments React to Negative EU Referendums' (2019) 26 *Journal of European Public Policy* 1056, 1061; A. Auer, 'The People Have Spoken: Abide? A Critical View of the EU's Dramatic Referendum (In)Experience' (2016) 12 *European Constitutional Law Review* 397, 404.

concerns, important as they are, occur almost entirely within the national public spheres. Without a European public sphere, these issues cannot be properly debated with a view to building European policy consensus and providing for implementation beyond national (and individualistic) Member State constituencies. It is my concern that this dynamic simply reinforces the tendency of Member State priorities to rule at the executive level and weakens the possibility for political decisions to be taken in the overall European interest, as debated by an informed public in a legitimate and deliberative process.

Meanwhile, in the legal dimension, the same tendency to reinforce Member State priorities plays out with respect to *Kompetenz-Kompetenz*. In my view, this tendency is deeply problematic; defining the jurisdiction of the European Union and its law is increasingly important due to the potential for European interpretations of the law to contribute so notably to resolving crises. As Stone Sweet has shown,[116] in areas such as sex equality and freedom of goods, the Court has forcefully demonstrated its capacity to drive forward institutional change by defining the limits of its own powers. Yet, in spite of this capacity, regrettably, the CJEU in *Pringle* failed to fully endorse any of the changes necessary. Instead, the Court chose to support actions by Member States even when those actions led to circumventing the EU institutions.[117]

Moreover, the adoption of the ESM outside the EU Treaty framework was criticized as a violation of the monetary policy competence.[118] The applicants argued that the ESM served to stabilize the currency and thus fell within the Treaty competence. However, the CJEU disagreed, characterizing the ESM as a financial policy that it deemed as being currently outside the scope covered by the Treaties. The Court thus endorsed a treaty design for an ESM that, although it relies on EU institutions such as the ECB and the EC, remains formally outside the EU law structure.[119] It is hard to see this approach as anything but a further contribution to the crisis in the receiving Member States. Conditions were proposed outside the EU legal framework and arguably in violation of its legal obligations in relation to, for instance, worker rights and

[116] Stone Sweet, 'The Judicial Construction of Europe'.

[117] *Pringle*.

[118] *Pringle*. On the 'fuzzy boundary' between the EU competences at issue, see M. Waibel, 'Monetary Policy: An Exclusive Competence Only in Name?' (2017) University of Cambridge Legal Research Paper No.11/2017, 15–20, https://ssrn.com/abstract=2915162.

[119] *Pringle*.

pension rules.[120] While the ESM arguably helped to stabilize the single currency quickly, it did not always respect EU law itself, in the process.[121] The policy debates in a European public sphere could have not only lessened the impacts of this deviation from ordinary constitutional practice but actually contributed to more considered solutions that integrated social, environmental and other European laws and policies.[122] The CJEU could have enabled such debate to take place had it been willing to find that the ESM was in fact adopted in violation of EU monetary policy competence.

Further, a key aspect of the recent European financial crisis has been the perception in certain Member States (but without any possibility of articulating it in an EU public sphere) that crisis management was not being carried out in accordance with the rule of law. Particularly in Greece, for example, the government suspended important social and political rights, and none of the proposals by the troika for the Greek bailout were subject to judicial review or full control.[123] It is embarrassing to the EU that it took an ILO committee to rule that the sweeping pension reforms in Greece constituted violations of international labour conventions when the CJEU should have constrained any sweeping reforms of doubtful EU legality.[124] The fact that the CJEU is tasked with reviewing the implementation of the Growth and Stability Pact might seem an effort to strengthen that institution; however, critics have pointed out that the CJEU's competence is so limited that one cannot avoid the impression that it is used only to lend broader legitimacy to the Pact rather than having any real judicial power with teeth. Undeniably, however, a stamp of approval from the CJEU will carry weight, given that it is the only EU institution that is still widely trusted and fully respected

[120] ILO, 'ILO Calls on Greece to Bring Its Labour Relations System Back to Fundamental Rights', 15 November 2012, www.ilo.org/brussels/press/press-releases/WCMS_193308/lang–en/index.htm.

[121] C. Wiesner, *Meanings of Europe: Changes and Exchanges of a Contested Concept* (Abingdon 2014).

[122] C. Kilpatrick and B. de Witte, 'Social Rights in Times of Crisis in the Eurozone: The Role of Fundamental Rights' Challenges' (22 April 2014), EUI Law Research Paper No. 2014/05, https://papers.ssrn.com/sol3/papers.cfm?abstract_id=2428855.

[123] See Chapter 1.

[124] See further S. Garben, 'The Problematic Interaction between EU and International Law in the Area of Social Rights' (2018) 7 *Cambridge International Law Journal* 77; N. A. Papadopoulos, 'Austerity-Based Labour Market Reforms in Greece vs Fundamental Rights in the Aftermath of the European Debt Crisis: An Analysis of Supranational and National Bodies' Jurisprudence' (forthcoming) *European Public Law* 24, https://ssrn.com/abstract=3276880.

across Member State boundaries.[125] The public has perceived the review powers of the CJEU in this regard to be merely a design feature and thus has continued to question the legitimacy of the EU's crisis management and bail-out. Curiously, many people sensed that the CJEU should have taken a more proactive approach to reviewing the legality of crisis management decisions. Actions such as closing the last remaining public broadcaster in Greece seemed, to some, a clear violation of EU law and, in the eye of the public, should have triggered a CJEU reaction.[126]

The crises are still ongoing, characterized by continuing concerns of further financial instability and the growing popularity of Eurosceptic parties in key national elections. To help address the constitutional dimensions of such crises, my study of the centre-periphery dialogues of the European Courts has identified the key obstacles and can guide the EU in focusing upon the issues that cannot be addressed simply by incrementalism.

According to Stephen Griffin[127] and not unlike many of the historical institutionalists who emphasize the importance of crises for state-building efforts,[128] Ackerman seems to presuppose the existence of a crisis:[129]

> At two of the greatest crises in their history Americans faced the very grave risk of a false negative. If they chose to play punctiliously by the rules of Art. 5, reconstruction republicans and New Deal democrats confronted the clear and present danger that their long and successful struggle to mobilize the People for fundamental change would be [lost in] legalistic nitpicking.[130]

In other words, as Ackerman advocates, in times of crisis, many constitutional polities rely on the people on whom the transformation itself (and thus the shape of the adaptive mechanisms themselves) relies.

Fundamentally, the options for addressing the constitutional dimensions of these continuing European crises might, especially where appropriate adaptive mechanisms exist, include incrementalism or formal amendment, but it may well be that a type of higher law-making is

125 See Chapter 1.
126 See Chapter 1.
127 S. M. Griffin, 'Constitutional Theory Transformed' (1999) 108 *Yale Law Journal* 2115, 2130.
128 See C. Bright and S. F. Harding (eds.), *Statemaking and Social Movements: Essays in History and Theory* (Ann Arbor, MI 1984).
129 Ackerman, *We the People: Vol. 2: Transformations*, 29.
130 Ibid.

actually necessary. The next sections turn to the recommendations that could advance European constitutionalization even in this context of significant remaining obstacles, based on my research and analysis.

5.6 Europe's Constitutional Moment and Potential Adaptive Mechanisms for European Constitutionalization

To chart a way forward that addresses the remaining obstacle and related challenges, the potential adaptive mechanisms for constitutional transitions in Europe can and must be identified.

An adaptive mechanism is a legitimate measure for changing the existing constitutional order and for enshrining popular democracy. As Christian Kirchner explains from an EU constitutional economics viewpoint, the role of an adaptive mechanism is to allocate competencies between the European Union and the Member States, and the search for such an adaptive mechanism is an 'institutional task'.[131] Generally, adaptive mechanisms are necessary only in dual democracies when higher law-making is different from general law-making.[132] Adaptive mechanisms can include formal constitutional amendments but also other measures such as legislative or judicial decisions.[133] In the European context, adaptive mechanisms could take the form of formally recognized and regularized amendments to constitutional documents, court decisions reinterpreting constitutional rules, or simply legitimate amendments of constitutional practices, among other measures.

In Ackerman's early works, he has pointed to the fact that the English constitution was far from monolithic and required a great deal of (unwritten) adaptation after the English Civil War.[134] Meanwhile, a similar adaptation process relative to the Canadian Constitution has taken place mainly through adaptations within the different branches of the government, rather than relying on a constitutional referendum by the Canadian people.[135] Indeed, as he notes in a recent study of the

[131] C Kirchner, 'The Principle of Subsidiarity in the Treaty on European Union: A Critique from a Perspective of Constitutional Economics' (1998) 6 *Tulane Journal of International and Comparative Law* 305.

[132] See Ackerman, *We the People: Vol. 2: Transformations*, 29.

[133] Kirchner.

[134] B. A. Ackerman and R. E. Charney, 'Canada at the Constitutional Crossroads' (1984) 34 *University of Toronto Law Journal* 117, 120.

[135] Ibid., 133.

American New Deal and the American civil rights revolution, no formal constitutional amendment was pursued due to the state-centred veto, which, while part of the formal US Constitution Article V Amendment process, was seen to be 'at odds with American political identity' in the twentieth century.[136]

While some observers argue that only formal amendments are relevant to constitutional law, English and Canadian constitutional changes are clear examples that non-formal constitutional amendment should not be trivialized. As Ackerman explains, it 'did succeed in adapting the separation-of-powers tradition to vindicate popular sovereignty in an America that had become a nation'.[137] In my view, the fundamental importance of such non-formal constitutional amendments is that they recognize that certain adaptive mechanisms depend on the existence of a common public sphere; a space that is currently weak, if not void, in Europe today.

In my view, there are essentially three European adaptive mechanisms that might be activated to address the remaining *demos* obstacle of a lack of European public space and its corollaries. One mechanism, which may be seen as somewhat Panglossian, would be to invoke further fundamental constitutional change whereby the *pouvoir constituant*, namely, the People, would join together in a massive expression of popular sovereignty and decide through higher law-making that a common public space should be created, addressing all of the corollary challenges in one moment of sympathetic pan-European decision-making.

The second option would be to rely upon the continued elite-led European institutional and administrative decision-making processes, for example through formal amendment of the European constitutional treaties or through engaging the Member State governments and EU institutions in finding and quietly applying a new *entente* or practice on each different issue that arises, crisis by crisis. Although this second option has been effective in addressing several of the potential obstacles to further constitutionalization demonstrated in this volume's analysis, it could prove particularly difficult as a way forward to address the lack of a European public space and its corollary challenges, which *par definition* depends upon the actual engagement of an informed and knowledgeable European public. As the dominance of these elite-led institutions has,

[136] B. A. Ackerman, *We the People: Vol. 3: The Civil Rights Revolution* (Cambridge, MA 2014), 311.

[137] Ibid., 312.

arguably, been part of the problem to date, this may be a less than satisfactory method of redressing this particular obstacle.

The third – and the most European – way to overcome this particular obstacle and its corollaries is for constitutional change by jurisprudence. This is a process in which the CJEU and the Member State courts activate their dialogue of the courts for the benefit of Europe and its people, taking up and deciding further key cases in a way that – while subject to certain caveats – can lay important foundations for a common European public space. As demonstrated in Chapters 2, 3 and 4, this method has proven remarkably successful in advancing solutions to certain other constitutional obstacles, along all three *demos*, *civitas* and *ius* dimensions of European constitutionalization; thus, it deserves careful attention in this study.

This section briefly discusses each of these options, before focusing on the third.

5.6.1 *European Popular Sovereignty and the Holy Grail of a Constitutional Moment*

What might be the first and best option for constitutional change, as Ackerman and others also suggest, is for our European political actors to become self-consciously engaged in higher law-making outside of the normal constitutional process. In essence, the idea is that, as the coming series of crises begins to deepen and anti-European voices become more strident in every country, higher law-making has an important role, even as the European economy, environment and society depend more heavily on deeper integration.

A moment of higher law-making depends on a 'failure of formal rules of constitutional amendment that are designed to constitute and regulate constitutional politics without becoming part of it'.[138] These rules will 'fail in situations where they cannot perform their central function which is to channel debates over constitutional change through procedures that yield institutional decisions that political actors accept as authoritative, i.e. constitutional decision procedures themselves are far from substantively neutral and reflect competing conceptions of the very sorts of values that are the gist of constitutional politics'.[139] In my view, the

[138] S. Choudhury, 'Ackerman's Higher Lawmaking', 197. Also on higher lawmaking, see Y. Roznai, *Unconstitutional Constitutional Amendments: The Limits of Amendment Powers* (Oxford 2017) 127.

[139] Ibid.

absence of a European public sphere has led the formal rules of constitutional amendment in the EU to 'fail' in the manner that Ackerman describes; without a sphere in which to channel debates about constitutional change, the formal rules lack the ability to effect such change. Higher law-making provides a solution.

As Ackerman and others have explained, higher law-making consists of a number of stages. First there is 'signalling', whereby a constitutional problem is signalled at an early stage. If the current constitutional status quo does not allow for any form of change, a popular movement 'earns the constitutional authority to claim that . . . its reform agenda should be placed at the centre of sustained public scrutiny'.[140] This is followed by the second stage – the proposal – a phase during which the popular movement translates its call for change 'into a series of more or less operational proposals for constitutional reform'.[141] While there might be many ways to solve a problem, constitutional moments all have in common the principle that their problems cannot be overcome by day-to-day politics in the normal political process. Operational proposals are unviable in the current constitutional setting. There are signals showing where fundamental change is needed and where the current constitutional order bars the exact institutions that are most necessary from triggering more fundamental constitutional change. The third stage is one of 'mobilized deliberation', which in itself comprises a series of sub-stages. This stage is characterized by a 'constitutional impasse' among different branches of the federal government, usually reflecting a resistance by conservative branches of the government to the proposed constitutional changes.

As with the remaining obstacles to further constitutionalization, these stages cannot easily be overcome by changed political or constitutional practice or changed judicial interpretation. What is needed, as Ackerman has shown, is a decisive electoral mandate for the institutional proponents of revolutionary constitutional change, where the proponents are prepared to advance an unconventional assault on the conservative institutions. This, as Ackerman has posited, is where the People play an important role; while revolutionary change is not always necessary, it is only overwhelming democratic support that can facilitate and trigger the change that will invariably lead us to a 'constitutional moment'. Then, the dissenting institutions will often come to endorse the constitutional change, which is concluded with a consolidating election in which the public

[140] Ackerman, *We the People: Vol. 1: Foundations*, 266.
[141] Ibid.

ratifies this 'inter-institutional settlement'.[142] This new constitutional order can be endorsed by the courts; a step that is crucial in a federal polity such as the European Union, where not only the central but also the periphery courts play a role in constitutional development and can influence acceptance of constitutional change.

The possibility of higher law-making may be favourable, yet, in order for this to work, it is the People of Europe themselves who need to be convinced that further constitutionalization of the European Union as a federal polity is both possible and necessary. Given the rampant misconceptions that were identified in constitutional press coverage, scholarship and jurisprudence throughout Europe – including among Member State courts themselves – it remains difficult to see how such conceptions could be swiftly, if at all, rectified without such higher law-making. If, through higher law-making, the People of Europe decided to directly establish a common European public sphere, it could have immediate repercussions in shaping how EU elections are conducted, in establishing and strengthening truly EU-wide political parties, in recognizing a functional number of working languages for Europe-wide policy debates in which more than an expert linguist could participate openly, in the selection of judges with Europe-wide legitimacy and knowledge, and in expanding the jurisdiction of the Court over that of the Member States.

It is my belief that a common EU public space could be established directly by the European people, as has been the case in other federal entities, through higher law-making. Some might even call the creation of a European public sphere a 'constitutional moment'. This moment must be significant, as explained by Walker,[143] but it must go beyond this; it must be built upon more than just abstract ideals or visionary political rhetoric. Such a development would require extraordinary public awareness and a popular movement across current national divides in order to fundamentally change the structure of the polity. For the remaining obstacle, this is particularly important. The very absence of a European public sphere actually *drives and is also driven by* the current dearth of deep popular involvement of the People to mobilize and activate this engagement. It is quite possible that the establishment of a common public space might, indeed, be one day achieved in Europe through a constitutional moment, led by the People. However, at present this is

[142] Ackerman, *We the People: Vol. 2: Transformations*, 18–20.
[143] Walker, 'Europe's Constitutional Momentum'.

unrealistic to expect for the very reason that, tautological though it may seem, such a public sphere does not yet exist to guide and stimulate the popular movement required for a 'constitutional moment'. Moreover, in my view, following the catastrophic failure of the Constitutional Convention in France and the Netherlands, it would be unreasonable to expect that an EU public sphere could be formed from either higher law-making or a constitutional moment.

In my view, where the possibility of a 'constitutional moment' is unlikely, as it is in the context of creating an EU public sphere, further adaptive mechanisms become all the more important and require particular consideration. I consider that there are two such mechanisms, based on the analysis, each of which I will now deal with in turn.

5.6.2 *The Challenge of Further Elite-Led European Institutional Reform*

The absence of a European public sphere and its corollary obstacles to further EU constitutionalization could conceivably be overcome simply by further incrementalism, either through formal amendment of the constitutional treaties or through elite-led and legitimized fundamental changes in constitutional practices. As discussed in Chapters 1 and 2 above, formal treaty change is possible under the Lisbon Treaty and can be combined with a convention process. As Art. 48 TEU mandates:

> If the European Council, after consulting the European Parliament and the Commission, adopts by a simple majority a decision in favour of examining the proposed amendments, the President of the European Council shall convene a Convention composed of representatives of the national Parliaments, of the Heads of State or Government of the Member States, of the European Parliament and of the Commission. ... The Convention shall examine the proposals for amendments and shall adopt by consensus a recommendation to a conference of representatives of the governments of the Member States as provided for in paragraph 4.

In other words, the final decision-making body on these matters remains the (IGC); a rationale that is justified by recognizing that any Convention is always negotiating in the shadow of the IGC and its European Member State governments.[144]

[144] On Art. 48, TEU, see E. Denza, 'Article 48' in H.-J. Blanke and S. Mangiameli (eds.), *The Treaty on European Union (TEU): A Commentary* (Berlin/Heidelberg 2013) 1331; S. Hug and T. König, 'In View of Ratification: Governmental Preferences and Domestic Constraints at the Amsterdam Intergovernmental Conference' (2002) 56 *International*

The Constitutional Convention and its IGC were the closest process that Europe offered, in terms of a formal Amendment procedure, where formal line-by-line Treaty modifications are included in incremental changes. EU history shows that the combination of the Convention process and the IGC can work reasonably well, as long as the members of the IGC defer to the Convention. Taking the Charter of Fundamental Rights as one such example, discussed in Chapter 4, we note that this document proceeded as an experts convention with relatively little political attention or pressure, where the most important controversy surrounded the reference to God in the preamble, on which conservative members tried unsuccessfully to insist.[145] The IGC adopted the Charter as a non-binding document at the Nice IGC and solemnly declared that all three institutions – the Commission, the Parliament and the Council – would be bound by its terms. In many ways, this level of non-interference with the work of the fundamental rights convention made the Charter a less controversial and, arguably, constitutionally, a more successful project.[146]

Any polity, including the European Union, could of course change its constitution through engagement with, and ultimately the will of, the European people, which could be achieved, for instance, by way of an elected Convention rather than an appointed one. However, there are fundamental structural problems with this approach. Even though the EU's constitutional text is easier to change than perhaps the US Constitution, its current adaptive mechanism neither involves nor is capable of invoking popular support. While governments could, by themselves, without the European People, change the constitutional text, in the absence of a referendum, any such amendment would not enshrine popular democracy.

The convention process outcome was substantively changed by the IGC and most convention discussions were conducted in the looming shadow of IGC debates. Member State governments, who often have very

Organization 447; J. Reinhard, J. Biesenbender and K. Holzinger, 'Do Arguments Matter? Argumentation and Negotiation Success at the 1997 Amsterdam Intergovernmental Conference' (2014) 6 *European Political Science Review* 283.

145 J. Meyer and N. Bernsdorff, *Kommentar zur Charta der Grundrechte der Europäischen Union* (Baden-Baden 2003) 15.

146 A. Maurer, 'Less Bargaining – More Deliberation: The Convention Method for Enhancing EU Democracy' (2003) *Internationale Politik und Gesellschaft* 167. On the pitfalls of lowest common denominator bargaining, see E. Jones, R. D. Kelemen and S. Meunier, 'Failing Forward? The Euro Crisis and the Incomplete Nature of European Integration' (2016) *Comparative Political Studies* 49.

distinct domestic agendas, find themselves discussing prospective treaty changes and can rarely advance beyond the lowest common denominator.[147] Europe's 2002 Constitutional Convention became rapidly very political and the subsequent IGC changed the draft Constitutional Treaty significantly.[148] While Walker has argued that the Convention itself might be considered a European 'constitutional moment',[149] it is difficult to agree if one takes the lack of popular mobilization, the IGC interference and the Member State ratification processes into account. Some commentators believe that even the ordinary legislative procedure adopted by the Constitutional Convention is incredibly cumbersome.[150] The Constitutional Convention and its Rome IGC therefore provide a case in point to demonstrate this problem.

A similar experience determined the Lisbon IGC, as well as the IGC in Brussels in 2011, to resolve the financial crisis and create the ESM.[151] In both instances, while fundamental change could have been on top of the agenda, the imagination of the people was not captured and governments divided on issues such as Council representation and qualified majority voting.[152] IGCs have proven to be the weakest point in the Constitutional Treaty process.[153] An IGC is limited *by its very nature* in what it can achieve to support the establishment and activation of a truly European public sphere. In my view, IGCs may be one of the reasons that such formal amendment procedures may not be the most effective adaptive mechanism.

Bruce Ackerman and others have long identified incrementalism as a further constitutional adaptive mechanism.[154] The process of incrementalism sees existing European constitutional institutions take advantage of their functions in unprecedented ways, creating modified institutional approaches and structures that contradict existing constitutional norms, using complex and heuristic methods. The changes

147 Hug and König.

148 E. O. Eriksen, J. E. Fossum and A. Menéndez (eds.), *Developing a Constitution for Europe* (London 2004) 14.

149 Walker, 'Europe's Constitutional Momentum'.

150 Craig and de Búrca, *The Evolution of EU Law.*

151 Council Regulation (EU) No. 407/2010 of 11 May 2010 establishing a European financial stabilisation mechanism, OJ L 118.

152 P. W. Thurner and F. U. Pappi, *European Union Intergovernmental Conferences: Domestic Preference Formation, Transgovernmental Networks and the Dynamics of Compromise* (London 2009) 23.

153 Reinhard, Biesenbender and Holzinger, 292.

154 Ackerman, *We the People: Vol. 2: Transformations*, 18–20.

brought about by the Treaty of Lisbon are one such example. In my view, this constitutional document, while propounded by elite-led reform, has spearheaded incrementalism, particularly with regard to the role of the European Parliament. As Chapter 3 has explored, the effect of the insertion of Art. 10 TEU has been to bring about a greater role for the European Parliament such that it now functions to rival other federal parliaments.[155]

In my view, the European Parliament has demonstrated a real willingness to fulfil the greater role that Art. 10 TEU envisages – as most clearly exemplified by the *Spitzenkandidaten* system.[156] The practice of *Spitzenkandidaten* refers to the designation of leading candidates for the different political parties in the European Union; a change that was practised in the 2014 European Parliament elections.[157] This system encouraged political discourse across Member State borders and, for the first time in almost four decades, the levels of participation in European elections did not drop.[158] Even though the system was not ultimately used in the 2019 von der Leyen Commission, two of the *Spitzenkandidaten* found themselves in leading positions in her Cabinet.[159] If such changes in constitutional practice provide a possible route for addressing the remaining overarching obstacle and its related challenges, this may offer a possible way forward. This discussion sits within the broader field of institutional constitutional law (*Staatsorganisationsrecht*), which has long been occupied with ideal forms of constitutional institutions and their interaction.[160] For example, building on the case law in different federal systems, governmental

155 See Section 3.8.

156 On the evolution of the *Spitzenkandidaten* system, see S. van Hecke, W. Wolfs and V. de Groof, '25 Years of Spitzenkandidaten: What Does the Future Hold?' (2018) Wilfred Martens Centre for European Studies Policy Brief, https://martenscentre.eu/sites/default/files/publication-files/ces_policybrief_spitzenkandidaten-web.pdf.

157 Hobolt, 'A Vote for the President?', 1–13. Reflecting on the most recent elections, see M. Dawson, 'Should the EU Think Twice before Dumping Its Spitzenkandidaten?', Verfassungsblog (2019), https://verfassungsblog.de/should-the-eu-think-twice-before-dumping-its-spitzenkandidaten/.

158 H. Schmitt, S. B. Hobolt and S. A. Popa, 'Does Personalization Increase Turnout? Spitzenkandidaten in the 2014 European Parliament Elections' (2015) 16 *European Union Politics* 347.

159 A. Gray, J. Barigazzi and M. de la Baume, 'Who Killed the Spitzenkandidat? No Shortage of Suspects in Drama over How EU Should Be Governed' (7 May 2019) *Politico*, www.politico.eu/article/who-killed-the-spitzenkandidat-european-parliament-election-2019-transition/.

160 M. Kloepfer, *Verfassungsrecht. 1. Grundlagen, Staatsorganisationsrecht, Bezüge zum Völker-und Europarecht* (Munich 2011).

decision-making is spread throughout different institutions in federal structures. Even in the best circumstances, the interaction between these different institutions is not always smooth. Indeed, the GFCC once felt itself forced to intervene when key competences were to be transferred from the Länder to the federal government, noting that their representation in the Bundesrat was not enough to safeguard their interests.[161] The increase in electoral participation that was witnessed as a result of this process illustrates the power of incrementalism to foster the creation of a European public sphere – the success of which is measured by, amongst other criteria, active participation by the electorate.

However, change in the mandates of European institutions through constitutional amendment or established practice is often a very long process. While the *Spitzenkandidaten* system did serve to increase engagement on EU issues at Member State level, without a European public sphere to openly debate these issues, we cannot be clear that these changes will actually contribute to wiser or better constitutionalization. In many respects, the Lisbon Treaty can be seen as actually rolling back some of the achievements under earlier EU Treaty iterations. Caroline Reh, for instance, has argued that in the post-Lisbon era, it is increasingly difficult to pinpoint executive power.[162] The increase in powers to the European Parliament through the EP budgetary powers and the right given to the European Parliament to elect the President of the Commission, combined with the simultaneous increase in Presidential powers through the establishment of a permanent European Council, is one factor that has led Reh to conclude that the Treaty of Lisbon is leading to 'deconstitutionalization'.[163]

Meanwhile, as other commentators have gone further to argue, constitutional development by incrementalism can lead the constitutionalization process in a dangerous and potentially fatal direction.[164] In a recent insightful book, Ackerman argues that such developments can accelerate and, if left unchecked, lead to serious pathologies in the future.[165] In the European context, the establishment of the European Growth and Stability Pact outside of the EU constitutional framework is

[161] See GFCC on *Länderfinanzausgleich*, Judgment of 11 November 1999, 2 BvF 1/99, ECLI: DE:BVerfG:1999:fs19991111.2bvf000298.

[162] C. Reh, 'The Lisbon Treaty: De-Constitutionalizing the European Union?' (2009) 47 *Journal of Common Market Studies* 625, 369.

[163] Ibid.

[164] Ackerman, *The Decline and Fall of the American Republic.*

[165] Ibid., 7.

one such example of the dangers of incrementalism. As mentioned in Chapter 1, the constitutional dimensions of this instrument remain problematic, despite its legitimization by the Grand Chamber of the CJEU in the *Pringle* judgment. This supports Ackerman's concerns that an incrementalist approach risks undermining the establishment of the very sphere that is necessary for open and transparent Europe-wide public political debates, as the example of the Stability Pact clearly demonstrates.

Finally, the recent bruising experience of the Constitutional Convention has, in my view, demonstrated that our usual elite-led amendment procedures of incrementalism will simply not work for the establishment of a common European public sphere. In essence, the Convention vision, process and outcomes could be seen as a 'memory of the days when the method of government was "diplomacy" rather than "democracy"'.[166] If this is the case, different adaptive mechanisms must be found and activated to lay the foundations for Europe's 'Second Constitution'. In essence, the best way to ensure popular democracy at the EU level would be not only through the Member States but rather through genuine, independent EU institutions, with little or no interference from Member State governments.[167]

In Chapters 2, 3 and 4, this book has shown that incremental changes in Europe have largely led to positive outcomes from a pro-European perspective. Yet the future of this approach may be less than adequate. We have left the worst and most intractable constitutional problems for last, and they do linger. Addressing them through formal amendment or incrementalism, while possibly effective, could take decades, and the outcome reached may still remain deficient in important areas. In a worst-case scenario, this strategy might even find itself characterized as increasingly undemocratic and illegitimate, feeding the anti-European nationalist movements at Member State levels and contributing to the social, economic and political series of crises that currently characterizes European integration. If a desired transformation truly centres on the people, incrementalism might fall far short in democratic legitimacy.[168]

Essentially, the time has come in Europe's constitutionalization process where we must question whether elite-led constitutional amendment or technocratic incremental change can genuinely provide the European

[166] D. M. Curtin, 'Judging EU Secrecy' (2012) 2 *Cahiers de Droit Européen* 459, 461.
[167] Cohn-Bendit and Verhofstadt; see also Piris, *The Future of Europe.*
[168] See, with the same idea, Cohn-Bendit and Verhofstadt.

public sphere necessary for further constitutionalization. Its absence has arguably contributed to the crises and cannot easily be addressed by the same approaches we have adopted in the past. Even though 'each crisis tends to have resulted in an intensification of communication about Europe',[169] there is currently no joint political space in which to debate solutions. The crises remain national in nature.

As one clear further indication, the failures of both IGCs and changes in the practices of European institutions to act as clear and forceful adaptive mechanisms for Europe do not inspire confidence that EU incrementalism will manage to overcome the remaining obstacles. As Section 5.6.3 will explore, this decision, although belonging in the hands of the People of Europe, has the power to be propounded by the European institutions, in particular by the Court.

5.6.3 *Potential Contributions of European Jurisprudence towards Constitutionalization*

A third and under-explored adaptive mechanism of the EU is the CJEU and its case law. In many ways the potential of what this jurisprudence can achieve for Europe and its continuing series of crises is remarkable. This adaptive mechanism must be taken into account for any attempt at comprehensive analysis of the continuing European constitutionalization process. As an adaptive mechanism, the CJEU operates on several levels, and not all are especially effective.

On the first level, the EU is demonstrably willing to translate constitutional reform into constitutional doctrine[170] Indeed, in the European Union, many of the fundamental changes suggested by the Court have eventually been codified into the formal constitutional text. There are several instances, most notably with regard to the findings of the Court in *Nold* concerning general principles,[171] when EU governments have codified the CJEU's decision in the treaty text (now Art. 5.3 TEU). Upon codification of the decision in *Nold* by way of the Charter of Fundamental Rights, the CJEU has further demonstrated its eagerness to translate this

169 A. Hepp and others, *The Communicative Construction of Europe: Cultures of Political Discourse* (London 2016) 33.

170 See on a theoretical level for common law countries, P. C. Oliver, *The Constitution of Independence: The Development of Constitutional Theory in Australia, Canada, and New Zealand* (Oxford/New York 2005) 315.

171 Case 4/73, *J. Nold, Kohlen- und Baustoffgroßhandlung* v. *Commission of the European Communities* [1974] ECR 00491.

constitutional reform (i.e. the existence of the Charter) into constitutional doctrine. In my view, the recently decided cases of *Volker/Eifert*[172] and *Test Achat*[173] demonstrate the CJEU's active engagement with Art. 52(4) of the Charter of Fundamental Rights – the obligation to interpret constitutional traditions that are common to Member States in a manner that is harmonious with the Charter.

Meanwhile, on the second level, the CJEU has been hesitant to review the Treaties, which it describes as the EU's constitutional charter.[174] In my view, this is disappointing, given the CJEU's eagerness to actively, and creatively, interpret the Charter of Fundamental Rights – a document of equal status to the Treaties. The Court has had instances where it has felt it has reached the limits of its own adaptive capacity, often, in my view, too early. The most prominent recent example involves the case of *UPA*, where the question that the CJEU sought to answer involved consideration of whether a more liberal interpretation of Art. 263 TFEU might be possible in order to provide individuals and companies with greater direct access to the Court. The Court highlighted the fundamental nature of this question and decided that the Court itself lacked the mandate to change the existing approach, instead calling on Member State governments to change the Treaties if they supported such a fundamental change.[175] It said:

> Finally, it should be added that, according to the system for judicial review of legality established by the Treaty, a natural or legal person can bring an action challenging a regulation only if it is concerned both directly and individually. Although this last condition must be interpreted in the light of the principle of effective judicial protection by taking account of the various circumstances that may distinguish an applicant individually . . ., such an interpretation cannot have the effect of setting aside the condition in question, expressly laid down in the Treaty, without going beyond the jurisdiction conferred by the Treaty on the Community Courts. While it is, admittedly, possible to envisage a system of judicial review of the legality of Community measures of general application different from that established by the founding Treaty and never amended as to its

[172] Joined Cases C-92/09 and C-93/09, *Volker und Markus Schecke GbR (C-92/09) and Hartmut Eifert (C-93/09)* v. *Land Hessen* [2010] ECR I-11063.

[173] Case C-236/09, *Association Belge des Consommateurs Test-Achats ASBL and Others* v. *Conseil des ministres* [2011] ECR I-00773.

[174] Case C-370/12, *Thomas Pringle* v. *Government of Ireland, Ireland and The Attorney General*, Judgment of the Court (Full Court) of 27 November 2012, not yet reported.

[175] C-50/00 P, *Unión de Pequeños Agricultores* v. *Council*, 2002 ECR I-6677.

> principles, it is for the Member States, if necessary, in accordance with Article 48 EU, to reform the system currently in force.[176]

The judgment in *UPA* has been criticized by many practitioners who would have hoped to see the CJEU be willing to take a bolder and more liberal approach to standing requirements. In my view, the extension of standing requirements in this way would not only be within the remit of the CJEU's powers but, owing to the nature of standing requirements themselves as determining the permissibility of when acts of the institutions can be reviewed, would, in turn, also assist in the creation of a European public sphere. Thus, in my opinion, further test cases on standing requirements should be given careful consideration by the CJEU; a solution that respects the criterion of 'individual concern' while simultaneously giving adequate recognition of the need to provide an effective remedy that is not only desirable but also plausible.

On the third level, the Court's jurisprudence may also be problematic as an adaptive mechanism, as it may be perceived as part of the elite project. As Karen Alter has shown, in spite of the imperfect selection procedures for European justices discussed in Chapter 4,[177], many European justices actually share the same convictions about the value and importance of further European integration, and even a certain trans-European ethos.[178]

Beyond these levels on which the CJEU operates, the Court, in other ways, can be seen as playing an instrumental role in giving power back to the citizens, which it has done mainly by allowing them to challenge decisions of their governments through its broad interpretations of the direct effect and jurisdiction of the Court. Owing to the fact that the preliminary reference procedure is not applicable to primary law, the validity of treaty provisions cannot be reviewed in the procedure that provides primary access for citizens to the Court, and because of this, the Court has started to interpret this provision widely.[179]

These qualified caveats aside, as discussed in Chapter 1 of this book, we find that the centre courts do have an important role to play in constitutionalization. Indeed, as Alec Stone Sweet has conclusively shown, the

176 Ibid., paras. 46, 47.

177 See Section 4.3.2.

178 Alter, *The European Court's Political Power*, 8.

179 Case 283/81, *Srl CILFIT and Lanificio di Gavardo SpA* v. *Ministry of Health* [1982] ECR 03415; see also B. W. Wegener, 'Commentary on TFEU Art. 267 (ex-Art. 234 TEC) [Vorabentscheidung]' in C. Calliess and M. Ruffert (eds.), *EUV/AEUV – Das Verfassungsrecht der Europäischen Union – Kommentar*, 4th ed. (Munich 2011).

Court does not routinely side with Member States.[180] Moreover, unlike treaty negotiations and constitutional conventions, it is clear that the Court is hearing real cases about constitutional matters every day as they affect people living within the evolving structures of Europe, and is interpreting the law to resolve the real-life problems.

The importance of the centre courts is further reiterated by appreciating that an adaptive constitutional mechanism that does not exclusively rely on the federated level has been proven very important in federal systems. In civil law systems, it is almost as though a reliance on supermajorities has grown into both parts of the federal parliaments, while federal common law systems such as the United States and Canada appear to experience greater degrees of constitutional change through their Supreme Courts. Given the continuing over-reliance of constitutional adaptive mechanisms at the Member State level, which can be prone to national capture, it is suggested that further adaptation post-Lisbon must rely on the Court as guardian of the Treaties and their spirit. The Court's role in exerting greater *Kompetenz-Kompetenz* could thus turn CJEU decisions into federal (rather than devolved) adaptive mechanisms. For example, the Lisbon Treaty includes an EU citizens' initiative, but the effect is not adaptive and serves only to force the Commission into developing a particular legislative proposal. This falls short of enshrining popular democracy at the European level.[181] As discussed in Chapter 4, however, the Court plays a key role in the constitutionalization of the European Union and has the potential to serve in a notably adaptive capacity.

As seen above, more far-reaching constitutional change could be prepared for by the courts of Europe, through jurisprudence on the key remaining obstacles to constitutionalization. The CJEU could highlight and signal the need for change as it did in *UPA* and, further still, it could exercise its powers more readily to formulate constitutional doctrine, as it failed to do in *UPA*. When it comes to the remaining constitutional obstacles, however, the Court has yet to fully play this role. As the *Pringle* judgment illustrates, the CJEU is hesitant to forcefully exert its own competence or to even highlight where EU constitutional development has not yet reached the stage of progressive development. Certain Advocate Generals have, however, been more forthcoming and have highlighted the need for change or opportunities for further development – an approach that I believe should be more

[180] Stone Sweet, *The Judicial Construction of Europe*.
[181] See discussion in Chapter 3.

frequently adopted.[182] Both through further judicial dialogue with Member State courts and by highlighting very explicitly wherever it reaches the limits of existing constitutional structures, the Court has a unique potential to facilitate the emergence of a European public sphere. Further, it can reach people across Europe with its decisions, making constitutional developments more relevant to people and their problems on the ground, altering Europeans' lived experience of justice and of Europe.

5.6.4 *The Centre-Periphery Dialogue of the European Courts as the Most Interesting Adaptive Mechanism*

European jurisprudence can be understood in a federal context, that is, as a judicial dialogue between the centre and its periphery.[183] This means, as noted in Chapter 1 and as argued by Stone Sweet,[184] Halberstam[185] and Ackerman,[186] that federal friction can occur and can result in conflicting judicial decisions or even the evolution of distinct trends or 'streams' of constitutional development. In Europe, the danger of such contradictions has been particularly acute until relatively recently. Even though there is a federalizing mechanism in the preliminary reference procedure, very few constitutional courts of Member States were using it to answer fundamental questions. In recent years, however, the majority of constitutional courts have begun to directly 'converse' with the CJEU; a dynamic that my research suggests has the potential to accelerate the constitutional judicial construction of Europe. It can be noted that certain constitutional courts on the periphery continue to voice important scepticism, such as the GFCC, which continues to signal both spurious and also serious obstacles to further constitutionalization. However, recently the GFCC for the first time engaged in the preliminary reference procedure, posing a question on monetary policy in *OMT*.[187] This federal centre–periphery dynamic is well

[182] See A.G. Sharpston in Case C-212/06, *Government of Communauté française and Gouvernement wallon* v. *Gouvernement flamand*, [2008] ECR I-01683.

[183] See more generally L. A. Jiménez, 'Constitutional Empathy and Judicial Dialogue in the European Union' (2018) 24 *European Public Law* 57 and F. Perrone, 'The Judicial Path to European Constitutionalism: The Role of the National Judge in the Multi-Level Dialogue' in P. Pinto de Albuquerque, *Judicial Power in a Globalized World: Liber Amicorum Vincent de Gaetano* (Cham 2019), 395.

[184] A. Stone Sweet, 'The Court of Justice' in P. Craig and G. de Búrca (eds.), *The Evolution of EU Law*, 2nd ed. (Oxford 2011).

[185] Halberstam and Reimann.

[186] Ackerman, *We the People: Vol. 2: Transformations.*

[187] GFCC, *OMT*.

documented.[188] In sociology and law, there is a long tradition of centre/core–periphery scholarship, especially in natural law, where organic development is seen as the basis for constitutionalization.[189] Equally, the role of courts in this dynamic has been theorized. As such, even in the United States or Canada, where the Supreme Court is supported by a federal court structure and the common law doctrine of precedent is followed, it is not uncommon for state- or province-level courts to decide in different – more peripheral – fashions, especially on constitutional matters.[190] This study applies this dynamic, which is understood among those studying federal systems in many countries of the world, to my consideration of the related judicial dialogues within the European Union.

However, the greater take-away point from this specific analysis is that the case law demonstrates that the dialogue among the courts of Europe is already developing the tools to highlight and signal which change via an alternative route might be necessary. In several of the identified remaining obstacles, the Court could, in dialogue with Member State courts, highlight the need for fundamental change in a more obvious way, as well as seeking to bring about change where possible.

Informed by the findings of this research, my view is that the central European Court alone, in itself, may not yet be functioning most effectively as an adaptive mechanism. However, the *interactional dialogue between* the myriad courts of Europe is already functioning as a highly flexible and profound adaptive mechanism. This dialogue engages the distinct voices of the highest Member State courts from the periphery together with the European Courts of the centre, and it is much more powerful than is yet understood.

5.7 The Way Forward: Recommendations for Further Constitutionalization of Europe

The Court of Justice is starting to draw certain bright lines with regard to the nature of the constitutional order of Europe. It has now declared that the EU, under international law, is not seeking to be viewed as a State but

188 See, for further references, D. J. Elazar, *Federalism and the Way to Peace* (Kingston, ON 1994).

189 Ibid., 19; D. J. Elazar, *Federal Systems of the World: A Handbook of Federal, Confederal, and Autonomy Arrangements* (Harlow 1991); V. Röben, 'Constitutionalism of the European Union after the Draft Constitutional Treaty: How Much Hierarchy?' (2004) 10 *Columbia Journal of European Law* 339, 346.

190 See Halberstam and Reimann.

rather has its own autonomous constitutional order.[191] In particular, most recently in Opinion 2/13 on the Accession to the European Convention on Human Rights (ECHR Opinion), it found that the EU has indeed its own constitutional order and that the courts on all levels play a special role in developing and interpreting this constitutional order towards further constitutionalization that respects distinctly European values and principles. The full Court explained that,

> [a]s the Court of Justice has repeatedly held, the founding treaties of the EU, unlike ordinary international treaties, established a new legal order, possessing its own institutions, for the benefit of which the Member States thereof have limited their sovereign rights, in ever wider fields, and the subjects of which comprise not only those States but also their nationals (see, in particular, judgments in *van Gend & Loos*, and *Costa* and *Opinion 1/09*).[192]

This was recently affirmed in *Achmea*: 'EU law is characterised by the fact that it stems from an independent source of law, the Treaties, by its primacy over the laws of the Member States, and by the direct effect of a whole series of provisions which are applicable to their nationals and to the Member States themselves' (para. 33) and repeated in the *CETA* Opinion (para. 109). It went on to highlight that the 'fact that the EU has a new kind of legal order, the nature of which is peculiar to the EU, its own constitutional framework and founding principles, a particularly sophisticated institutional structure and a full set of legal rules to ensure its operation, has consequences as regards the procedure for and conditions of accession to the ECHR'.[193] It thus highlighted its own most fundamental and important case law on direct effect in *Van Gend en*

[191] Opinion 2/13 of the Court (Full Court) of 18 December 2014 on the draft agreement providing for the accession of the European Union to the Convention for the Protection of Human Rights and Fundamental Freedoms (ECHR), para 170 [Opinion 2/13 of the Court (Full Court) of 18 December 2014]. See also, most recently: Opinion 1/17, *CETA* [2019] EU:C:2019:341, paras. [107]–[110] (for a comment, see P. Koutrakos, 'More on Autonomy – Opinion 1/17 (CETA)' (2019) 3 *European Law Review* 293); Case C-284/16, *Slovak Republic* v. *Achmea* [2018] EU:C:2018:158, paras. [32]–[35] and [57]-[59]. On EU external autonomy, see J. Odermatt, 'When a Fence Becomes a Cage: The Principle of Autonomy in EU External Relations Law' EUI Working Paper MWP 2016/17; C. Contartese, 'The Autonomy of the EU Legal Order in the ECJ's External Relations Case Law: From the "Essential" to the "Specific Characteristics" of the Union and Back Again' (2017) 54 *Common Market Law Review* 1627; N. Nic Schuibhne, 'What Is the Autonomy of EU Law, and Why Does that Matter?' (2019) 88 *Nordic Journal of International Law* 9, 22–3, 38.

[192] Opinion 2/13 of the Court (Full Court) of 18 December 2014, para. 157.

[193] Opinion 2/13 of the Court (Full Court) of 18 December 2014, paras. 157, 158.

Loos and supremacy in *Costa* as clarifying the constitutional order (together with the *Patent Court Opinion*, which explains that there cannot be any legally binding decision from outside the EU that would bind the Court of Justice) that includes the citizens, not just the Member States themselves.

This reference is particularly important. When considering the role of the Court, it becomes clear that the Court sees its function as not just defending the EU legal order but increasingly also defending Member State nationals as part of that legal order. It further highlighted:

> These essential characteristics of EU law have given rise to a structured network of principles, rules and mutually interdependent legal relations linking the EU and its Member States, and its Member States with each other, which are now engaged, as is recalled in the second paragraph of Article 1 TEU, in a 'process of creating an ever closer union among the peoples of Europe'. This legal structure is based on the fundamental premise that each Member State shares with all the other Member States, and recognizes that they share with it, a set of common values on which the EU is founded, as stated in Article 2 TEU.[194] That premise implies and justifies the existence of mutual trust between the Member States that those values will be recognized and, therefore, that the law of the EU that implements them will be respected.[195]

Implicitly, at least, the Court recognizes the federal structure of the EU and that the main source of legitimacy in the Union is a question of mutual trust.

5.7.1 *Building on Key Threads of European Jurisprudence towards the Construction of a European Public Space*

The role of the courts has been largely neglected in triggering fundamental constitutional change and, as highlighted, there seems to be a lack of understanding about the role of the courts in overcoming fundamental constitutional obstacles. The courts' signalling function has not yet been fully developed. In dialogue with periphery courts, the Court of Justice has been instrumental in overcoming some but not all obstacles to further constitutionalization in Europe. This can change; there is an active role for the Court to play.

[194] Klamert and Kochenov, 22.
[195] Opinion 2/13 of the Court (Full Court) of 18 December 2014, paras. 167, 168.

5.7.1.1 European Public Sphere and Common Citizenship

In the jurisprudence of the central courts, further steps can and should be taken to help provide for a European public space. In addressing *demos* deficits with regard to the development of a truly European citizenship, the Court of Justice has made certain progress, discussed in detail in Chapter 2. In *Ruiz Zambrano*, the Court found that merely being the holder of citizenship was insufficient action on behalf of Member States. Rather, according to the CJEU, Member States are required to ensure that 'genuine enjoyment' of citizenship rights[196] can be guaranteed, across Europe. By this judgment, the CJEU gave force to the citizenship rights of Union members in a way that the Lisbon Treaty, by virtue of its wholly non-adaptive EU citizens' initiative, was not capable of providing. The line of jurisprudence has thus contributed to the development of a European *demos*, addressing the otherwise serious obstacle raised by periphery Member State courts that Europe does not even have a citizenry.

The Court could play a similar, indeed decisive role in overcoming the other remaining obstacles to European constitutionalization, with only a little more courage, a more nuanced conception of federalism and a stronger commitment to establishing the preconditions necessary for Europe's constitutional moment. With regard to this one remaining obstacle, a great deal of effort is still needed to secure a truly common European public space, and a series of test cases could prove to be instrumental in this regard. Future decisions of the Court have the opportunity to either frustrate or foster this effort. In particular, the Court of Justice is advised to consider the arguments of the Advocate General in C-280/11P *Council* v. *Access Info Europe*,[197] initially raised in Chapter 2, and to further crystallize the link between transparency and democracy.[198] This course of reasoning is not uncharted, nor is it inconceivable to extend. As the Court of Justice has highlighted, 'the intention

[196] Case C-34/09, *Gerardo Ruiz Zambrano* v. *Office national de l'emploi (ONEm)* [2011] ECR I-1177.

[197] Case C-280/11 P, *Council of the European Union* v. *Access Info Europe*, Judgment of the Court (First Chamber) of 17 October 2013, not yet reported, para. 63.

[198] For diverse views on transparency and democracy in the EU, see A. Alemanno, 'Unpacking the Principle of Openness in EU Law: Transparency, Participation and Democracy' (2014) 39 *European Law Review* 72; H. Michel, 'La transparence dans l'Union européenne: réalisation de la bonne gouvernance et redéfinition de la démocratie' (2018) 165 *Revue française d'administration publique* 109; J. B. Hollyer, B. P. Rosendorff and J. R. Vreeland, *Transparency, Democracy, and Autocracy: Economic Transparency and Political (In)Stability* (Cambridge 2018), 318.

expressed in the second paragraph of Article 1 TEU of marking a new stage in the process of creating an ever closer union among the peoples of Europe, in which decisions are taken as openly as possible and as closely as possible to the citizen ... is related to the democratic nature of those institutions'.[199] Although, in *Access Info Europe*, the Court allowed access to Council negotiation documents by Member States, the Court has yet to fully endorse or extend the high level of EU transparency to the spheres of Member State jurisdiction even when these are implementing EU law or better, as with fundamental rights 'acting in the sphere of EU law'. The Court could go further, in support of the European *demos*. Federal and federated transparency is the first step for a common public space; a necessary precondition. The Court can create the preconditions for such a development to take place, by building equal trans-European transparency and access to information for all people of Europe, across all Member States.

The challenge raised by the *demos* analysis in Chapter 2 is whether the lack of a common public space could be addressed through further central jurisprudence. One could think of judgments of the ECJ, such as in *Vodafone*[200] on mobile phone charges. The Court decided that mobile phone roaming charges could be regulated by the EU and thus, in this decision, the Court provided a direct benefit for consumers across the Union now facing lower charges when crossing EU borders. In parallel, media outlets across the Union discussed the implications of this judgment, which many deemed to be of direct relevance to consumers. The Court was conscious of this impact when it highlighted that the roaming charge limitation was proportionate because

> [f]inally, in the light of the importance of the objective of consumer protection within the context of Article 95(3) EC, intervention that is limited in time in a market that is subject to competition, which makes it possible, in the immediate future, to protect consumers against excessive prices, such as that at issue, even if it might have negative economic

[199] *Supra* note 197, citing Joined Cases C-39/05 P and C-52/05 P *Sweden and Turco* v. *Council* [2008] ECR I-4723, para. 34; Joined Cases C-514/07 P, C-528/07 P and C-532/07 P *Sweden and Others* v. *API and Commission* [2010] ECR I-8533, para. 68; and Case C-506/08 P *Sweden* v. *MyTravel and Commission* [2011] ECR I-6237, para. 72.

[200] C-58/08 *Vodafone and Others* v. *Secretary of State for Business, Enterprise and Regulatory Reform* [2010] ECR I-4999. For a commentary, see I. Maletic, 'The Story of the EU and the Happily Roaming Consumers Case No. C58/08, Vodafone Ltd, et al. v. Secretary of State for Business, Enterprise and Regulatory Reform' (2011) 38 *Legal Issues of Economic Integration* 199.

consequences for certain operators, is proportionate to the aim pursued.[201]

In similar vein, issues were raised in the *Google* 'right to be forgotten'[202] judgment, which also triggered pan-European discussions.[203] In the judgment, the Court decided that the global search engine Google had to remove certain results from its searches if they violated the privacy of individuals. This judgment, even though it was rendered only for a Spanish case, was hotly debated across the European Union because of the close interconnection among EU countries and the legal validity of Google's policies in all Member States.

However, to address the obstacle of a lack of common public space, a more direct intervention is also needed. For example, while the CJEU was willing to recognize the principle of subsidiarity in cases such as *Vodafone*, it has consistently avoided annulling any act for breaching this fundamental principle.[204] The impact of annulling such acts that fail to comply with this important principle could have a real impact on the development of a public sphere.

The Lisbon Treaty does allow for a common public space to be developed over time. As we have seen, for instance, the citizens' initiative introduced in 2009 might develop further in the coming years, leading to the opening of a common public space in Europe. Yet, as discussed in Chapter 2, the problem is that even a successful initiative only forces the Commission to develop a legislative proposal; it cannot force EU legislation on an issue. So, while the establishment of a common public space cannot be excluded a priori, it remains a distant possibility even with the most dynamic interpretation of the current provisions. The same Art. 11

[201] Further on *Vodafone* and proportionality, see N. Foster, *EU Law Directions* (Oxford 2018) 88.

[202] C-131/12 *Google Spain SL and Google Inc.* v. *Agencia Española de Protección de Datos (AEPD) and Mario Costeja González*, Grand Chamber of 13 May 2014, not yet reported.

[203] The Economist, 'Google and the EU: On Being Forgotten: The Right to be Forgotten Sounds Attractive. But It Creates More Problems than It Solves' (17 May 2014), www.economist.com/leaders/2014/05/17/on-being-forgotten.

[204] For example: Case C-491/01 *The Queen* v. *Secretary of State for Health, ex parte British American Tobacco (Investments) Ltd and Imperial Tobacco Ltd* [2002] I-11453; Joined Cases C-154/04 and C-155/04 *The Queen, on the application of Alliance for Natural Health and Nutri-Link Ltd* v. *Secretary of State for Health (C-154/04)* and *The Queen, on the application of National Association of Health Stores and Health Food Manufacturers Ltd* v. *Secretary of State for Health and National Assembly for Wales (C-155/04)* [2005] ECR I-6451.

TEU that introduced the citizens' initiative, discussed in Chapter 3, also invites EU citizens to participate in policy-making at the Union level:

> The institutions shall, by appropriate means, give citizens and representative associations the opportunity to make known and publicly exchange their views in all areas of Union action. 2. The institutions shall maintain an open, transparent and regular dialogue with representative associations and civil society. 3. The European Commission shall carry out broad consultations with parties concerned in order to ensure that the Union's actions are coherent and transparent.

This provision alone will not trigger a greater common space but, if interpreted by the Court in a way that facilitates exchanges between the citizens of different Member States, a common public space could develop.

Another case to advance a common public space could therefore involve the new EU citizens' initiative. If the Court forcefully defended the rights of the initiative authors and mandated the Commission to come up with a meaningful proposal, given that citizens from a significant number of Member States must participate, it would inevitably create trans-European discussions, which may, in turn, transcend this one particular matter. Arguably, the CJEU itself, as an EU institution, could apply Art. 11(2) TEU to its own case management procedures. If there are cases involving a significant number of Member States and their citizens, for example, the Court could decide to fast-track them in these circumstances, creating an incentive for litigants to find like-minded counterparts in other Member States. In academia, for example, pan-European cooperation already exists because applicants must compete for EU funding within a wide range of different Member State institutions. While, arguably, this is possible in academia due to the at least tangential existence of an *academic* public sphere, this example illustrates that cross-cooperation between individuals and concerned organizations across Europe is possible and, to some extent, is already being done.

Another area for a European public space is the Internet. Interestingly, here it was Lord Sumption of the UK Supreme Court who made this clear, when considering a preliminary reference. Despite considering EU law to be clear on the matter, Lord Sumption supported such a question with the following reason:

> However, I recognise the issue has a transnational dimension and that the application of copyright law to internet use has important implications for many millions of people across the EU making use of what has become a basic technical facility. These considerations make it desirable that any

> decision on the point should be referred to the Court of Justice for a preliminary ruling, so that the critical point may be resolved in a manner which will apply uniformly across the European Union.[205]

The CJEU should give consideration to the message propounded here by one of its periphery courts. While the CJEU has confirmed the domestic and territorial nature of copyright, in its *Lagardère* judgment,[206] I believe that a willingness on behalf of the CJEU to innovate in this field could generate real and sustained debate on this topic, in a similar manner to that created by the recent *Google* judgment. Further, pronouncement by the CJEU has already been proven to be effective in driving reform in this area; the CJEU's refusal to find a rule of Community exhaustion in the case of secondary cable transmission in *Coditel I*[207] was subsequently debated and codified by the EU legislature in Art. 3(3) of the Information Society Directive.[208] A bold and nuanced approach by the Court in this area is therefore to be welcomed.

5.7.1.2 European Public Sphere and Member State Languages

In addition, and related to the creation of this public space, is the question of Member State languages. As my assessment has concluded in Chapter 2, this is not itself a serious obstacle to further constitutionalization, and it is commonly accepted in federal legal scholarship that many languages can be accommodated in a common federal polity.[209] In my view, however, this question would greatly benefit from discussions in a future European public space and in turn also impacts on the ability of a polity to create a European public space. It is thus not the question whether a polity with more than just a couple of official or at least working languages can be functioning; the comparative and particularized European treaty and case law analysis suggests that, for a common public space, there is a role for jurisprudence in the dialogue also concerning languages. The Court of Justice has taken certain significant steps in this direction, but, again, it could be clearer in its desire to create a workable policy space without reducing diversity. In *Spain and Italy*

205 Lord Sumption in *Public Relations Consultants Association Ltd* v. *The Newspaper Licensing Agency Ltd & Ors* [2013] UKSC 18 (17 April 2013), para. 38.

206 *Lagardère Active Broadcast* v. *Société pour la perception de la rémunération équitable* (C-192/04) [2005] ECR 1-7199.

207 *Compagnie Général pour la Difusion de la Télévision* v. *Ciné Vog Films* (C-62/79) [1980] ECR 881 ('Coditel I').

208 Information Society Directive [2001] OJ L 167/10.

209 See Section 4.3.2.

v. *Council*,[210] the Court of Justice was asked to consider an encroachment of Member State rights when an enhanced cooperation measure, that is, a smaller subset of Member States agreeing on a measure, was adopted that included only three official languages, English, French and German. The CJEU decided:

> Nothing in the contested decision prejudices any competence, right or obligation of those two Member States. In particular, the prospect, indicated by that decision, of the introduction of the language arrangements objected to by the Kingdom of Spain and the Italian Republic may not be described as prejudicial to the competences, rights or obligations of those latter States. While it is, admittedly, essential for enhanced cooperation not to lead to the adoption of measures that might prevent the non-participating Member States from exercising their competences and rights or shouldering their obligations, it is, in contrast, permissible for those taking part in this cooperation to prescribe rules with which those non-participating States would not agree if they did take part in it.[211]

In my view, while in this instance the CJEU is essentially defending the right of Member States to adopt language arrangements with fewer than all official languages, it could have made this more explicit, perhaps echoing the concern of the majority of Member States that too many working languages may become unwieldy or impact negatively on a common political space in the European Union.[212] In other words, the Court could have been much clearer that, in an ever-closer Union, perhaps not all languages can play the same role, irrespective of the number of speakers.

The issue of a certain level of linguistic homogeneity has already received the kind of test cases that the Court could also decide in other areas concerning the European public space. As discussed in Chapter 1, there are already approaches supported by the central court to address this obstacle to further constitutional development. With its *Patent Court*

[210] Joined Cases C-274/11 and C-295/11, *Kingdom of Spain and Italian Republic* v. *Council of the European Union*, Judgment of the Court (Grand Chamber) of 16 April 2013, not yet reported.

[211] Ibid., para. 82.

[212] Further on language-related barriers in the EU in the public sphere, see J.-C. Barbier, 'The Myth of English as a Common Language in the European Union (EU) and Some of Its Political Consequences' in M. Gazzola, T. Templin and B.-A. Wickstrom, *Language Policy and Linguistic Justice: Economic, Philosophical and Sociolinguistic Approaches* (Cham 2018), 209, 224.

decision,[213] the CJEU dismissed objections from Spain and Italy to a language regime focused on three languages in which all EU states were invited to participate. Here, the CJEU refused to follow the arguments by those two Member States that a decision akin to the one on the EU patent could not be implemented through enhanced cooperation. In rejecting these arguments, the Court highlighted that in situations where there is a deadlock on languages, a subset of Member States are permitted to agree among themselves to introduce working languages. I believe that, constitutionally, this approach needs to be developed further by the CJEU in any forthcoming case law on this issue. Member States and their citizens can be persuaded to voluntarily participate in a linguistic regime that reduces linguistic diversity for certain documents or procedures, the evolution of a set of 'working languages' that allows the institutions to function. The factual outcome will result in an overall move to a higher level of linguistic homogeneity, while also recognizing and granting support to the many languages of Europe – support and protection that the smaller languages lack, without a strong Europe.

5.7.1.3 European Public Sphere and EU Elections

The limitations on a European public space also impact on the *civitas* dimension of EU constitutionalization. Questions raised concerning the structure of EU elections and the European Parliament being recognized as the institutional body most closely associated with a European public space have largely been answered by the central courts. In the case of *Donnici*, the CJEU gave the Member State a large margin of discretion when determining EU election results, while simultaneously establishing a set of minimum criteria for elections from a central European perspective. In *Pringle*, as discussed in Chapter 3, the CJEU highlighted that Member States are free to conclude international agreements among themselves in Council in areas outside of EU competences and that they are free to attribute further functions to the EU institutions if they so decide.

Now, constitutional structures can evolve over time and therefore a high degree of centralization is not required for these institutions to develop or for further constitutionalization to advance. The potential effect of the CJEU's judgments in cases such as *Donnici* and *Pringle* is

[213] Joined Cases C-274/11 and C-295/11, *Kingdom of Spain and Italian Republic* v. *Council of the European Union*, Judgment of the Court (Grand Chamber) of 16 April 2013, not yet reported.

that, by giving Member States the freedom to determine their own arrangements with respect to EU elections and international agreements, while acknowledging minimum specified criteria and/or boundaries, a sharing of best practices among Member States becomes possible and, with it, public discourse on these issues has the ability to form.

However, while the CJEU has a key role to play in the construction of a European public sphere, as the analysis in Chapter 2 has shown, both the European institutions and the treaties continue to be perceived as very much an elite project. The key obstacles that remain clearly evoke the absence of popular support from the developing constitutional structures of the EU. These European public space limitations also prevent the increase of popular interest in the European elections, hold back the deeper engagement of cross-European political parties and continue to constrain the treaty structure of the current basic law of the EU.

Fundamentally, I believe that the Court could play a decisive role in overcoming these key obstacles, with future decisions having the chance to either frustrate or foster the effort for a common European public space. While it is true that one key element in this area would be to bring the Member State courts from the periphery more towards the centre, the Court of Justice could also consider going further than it did in the case of *Donnici*. In this instance, the CJEU only theoretically erected a boundary for the Member States and, in essence, it left the entire administration and communication of election results to the Member States, displaying a more federalist interpretation of the rules, particularly regarding the election of EU institutions. This course of reasoning is neither uncharted nor inconceivable to extend. As the Court of Justice has highlighted in *Donnici*:

> That legislative framework does not suggest that the Parliament has a general power to assess the compliance of Member States' electoral procedures and their application to the present case with regard to Community law. It follows that the Parliament's powers are limited, in the context of the verification of the credentials of its Members, to the rights and powers that are clearly set out in the relevant provisions of the 1976 Act.[214]

Notably, however, the Court has yet to go as far as to fully endorse federal elections.

[214] Joined Cases C-393/07 and C-9/08, *Italian Republic and Beniamino Donnici* v. *European Parliament* [2009] ECR I-03679.

In my view, while a truly European *civitas* might be created only through the further development of a European public space – which, as I have suggested, may be triggered by the sharing of best practices among Member States or, alternatively, by related higher law-making – the Court can still assist in creating the preconditions for such a moment, by expanding the principle of equal elections to the European level. While certain levels of imbalances are inevitable for federal systems, most federal directly elected institutions follow the same rules regarding the equality of votes. If the CJEU recognized such a principle in its case law, a precondition for more equal trans-European elections and parties for all people of Europe across all Member States would be created, requiring great administrative control over EU elections at the EU level and less deference to the Member States themselves, even in election matters.

5.7.1.4 European Public Sphere and Pan-EU Parties

A good example of the nucleus of a European public space and changed administrative practices can be found in the second area of *civitas* that is heavily influenced by the question concerning an EU public space: pan-European parties. The EU has seen significant developments in 2014 by the decision of all the major political groups in the European Parliament to nominate a *Spitzenkandidaten* for the EU elections. As noted, this practice brought, for the first time, representatives from all Member States and their political parties together to decide on one key personality. It also resulted in televised debates between the candidates for the Commission President; the two main contenders were later elected into the Commission Presidency (Jean-Claude Juncker) and the Parliament Presidency (Martin Schulz).[215] This new constitutional practice, while not completely followed in 2019, also because it was met by criticism from the Member States, has nevertheless left a mark on the Union.[216] For these reasons, it is my view that the Court's support for this changed constitutional practice should be sought only tacitly. While the Court of Justice could have strengthened pan-European party structures, it is clear that the new *Spitzenkandidaten* system, which was ultimately successful in 2014 even against some Member State preferences, has a lasting impact

[215] On the effects of this debate, see J. Maier and others, 'This Time It's Different? Effects of the Eurovision Debate on Young Citizens and Its Consequence for EU Democracy: Evidence from a Quasi-experiment in 24 Countries' (2018) 25 *Journal of European Public Policy* 606.

[216] A. Kocharov, 'This Time It's Different? Constitutional Complexities of the Spitzenkandidaten Arrangement' (2014) *Berliner Online-Beiträge zum Europarecht* 95.

on the constitutional development and landscape of the Union. As a result of this system, European political parties could come together not just as parliamentary groups but also by virtue of an EU legislative basis for party organization. These federal political party structures could be established in a European public sphere, with tactical support from the CJEU where necessary.

5.7.1.5 European Public Space and Federal Competence

As I have demonstrated in Chapter 4, there are no inherent or fundamental obstacles that would hinder EU constitutionalization in relation to the *ius* dimension. The EU, as a Union, is based on the rule of law; very few legal obstacles stand in the way of the Union. The main challenges concerning this *ius* dimension have either already been developed by the Court of Justice or constitute misconceptions about the requirements for a federal polity. For instance, as discussed in Chapter 4, there is a strong argument that because the EU has to rely on Member States to enforce 'federal' laws, this undermines the *ius* dimension of constitutionalization. Others have argued that, despite a similar recognition of the areas where federal law has supremacy across the EU, there are significant differences among Member States in terms of compliance, inconsistencies in enforcement and the ability to mandate action of federal institutions.[217] Yet, nonetheless, I support the view that these objections do not give cause for constitutional concern and, as Schütze has conclusively shown, there are different forms of executive federalism that extend as far as a German model that relies on the Länder level for all enforcement.[218] As Chapter 4 of this book has demonstrated, the other obstacles raised against the *ius* dimension of EU constitutionalization either are no longer valid under the new legal yardstick that is the Lisbon Treaty, as interpreted by the courts of the centre, or are simply unnecessary for constitutionalization after a federal comparative analysis.

The fact that Europe has developed over time to address these issues is not unusual. It is clear that certain features of constitutionalization have existed in the early federal experiences of other polities *ab initio*, while others gradually became more pronounced, in essence evolving over time. An important outstanding question involves the interaction of different elements of the constitution. But the real debate is whether the lack of certain elements can really mount a persuasive argument

[217] See Chapter 4.
[218] Schütze, 'From Rome to Lisbon'.

against further constitutionalization or whether such gaps simply suggest the need for further constitutional reform of the European Union as a 'constitutionalizing' polity.

However, as noted, the EU legal order arguably still demonstrates some gaps where further constitutionalization is required, in particular with regard to the question of *Kompetenz-Kompetenz.* While in the other federal contexts, federal judiciaries defined the limits of federal powers autonomously relatively early on, without reference to the federated component states, the CJEU has yet to fully exert its *Kompetenz-Kompetenz* beyond merely interpreting the precise limits of its jurisdiction. As Chapter 4 explains, this question is also closely related to the European public sphere; the *Kompetenz-Kompetenz* would be debated and communicated in one public space and thus seem much less controversial. But, again, perhaps a leading test case could initially advance this area of constitutionalization.

In my view, there is a genuine possibility for the EU Courts to act in a way so as to interpret the current structure of power and their own jurisdiction in a manner much more closely resembling full *Kompetenz-Komptenz.* The CJEU has shown, and forcefully reiterated in the *Patent Court Opinion,*[219] that, as a judicial institution, it is the only Court that can authoritatively interpret EU law. Here, the Court of Justice highlighted that a new judicial institution could not be created outside the jurisdiction of the CJEU. It held conclusively that the '... national court, in collaboration with the Court of Justice, fulfils a duty entrusted to them both of ensuring that in the interpretation and application of the Treaties the law is observed'.[220] However, as I argued in Chapter 4, this remains a contested notion, with certain periphery courts also claiming that they continue to hold clear *Kompetenz-Kompetenz* over questions regarding the transfer of power to the EU level and indeed over the democratic legitimacy of such transfers.

Constitutional practice might be activated to address this obstacle. In particular, Member State institutions could begin to defer more definitively to the Court of Justice of Europe, allowing it to set its own

[219] Opinion 1/09, Opinion of the Court (Full Court) of 8 March 2011 on the draft agreement for the creation of a unified patent litigation system – European and Community Patents Court [2011] ECR I-01137 [Patent Court Decision]. In the *CETA* Opinion, the Court further 'secured its monopoly to give the definitive interpretation of EU law': C. Riffel, 'The CETA Opinion of the European Court of Justice and Its Implications: Not That Selfish After All' (2019) 22(3) *Journal of International Economic Law* 1, 3.

[220] Patent Court Decision, para. 69.

limitations. It is not, however, clear that outlying periphery courts such as Germany will ever be willing to fully defer to the European courts or to play a significant role in establishing a valid and legitimate European public sphere. As I have shown, for example, while there has been willingness by some of the periphery courts to defer to the CJEU on matters of linguistic politics,[221] there has been, on the other hand, noted resistance by the GFCC to defer fully, or at all, on matters concerning social and political homogeneity.[222] In my view, full deference will not be possible unless the central Court complies with the standards that national courts expect of them. In a 2010 essay, Lady Justice Arden of the Court of Appeal of England and Wales discusses the benchmarks of success for the central European Court from the perspective of the periphery courts.[223] It is compelling that Lady Justice Arden points to the need for the central courts to pass judgments that are clear, both in form and in substance. As she observes: '[T]he Luxembourg court rarely discusses the constitutional ramifications or policy considerations of its decisions. If it did this more often, national courts could engage with these issues and make a contribution to their solution.' This sentiment is, as I see it, a compelling one; a clearer debate on thematic issues of European Union law by the CJEU is desired by its periphery courts. In turn, the dialogue between the central and the periphery courts would thus become more transparent and the boundaries of the CJEU's *Kompetenz-Kompetenz* could be properly debated and more readily formed.

But, while a changed approach by the CJEU would be of assistance, I think that the Court could play a further, even greater role in overcoming this obstacle to European constitutionalization. With only a little more courage, a more nuanced conception of federalism and a stronger commitment to the preconditions necessary for Europe's constitutional moment, it could, of its own initiative, be more active in addressing the one remaining *ius* obstacle of *Kompetenz-Kompetenz.* In the *Pringle* case, for example, the CJEU was invited to exert forcefully the borders of EU law even over the approach favoured by Member States, but the Court

221 See, for example, Case No 51/2006, 19 April 2006, Belgian Constitutional Court, www.const-court.be/public/f/2006/2006-051f.pdf.

222 See Section 2.5.3.

223 The Rt Hon. Lady Justice Arden, 'Peaceful or Problematic? The Relationship between National Supreme Courts and Supranational Courts in Europe' (2010) 29(1) *Yearbook of European Law* 3.

agreed that the Member States had the liberty to conduct their relations within or outside the Treaty. It decided that

> ... it is apparent from the case-law of the Court that the Member States are entitled, in areas which do not fall under the exclusive competence of the Union, to entrust tasks to the institutions, outside the framework of the Union, such as the task of coordinating a collective action undertaken by the Member States or managing financial assistance, provided that those tasks do not alter the essential character of the powers conferred on those institutions by the EU and FEU Treaties.[224]

It should also be noted that in *Ledra Advertising*, the ECJ said in principle that the institutions acting in such capacities could nevertheless trigger non-contractual liability (though the conditions were not met in that case).[225]

The Court could have gone further here and decided precisely which powers it regards as essential (which it denied for the ESM), in support of the European *ius*. A bolder approach here, combined with clearer reasoning about the constitutional considerations for this decision, would be an important first step for overcoming this obstacle to further constitutionalization.

5.7.2 *Raising Public Awareness and Engagement with the Decisions of the European Courts*

I have demonstrated the power of the central Courts in clarifying aspects of constitutional significance in their dialogue with the periphery courts. However, periphery courts can also be helpful in clarifying existing legal structures to the general public. Their role in explaining the rationale and reasons behind certain decisions has been highlighted, especially in the European context.[226] I believe that they could do much more. They could signal the need for change or assess the current obstacles to further

224 Case C-370/12, *Thomas Pringle* v. *Government of Ireland, Ireland and The Attorney General*, Judgment of the Court (Full Court) of 27 November 2012.

225 Joined Cases C-8/15 P to C-10/15 P, *Ledra Advertising* [2016] EU:C:2016:701, discussed e.g. in G. Zaccaroni, 'Procedural Rights within the European Economic Constitution: Which Remedies for the Rights and Interests of Those Affected by the Legal Measures Enacted to Counter the Economic Crisis?' in H. C. H. Hoffmann, K. Pantazatou and G. Zaccaroni (eds.), *The Metamorphosis of the European Economic Constitution* (2019), 11, orbilu.uni.lu/bitstream/10993/37508/1/08_Chapter%208_Zaccaroni_Metamorphosis.pdf.

226 See C. Barnard, M., Gehring and I. Solanke (eds.), 'The Advocate General: Securing Trust and Democracy in the EU Judicial Order' in (2011–2012) 14 *Cambridge Yearbook of European Legal Studies* 1.

constitutionalization from their judicial perspective. They could also highlight decisions of a constitutional nature much more prominently and in a publicly accessible manner. For instance, the Court of Justice's website is instrumental and reaches far beyond a small circle of interested lawyers and jurists. As another example, the press in all European countries reports on major cases of importance to Europe, providing one of the only examples of a pan-European public conversation that can be observed today in Europe. In my view, the old dynamic, highlighted by Stein as to the making of a transnational constitution,[227] has changed. Today, many more actors other than just legal experts in Europe and its Member States are included, and each dispute decided by the CJEU can touch upon many aspects of our lives as Europeans. Moreover, the Court is arguably the institution with the greatest amount of credibility and respect within the European Union structure.[228] This public trust is important and has significant constitutional weight. While some have criticized the culture of the Court of Justice,[229] it has been remarkably resilient against broad criticism and capture by political interests.[230]

As discussed, the Court of Justice plays a crucial role in the constitutional development of the Union. Yet, despite its significant role and the general perception of it as a credible institution, greater effort is needed by the Court for it to be noted and understood by the European people and, in this role, to facilitate the creation of a European public space. The internet presence of the Court is a valuable resource and its press section supplies EU media in a large variety of languages, but more is required so that its role in the EU constitutional order is better understood by lay persons and specialists alike. Certain commentators might feel that the Court of Justice is the most elite-driven of all EU institutions,[231] but I beg to differ. The vast majority of its caseload is preliminary references, that is, cases launched in Member State courts and answered by the Court of Justice. These cases most often concern private parties and as such are

227 Stein.

228 See an early study by J. L. Gibson and G. A. Caldeira, 'Changes in the Legitimacy of the European Court of Justice: A Post-Maastricht Analysis' (1998) 28 *British Journal of Political Science* 63.

229 See the recent speech by Lord Neuberger: D. Neuberger, 'The British and Europe', Annual Freshfields Lecture, Faculty of Law, University of Cambridge, 12 February 2014, www.supremecourt.uk/docs/speech-140212.pdf.

230 Though not void of politics, see Alter, *The European Court's Political Power*.

231 On the elite composition of the CJEU, see, for example, N. Kauppi and M. R. Madsen, 'Non-elected Political Elites in the EU' in H. Best and H. Higley (eds.), *The Palgrave Handbook of Political Elites* (London 2018), 381.

driven not by the highest level of decision-making but rather by those same private concerns. In essence, the Court of Justice decides cases in public about real people, with real European problems, even if, as Lady Justice Arden argues, the delivery of such judgments is currently 'impersonal' and contains little by way of reasoning.[232] I suggest that there are two practical courses of action that the central Courts could take to overcome this: either to personalize their written judgments so that they more clearly identify and comment upon the real people and the real European problems on which they are based or, alternatively, through mediums such as the Internet and popular media, they could seek alternative means of making their judgments more publicly 'relevant' to the People of Europe. This strategy will involve securing greater priority of EU judgments across Europe, both in intellectual forums (law journals, universities) and in the public media (beyond Eurovision, into pan-European newspapers, television and internet discussion forums). It is worth noting that while leading lawyers in various jurisdictions such as the United Kingdom and the United States have come together to create dedicated and continually updated blogs detailing the activities of their respective Supreme Courts,[233] there appears to be no equivalent cohort of European lawyers or commentators processing judgments of the central Courts to the same degree or intensity.

5.8 Key Findings

In this chapter, I have highlighted that the remaining obstacle is not merely a misconception; a common European public sphere is not just relevant for the European crises but remains problematic for further constitutional development, which cannot be achieved by an incremental process but, rather, must be fundamental. In my view, critics are wrong to focus on all the other obstacles to constitutionalization as are perceived to exist within the EU constitutional order; I have addressed concerns in relation to these throughout this work. Instead, I find that it is the lack of a common European public sphere or, better, the lack of sufficient degrees of interconnectedness among the public spheres of the Member States that continues to fundamentally hamper further constitutionalization.

232 Arden.

233 See, for example, the UK Supreme Court blog, http://ukscblog.com and the US Supreme Court blog, www.scotusblog.com.

This book has shown that, in virtually all but one area, the central Courts, in dialogue with Member State courts, have provided sufficient clarity from which we can discern that many of the perceived obstacles either are misconceptions (due to a misunderstanding of federalism) or have been advanced by the courts to a point where they are now no longer obstacles in the EU constitutional order. Moreover, with regard to the final, remaining obstacle, this book has delved into political science research from which it becomes clear that an increased politicization of the EU in turn leads to greater interconnectedness of the EU public spheres. The current absence of an EU-wide media platform and EU-specific public discussions is presently hindering the development of a European public sphere. As of yet, discussions on issues of European law are almost exclusively at the individual Member State level and there is a lack of reception or understanding among these respective national spheres.

As I have shown, the central Courts have a crucial role to play in paving the way for a European public sphere to exist. The cases that I have selected for the purpose of this book are those that concern key European policy issues of general European interest and whose relevance transcends the particular Member State to whom they are addressed. The findings of the Court of Justice in controversial cases such as *Melloni* on the scope of fundamental rights, *Pringle* on the ability of Member States to conclude international agreements outside of EU competences and *Angongese* on linguistic diversity would, if such a public sphere existed, be important topics of European-wide debate. The fact that the central Courts are, almost daily, ruling on questions of considerable political and constitutional significance means that if a European public sphere did exist, it would benefit from a ready-made agenda rich in diverse topics for debate.

Beyond establishing *how* and *in what form* a European public sphere could develop, I have also established *why* such a common sphere is necessary, as a crucial ingredient for overcoming both the existing crisis and further constitutional development. While changed constitutional practice may be capable of overcoming obstacles such as the number of working languages, or the lack of European elections and European-wide parties, the absence of a common public space remains the obstacle that is unlikely to be addressed through mere reinterpretation or altered constitutional practice alone.

Significantly, in my view, the creation of a common European public sphere is the obstacle closest to the people and thus probably the main element that could be changed by a movement of 'We, the European People'. This is a crucial aspect of future constitutionalization that will require momentum from the People of Europe. In this regard, there is a real need for the People of Europe to better understand the role of the Courts; an institution relatively close to the People when compared with other elite institutions, and the institution with the potential to actively adopt the role as facilitator of European integration. It is hoped that this book has highlighted the need for the CJEU to realize its full potential and, in doing so, to foster the popular support that is required for the transition into Europe's Second Constitution.

6

Conclusions

6.1 European Constitutionalization Answered

European constitutionalization continues to advance along the path that has been paved over recent decades. Contrary to the view advanced by many critics, many obstacles revered as insurmountable for Europe on this long journey, are either misconceptions or have been redressed by the Court of Justice to a degree such that they no longer stand in the way of further constitutionalization. However, as discussed at length in Chapter 5, there is one, remaining obstacle to be addressed. One point of contention continues to stand firm: the continuing and notable lack of a common European public sphere. It would be a mistake to view this as a practical or factual issue; rather, it is a legally constructed dilemma and, indeed, it can be addressed in legal ways.

So, what does this mean for further constitutionalization and constitutionalization research? In this book, I have challenged the conventional wisdom that further constitutionalization of the EU can be achieved only by a fundamental change, such as a new treaty among the Member States. I have also shown that those continental critics (including periphery courts in Member States) that believe that the EU in its current form cannot further constitutionalize do not fully grasp the potential contributions of a 'common law' approach to constitutionalization. Given the revelations uncovered with the adoption of my suggested common law approach so far, my first recommendation is that further constitutionalization research needs to continue and deepen along this vein.

This research also provides some guidance on potentially successful approaches to further constitutionalization. The CJEU has played a pivotal role in overcoming many of the initially raised obstacles to EU constitutionalization. As I have discussed, this common law analysis of EU constitutionalization and its related federalist dialogue by all courts in the system can significantly assist in understanding how to overcome bstacles to constitutionalization. The Court has performed an understated and crucial role to date and is key to all future constitutionalization.

With this is mind, how, then, should the EU constitutionalize? The EU, being essentially federal in nature and sharing many similarities with early forms of constitutional polities, faces very few obstacles to further constitutionalization in the three dimensions of constitutional development. The one remaining key obstacle, which is crucial to overcome in order to address the continuing succession of European crises, remains the lack of a common European public sphere, compounded by several corollary or related challenges. To address it and best achieve further constitutionalization in Europe, in particular, there is a great deal to be contributed by a more developed and intensive dialogue between the central and periphery courts in the European Union. This third way has great potential, as demonstrated with reference to many of the earlier perceived obstacles to constitutionalization.

Courts remain one of the most important political actors in the European Union and, through the interactional dialogue between centre and periphery, their decisions could help establish the European public space much needed for future constitutionalization. It is very much conceivable that EU and Member State courts could act not in an atmosphere of tension over constitutional issues but, rather, together to better define and refine European public debates, taking on important decisions in dialogue with each other. Such a 'common EU judicial approach' could prepare the still missing common public sphere that remains so key to policy debate and political decision-making.

6.2 Intersections of Law and Political Science for Constitutionalization Theory

6.2.1 Advancing New Ideas of Constitutionalization

Constitutionalization, in this study, refers to the process by which a polity submits governmental power to a constitution. As Martin Loughlin writes:

> Constitutionalization involves the attempt to subject all governmental action within a designated field to the structures, processes, principles, and values of a 'constitution'. Although this phenomenon is having an impact across government, its prominence today is mainly attributable to

> the realization that the activity of governing is increasingly being exercised through transnational or international arrangements that are not easily susceptible to the controls of national constitutions. Constitutionalization is the term used for the attempt to subject the exercise of all types of public power, whatever the medium of its exercise, to the discipline of constitutional procedures and norms.

As such, it is possible to analyse the 'character of this phenomenon, offer an account of its dynamic, and raise some questions about the processes it engenders',[1] whereby constitutionalization is best understood by reference to the related concepts of constitution and constitutionalism.

As Loughlin and Walker explain, the paradox of constitutionalism has certain key features, including

> whether those who have the authority to make a constitution – the 'constitutive power' – can do so without effectively surrendering that authority to the institutional sites of power 'constituted' by the constitutional form they enact. In particular, is the constitutive power exhausted in the single constitutive act or does it retain a presence, acting as critical check on the constitutional operating system and/or an alternative source of authority to be invoked in moments of crisis?[2]

Although at its creation, perhaps, the people of Europe played a minor role, I consider the constitutionalization of the EU to be, in the end, ours. The European peoples, acting together, should be the ones who exert this kind of constitutive power for the EU.

As Christian Joerges concludes:

> One cannot be more passionately committed to the European project than Jürgen Habermas and Hauke Brunkhorst. Both agree in their diagnoses. They see Europe on course towards an 'executive federalism' and 'technological (mis)management', which is threatening democracy and the rule of law. However, both also believe that the crisis will impose constraints which may be transformed into a democratic constitutional moment. . . . The federal vision of Europe has, although often proclaimed, never been realistic. However, a return to autonomous nation states is neither likely nor desirable.[3]

1 M. Loughlin, 'What Is Constitutionalism' in P. Dobner and M. Loughlin, *The Twilight of Constitutionalism?* (New York 2010) 42.

2 N. Walker and M. Loughlin, *The Paradox of Constitutionalism: Constituent Power and Constitutional Form* (Oxford 2007).

3 C. Joerges, 'Justum facere in the European Integration Process: How Should the Law Promote the Constitutionalization of Europe?' Helsinki Legal Studies Research Paper No. 23, 19, http://ssrn.com/abstract=2214814.

In my view, constitutionalization represents a focus for rule of law and democracy, rather than a threat to it. While federal experiences are directly relevant to our analysis, as the Court itself has recognized, further constitutionalization does not need to lead to a new federal State, nor is progress dependent on this single end.[4] Rather, the constitutional polity will strive towards a transparent and accountable governance structure that is fit for purpose. Without a constitutional order that can guarantee a basic minimum respect for *demos*, *civitas* and *ius* within its jurisdiction, responses to the current succession of European crises will simply make things worse.

The concept of constitutionalization is not without its rational critics, however. As David Feldman explains, constitutionalization enthusiasts seem to only compare entities with the US Constitution, or some other idealized form, which would be hard for most countries to attain and, in doing so, they fail to take into account the diversity of possible approaches.[5] Others dispute the disparity between the European experience and the traditionally invoked 'case studies' of constitutionalization. For instance, as Wojciech Sadurski argues, it is possible that Europe is primarily an example of constitutionalism: 'The EU represents the most formidable case of "constitutionalism beyond the nation-state" and the Council of Europe has also manifested a move towards constitutionalism in so far as the European Court of Human Rights has evolved towards becoming a human-rights constitutional court for Europe ....' According to such theorists, it is possible to show that 'the constitutionalization of these two European legal and political structures has been strictly related to the enlargement of both structures, made possible by the fall of Communism in Central and Eastern Europe'.[6] Interestingly this approach underlines the role of judicial institutions.

Taking this scholarly work into account, constitutionalization, for the purposes of this book, is the process by which a polity submits governmental power to a constitution in whatever formal and substantive form. Constitutionalization is a process that all constitutional entities undergo. As long as constitutional text is used, interpreted, applied and amended, constitutionalization occurs. It also means that, in the EU, the

[4] Opinion 2/13 of the Court (Full Court) of 18 December 2014 on the draft agreement providing for the accession of the European Union to the Convention for the Protection of Human Rights and Fundamental Freedoms (ECHR), para. 157.

[5] D. Feldman, '"Which in Your Case You Have Not Got": Constitutionalism at Home and Abroad' (2011) 64 *Current Legal Problems* 117.

[6] W. Sadurski, *Constitutionalism and the Enlargement of Europe* (Oxford 2012) xvii.

importance of the Court of Justice and the Member State courts should not be underestimated. Both are 'norm users' of the constitutional order of the EU and thus can have a dramatic influence on its constitutionalization.

6.2.2 *Federalism in the Context of Constitutionalization*

As discussed, federalism can be defined in many ways, but in essence it refers to a structure of governance with two or more tiers.[7] It forms a constitutional continuum between looser alliances and more centralized forms of governance, such as a unitary state.[8] Courts can often provide some valuable insight into where a given entity should be placed on this sliding scale, and federalist thought is often manifest in court decisions. The best studied example is the US Supreme Court, which moved from a strictly dual to a much more cooperative vision of federalism in its jurisprudence. Shifting visions of federalism appear in many court decisions, as discussed in Chapters 2 to 4, but a clear and nuanced perspective remains rare. It is important to address this gap because, otherwise, federalism can be seen as 'being in the eyes of the beholder' – where some see central government authority, others hail an advanced form of federal governance. The best way to analyse courts' understanding of the EU as a federal polity is to consider how federalism itself is understood and lived in different polities. Elements of a consensus are emerging, along the constitutional continuum starting with a unitary state, a federation towards less unified forms of state integration such as a confederation, league or alliance.

Member State courts regularly contribute to our understanding of federalism within the European context. The *Maastricht* decision of the GFCC, for example, highlights the differing perceptions of federalism. Faced with an argument that the EU is just a normal international organization, the German Court recognized the special character of the EU by distinguishing it from a federation and alliance of states. It coined a new term in German, *Staatenverbund*, which means not just an alliance (*Staatenbund*) but not yet a federation (*Bundesstaat*); in doing so, it

[7] Hueglin and Fenna; Burgess, *Comparative Federalism*; Burgess, *In Search of the Federal Spirit*; Halberstam and Reimann; Erk.

[8] Hueglin and Fenna, 35.

characterized the EU as a unique polity. In the *Lisbon* judgment, the Court explained its use of the term:

> European Union designed as an association of sovereign states (Staatenverbund) to which sovereign powers are transferred [*sic*]. The concept of *Verbund* covers a close long-term association of states which remain sovereign, a treaty-based association which exercises public authority, but whose fundamental order is subject to the decision-making power of the Member States and in which the peoples, i.e. the citizens of the Member States, remain the subjects of democratic legitimation.[9]

Given the dual source of democratic legitimacy in the EU, through the Parliament directly and indirectly through the Council, the Court could thus be said to misconceive the nature of the European Union.

The varying degrees of constitutionalization in Europe have informed this research, adding analytical clarity to the constitutional dialogues between the European Courts and the Member State constitutional courts. These dialogues, which have extensively debated the modern conceptions of federalism in Europe, enrich our understanding of the constitutionalization process for the EU.[10] They are essential when discussing the remaining obstacles to constitutionalization, especially when faced with the continuing economic, political and legitimacy crises within the European Union. It is when there are large degrees of interaction between the courts, which lead towards a better, less impoverished understanding of the federal nature of the Union, that the real obstacles to constitutionalization can be highlighted and brought to the attention of the People.

One of the key questions in a federal structure involves the role of different levels of jurisprudence and their interaction. As noted by Pierre Pescatore:

> [T]he methods of federalism are not only a means of organising states. [F] ederalism is a political and legal philosophy which adapts itself to all political contexts on both the municipal and the international level, wherever and whenever two basic prerequisites are fulfilled: the search

[9] GFCC, *Lisbon Decision*, para. 229.
[10] Weiler, 'The Transformation of Europe'.

> for unity, combined with genuine respect for the autonomy and the legitimate interests of the participant entities.[11]

Here, the focus is on the theory of constitutional federalism, which involves the examination of a distinctive order of a state and seeks to 'accommodate the constituent units of a union in the decision-making procedure of the central government by means of constitutional entrenchment'.[12] Which forms of such federalism are most helpful for comparison with Europe? There is no straightforward, single answer. Insights as to different dimensions of federalism may be gleaned from a variety of international and historical comparisons. Political scientists have long been comparing Europe with 'more mature' federal states.[13] As David McKay writes:

> It is well accepted that federalism is beset with problems of definition. In many federations power is decentralized and in others centralized. Centralization can be measured in constitutional/institutional terms and in terms of political, administrative, and fiscal as well as cultural/commercial criteria. The sometimes radical shifts towards centralization – and, more rarely, decentralization – experienced by federal systems are naturally a function of a complex mix of institutional structure and unique historical circumstances.[14]

Taking federalism theories of this kind into consideration does account for the use of comparisons between mature federations and the European Union (EU); indeed, from the view of certain scholars, it even suggests that 'the post-Maastricht EU has developed into a species of federal state'.[15]

Of course, this constitutional federalism is not the only understanding of European federalism. As Joseph Weiler argues, it is also possible that Europe has federalism without constitutionalism: 'Europe has charted its own brand of constitutional federalism. It works. Why fix

[11] P. Pescatore, 'Preface' in T. Sandalow and E. Stein (eds.), *Courts and Free Markets*, Vol. 1 (Oxford 1982) ix–x.

[12] Ibid., at 2.

[13] See, for example, Lacey; W. Swenden, 'What – If Anything – Can the European Union Learn from Belgian Federalism and Vice Versa?' (2005) 15 *Regional and Federal Studies* 187; P. Dardanelli, 'Conclusions: Comparative Federalism and the Constitutional Treaty' (2005) 15 *Regional and Federal Studies* 259; Church and Dardanelli; Börzel.

[14] McKay, 8.

[15] Ibid.

it?'[16] This, according to scholars such as Dan Elazar, can be explained by the argument that Europe is already a federal entity, as the 'federal principle should not be confused with its specific manifestation in the federal state'.[17] As such, comparisons between the United States and Europe become a 'staple feature'.[18] In essence, according to this argument, the EU can be considered federal without being also constitutional. I disagree, if this stance evokes no willingness to look forward, towards further constitutionalization. In my view, it does matter how the EU understands federalism and, in particular, how we perceive our own federal vision.

A careful study of the key factors necessary for constitutionalization can assist in understanding how relevant Albert Venn Dicey's analysis continues to be for the European Union today. As this research has shown, certain indications of Dicey's 'desire for union not unity' can be found in the relevant jurisprudence of the EU courts, but this can be deepened only if a European public itself, in a transparent and deliberative manner, is able to consider and address these questions together, jointly defining their common 'desire'.

The United States and other federal entities have experienced these tensions and gaps, and illustrations from their own stories of constitutionalization can help to identify and highlight existing misconceptions in the Member State courts. Superficially, the reasons given by the Federalists for choosing the original US constitutional structure[19] do not appear so very different from those advanced by the European Federalists in their failed constitutional project.[20] However, there is no need to convert the US Constitution – evolved in specific circumstances and historical context – into the only reference point.[21] The reference point, at each step in any analysis, must return to Europe,

16 J. H. H. Weiler, 'Federalism without Constitutionalism: Europe's Sonderweg' in Nicolaidis and Howse, 70.

17 D. J. Elazar, 'Options, Problems and Possibilities in Light of the Current Situation' in D. J. Elazar (ed.), *Self Rule – Shared Rule: Federal Solutions to the Middle East Conflict* (Ramat Gan 1979) 3.

18 R. R. Bowie and C. J. Friedrich (eds.), *Studies in Federalism* (Boston 1954); A. W. Macmahon (ed.), *Federalism Mature and Emergent* (New York 1955); and, later, T. Sandalow and E. Stein, *Courts and Free Markets* (Oxford 1982); M. Cappelletti, M. Seccombe and J. H. H. Weiler (eds.), Integration *through* Law: Europe and the American Federal Experience (Berlin/New York 1985–87); K. Lenaerts (ed.), *Two Hundred Years of U.S. Constitution and Thirty Years of EEC Treaty* (Brussels 1988).

19 See Ackerman, *We the People: Vol. 2: Transformations*, 18.

20 See, for example, UK Federal Union, 'Implementation of Federalism in Europe', https://federalunion.org.uk/.

21 Feldman.

authentic to the European historical, political and legal context and experience.[22]

But what precisely is the focus of the common law analysis and the related illustrative examples? As explained by Cloots, de Baere and Sottiaux in *Federalism in the European Union*, existing federal structures in the EU are important, but the actual practice of federalism in the Member States must also be closely examined. This is due to a certain paradox:

> On the one hand, numerous formerly unitary Member States have embarked on a path towards a (quasi-) federal governance structure. On the other hand, the EU itself is sometimes qualified as a federal system. Significantly, the concept of federalism has a very different, even opposite, connotation in both contexts. When associated with Member State reform, federalism is regarded as a technique for accommodating autonomy claims of sub-state nations. By contrast, when federalism is used as a label for the EU itself, it is conceived as a far-reaching way of integrating the nations of Europe.[23]

In other words, federalism in the EU has many connotations – and not all of them apply to the Union as such when actual constitutional practice is examined.

As Schütze explains, legal historians and political scientists can distinguish three different historical conceptions of federalism.[24] First, there is an international law approach, which in essence equates federation with any kind of international organization. From this conception, even the earliest emanation of the European Union would have to be considered a federation of States. Second, a continental European conception can also be used, which reserves the term 'federation' for a sovereign State not unlike the German Federal Republic. Finally, as Schütze notes, there is a pragmatic approach that recognizes the possibility of change over time within the federation that changes the federal character or might swing back and forth like a pendulum. Schütze argues that it is this third model, rather than the traditional continental (German) approach, that can be used to assess the constitutionalization of the European Union.[25]

For most scholars, federalism is a continuum and most federal polities can be distinguished by their degree of centralization. Some federal structures have very weak central institutions, but this does not

[22] Ackerman, *The Future of Liberal Revolution*.
[23] Cloots, de Baere and Sottiaux.
[24] Schütze, *From Dual to Cooperative Federalism*, 3.
[25] Ibid., 5.

undermine the utility of analysing the EU in federal terms. In European political terms, the failed European Convention highlighted some of the discussions about the federal nature of the EU.[26] The Convention's mandate in this area was to achieve '[a] better division and definition of competence in the European Union'.[27] The Heads of State decided to

[26] See E. A. Young, 'Protecting Member State Autonomy in the European Union: Some Cautionary Tales from American Federalism' (2002) 77(6) *New York University Law Review* 1612.

[27] See Laeken Declaration:

> Citizens often hold expectations of the European Union that are not always fulfilled. And vice versa – they sometimes have the impression that the Union takes on too much in areas where its involvement is not always essential. Thus the important thing is to clarify, simplify and adjust the division of competence between the Union and the Member States in the light of the new challenges facing the Union. This can lead both to restoring tasks to the Member States and to assigning new missions to the Union, or to the extension of existing powers, while constantly bearing in mind the equality of the Member States and their mutual solidarity. A first series of questions that needs to be put concerns how the division of competence can be made more transparent. Can we thus make a clearer distinction between three types of competence: the exclusive competence of the Union, the competence of the Member States and the shared competence of the Union and the Member States? At what level is competence exercised in the most efficient way? How is the principle of subsidiarity to be applied here? And should we not make it clear that any powers not assigned by the Treaties to the Union fall within the exclusive sphere of competence of the Member States? And what would be the consequences of this? The next series of questions should aim, within this new framework and while respecting the 'acquis communautaire', to determine whether there needs to be any reorganisation of competence. How can citizens' expectations be taken as a guide here? What missions would this produce for the Union? And, vice versa, what tasks could better be left to the Member States? What amendments should be made to the Treaty on the various policies? How, for example, should a more coherent common foreign policy and defence policy be developed? Should the Petersberg tasks be updated? Do we want to adopt a more integrated approach to police and criminal law cooperation? How can economic-policy coordination be stepped up? How can we intensify cooperation in the field of social inclusion, the environment, health and food safety? But then, should not the day-to-day administration and implementation of the Union's policy be left more emphatically to the Member States and, where their constitutions so provide, to the regions? Should they not be provided with guarantees that their spheres of competence will not be affected? Lastly, there is the question of how to ensure that a redefined division of competence does not lead to a creeping expansion of the competence of the Union or to encroachment upon the exclusive areas of competence of the Member States and, where there is provision for this, regions. How are we to ensure at the same time that the European dynamic does not come to a halt? In the future as well the Union must continue to be

ask the Convention to focus specifically on three issues in simplifying and adjusting the division of competence between the Union and the Member States: (1) transparency in the division of competences, (2) the need for reorganization of competence (while respecting the existing *aquis communitare*) and (3) prevention against the creeping expansion of the competence of the Union or encroachment upon the exclusive areas of competence of the Member States. The dynamic tension of the mandate becomes clear from the issues. It is thus not surprising that conflicting visions are pulling Europe apart.

6.3 Future Directions for Legal and Historical Research

Of course, this book has only ignited what will hopefully be an energetic and renewed commitment to the task of asking all the necessary questions about constitutional development. Ideally, we would know more about what constitutes a bad or hopeless constitutional design, bad court decisions or a lack of democratic will sufficient to stifle a constitutionalization project of the vast majority of the people. Further, in the European Union, courts at both the Member State and EU levels play a very important role and it is understood that, in many ways, this is a valid precondition for court-led constitutional development, but can some of these insights be transferred to other polities? Could a federal nature help many countries with strong linguistic or other minorities and thus keep established political entities together rather than splitting them up? And, more importantly, is the historic achievement that constitutes the EU irreversible? Could its federation never unravel?

Unfortunately, even the most comprehensive analysis could not answer these questions. Historically, federations have found it necessary to split in order to better represent their people, but, in the globalized world, this endeavour seems a folly. With the Scottish and other peoples aiming to split from their Unions, a broader question remains: Can a single referendum, perhaps only by a part of the Union, truly reflect the will of We, the European People?

However, with a stable court system, there is hope that Union will prevail over disunity. The significance of the court as the key to future constitutionalization and Union stability has, to date, been severely understated. But it is in this respect that my work in this book offers an

able to react to fresh challenges and developments and must be able to explore new policy areas. Should Articles 95 and 308 of the Treaty be reviewed for this purpose in the light of the 'acquis jurisprudentiel'?

original and insightful perspective, both for Europe and for the world more broadly.

6.4 Recommendations for a Process of Constitutional Change

This study does not focus on whether the Union would be better off in its current state, lurching unsteadily from crisis to crisis, or whether it might function more decisively as a more federal Union with a common European public sphere. Rather, it argues that, for those who agree that a Union is better than a Division for Europe, there are a few concrete recommendations that could greatly advance our efforts regarding further constitutionalization, namely in addressing the crucial need for a European public sphere and the corollary issues identified with its current absence.

First, a more detailed and nuanced understanding of current, interactional dialogue between the central and periphery courts in the Union of the federal nature is necessary. For this, misconceptions on the part of the Member State courts need to be cleared away and, as far as possible, the central courts can and should seize current opportunities to be more assertive on key issues for constitutionalization. They have the power and authority to send strong messages on these crucial issues.

Second, it is important to take the 'common law' constitutionalization of the EU seriously, recognizing that forward-looking jurisprudence at all levels can work to help overcome both the lack of a European public sphere and minor corollary *demos*, *civitas* and *ius* obstacles standing in the way of further constitutionalization.

Third, the one obstacle identified by Member State courts that is not easily overcome is the lack of a common European public sphere. For this obstacle, new approaches, along with new dialogues between the central courts and the periphery courts regarding the development of a shared, common federal understanding of their role, are needed. In particular, by developing certain lines of jurisprudence that move Europe away from current isolated nationalist debates, into broader public policy discussions on matters of common concern, courts can play a crucial role in building Europe's 'Second Constitution'.

Finally, it should be underlined that further constitutionalization, while fatally restrained by the dearth of a real EU public sphere, will still in the end depend on 'We, the European People'. Our people are the key to Europe's Second Constitution, as they could either ratify elite proposals or trigger fundamental change for the polity.

This public sphere remains under-explored in the law. It is still headline news for politicians to speak of European values or a European people; for example, when the Italian Prime Minister Matteo Renzi commented on the terror attack in Paris and the demonstration of solidarity on the subsequent Sunday:

> This is a very important event because for the first time we give the message Europe will be the place for the future, not only the place that has given freedom for 70 years. If terrorism tries to destroy our values the answer will come altogether. I represent my people but I am also a part of the European people. This is a moment of solidarity, but also of hope.[28]

A truly European public sphere, very much like the European Union itself, will be a constructed historic achievement. There is firm hope that, with the dawn of a European public space, key *demos*, *civitas* and *ius* dimensions of the EU integration project will also become progressively much harder to unravel. At the moment, in the absence of this much needed European public sphere, we are seeing a counter-tendency. The renewed Greek crisis does not seem to catch the same headlines, with financial institutions less involved and key actors therefore much less exposed to any Greek regulatory action. Similarly, the renewed nationalism in the Brexit debates, while exercising EU politicians, is not debated as a pan-EU issue.

This is a very dangerous tendency. If Member States re-start to perceive themselves as the only important actors, shrouded in nationalistic dialogue, and are able to characterize their populations as non-occupants of a 'common European house', as Gorbachev called it, the dearth of engagement could indeed signal the end of the Union.[29] So, in many ways, establishment and strengthening of a European public sphere is the antidote to the disease of nationalistic sentiment, serving to reinforce and safeguard the entire integration project. This has been, by and large, the ethos of the Court of Justice,[30] but its insights have not yet reached all Member State courts in their interactions with the European Union.

[28] M. Bonucci, 'Italian PM Vows to Push for United States of Europe during Presidency' (9 May 2014), EUROACTIV, www.euractiv.com/section/future-eu/news/italian-pm-vows-to-push-for-united-states-of-europe-during-presidency/.

[29] M.-L. von Plessen and F. Ausstellung, *Idee Europa: Entwürfe zum 'Ewigen Frieden'; Ordnungen und Utopien für die Gestaltung Europas von der pax romana zur Europäischen Union [Idea Europe: Drafts for 'Eternal Peace'; Orders and utopias for shaping Europe from the pax romana to the European Union]*, Exhibition (as a historical topography) at German Historical Museum, Berlin, for the reopening of the exhibition hall by I. M. Pei, 25 May to 25 August 2003.

[30] Alter, *The European Court's Political Power*, p.4.

6.5 A European Contribution to Our Understanding of Post-Regional Constitutional Entities

By taking federalism in Europe seriously and showing how its ideas, though perhaps not in the same language, have long entered EU court decisions, as I have done throughout this book, I hoped to challenge our understanding of both EU constitutionalization and, potentially, federalism more generally. The Court of Justice has now authoritatively stated that the European Union is 'precluded by its very nature from being considered a State', but also that the EU constitutes a 'new kind of legal order, the nature of which is peculiar to the EU, its own constitutional framework and founding principles, a particularly sophisticated institutional structure and a full set of legal rules to ensure its operation'.[31] This constitutional situation is not restricted to the EU as such. Rather, many varying constitutional entities exist, especially at the regional level, where certain Member States have pooled their sovereignty to achieve a collective objective. For these reasons, insights from the European Union are thus highly relevant for all federal entities.

In light of this, conclusions in this work are not to be regarded as confined to the European model; in fact, they provide wider lessons on the approach and perspective that we should adopt going forward in our efforts to form a fuller understanding of federalism more generally. Entities that are perceived as pre-federal might indeed be federal in the way that their courts decide and interact. In other words, there is a viable 'common law' approach to federalism that would rely less on the formal constitutional texts and treaties and much more on the decisions and interactions of central and periphery courts. This approach challenges the over-reliance on fundamental treaty change projects and pure incrementalism by establishing a middle way, where higher law-making is possible through courts and their interactions. It is a fundamentally European contribution to our understanding of post-regional entities; a 'common law' lens could magnify and clarify our vision of federalism in a way not previously anticipated.

In this research, having eliminated many of the commonly held concerns, we have identified the European public sphere as the main existing obstacle to further constitutionalization and shown how several other challenges are corollaries of this particular lack. This insight is, however, important not only for this particular constitutionalization project; it is

[31] *Opinion 2/2013*, paras. 156 and 158.

also fundamental for all forms of constitutional transition – namely, it can inform us on how to transition from one constitutional arrangement to another when normal amendment procedures are not being effective. In this respect, the contribution of this book is largely to a legal scholarship that is still struggling to define and understand the characteristics of 'a constitutional polity' as such; in this, it emphasizes that, in any federal entity, rulings by courts should be studied more closely. To a large degree, my work here has confirmed Ackerman when he argues that there is actually no single template for constitutionalization, as each constitutional polity must understand itself in its own terms.

From this perspective, the courts play a crucial and currently underestimated role in achieving this understanding. The analysis of the often dynamic tension between central and periphery courts serves to highlight the beginnings of and to contribute to the understanding of Europe in its own terms as a constitutional polity. As shown, when courts share an understanding of federalism, many constitutional obstacles dissipate. This is a situation that will be no different for Europe. Direction and leadership from the central courts, in the areas that were identified, have the ability to overcome Europe's single remaining constitutional obstacle – the lack of a European public sphere. By being more courageous and creative in its judgments on areas of key transnational importance, by engaging in dialogue with the People of Europe about the constitutional ramifications of its judgments and, perhaps most significantly, by full assertion of its own *Kompetenz-Kompetenz*, the CJEU is uniquely positioned to propound the creation of a European public sphere and pave the way for Europe's future constitutionalization success story.

The relevance of this research is therefore threefold. First, it is important for the further development of Europe itself. Second, it is relevant because other parts of the world are currently engaged in pre-federal economic integration projects, such as CARICOM, Mercosur and perhaps even SADC, if they continue down their current paths. At the very least, the book offers important insights towards a stronger theory of managing and adapting to constitutional change in cases that involve post-regionalism, a theory that recognizes the legal importance of the popular mobilization of a European People and the decisions of the European courts.

Third, even existing federal nation states can benefit from the lessons currently being learnt in Europe during this critical period of its development. One such example is the recent establishment of the ECB as the securities regulator for the largest European banks. The ECB operates a unique, multi-tiered system in which Member States still retain control and responsibility over the regulation of smaller banks.[32] There is no doubt that such an approach would have been favoured by the Supreme Court of Canada, which found itself with no option other than to strike down the Canadian Securities Act on the basis that the legislation infringed provincial competences.[33] In other words, even cooperative federalism can benefit from the lessons learnt in Europe.

For Europe, and the world, these lessons are much needed. The crises that have crippled Europe in recent years cannot go unaddressed; Europe cannot keep limping forwards in darkness. The 'quick fixes' sought by the elite institutions that continue to hold sway in Europe have failed and will continue to fail in forming and pursuing a long-term solution to Europe's constitutional dilemmas. Having identified the legitimate obstacles that remain to a stable and cohesive Europe, I consider that further constitutionalization as the answer for Europe is not only clear; it is an achievable goal. In their journey towards this solution, my book's insights seek to shine the necessary light onto the path that We, the People of Europe, should take towards our Second Constitution.

[32] N. Moloney, *EU Securities and Financial Markets Regulation* (Oxford 2014).

[33] Canada Supreme Court, *In the Matter of a Reference by the Governor in Council concerning the proposed Canadian Securities Act, as set out in Order in Council P.C.* 2010–667, May 26, 2010, 2011 SCC 66.

BIBLIOGRAPHY

Abrams, K., 'On Reading and Using the Tenth Amendment' (1984) 93 *Yale Law Journal* 723.

Ackerman, B. A., 'A Generation of Betrayal?' (1996–97) 65 *Fordham Law Review* 1519.

'Constitutional Politics/Constitutional Law' (1989) 99 *Yale Law Journal* 453.

The Decline and Fall of the American Republic (Cambridge, MA 2010).

'The Emergency Constitution' (2004) 113 *Yale Law Journal* 1029.

The Failure of the Founding Fathers: Jefferson, Marshall, and the Rise of Presidential Democracy (Cambridge, MA 2005).

The Future of Liberal Revolution (New Haven, CT 1992).

'The Holmes Lectures: The Living Constitution' (2007) 120(7) *Harvard Law Review* 1737.

'The Rise of World Constitutionalism' (1996) 83 *Virginia Law Review* 771.

'Three Paths to Constitutionalism – and the Crisis of the European Union' (2015) 45 *British Journal of Political Science* 705.

We the People: Vol. 1: Foundations (Cambridge, MA 1991).

We the People: Vol. 2: Transformations (Cambridge, MA 2000).

We the People: Vol. 3: The Civil Rights Revolution (Cambridge, MA 2014).

Ackerman, B. A. and Charney, R. E., 'Canada at the Constitutional Crossroads' (1984) 34 *University of Toronto Law Journal* 117.

Ackerman, L., 'Tenth Amendment: The United States' Defining Compromise' (2019) 20(1) *Federalism-E* 44.

Adam, J. and Möllers, C., 'Unification of Laws in the Federal System of Germany' in D. Halberstam and M. Reimann (eds.), *Federalism and Legal Unification: A Comparative Empirical Investigation of Twenty Systems*, Vol. 28 of the Ius Gentium: Comparative Perspectives on Law and Justice book series (Berlin/Heidelberg 2014).

Adam, S. and van Elsuwege, P., 'Citizenship Rights and the Federal Balance between the European Union and Its Member States: Comment on Dereci' (2012) 37(2) *European Law Review* 176.

Ahlstrom, S. E. and Hall, D. D., *A Religious History of the American People* (New Haven, CT 2004).

Albors-Llorens, A., 'A Broader Construction of the EC Treaty Provisions on Citizenship?' (1998) 57 *Cambridge Law Journal* 461.

Albors-Llorens, A., 'The Direct Effect of EU Directives: Fresh Controversy or a Storm in a Teacup? Comment on Portgas' (2014) 39(6) *European Law Review* 851.

Alemanno, A., 'Unpacking the Principle of Openness in EU Law: Transparency, Participation and Democracy' (2014) 39 *European Law Review* 72.

Alen, A. and Muylle, K., *Compendium van het Belgisch staatsrecht, Diegem* (The Hague 2004).

Alleman, R. and Mazzone, J., 'The Case for Returning Politicians to the Supreme Court' (2010) 61 *Hastings Law Journal* 1353.

Alter, K. J., *The European Court's Political Power: Selected Essays* (Oxford 2009).

Alter, K. J., 'The Global Spread of European Style International Courts' (2012) 35 (1) *West European Politics* 135.

Alter, K. J., 'Who Are the "Masters of the Treaty"? European Governments and the European Court of Justice' (1998) 52 *International Organization* 121.

Ambos, K., *European Criminal Law* (Cambridge 2018).

Amirfar, C. and Singh, A., 'The Trump Administration and the "Unmaking" of International Agreements' (2018) 59 *Harvard International Law Journal* 443.

Ansell, C. K. and di Palma, G. (eds.), *Restructuring Territoriality: Europe and the United States Compared* (Cambridge 2004).

Ansell, S. T., *Legal and Historical Aspects of the Militia* (New Haven, CT 1917).

Arden, Rt Hon. Lady Justice, 'Peaceful or Problematic? The Relationship between National Supreme Courts and Supranational Courts in Europe' (2010) 29(1) *Yearbook of European Law* 3.

Arestis, P. and Sawyer, M., *The Euro Crisis* (Basingstoke 2012).

Arnull, A., 'A Constitutional Court for Europe?' (2003–2004) 6 *Cambridge Yearbook of European Legal Studies* 24.

Arnull A., Barnard C., Dougan M. and Spaventa E. (eds.), *A Constitutional Order of States? Essays in EU Law in Honour of Alan Dashwood* (Oxford/Portland, OR 2011).

Aroney, N. and Kincaid, J. (eds.), *Federal Countries: Federalists or Unitarists* (Toronto 2017).

Atik, J., 'From No Bailout to the European Stability Mechanism' (2015–2016) 39 *Fordham International Law Journal* 1201.

Auer, A., 'The People Have Spoken: Abide? A Critical View of the EU's Dramatic Referendum (In)Experience' (2016) 12 *European Constitutional Law Review* 397.

Augustin, A., *Das Volk der Europäischen Union. Zu Inhalt und Kritik eines normativen Begriffs* (Berlin 2000).

Aumaitre, A., 'From the SGP to the TSCG through the Lenses of European Integration Theories' (2018) Bruges Political Research Papers 67/2018, aei .pitt.edu/97356/1/wp67_aumaitre.pdf.

Awe, B. M., 'Religion in the EU: Using Modified Public Reason to Define European Human Rights' (2009) 10 *German Law Journal* 1439.

Bahlmann, K., 'Europäische Grundrechtsperspektiven' in B. Börner and K. Carstens (eds.), *Einigkeit und Recht und Freiheit – Festschrift für Karl Carstens zum* 70 (Cologne 1984).

Bakke, K. M. and Wibbels, E., 'Diversity, Disparity, and Civil Conflict in Federal States' (2006) 59 *World Politics* 1.

Ballas, D., Dorling, D. and Hennig, B., *The Social Atlas of Europe* (Bristol 2014).

Barager, J. R., *Why Perón Came to Power: The Background to Peronism in Argentina* (New York 1968).

Barber, N., Hickman, T. and King, J., 'Pulling the Article 50 "Trigger": Parliament's Indispensable Role', UK Constitution Law blog (27 June 2016), https://ukconstitutionallaw.org.

Barber, T., 'Europe Must Confront Crisis of Legitimacy' (23 April 2012), *Financial Times*, www.ft.com/content/4e2c793c-8d50-11e1-8b49-00144feab49a.

Baratta, R., 'National Courts as "Guardians" and "Ordinary Courts" of EU Law: Opinion 1/09 of the ECJ' (2011) 38(4) *Legal Issues of Economic Integration* 297.

Barbier, J.-C., 'The Myth of English as a Common Language in the European Union (EU) and Some of Its Political Consequences' in M. Gazzola, T. Templin and B.-A. Wickstrom, *Language Policy and Linguistic Justice: Economic, Philosophical and Sociolinguistic Approaches* (Cham 2018).

Barnard, C., 'Case C-209/03, R (on the application of Danny Bidar) v London Borough of Ealing, Secretary of State for Education and Skills, Judgment of the Court (Grand Chamber) 15 March 2005, not yet reported' (2005) 42 *Common Market Law Review* 1465.

EU Employment Law (Oxford 2012).

The Substantive Law of the EU: The Four Freedoms, 3rd ed. (Oxford 2010).

'Viking and Laval: An Introduction' (2007–2008) 10 *Cambridge Yearbook of European Legal Studies* 463.

Barnard, C. and de Vires, S., 'The "Social Market Economy" in a (Heterogeneous) Social Europe: Does It Make a Difference?' (2019) 15 *Utrecht Law Review* 47.

Barnard, C., Gehring, M. and Solanke, I. (eds.), 'The Advocate General: Securing Trust and Democracy in the EU Judicial Order' (2011–2012) 14 *Cambridge Yearbook of European Legal Studies* 697.

Barnard, C. and Odudu, O., *The Outer Limits of European Union Law* (Oxford/Portland, OR 2009).

Barnard, C. and Peers, S., *European Union Law* (Oxford 2014).

Barroso, J. M., 'State of the Union 2012 Address', Plenary Session of the European Parliament, Strasbourg, vol. 12 (2012).

Bassett, D. L., 'Recusal and the Supreme Court' (2005) 56 *Hastings Law Journal* 657.

BBC News, 'Germany and France Vow to Strengthen Ties', 22 September 2012, www.bbc.co.uk/news/world-europe-19684532.

BBC News, 'MPs Back EU Arrest Warrant in Commons Motion Brought by Labour', 19 November 2014, www.bbc.co.uk/news/uk-politics-30118664.

Beaud,O., 'Fédéralisme et souveraineté. Notes pour une théorie constitutionnelle de la Fédération' (1998) 1 *Revue du droit public* 83.

Beblavý, M., Cobham, D. and Ódor, L. u., *The Euro Area and the Financial Crisis* (Cambridge 2011).

Beck, G., 'Judicial Activism in the Court of Justice of the EU' (2017) 36 *University of Queensland Law Journal* 333.

Beck, G., 'The Legal Reasoning of the Court of Justice and the Euro Crisis: The Flexibility of the Court's Cumulative Approach and the Pringle Case' (2012) 20 *Maastricht Journal of European and Comparative Law* 635.

Beck, G., 'The Lisbon Judgment of the German Constitutional Court, the Primacy of EU Law and the Problem of Kompetenz-Kompetenz: A Conflict between Right and Right in Which There Is No Praetor' (2011) 17 *European law Journal* 470.

Bell, J., 'The Role of European Judges in an Era of Uncertainty' in P. Birkinshaw and M. Varney (eds.), *The European Union Legal Order after Lisbon* (Alphen Aan Den Rijn 2010).

Bellamy, R., *A Republican Europe of States: Cosmopolitanism, Intergovernmentalism and Democracy in the EU* (Cambridge 2019).

Bellamy, R. (ed.), *Constitutionalism, Democracy and Sovereignty: American and European Perspectives* (Aldershot 1996).

Bergström, M. and Cornell, A. J., *European Police and Criminal Law Co-operation* (Oxford 2014).

Bermann, G. A., 'Executive Power in the New European Constitution' (2005) 3 *International Journal of Constitutional Law* 440.

Bermann, G. A., 'Taking Subsidiarity Seriously: Federalism in the European Community and the United States' (1994) 94 *Columbia Law Review* 331.

'The Role of Law in the Functioning of Federal Systems' in K. Nicolaidis and R. Howse (eds.), *The Federal Vision: Legitimacy and Levels of Governance in the United States and the European Union* (Oxford 2001).

Besselink, L. and Bonelli, M., 'Back and Forth between Sovereignty and Constitutionalism: The Court of Justice's Constitutional Case Law' (2018) 14 *European Constitutional Law Review* 665.

Besselink, L. and Reestman, J. H., 'The Fiscal Compact and the European Constitutions: "Europe Speaking German"' (2012) 8 *European Constitutional Law Review* 1.

Betten, L. and Grief, N., *EU Law and Human Rights* (Harlow 1998).

von Beyme, K., 'Fischers Griffnacheiner EuropäischenVerfassung' in C. Joerges, Y. Mény and J. H. H. Weiler (eds.), *What Kind of Constitution for What Kind of Policy? Responses to Joschka Fischer* (Cambridge, MA 2000).

Bickel, A. M., *The Least Dangerous Branch: The Supreme Court at the Bar of Politics* (Indianapolis, IN 1962).

The Least Dangerous Branch: The Supreme Court at the Bar of Politics, 2nd ed. (New Haven, CT 1986).

Bickerton, C. J., Hodson, D. and Puetter, U. (eds.), *The New Intergovernmentalism: States and Supranational Actors in the Post-Maastricht Era* (Oxford 2015).

Bieber, R., 'Verfassungsentwicklung und Verfassungsgebung in der Europäischen Gemeinschaft' in R. Wildenmann (ed.), *Staatswerdung Europas? Optionen für eine Europäische Union* (Baden-Baden 1991).

Bilder, M. S., 'The Corporate Origins of Judicial Review' (2006) 116 *Yale Law Journal* 502.

Biondi, A., Dagilytė, E. and Küçük, E., *Solidarity in EU Law: Legal Principle in the Making* (Cheltenham/Northampton, MA 2018).

Birkinshaw, P. and Varney, M. (eds.), *The European Union Legal Order after Lisbon* (Alphen aan den Rijn 2010).

Bitsch, M.-T., *Histoire de la construction européenne de 1945 à nos jours* (Brussels 1999).

Blackett, A., '"This Is Hallowed Ground": Canada and International Labour Law' (2018) CIGI Papers No. 22, www.cigionline.org/sites/default/files/documents/Reflections%20Series%20Paper%20no.22%20Blackett.pdf, 5–10.

Blanke, H.-J., 'Der Unionsvertragvon Maastricht–EinSchrittaufdem Wegzueinem europäischen Bundesstaat' (1993) Die Öffentliche Verwaltung 412.

Blokker, P., 'Constitutional Mobilization and Contestation in the Transnational Sphere' (2018) 45 *Journal of Law and Society* S52.

Blundell-Wignall, A., 'Solving the Financial and Sovereign Debt Crisis in Europe' (2012) 2011(2) *OECD Journal: Financial Market Trends* 201.

Bobek, M., *Selecting Europe's Judges: A Critical Review of the Appointment Procedures to the European Courts* (Oxford 2015).

Böckenförde, E., 'Die Nation: Identität in Differenz' (1995) Politische Wissenschaft 974.

Boerger, A. and Davies, B., 'Imagining the Course of European Law?' in F. Nicola and B. Davies (eds.), *EU Law Stories: Contextual and Critical Histories of European Jurisprudence* (Cambridge 2017).

von Bogdandy, A., 'The European Constitution and European Identity: Text and Subtext of the Treaty Establishing a Constitution for Europe' (2005) 3 *International Journal of Constitutional Law* 295–315.

von Bogdandy, A., 'The European Union as a Human Rights Organization? Human Rights and the Core of the European Union' (2000) 37 *Common Market Law Review* 1307.

von Bogdandy, A. and Bast, J. (eds.), *Principles of European Constitutional Law* (Oxford/Portland, OR 2006).

von Bogdandy, A. and Krenn, C., 'On the Democratic Legitimacy of Europe's Judges' in M. Bobek, *Selecting Europe's Judges: A Critical Review of the Appointment Procedures to the European Courts* (Oxford 2015).

Bogdanor, V., 'Legitimacy, Accountability and Democracy in the European Union' (2007) Federal Trust Report.

Bonfield, L., 'The Foreign Affairs' Power of the European Union: All Hat and No Cattle?' (2011) 20 *Tulane Journal of International and Comparative Law* 123.

Borger, V., 'The ESM and the European Court's Predicament in Pringle' (2013) 14 *German Law Journal* 113.

Börzel, T. A., 'What Can Federalism Teach Us about the European Union? The German Experience' (2005) 15 *Regional and Federal Studies* 245.

Börzel, T. A. and Risse, T., 'A Litmus Test for European Integration Theories: Explaining Crises and Comparing Regionalisms' (2018) KFG Working Paper 85, www.ssoar.info/ssoar/handle/document/57753#.

Bowie, R. R. and Friedrich, C. J. (eds.), *Studies in Federalism* (Boston 1954).

Brando, N. and de Schutter, H., 'Federal Commons' in S. Cogolati and J. Wouters (eds.), *The Commons and a New Global Governance* (Cheltenham/Northampton, MA 2018).

Bräuninger, T. and König, T., 'The Checks and Balances of Party Federalism: German Federal Government in a Divided Legislature' (1999) 36 *European Journal of Political Research* 207.

Brennan, Jr., W. J., 'State Constitutions and the Protection of Individual Rights' (1977) 90 *Harvard Law Review* 489.

Brewer Carías, A.-R., *Constitutional Courts as Positive Legislators: A Comparative Law Study* (New York 2011).

Breyer, S., *America's Supreme Court: Making Democracy Work* (Oxford 2010).

Breyer, S., 'Changing Relationships among European Constitutional Courts' (1999–2000) 21 *Cardozo Law Review* 1045.

Bright, C. and Harding, S. F. (eds.), *Statemaking and Social Movements: Essays in History and Theory* (Ann Arbor, MI 1984).

Broberg, M. and Fenger, N., *Preliminary References to the European Court* (New York 2010).

Brown, L. and Kennedy, T., *The Court of Justice of the European Communities*, 4th ed. (London 1994).

Brown, J. and Lloyd, C., *Federal-Type Solutions and European Integration* (Lanham, MD 1993).

C. L. Brown-John, Federal-Type Solutions and European Integration (1993).

Brunell, T. and Stone Sweet, A., 'The European Court, National Judges and Legal Integration: A Researcher's Guide to the Data Base on Preliminary References in European Law, 1958–98' (2000) 6 *European Law Journal* 117.

Bumke, C. and Voßkuhle, A., *German Constitutional Law: Introduction, Cases, and Principles* (Oxford 2019).

de Búrca, G., 'The Evolution of EU Human Rights Law' in P. Craig and G. de Búrca (eds.), *The Evolution of EU Law*, 2nd ed. (Oxford 2011).

de Búrca, G., 'The Road Not Taken: The EU as a Global Human Rights Actor' (2011) 105 *American Journal of International Law* 649.

Burgess, M., *Comparative Federalism: Theory and Practice* (New York 2006).

M. Burgess, 'Federal Democracy: Federalism as Political Culture, Civil Society, and Liberal Democratic Constitutionalism' in M. Burgess, *In Search of the Federal Spirit: New Comparative Empirical and Theoretical Perspectives* (Oxford 2012).

Burgess, M., *Federalism and European Union: The Building of Europe, 1950–2000* (London 2000).

Burgess, M., *In Search of the Federal Spirit: New Comparative Empirical and Theoretical Perspectives* (Oxford 2012).

Burgess, M. and Gagnon, A.-G. (eds.), *Comparative Federalism and Federation: Competing Traditions and Future Directions* (London 1993).

Burghardt, G., 'Die Europäische Verfassungsentwicklung aus dem Blickwinkel der USA' in A. Golze and E. Lenski (eds.), *Die europäische Verfassung im globalen Kontext* (Baden-Baden 2004).

Burley, A.-M. and Mattli, W., 'Europe before the Court: A Political Theory of Legal Integration' (1993) 47(1) *International Organization* 41.

Butler, G., *Constitutional Law of the EU's Common Foreign and Security Policy: Competence and Institutions in External Relations* (Oxford 2019).

Calhoon, R. M., *The Loyalists in Revolutionary America, 1760–1781* (New York 1973).

C. Calliess, 'From Fiscal Compact to Fiscal Union? New Rules for the Eurozone' (2011–2012) 14 *Cambridge Yearbook of European Legal Studies* 101.

Cameron, D., 'EU Speech at Bloomberg' (23 January 2013), www.number10.gov.uk/news/eu-speech-at-bloomberg/.

Cappelletti, M., Seccombe, M. and Weiler, J. H. H. (eds.), *Integration through Law: Europe and the American Federal Experience* (Berlin/New York 1985–87).

Carbone, S. M., 'The Principle of the Primacy of EU Law over the National Legal Systems of Member States' in G. Amato, E. Moavero-Milanesi, G. Pasquino and L. Reichlin (eds.), *The History of the European Union: Constructing Utopia* (Oxford 2018).

Cardwell, P. J. and French, D., 'Who Decides? The CJEU's Judgment on Jurisdiction in the MOX Plant Dispute' (2007) 19(1) *Journal of Environmental Law* 121.

Carreau, D., 'Droit communautaire et droits nationaux: concurrence ou primauté? La contribution de l'arrêt Simmenthal' (1978) *Revue trimestrielle de droit européen* 381.

Carty, K. and Cross, W., 'Political Parties and the Practice of Brokerage Politics' in J. Courtney and D. Smith (eds.), *The Oxford Handbook of Canadian Politics* (New York 2010).

Cashin Ritaine, E. and Papeil, A.-S., 'Federalism and Legal Unification in Switzerland' in D. Halberstam and M. Reimann (eds.), *Federalism and Legal Unification: A Comparative Empirical Investigation of Twenty Systems*, Vol. 28 of the Ius Gentium: Comparative Perspectives on Law and Justice book series (Berlin/Heidelberg 2014).

Castells, M. and others (eds.), *Europe's Crises* (Cambridge, UK/Medford, MA 2018).

Ceasar, J., *Presidential Selection: Theory and Development* (Princeton, NJ 1979).

Chalmers, D., 'Judicial Authority and the Constitutional Treaty' (2005) 3 *International Journal of Constitutional Law* 448.

Chalmers, D., 'The Single Market: From Prima Donna to Journeyman' in J. Shaw and G. More (eds.), *New Legal Dynamics of European Union* (Oxford 1996).

Chalmers, D., Davies, G. T. and Monti, G., *European Union Law: Cases and Materials*, 2nd ed. (Cambridge 2010).

Chaltiel, F., 'Les crises de l'Europe' (September 2011) No. 551 *Revue de l'Union européenne* 485.

Chemerinsky, E., *Constitutional Law: Principles and Policies*, 6th ed. (New York 2019).

Choudhry, S., 'Ackerman's Higher Lawmaking in Comparative Constitutional Perspective: Constitutional Moments as Constitutional Failures?' (2008) 6(2) *International Journal of Constitutional Law* 193.

Choudhry, S., 'Citizenship and Federations: Some Preliminary Reflections' in K. Nicolaidis and R. Howse (eds.), *The Federal Vision: Legitimacy and Levels of Governance in the United States and the European Union* (Oxford 2001).

Chryssochoou, D. N., *Democracy in the European Union* (London 1998).

Church, C. H. and Conrad, H. R., *A Concise History of Switzerland* (Cambridge 2013).

Church, C. H. and Dardanelli, P., 'The Dynamics of Confederalism and Federalism: Comparing Switzerland and the EU' (2005) 15 *Regional and Federal Studies* 163.

Cini, M. and Verdun, A., 'The Implications of Brexit for the Future of Europe' in B. Martill and U. Staiger (eds.), *Brexit and Beyond: Rethinking the Futures of Europe* (London 2018).

Claes, M., 'The Primacy of EU Law in European and National Law' in A. Arnull and D. Chalmers (eds.), *The Oxford Handbook of European Union Law* (Oxford 2015).

Clement-Wilz, L., 'Advocate General: A Key Actor of the Court of Justice of the European Union' (2011–2012) 14 *Cambridge Yearbook of European Legal Studies* 587.

Cline, W. R., *Managing the Euro Area Debt Crisis* (New York 2014).

Cloots, E., de Baere, G. and Sottiaux, S. (eds.), *Federalism in the European Union* (Oxford/Portland, OR 2012).

Closa, C. and Kochenov, D. (eds.), *Reinforcing the Rule of Law Oversight in the European Union* (Cambridge 2016).

Cocks, B., *The European Parliament; Structure, Procedure and Practice* (London 1973).

Cohen, J. C., 'The European Preliminary Reference and U. S. Supreme Court Review of State Court Judgments: A Study in Comparative Judicial Federalism' (1996) 44 *American Journal of Comparative Law* 421.

Cohen, J. L., 'Changing Paradigms of Citizenship and the Exclusiveness of the Demos' (1999) 14 *International Sociology* 245.

Cohn-Bendit, D. and Verhofstadt, G., *For Europe! Manifesto for a Postnational Revolution in Europe* (Munich 2012) (the French original makes clear that the authors were both interviewed by Jean Quatremer (Debout l'Europe!: manifeste pour une révolution postnationale en Europe; Suivi d'un entretien avec Jean Quatremer / Daniel Cohn-Bendit, Guy Verhofstadt (Brussels 2012)).

Condorelli, L., 'Il caso Simmenthal e il primato del diritto comunitario: due corti a confronto' (1978) I *Giurisprudenza costituzionale* 669.

Contartese, C., 'The Autonomy of the EU Legal Order in the ECJ's External Relations Case Law: From the "Essential" to the "Specific Characteristics" of the Union and Back Again' (2017) 54 *Common Market Law Review* 1627.

Conti, N. (ed.), *Party Attitudes towards the EU in the Member States: Parties for Europe, Parties against Europe* (Abingdon/New York 2014).

Corbett, R., Jacobs, F. and Shackleton, M., *The European Parliament*, 8th ed. (London 2011).

Cordonier Segger, M. C., Gehring, M. and Newcombe, A., *Sustainable Development in World Investment Law* (Alphen aan den Rijn 2010).

Costanzo, P., Mezzetti, L. and Ruggeri, A., *Lineamenti di Diritto costituzionale dell'Unione Europea: Quarta edizione* (Torino 2014).

Court of Justice of the European Union, Annual Report 2012 (Luxembourg 2013).

Craig, P., 'Competence and Member State Autonomy: Causality, Consequences and Legitimacy' (2009) Oxford Legal Studies Research Paper No. 57/2009, http://papers.ssrn.com/soL3/papers.cfm?abstract_id=1474325.

Craig, P., 'Constitutional Process and Reform in the EU: Nice, Laeken, The Convention and the IGC' (2004) 10 *European Public Law* 635.

Craig, P., 'European Governance: Executive and Administrative Powers under the New Constitutional Settlement' (2005) 3 *International Journal of Constitutional Law* 407.

Craig, P., 'Integration, Democracy, and Legitimacy' in P. Craig and G. de Búrca (eds.), *The Evolution of EU Law*, 2nd ed. (Oxford 2011).

Craig, P., 'Pringle and Use of EU Institutions Outside the EU Legal Framework: Foundations, Procedure and Substance' (2013) 9 *European Constitutional Law Review* 263.

Craig, P., 'Pringle: Legal Reasoning, Text, Purpose and Teleology' (2013) 20 *Maastricht Journal of European and Comparative Law* 3.

Craig, P., 'The EU, Democracy and Institutional Structure: Past, Present and Future', in W. Heusel and J.-P. Regeade (eds.), *The Authority of EU Law* (Berlin/Heidelberg 2019).

Craig, P., 'Treaty Amendment, the Draft Constitution and European Integration' in N. W. Barber, M. Cahill and R. Ekins (eds.), *The Rise and Fall of the European Constitution* (Oxford 2019).

Craig, P. and de Búrca, G., *EU Law: Text, Cases, and Materials*, 5th ed. (Oxford 2011)

Craig, P. and de Búrca, G. (eds.), *The Evolution of EU Law*, 2nd ed. (Oxford 2011).

Crawford, J., *The Creation of States*, 2nd ed. (Cambridge 2008).

Creech, R. L., *Law and Language in the European Union: The Paradox of a Babel 'United in Diversity'* (Groningen 2007).

Cremona, M., 'The Position of CFSP/CSDP in the EU's Constitutional Architecture' in S. Blockmans and P Koutrakos (eds.), *Research Handbook on the EU's Common Foreign and Security Policy* (Cheltenham/Northampton, MA 2018).

Crook, S. B. and Hibbing, J. R., 'A Not-So-Distant Mirror: The 17th Amendment and Congressional Change' (1997) 91 *American Political Science Review* 845.

Cross, D. and Mai'a, K., 'Identity Politics and European Integration' (2012) 44 *Comparative Politics* 229.

Crum, B. and Fossum, J., 'The Multilevel Parliamentary Field: A Framework for Theorizing Representative Democracy in the EU' (2009) 1(2) *European Political Science Review* 249.

Curtin, D. M., 'Judging EU Secrecy' (2012) 2 *Cahiers de Droit Européen* 459.

Curtin, D. M., *Postnational Democracy: The European Union in Search of a Political Philosophy* (London 1997).

Cushman, C., *Supreme Court Decisions and Women's Rights: Milestones to Equality*, 2nd ed. (Washington, DC 2011).

Danaci, D., 'The Minaret Ban in Switzerland: An Exception to the Rule?' in W. Marxer (ed.), *Direct Democracy and Minorities* (New York/Heidelberg 2012).

Dardanelli, P., 'Conclusions: Comparative Federalism and the Constitutional Treaty' (2005) 15 *Regional and Federal Studies* 259.

Dardanelli, P. and others, 'Dynamic De/Centralization in Federations: Comparative Conclusions' (2019) 49 *Publius: The Journal of Federalism* 194.

Dashwood, A., 'The Relationship between the Member States and the European Union/European Community' (2004) 41 *Common Market Law Review* 355.

Davey, M., 'Governor Accused in Scheme to Sell Obama's Senate Seat' (9 December 2008) *New York Times*, www.nytimes.com/2008/12/10/us/politics/10Illinois.html.

Davies, G., 'Interpretative Pluralism within EU Law' in G. Davies and M. Avbelj (eds.), *Research Handbook on Legal Pluralism and EU Law* (Cheltenham/ Northampton, MA 2018).

Davies, G., 'The European Union Legislature as an Agent of the European Court of Justice' (2016) 54 *Journal of Common Market Studies* 846.

Davis, D. M., 'Constitutional Borrowing: The Influence of Legal Culture and Local History in the Reconstitution of Comparative Influence: The South African Experience' (2003) 1 *International Journal of Constitutional Law* 181.

Davis, R., *Electing Justice: Fixing the Supreme Court Nomination Process* (New York 2005).

Dawson, M., 'Should the EU Think Twice before Dumping Its Spitzenkandidaten?', Verfassungsblog (2019), https://verfassungsblog.de/should-the-eu-think-twice-before-dumping-its-spitzenkandidaten/.

Dawson, M. and de Witte, F., 'Constitutional Balance in the EU after the Euro-Crisis' (2013) 76 *Modern Law Review* 817.

Deakin, S., 'Social Policy, Economic Governance and EMU: Alternatives to Austerity', Cambridge Working Papers (Cambridge 2013).

Deakin, S. and Browne, J., 'Social Rights and Market Order' in T. K. Hervey and J. Kenner (eds.), *Economic and Social Rights under the EU Charter of Fundamental Rights: A Legal Perspective* (Portland, OR 2003).

Defeis, E., 'The Treaty of Lisbon and Human Rights' (2009–2010) 16 *ILSA Journal of International and Comparative Law* 413.

Delaney, E., 'Managing in a Federal System without an "Ultimate Arbiter": Kompetenz-Kompetenz in the EU and the Ante-Bellum United States' (2005) 15(2) *Regional and Federal Studies* 225.

Delledonne, G. and Fabbrini, F., 'The Founding Myth of European Human Rights Law: Revisiting the Role of National Courts in the Rise of EU Human Rights Jurisprudence' (2019) 2 *European Law Review* 178.

Dembart, L., 'Giscard's Summer Reading: Federalism in the U.S.: The Future Europe Takes Form' (3 September 2002), *New York Times*.

Denza, E., 'Article 48' in H.-J. Blanke and S. Mangiameli (eds.), *The Treaty on European Union (TEU): A Commentary* (Berlin/Heidelberg 2013).

Devuyst, Y., 'The European Union's Constitutional Order? Between Community Method and Ad Hoc Compromise' (2000) 18 *Berkeley Journal of International Law* 1.

DeWitt, J., et al., *Anti-Federalist Papers* (1787).

Dicey, A. V., *Introduction to the Study of the Law of the Constitution*, 8th ed. (London 1915).

Dimitrakopoulos, D. G., 'Incrementalism and Path Dependence: European Integration and Institutional Change in National Parliaments' (2001) 39 *Journal of Common Market Studies* 405.

Dinan, D., *Europe Recast: A History of European Union*, 2nd ed. (London 2017).

Doherty, M., 'W(h)ither Social Europe? Labour Rights in a Social Market Economy' in D. Ferri and F. Cortese (eds.), *The EU Social Market Economy and the Law: Theoretical Perspectives and Challenges for the EU* (Abingdon/New York 2019).

Dombert, M., 'Landesverfassungen und Landesverfassungsgerichte in ihrer Bedeutung für den Föderalismus' in I. Härtel (ed.), *Handbuch Föderalismus – Föderalismus als demokratische Rechtsordnung und Rechtskultur in Deutschland, Europa und der Welt* (Berlin/Heidelberg 2012).

Döpfner, M., 'Juncker muss Präsident werden' (30 May 2014), www.bild.de/news/standards/mathias-doepfner/juncker-muss-praesident-werden-36187236.bild.html.

Dorau, C. and Jacobi, P., 'The Debate over a "European Constitution": Is It Solely a German Concern?' (2000) 6(3) *European Public Law* 413.

van Dorp, J. and Phoa, P., 'How to Continue a Meaningful Judicial Dialogue about EU Law? From the Conditions in the CILFIT Judgment to the Creation of a New European Legal Culture' (2018) 34 *Utrecht Journal of International and European Law* 73.

Dorsen, N., 'The Selection of U.S. Supreme Court Justices' (2006) 4 *International Journal of Constitutional Law* 652.

Dosenrode, S., 'Policy-making in Federations and in the EU' in S. Dosenrode (ed.), *Approaching the EUropean Federation?* (London 2013).

Dougan, M., 'The Treaty of Lisbon 2007: Winning Minds, Not Hearts' (2008) 45 *Common Market Law Review* 617.

Douglas-Scott, S., 'A Tale of Two Courts: Luxembourg, Strasbourg and the Growing European Human Rights Acquis' (2006) 43 *Common Market Law Review* 629.

Drinoczi, T., 'Constitutional Identity in Europe: The Identity of the Constitution: A Regional Approach' (2020, forthcoming) *German Law Journal*, https://ssrn.com/abstract=3448407.

Duer, A. and Konstantinidis, N., 'Ratifying International Treaties by Referendum: The Case of the EU's Constitutional Treaty', LSE Working Paper (2012).

Duff, J., 'Annual Report of the Director of the Administrative Office of the United States Courts' (2009).

Dumbrovský, T., Petkova, B. and van der Sluis, M., 'Judicial Appointments: The Article 255 TFEU Advisory Panel and Selection Procedures in the Member States' (2014) 51 *Common Market Law Review* 455.

Dyck, R., 'Links between Federal and Provincial Parties and Party Systems' (1991) 14 *Representation, Integration and Political Parties in Canada* 129.

Dyzenhaus, D., *The Constitution of Law: Legality in a Time of Emergency* (Cambridge, 2006).

Economist, The, 'Charlemagne: A Flawed Temple: The Loss of Legitimacy May Now Be the Biggest Threat to the European Project' (16 March 2013), www.economist.com/europe/2013/03/16/a-flawed-temple.

Economist, The, 'The Euro Crisis: An Ever-Deeper Democratic Deficit: The Level of Further Integration Necessary to Deal with the Euro Crisis Will Be Hard to Square with the Increasing Cantankerousness of Europe's Voters' (26 May 2012), www.economist.com/briefing/2012/05/26/an-ever-deeper-democratic-deficit.

Economist, The, 'European Union: The Right Verdict on the Constitution: European Voters Should Reject the New Constitutional Treaty and Demand Something Better' (24 June 2004), www.economist.com/leaders/2004/06/24/the-right-verdict-on-the-constitution.

Economist, The, 'Google and the EU: On Being Forgotten: The Right to Be Forgotten Sounds Attractive. But It Creates More Problems than It Solves' (17 May 2014), www.economist.com/leaders/2014/05/17/on-being-forgotten.

Economist, The, 'Great Britain or Little England? Fingers Crossed that the Country Will Choose Wisely', Special Report (9 November 2013), www.economist.com/special-report/2013/11/07/great-britain-or-little-england.

Economist, The, 'The European Union Constitution: Dead, but Not Yet Buried: Voters in France and the Netherlands Have Killed the EU Constitution' (2 June 2005), www.economist.com/europe/2005/06/02/dead-but-not-yet-buried.

Economist, The, 'The Future of Europe: The Europe that Died; And the One that Should Live On' (2 June 2005), www.economist.com/leaders/2005/06/02/the-europe-that-died.

Eeckhout, P., 'The EU Charter of Fundamental Rights and the Federal Question' (2002) 39 *Common Market Law Review* 945.

Eeckhout, P. and Lopez-Escudero, M., 'Introduction' in P. Eeckhout and M. Lopez-Escudero (eds.), *The European Union's External Action in Times of Crisis* (London 2016).

Eijsbouts, T., 'People and Peoples in EU Law: To Debunk the No-Demos Myth' in L. Papadopoulou, I. Pernice and J. H. H. Weiler (eds.), *Legitimacy Issues of the European Union in the Face of Crisis* (Baden-Baden 2017), 113.

Eisgruber, C. and Weiler, J. H. H., 'Preface' (2005) 3 *International Journal of Constitutional Law* 163.

Elazar, D. J., *Federal Systems of the World: A Handbook of Federal, Confederal, and Autonomy Arrangements* (Harlow 1991).

Elazar, D. J., *Federalism and the Way to Peace* (Kingston, ON 1994).

Elazar, D. J., 'Options, Problems and Possibilities in Light of the Current Situation' in D. J. Elazar (ed.), *Self Rule – Shared Rule: Federal Solutions to the Middle East Conflict* (Ramat Gan 1979).

Elliott, M. and Thomas, R., *Public Law*, 2nd ed. (Oxford 2014).

Elsig, M., *The EU's Common Commercial Policy: Institutions, Interests and Ideas* (Abingdon/New York 2017).

Epstein R. A., 'Executive Power, the Commander in Chief, and the Militia Clause' (2005–2006) 34 *Hofstra Law Review* 317.

Eriksen, E. O. and Fossum, J. E. (eds.), *Democracy in the European Union: Integration through Deliberation?* (London 2000).

Eriksen, E. O., Fossum, J. E. and Menéndez, A. (eds.), *Developing a Constitution for Europe* (London 2004).

Erk, J., *Explaining Federalism: State, Society and Congruence in Austria, Belgium, Canada, Germany and Switzerland* (New York 2007).

Eskandari, V. and Banfi, E., 'Institutionalising Islamophobia in Switzerland: The Burqa and Minaret Bans' (2017) 4 *Islamophobia Studies Journal* 53.

Esty, D. C. and Geradin, D. (eds.), *Regulatory Competition and Economic Integration: Comparative Perspectives* (New York 2001).

European Commission, 'White paper on the future of Europe: Reflections and scenarios for the EU27 by 2025' COM(2017)2025.

European Parliament News, 'Eurobarometer Survey Shows Highest Support for the EU in 35 Years', 23 May 2018, www.europarl.europa.eu/news/en/headlines/eu-affairs/20180522STO04020/eurobarometer-survey-highest-support-for-the-eu-in-35-years.

Fabbrini, F., 'The Principle of Subsidiarity' in R. Schütze and T. Tridimas (eds.), *Oxford Principles of European Union Law: Volume 1: The European Union Legal Order* (Oxford 2018) 14–18, https://ssrn.com/abstract=2781845.

Fabbrini, F. and Maduro, M. P., 'Supranational Constitutional Courts', iCourts Working Paper Series, No. 98 (2017) 14, https://papers.ssrn.com/sol3/papers.cfm?abstract_id=2990277.

Fabbrini, S., 'Alternative Governance Models: "Hard Core" in a Differentiated Europe' (2019) 17 *Comparative European Politics* 278.

Fabbrini, S., *Compound Democracies: Why the United States and Europe Are Becoming Similar* (New York 2007).

Fabbrini, S. (ed.), *Democracy and Federalism in the European Union and the United States: Exploring Post-National Governance* (Abingdon/New York 2005).

Falkner, G., 'The EU's Problem-Solving Capacity and Legitimacy in a Crisis Context: A Virtuous or Vicious Circle?' (2016) 39 *West European Politics* 953.

Faraguna, P., 'Constitutional Identity in the EU: A Shield or a Sword?' (2017) 18 *German Law Journal* 1617.

D. A. Farber, 'The Inevitability of Practical Reason: Statutes, Formalism, and the Rule of Law' (1992) 45 *Vanderbilt Law Review* 533.

FBI, *The FBI: A Centennial History, 1908–2008* (Washington, DC 2008).

Feldman, D., '"Which in Your Case You Have Not Got": Constitutionalism at Home and Abroad' (2011) 64 *Current Legal Problems* 117.

Fernandes, S. P., 'Fundamental Rights at the Crossroads of EU Constitutionalism: Decoding the Member States' Key(s) to the Charter' (2018) 60 *Revista de Derecho Comunitario Europeo* 677.

Fichera, M., *The Foundations of the EU as a Polity* (Cheltenham/Northampton, MA 2018).

Finkelman, P., 'James Madison and the Bill of Rights: A Reluctant Paternity' (1990) 9 *Supreme Court Review* 301.
L. Fisher, *Defending Congress and the Constitution* (Lawrence, KS 2010).
Fleiner, T., Misic, A. and Töpperwien, N., *Constitutional Law in Switzerland* (Alphen aan den Rijn 2012).
Fleiner-Gerster, T., 'Problèmes de la souveraineté intérieure et extérieure' in T. Fleiner-Gerster and S. Hutter (eds.), *Federalism and Decentralization* (Fribourg 1987).
Fleiner-Gerster, T. and Misic, A., 'Föderalismus als Ordnungssprizip der Verfassung' in D. Thürer, J.-F. Aubert and J.-P. Müller (eds.), *Verfassungsrecht der Schweiz* (Zürich 2001).
Foner, E. and Garraty, J. A. (eds.), *The Reader's Companion to American History* (New York 1991).
Forsyth, M., 'The Political Objectives of European Integration' (1967) 43(3) International Affairs 483.
Fortin-Rittberger, J. and Rittberger, B., 'Do Electoral Rules Matter? Explaining National Differences in Women's Representation in the European Parliament' (2014) *European Union Politics* 1.
Fossum, J. E. and Jachtenfuchs, M., 'Federal Challenges and Challenges to Federalism: Insights from the EU and Federal States' (2017) *Journal of European Public Policy* 467.
Fossum, J. E. and Menéndez, A. J., *The Constitution's Gift: A Constitutional Theory for a Democratic European Union* (Lanham, MD 2011).
Fossum, J. E. and Schlesinger, P., *The European Union and the Public Sphere: A Communicative Space in the Making?* (Abingdon/New York 2007).
Foster, N., *EU Law Directions* (Oxford 2018).
Fouskas, V. K. and Dimoulas, C., 'The Greek Workshop of Debt and the Failure of the European Project' (2012) 14 *Journal of Balkan and Near Eastern Studies* 1.
Freeman, J., *Affairs of Honor: National Politics in the New Republic* (New Haven, CT 2002).
Fritz, C. G., *American Sovereigns: The People and America's Constitutional Tradition before the Civil War* (Cambridge 2007).
Full Fact, 'Was the EU Referendum "Advisory"?' (8 November 2016), https://fullfact.org/europe/was-eu-referendum-advisory.
Galinas, F. and Sirota, L., 'Constitutional Conventions and Senate Reform' (2013) 5 *Revue québécoise de droit constitutionnel* 107.
Garben, S., 'The Problematic Interaction between EU and International Law in the Area of Social Rights' (2018) 7 *Cambridge International Law Journal* 77.
Garrett, G., 'International Cooperation and Institutional Choice: The European Community's Internal Market' (1992) 46(2) *International Organization* 533.
Gaudreault-DesBiens, J.-F. and Karazivan, N., 'Canada: Upcoming Appointment of Supreme Court Judges' (October 2011) *Canada Public Law* 827.

Gazzola, M. and Grin, F., 'Is English as Lingua Franca More Effective and Fair than Translation? An Evaluation of the EU's Multilingual Regime' (2013) 23 *International Journal of Applied Linguistics* 93.

Gazzola, M. and Ronza, R. W., 'The Politics and Policy of Multilingualism in the European Union' (2018) 1 *Brown Journal of World Affairs* 55.

Gehring, M., 'Brexit and EU–UK Trade Relations with Third States' EU Law Analysis (6 March 2016), http://eulawanalysis.blogspot.com/2016/03/brexit-and-eu-uk-trade-relations-with.html.

Gehring, M., 'Subnational Participation in International Trade Law: Options for the European Union' (2018) CIGI Papers No. 167, www.cigionline.org/sites/default/files/documents/Paper%20no.167_web_1.pdf.

Gehring, M., 'The German Constitutional Court's Latest Decision on European Elections: No Protection Needed', International Journal of Constitutional Law blog (28 February 2014) www.iconnectblog.com/2014/02/the-german-constitutional-courts-latest-decision-on-european-elections-no-protection-needed.

Gehring, M. and Cordonier Segger, M. C., *Sustainable Development in World Trade Law* (Alphen aan den Rijn 2005).

Genovese, M. A., *A Presidential Nation: Causes, Consequences, and Cures* (New York/Abingdon 2013).

Genovese, M. A., *Presidential Leadership in an Age of Change* (Abingdon/New York 2017).

Georgosouli, A., 'The Financial Crisis in Constitutional Perspective: The Dark Side of Functional Differentiation' (2012) 10(4) *International Journal of Constitutional Law* 1174.

Gerhards, J. and Neidhart, F., 'Strukturen und Funtionen moderner Offentlichkeit. Fragestellungen und Ansatze' in S. Muller-Dohm and K. Neumann-Braun (eds.), *Offentlichkeit, Kultur, Massenkommunikation. Beitrage zur Medienkommunikationssoziologie* (Oldenburg 1991).

Gibson, J. L. and Caldeira, G. A., 'Changes in the Legitimacy of the European Court of Justice: A Post-Maastricht Analysis' (1998) 28 *British Journal of Political Science* 63.

Glencross, A., *E Pluribus Europa? Assessing the Viability of the EU Compound Polity by Analogy with the Early US Republic* (Florence 2007).

Glencross, A., 'The Spitzenkandidaten Process Has "Presidentialised" the Commission, But Only Time Will Tell Whether It Allows for Better Representation of Citizens' Views', LSE EUROPP blog (10 Sep 2014), http://blogs.lse.ac.uk/europpblog/2014/09/10/the-spitzenkandidaten-process-has-presidentialised-the-commission-but-only-time-will-tell-whether-it-allows-for-better-representation-of-citizens-views.

Glencross, A., *What Makes the EU Viable? European Integration in the Light of the Antebellum US Experience* (Basingstoke/New York 2009).

Glenn, H. P., *Legal Traditions of the World: Sustainable Diversity in Law* (Oxford 2000).

Glick, J., 'On the Road: The Supreme Court and the History of Circuit Riding' (2002–2003) 24 *Cardozo Law Review* 1753.

Goebel, Jr., J., 'Constitutional History and Constitutional Law' (1938) 38 *Columbia Law Review* 555.

Goerlich, H., Huber, W. and Lehmann, K., *Verfassung ohne Gottesbezug?: Zu einer aktuellen europäischen Kontroverse* (Leipzig 2004).

Goldner Lang, I., 'The EU Financial and Migration Crises: Two Crises – Many Facets of EU Solidarity' in A. Biondi, E. Dagilyte and E. Kucuk (eds.), *Solidarity in EU Law: Legal Principle in the Making* (Cheltenham/Northampton, MA 2018).

Goldstein, A., 'History, Homosexuality, and Political Values: Searching for the Hidden Determination of Bowers v. Hardwick' (1987) 97 *Yale Law Journal* 1073.

Goldstein, L. F., *Constituting Federal Sovereignty: The European Union in Comparative Context* (Baltimore, MD 2001).

Gonzales, A., 'Presidential Powers, Immunities, and Pardons' (2018–2019) 96 *Washington University Law Review* 905.

Govender, K., 'Federalism and Legal Unification in South Africa' in D. Halberstam and M. Reimann (eds.), *Federalism and Legal Unification: A Comparative Empirical Investigation of Twenty Systems*, Vol. 28 of the Ius Gentium: Comparative Perspectives on Law and Justice book series (Berlin/Heidelberg 2014).

Grammond, S., *Identity Captured by Law: Membership in Canada's Indigenous Peoples and Linguistic Minorities* (Montreal, QC/Kingston, ON 2009).

Gray, A., Barigazzi, J. and de la Baume, M., 'Who Killed the Spitzenkandidat? No Shortage of Suspects in Drama over How EU Should Be Governed' (7 May 2019) *Politico*, www.politico.eu/article/who-killed-the-spitzenkandidat-european-parliament-election-2019-transition/.

Greenwood, J., 'The European Citizens' Initiative: Bringing the EU Closer to Its Citizens?' (2018) *Comparative European Politics* 940.

Grekousis, G., 'Further Widening or Bridging the Gap? A Cross-Regional Study of Unemployment across the EU Amid Economic Crisis' (2018) 10 *Sustainability*, www.mdpi.com/2071-1050/10/6/1702.

Grenon, A., 'Unification of Laws in Federal Systems: The Canadian Model' in D. Halberstam and M. Reimann (eds.), *Federalism and Legal Unification: A Comparative Empirical Investigation of Twenty Systems*, Vol. 28 of the Ius Gentium: Comparative Perspectives on Law and Justice book series (Berlin/Heidelberg 2014).

Griffin, P. B., 'The European Union and Its Issue with Democracy: A Closer Look at the Irish Rejection of the Lisbon Treaty' (2018) https://ssrn.com/abstract=3205274.

Griffin, S. M., 'Constitutional Theory Transformed' (1999) 108 *Yale Law Journal* 2115.

Grimm, D., 'Braucht Europa eine Verfassung?' (1995) *Juristenzeitung* 581.

Grimm, D., *Braucht Europa eine Verfassung?*, vol. 60 Siemens Stiftung (Munich 1995).

Grimm, D., 'Integration by Constitution' (2005) 3 *International Journal of Constitutional Law* 193.

Grimm, D., *The Constitution of European Democracy* (Oxford 2017).

Grimm, D., 'The European Court of Justice and National Courts: The German Constitutional Perspective after the Maastricht Decision' (1997) 3 *Columbia Journal of European Law* 229.

Grosman, L. S., 'Argentine Constitutional Law: An Overview' (2015) 43 *International Journal of Legal Information* 1.

Grote, R., 'Constitutional Courts in Federal States: The Case of Germany' (2017) 17 *Fédéralisme Régionalisme*, https://popups.uliege.be/1374-3864/index.php?id=1691.

Groussot, X., *Creation, Development and Impact of the General Principles of Community Law: Towards a Ius Commune Europaeum?* (Lund 2005).

Häberle, P., *Europäische Rechtskultur* (Baden-Baden 1994).

Häberle, P., *Europäische Verfassungslehre* (Baden-Baden 2009).

Häberle, P., 'Gemeineuropäisches Verfassungsrecht' (1991) Europäische Grundrechte Zeitschrift 261.#

Habermans, J., *Between Facts and Norms: Contributions to a Discourse Theory of Law and Democracy*, translated by William Rehg (Cambridge 1996).

Habermas, J., 'Citizen and State Equality in a Supranational Political Community: Degressive Proportionality and the *Pouvoir Constituant Mixte*' (2017) 55 *Journal of Common Market Studies* 171.

Habermas, J., *Die Einbeziehung des Anderen. Studien zur politischen Theorie* (Frankfurt 1996).

Habermas, J., 'Religion in the Public Sphere' (2006) 14 *European Journal of Philosophy* 7.

Habermas, J., 'Remarks on Dieter Grimm's "Does Europe Need a Constitution?"' (1995) 1 *European Law Journal* 303.

Hagedorn, H., 'Föderalismus und die deutsche Staatsangehörigkeit: die Einbürgerungspolitik der Bundesländer' in L. Akgün and D. Thränhardt (eds.), *Integrationspolitik in föderalistischen Systemen* (Münster 2001).

Halberstam, D., '"A People for Certain Purposes": On the History and Philosophy of Federalism(S) in the United States And Europe' (2018) University of Michigan Public Law Research Paper No. 619, 25, https://ssrn.com/abstract=3241597.

Halberstam, D. and Mollers, C., 'The German Constitutional Court Says "Ja zu Deutschland!"' (2009) 10 *German Law Journal* 1241.

Halberstam, D. and Reimann, M., 'Federalism and Legal Unification: Comparing Methods, Results, and Explanations across Twenty Systems' in D. Halberstam and M. Reimann (eds.), *Federalism and Legal Unification: A Comparative Empirical Investigation of Twenty Systems*, Vol. 28 of the Ius Gentium: Comparative Perspectives on Law and Justice book series (Berlin/Heidelberg 2014).

Halberstam, D. and Reimann, M. (eds.), *Federalism and Legal Unification: A Comparative Empirical Investigation of Twenty Systems* (Berlin/Heidelberg 2014), Vol. 28 of the ongoing Ius Gentium: Comparative Perspectives on Law and Justice book series (2007–).

Hall, K. (ed.), *The Oxford Companion to the Supreme Court of the United States*, 2nd ed. (New York 2005).

Hall, M., 'Mixed Reaction to "Opt-Out" from EU Charter of Fundamental Rights' (2007) 7 European Industrial Relations Observatory Online.

Haller, W., 'The New Swiss Constitution: Foreign and International Influences' (2002) 30 *International Journal of Legal Information* 256.

Halstein, W., Götz, H. H. and Narjes, K.-H., *Der unvollendete Bundesstaat – Europäische Erfahrungen und Erkenntnisse* (Dusseldorf 1969).

Hamburger, P., 'Law and Judicial Duty' (2003) 72 *George Washington Law Review* 1.

Hamilton, A., 'The Federalist No. 17' in *The Federalist Papers* (1787–1788).

Hamilton, A., 'The Federalist No. 33' in *The Federalist Papers* (1787–1788).

Hamilton, A., 'The Federalist No. 69' in *The Federalist Papers* (1787–1788).

Hamilton, A., 'The Federalist No. 80' in *The Federalist Papers* (1787–1788).

Hamilton, A., 'The Federalist No. 84' in *The Federalist Papers* (1787–1788).

Hansen, R. and Weil, P., *Dual Nationality, Social Rights and Federal Citizenship in the US and Europe: The Reinvention of Citizenship* (New York/Oxford 2002).

Hart, H. L. A., *The Concept of Law*, 3rd ed. (Oxford 2010).

Haskins, G. and Johnson, H., *History of the Supreme Court of the United States: Foundations of Power, John Marshall 1801–15* (New York 1981).

Hatton, R. M., Oresko, R., Gibbs, G. C. and Scott, H. M., *Royal and Republican Sovereignty in Early Modern Europe: Essays in Memory of Ragnhild Hatton* (Cambridge 1997).

Heater, D. B., *A Brief History of Citizenship* (New York 2004).

Heath, J. N., 'Exposing the Second Amendment: Federal Preemption of State Militia Legislation' (2001–2002) 79 *University of Detroit Mercy Law Review* 39.

van Hecke, S., Wolfs, W. and de Groof, V., '25 Years of Spitzenkandidaten: What Does the Future Hold?' (2018) Wilfred Martens Centre for European Studies Policy Brief, https://martenscentre.eu/sites/default/files/publication-files/ces_policybrief_spitzenkandidaten-web.pdf.

Heinemann-Gruder, A., *Federalism Doomed? European Federalism between Integration and Separation* (New York/Oxford 2002).

Held, D., *Models of Democracy*, 3rd ed. (Cambridge 2006).

Heller, H., *Gesammelte Schriften*, Vol. 2 (Leiden 1971).

Henkin, L., 'The Constitution for Its Third Century: Foreign Affairs' (1989) 83(4) *American Journal of International Law* 713.

Henri, D., Le Quintrec, G., Geiss, P., Prass, R. and Mursa, E., *Histoire/Geschichte* (Stuttgart/Leipzig 2008).

Hepp, A. and others, *The Communicative Construction of Europe: Cultures of Political Discourse* (London 2016).

Herlin-Karnell, E., 'The Domination of Security and the Promise of Justice: On Justification and Proportionality in Europe's "Area of Freedom, Security and Justice"' (2017) 8 *Transnational Legal Theory* 79.

Hernández, A. M., *Sub-national Constitutional Law in Argentina* (Alphen aan den Rijn 2011).

Herrmann, R. K. and others, *Transnational Identities: Becoming European in the EU* (Oxford 2004).

Hesse, J. J. and Wright, V., *Federalizing Europe? The Costs, Benefits and Preconditions of Federal Political Systems* (Oxford 1996).

Higgins, R., 'The ICJ, the CJEU, and the Integrity of International Law' (2003) 52 *International and Comparative Law Quarterly* 1.

Hilbink, L., *Judges beyond Politics in Democracy and Dictatorship: Lessons from Chile* (New York 2007).

Hinarejos, A., 'El diálogo judicial en curso y los poderes del Banco Central Europeo: la sentencia Weiss' (2019) 23 *Revista de Derecho Comunitario Europeo* 651.

Hinarejos, A., 'Fiscal Federalism in the European Union: Evolution and Future Choices for EMU' (2013) 50(6) *Common Market Law Review* 1621.

Hinarejos, A., 'The Euro Area Crisis and Constitutional Limits to Fiscal Integration' (2011–2012) 14 *Cambridge Yearbook of European Legal Studies* 243.

Hinarejos, A., *The Euro Area Crisis in Constitutional Perspective* (Oxford 2015).

Hirsch, G., 'Kein Staat, aber eine Verfassung' (2000) Neue Juristische Wochenschrift 46.

Hirschl, R., 'Preserving Hegemony? Assessing the Political Origins of the EU Constitution' (2005) 3 *International Journal of Constitutional Law* 269.

His, E., *Schweizer Verfassungsgeschichte: Der Bundesstaat von 1848 bis 1914. Register zu Band I–III* (Zurich 1938).

Hix, S., 'Decentralised Federalism: A New Model for the EU' in B. Martill and U. Staiger (eds.), *Brexit and Beyond: Rethinking the Futures of Europe* (London 2018) 72–80.

Hix, S., 'Elections, Parties and Institutional Design: A Comparative Perspective on European Union Democracy' (1998) 21 *West European Politics* 19.

Hobolt, S. B., 'A Vote for the President? The Role of Spitzenkandidaten in the 2014 European Parliament Elections' (2014) 21(10) *Journal of European Public Policy* 1528.

Hobolt, S. B., 'The Crisis of Legitimacy of European Institutions' in M. Castells and others (eds.), *Europe's Crises* (Cambridge, UK/Medford, MA 2018).

Hobson, C. F., *The Great Chief Justice: John Marshall and the Rule of Law* (Lawrence, KS 1996).

Hodson, D. and Maher, I. (eds.), *The Transformation of EU Treaty Making* (Cambridge 2018).

Hodson, D. and Peterson, J. (eds.), *The Institutions of the European Union* (Oxford 2017).

Hodson, D. and Puetter, U., 'The Euro Crisis and European Integration' in M. Cini and N. Pérez-Solórzano Borragán, *European Union Politics*, 5th ed. (Oxford 2016).

Hodson, D. and Puetter, U., 'The European Union in Disequilibrium: New Intergovernmentalism, Postfunctionalism and Integration Theory in the Post-Maastricht Period' (2019) 26 *Journal of European Public Policy* 1153.

Hofmann, A., 'Resistance against the Court of Justice of the European Union' (2018) 14 *International Journal of Law in Context* 258.

Hofmeister, H., 'To Bail Out or Not to Bail Out? Legal Aspects of the Greek Crisis' (2011) 13 *Cambridge Yearbook of European Legal Studies* 113.

Hogg, P. W., *Constitutional Law of Canada*, 6th ed. (Toronto 2013).

Holdgaard, R., Elkan, D. and Schaldemose, G. K., 'From Cooperation to Collision: The ECJ's Ajos Ruling and the Danish Supreme Court's Refusal to Comply' (2018) 55 *Common Market Law Review* 17.

Hollyer, J. B., Rosendorff, B. P. and Vreeland, J. R., *Transparency, Democracy, and Autocracy: Economic Transparency and Political (In)Stability* (Cambridge 2018).

Hopp, G., Sebaldt, M. and Zeitler, B., *Die CSU Strukturwandel, Modernisierung und Herausforderungen einer Volkspartei* (Wiesbaden 2010).

Höreth, M., *Die Selbstautorisierung des Agenten: der Europäische Gerichtshof im Vergleich zum U.S. Supreme Court* (Baden-Baden 2008).

Hottelier, M., 'La justice constitutionnelle en Suisse' (2017) 17 *Fédéralisme Régionalisme* 5–6, http://archive-ouverte.unige.ch/unige:102293.

Howart, D. and Spendzharova, A., 'Accountability in Post-Crisis Eurozone Governance: The Tricky Case of the European Stability Mechanism' (2019) 57 *Journal of Common Market Studies* 894.

Hueglin, T. O. and Fenna, A., *Comparative Federalism: A Systematic Inquiry* (Toronto 2006).

Hug, S. and König, T., 'In View of Ratification: Governmental Preferences and Domestic Constraints at the Amsterdam Intergovernmental Conference' (2002) 56 *International Organization* 447.

Huhe, N., Naurin, D. and Thomson, R., 'Don't Cry for Me Britannia: The Resilience of the European Union to Brexit' (2019) *European Union Politics* 1.

Innerarity, D., *Democracy in Europe* (Cham 2018).

Ipsen, H. P., *Europäisches Gemeinschaftsrecht* (Heidelberg 1972).

Ipsen, H.-P., 'Europäische Verfassung – Nationale Verfassung' (1987) *Europarecht* 195.

Ipsen, H.-P., *Verfassungsperspektiven der Europäischen Gemeinschaften* (Berlin 1970).

Jackson, V. C., 'Constitutional Comparisons: Convergence, Resistance, Engagement' (2005) *Harvard Law Review* 109.

Jackson, V. C., 'US Constitutional Law and History' in R. Masterman and R. Schütze (eds.), *The Cambridge Companion to Comparative Constitutional Law* (Cambridge 2019).

Jacobs, F. B., *The EU after Brexit: Institutional and Policy Implications* (Cham 2018).

Jančić, D., 'TTIP and Legislative-Executive Relations in EU Trade Policy' (2016) 40 *West European Politics* 202.

Jansson, J., 'Building Resilience, Demolishing Accountability? The Role of Europol in Counter-Terrorism' (2018) 28(4) *Policing and Society* 432.

Jellinek, G., *Die Lehre von den Staatenverbindungen* (Vienna 1882).

Jimenez, A. de la Fuente, J. M. and Duran, J. J., 'Is There an East–West Structure in the Location of FDI in Europe? The Role of Institutions and Political Risk' (2013) 3 *Research in Economics and Business: Central and Eastern Europe.*

Jiménez, L. A., 'Constitutional Empathy and Judicial Dialogue in the European Union' (2018) 24 *European Public Law* 57.

Jin, Q., 'Linguistic Hegemony in the EU' (2017) Proceedings of 3rd International Symposium on Social Science.

Joerges, C., 'Europe's Economic Constitution in Crisis', ZenTra Working Papers in Transnational Studies 6/2012 (Bremen 2013), http://ssrn.com/abstract=2179595.

Joerges, C., 'Justum facere in the European Integration Process: How Should the Law Promote the Constitutionalization of Europe?' Helsinki Legal Studies Research Paper No. 23, 19, http://ssrn.com/abstract=2214814.

Joerges, C., 'What Is Left of the European Economic Constitution? A Melancholic Eulogy' (2005) 30 *European Law Review* 461.

Joerges, C. and Roedl, F., 'Informal Politics, Formalised Law and the "Social Deficit" of European Integration: Reflections after the Judgments of the ECJ in Viking and Laval' (2009) 15 *European Law Journal* 1.

Jolly, M., *The European Union and the People* (New York 2007).

Jones, E., Kelemen, R. D. and Meunier, S., 'Failing Forward? The Euro Crisis and the Incomplete Nature of European Integration' (2016) *Comparative Political Studies* 49.

Joppke, C., 'Transformation of Citizenship: Status, Rights, Identity' (2007) 11 *Citizenship Studies* 37.

Joutsen, M., 'The European Union and Cooperation in Criminal Matters' in M. Natarajan (ed.), *International and Transnational Crime and Justice*, 2nd ed. (Cambridge 2019).

Junker, D., *Cornerstone of Democracy: The West German Grundgesetz, 1949–1989* (Washington, DC 1995).

Kadelbach, S. (ed.), *Verfassungskrisen in der Europäischen Union* (Baden-Baden 2018).

Kahn, P. W., 'Interpretation and Authority in State Constitutionalism' (1993) 106 *Harvard Law Review* 1147.

Kauppi, N. and Madsen, M. R., 'Non-elected Political Elites in the EU' in H. Best and H. Higley (eds.), *The Palgrave Handbook of Political Elites* (London 2018).

Kelemen, R. D., 'Selection, Appointment, and Legitimacy' in M. Bobek, *Selecting Europe's Judges: A Critical Review of the Appointment Procedures to the European Courts* (Oxford 2015).

Kelemen, R. D., 'The Dangers of Constitutional Pluralism' in G. Davies and M. Avbelj (eds.), *Research Handbook on Legal Pluralism and EU Law* (Cheltenham/Northampton, MA 2018).

Ketcham, R. (ed.), *The Anti-Federalist Papers and the Constitutional Convention Debates* (New York 2003).

Kilpatrick, C. and de Witte, B., 'Social Rights in Times of Crisis in the Eurozone: The Role of Fundamental Rights' Challenges' (22 April 2014), EUI Law Research Paper No. 2014/05, https://papers.ssrn.com/sol3/papers.cfm?abstract_id=2428855.

Kingsbury, B., *The Emergence of Global Administrative Law* (Durham, NC 2005).

Kirchhof, P., 'The Balance of Powers between National and European Institutions' (1999) 5 *European Law Journal* 225.

Kirchner, C., 'The Principle of Subsidiarity in the Treaty on European Union: A Critique from a Perspective of Constitutional Economics' (1998) 6 *Tulane Journal of International and Comparative Law* 305.

Kjaer, P. F., Teubner, G. and Febbrajo, A., The Financial Crisis in Constitutional Perspective: The Dark Side of Functional Differentiation (Oxford 2011).

Klamert, M. and Kochenov, D., 'Article 2 TEU' in M. Kellerbauer, M. Klamert and J. Tomkin (eds.), *The Treaties and the Charter of Fundamental Rights: A Commentary* (Oxford 2019).

Kleine, M., 'Informal Governance and Legitimacy in EU Politics' (2018) 40 *Journal of European Integration* 873.

Kleine, M. and Pollack, M., 'Liberal Intergovernmentalism and Its Critics' (2018) 56 *Journal of Common Market Studies* 1493.

Kloepfer, M., *Verfassungsrecht. 1. Grundlagen, Staatsorganisationsrecht, Bezüge zum Völker-und Europarecht* (Munich 2011).

Knapp, A. T., 'Law's Revolution: Benjamin Austin and the Spirit of '86' (2013) 25 *Yale Journal of Law and the Humanities* 271.

Kobach, K. W., *The Referendum: Direct Democracy in Switzerland* (Aldershot 1993).

Kocharov, A., 'This Time It's Different? Constitutional Complexities of the Spitzenkandidaten Arrangement' (2014) *Berliner Online-Beiträge zum Europarecht* 95.

Komárek, J., 'Czech Constitutional Court Playing with Matches: The Czech Constitutional Court Declares a Judgment of the Court of Justice of the EU

Ultra Vires; Judgment of 31 January 2012, Pl. ÚS 5/12, Slovak Pensions XVII' (2012) 8 *European Constitutional Law Review* 323.

Koopmans, R. and Statham, P. *The Making of a European Public Sphere: Media Discourse and Political Contention* (New York 2010).

Koschnik, A., 'The Democratic Societies of Philadelphia and the Limits of the American Public Sphere, circa 1793–1795' (2001) 58 *The William and Mary Quarterly* 615.

Kostakopoulou, T., 'Democracy-Talk in the European Union: The Need for a Reflexive Approach' (2003) 9 Columbia Journal of European Law 411.

Koutrakos, P., 'More on Autonomy – Opinion 1/17 (CETA)' (2019) 3 *European Law Review* 293.

Kovács, K., 'Ethnocultural Identity in East Central European Courts' (2017) 18 *German Law Journal* 1703.

Krämer, L., *EC Environmental Law*, 7th ed. (London 2011).

Kreppel, A., *The European Parliament and Supranational Party System: A Study in Institutional Development* (Cambridge 2001).

Kühn, Z., 'Ultra Vires Review and the Demise of Constitutional Pluralism: The Czecho-Slovak Pension Saga, and the Dangers of State Courts' Defiance of EU Law' (2016) 23 *Maastricht Journal of European and Comparative Law* 185.

Kuisma, M., 'Jurisdiction, Rule of Law, and Unity of EU Law in Rosneft' (2018) 37 *Yearbook of European Law* 3.

Kukk, M., 'Enhanced Fiscal Governance in the European Union: The Fiscal Compact' (2018) 5 *Baltic Journal of European Studies* 73.

Kumm, M., 'Beyond Golf Clubs and the Judicialization of Politics: Why Europe Has a Constitution Properly So Called' (2006) 54 *American Journal of Comparative Law* 505.

Kumm, M. and Comella, V. F., 'The Primacy Clause of the Constitutional Treaty and the Future of Constitutional Conflict in the European Union' (2005) 3 *International Journal of Constitutional Law* 473.

Kuniholm, B., Turkey's Accession to the European Union: Differences in European and US Attitudes, and Challenges for Turkey' (2001) 2 *Turkish Studies* 25.

Lacey, J., 'Must Europe Be Swiss? On the Idea of a Voting Space and the Possibility of a Multilingual Demos' 44 *British Journal of Political Science* 61.

Lacorne, D., 'European Citizenship: The Relevance of the American Model' in K. Nicolaidis and R. Howse (eds.), *The Federal Vision: Legitimacy and Levels of Governance in the United States and the European Union* (Oxford 2001).

Lacroix, J., 'Does Europe Need Common Values? Habermas vs Habermas' (2009) 8 *European Journal of Political Theory* 141.

Laffan, B. and Schlosser, P., 'Public Finances in Europe: Fortifying EU Economic Governance in the Shadow of the Crisis' (2016) 38 *Journal of European Integration* 237.

Landfried, C., *Constitutional Review and Legislation: An International Comparison* (Baden-Baden 1988).

Lane, P. R., 'The European Sovereign Debt Crisis' (2012) 26 *The Journal of Economic Perspectives* 49.

Lane, P. R., 'The Irish Crisis' in M. Beblavý, D. Cobham and L. Ódor (eds.), *The Euro Area and the Financial Crisis* (Cambridge 2011).

Larkin, P. M., 'Incapacity, the Labour Market and Social Security: Coercion into "Positive" Citizenship' (2011) 74 *Modern Law Review* 385.

Laursen, F., *The EU and Federalism: Polities and Policies Compared* (Farnham 2011).

Laursen, F. (ed.), *The EU and the Eurozone Crisis: Policy Challenges and Strategic Choices* (Farnham 2013).

Lawson, G., 'A Truism with Attitude: The Tenth Amendment in Constitutional Context' (2007–2008) 83 *Notre Dame Law Review* 469.

Lee, M., 'The Ambiguity of Multi-Level Governance and (De-)Harmonisation in EU Environmental Law' (2012–2013) 15 *Cambridge Yearbook of European Legal Studies* 357.

Lehner, F., 'Consociational Democracy in Switzerland: A Political-Economic Explanation and Some Empirical Evidence' (1984) 12 *European Journal of Political Research* 25.

Leino, P. and Petrov, R., 'Between "Common Values" and Competing Universals: The Promotion of the EU's Common Values through the European Neighbourhood Policy' (2009) 15 *European Law Journal* 654.

Lenaerts, K., 'Constitutionalism and the Many Faces of Federalism' (1990) 38(2) *American Journal of Comparative Law* 205.

Lenaerts, K., 'The Basic Constitutional Charter of a Community Based on the Rule of Law' in M. P. Maduro and L. Azoulai (eds.), *The Past and Future of EU Law: The Classics of EU Law Revisited on the 50th Anniversary of the Rome Treaty* (Oxford 2010).

Lenaerts, K. (ed.), *Two Hundred Years of U.S. Constitution and Thirty Years of EEC Treaty* (Brussels 1988).

Lenaerts, K. and Gutierrez-Fons, J. A., 'A Constitutional Perspective' in R. Schütze and T. Tridimas (eds.), *Oxford Principles of European Union Law: Volume 1: The European Union Legal Order* (Oxford 2018).

Létourneau, J., '"Silent Revolution": The Transformation of the Québécois Identity' (2017) 32 *London Journal of Canadian Studies* 98.

Levinson, S., 'Transitions' (1999) 108 *Yale Law Journal* 2215.

Liebert, U., 'Civil Society, Public Sphere and Democracy in the EU' in E. O. Eriksen and J. E. Fossum (eds.), *Rethinking Democracy and the European Union* (London 2013).

Liedhegener, A. and Gerstenhauer, D., 'Auf dem Weg zu einem kooperativen Verhaeltnis Religion und die Vertiefung der Europaeischen Union' in O. Leisse (ed.), *Die Europaeische Union nach dem Vertrag von Lissabon* (Wiesbaden 2010).

Lienhard, A. and others, 'The Federal Supreme Court of Switzerland: Judicial Balancing of federalism without Judicial Review' in N. Aroney and J. Kincaid (eds.), *Courts in Federal Countries: Federalists or Unitarists?* (Toronto 2017).

Lijphart, A., *Democracy in Plural Societies: A Comparative Exploration* (New Haven, CT 1977).

Lindeboom, J., 'Why EU Law Claims Supremacy' (2018) 38 *Oxford Journal of Legal Studies* 328.

Lindseth, P. L., 'Law, History and Memory: "Republican Moments" and the Legitimacy of Constitutional Review in France' (1996–1997) 3 *Columbia Journal of European Law* 49.

Lindseth, P. L., *Power and Legitimacy: Reconciling Europe and the Nation-State* (New York 2010).

Lingren, K.-O. and Persson, T., 'Participatory Governance in the European Union' in H. Heinelt (ed.), *Handbook on Participatory Governance* (Cheltenham/ Northampton, MA 2018).

de Londras, F., 'Convergence Gaps in EU Counter-Terrorism' in F. de Londras and J. Doddy (eds.), *The Impact, Legitimacy and Effectiveness of EU Counter-Terrorism* (London/New York 2015).

Longo, M. A., *Constitutionalising Europe: Processes and Practices* (Farnham/ Burlington, VT 2006).

Lord, C., *Democracy in the European Union* (Sheffield 1998).

Loughlin, M., 'What Is Constitutionalism' in P. Dobner and M. Loughlin, *The Twilight of Constitutionalism?* (New York 2010).

Low, P. W. and Jeffries, J. C., *Federal Courts and the Law of Federal-State Relations*, 4th ed. (New York 1998).

Lustig, D. and Weiler, J. H. H., 'Judicial Review in the Contemporary World: Retrospective and Prospective' (2018) 16 *International Journal of Constitutional Law* 315.

Mac Amhlaigh, C., 'The Anatomy of Constitutional Pluralism in the European Union' in G. Davies and M. Avbelj (eds.), *Research Handbook on Pluralism and EU Law* (Cheltenham/Northampton, MA 2018).

Machill, M., Beiler, M. and Fischer, C., 'Europe-Topics in Europe's Media: The Debate about the European Public Sphere: A Meta-Analysis of Media Content Analyses' (2006) 21 *European Journal of Communication* 57.

Maclure, J., 'Le projet d'une charte de la laïcité: les raisons d'un sain scepticisme' (2013) 34 *La Revue Tocqueville* 155.

Maclure, J. *Quebec Identity: The Challenge of Pluralism* (Montreal/Kingston, Ontario 2013) 10–11.

Macmahon, A. W. (ed.), *Federalism Mature and Emergent* (New York 1955).
Maddex, R. L., *Constitutions of the World* (New York 1996).
Madison, J., 'The Federalist No. 40' in *The Federalist Papers* (1787–1788).
Madison, J., 'The Federalist No. 44' in *The Federalist Papers* (1787–1788).
Madison, J., 'The Federalist No. 50' in *The Federalist Papers* (1787–1788).
Madsen, M. R., Olsen, H. P. and Šadl, U., 'Competing Supremacies and Clashing Institutional Rationalities: The Danish Supreme Court's Decision in the Ajos Case and the National Limits of Judicial Cooperation' (2017) 23 *European Law Journal* 140.
Maduro, M. P., 'The Importance of Being Called a Constitution: Constitutional Authority and the Authority of Constitutionalism' (2005) 3 *International Journal of Constitutional Law* 332.
Magen, A. and Pech, L., 'The Rule of Law and the European Union' in C. May and A. Winchester (eds.), *Handbook on the Rule of Law* (Cheltenham/Northampton, MA 2018).
Maier, J. and others, 'This Time It's Different? Effects of the Eurovision Debate on Young Citizens and Its Consequence for EU Democracy: Evidence from a Quasi-experiment in 24 Countries' (2018) 25 *Journal of European Public Policy* 606.
Maier, M., Strömbäck, J. and Lee Kaid, L., *Political Communication in European Parliamentary Elections* (Farnham 2011).
Mair, P. and Thomassen, J., 'Electoral Democracy and Political Representation in the European Union' (1 April 2008) Paper prepared for the Conference on Representation, Immigration and the 2009 Election to the European Parliament, Indiana University, Bloomington, www.indiana.edu/~west/documents/electoral_democracy_mair_2008.pdf.
Maletic, I., 'The Story of the EU and the Happily Roaming Consumers Case No. C58/08, Vodafone Ltd, et al. v. Secretary of State for Business, Enterprise and Regulatory Reform' (2011) 38 *Legal Issues of Economic Integration* 199.
Mancini, G. F., *Democracy and Constitutionalism in the EU* (Oxford 2000).
Mancini, G. F., 'The Making of a Constitution for Europe' in R. Keohane and S. Hoffman (eds.), *The New European Community: Decisionmaking and Institutional Change* (Boulder, CO 1991).
Mancini, S., 'Taking Secularism (Not Too) Seriously: The Italian "Crucifix Case"' (2006) 1 *Religion and Human Rights* 179.
Mann, D., *'We, the People' vs. 'We, the Peoples': The Debate over the Nature of the Union in the USA and Canada and Its Lessons for European Integration* (Florence 2012).
Manners, I., 'The Normative Ethics of the European Union' (2008) 84 *International Affairs* 45.
J. F. Manning, 'Textualism and Legislative Intent' (2005) 91(2) *Virginia Law Review* 419.

J. F. Manning, 'Textualism and the Equity of the Statute' (2005) 101(1) *Columbia Law Review* 1.

Mantu, S. and Minderhoud, P., 'EU Citizenship and Social Solidarity' (2017) 24 *Maastricht Journal of European and Comparative Law* 703.

Martí, J. L., 'European Democracy and the No-Demos Thesis' in D. Innerarity and others (eds.), *A New Narrative for a New Europe* (2018).

Márton, P., 'Europe's Crises: Preparing to Study Disintegration' (2018) 14 *Journal of Contemporary European Research* 274.

Maśnicki, J., 'From Integration to Fragmentation? The Late and Incorrect Transposition of the EU Directives' in R. Grzeszczak (ed.), *Renationalisation of the Integration Process in the Internal Market of the European Union* (Baden-Baden 2018).

Mason, H. L., *The European Coal and Steel Community: Experiment in Supranationalism* (The Hague 1955).

Massey, C. R.., 'The Locus of Sovereignty: Judicial Review, Legislative Supremacy, and Federalism in The Constitutional Traditions of Canada and the United States' (1990) *Duke Law Journal* 1229.

Maurer, A., 'Less Bargaining – More Deliberation: The Convention Method for Enhancing EU Democracy' (2003) *Internationale Politik und Gesellschaft* 167.

Maurer, H. and Manssen, G., *Staatsrecht I* (2003).

de Mauro, T., *In Europa son già 103. Troppe lingue per una democrazia?* (Laterza 2014).

Mayer, F. C., 'Competences – Reloaded? The Vertical Division of Powers in the EU and the New European Constitution' (2005) 3 *International Journal of Constitutional Law* 493.

Mayer, J.-F., 'A Country without Minarets: Analysis of the Background and Meaning of the Swiss Vote of 29 November 2009' (2011) 41(1) *Religion* 11.

McBain, H. L., *The Living Constitution: A Consideration of the Realities and Legends of Our Fundamental Law* (1927).

McDougal, M. S., 'The Comparative Study of Law for Policy Purposes: Value Clarification as an Instrument of Democratic World Order' (1952) 1 *American Journal of Comparative Law* 24.

McKay, D. H., *Designing Europe: Comparative Lessons from the Federal Experience* (New York 2001).

McManners, J., *The Oxford History of Christianity* (New York 1993).

Meissner, K., 'Democratizing EU External Relations: The European Parliament's Informal Role in SWIFT, ACTA, and TTIP' (2016) 21 *European Foreign Affairs Review* 269.

Menéndez, A. J., 'A Christian or a Laic Europe? Christian Values and European Identity' (2005) 18 *Ratio Juris* 179.

Merler, S. and Pisani-Ferry, J., 'Sudden Stops in the Euro Area' (2012) 3(3) *Review of Economics and Institutions* 23.

Mestmacker, E.-J., 'On the Legitimacy of European Law' (1994) *The Rabel Journal of Comparative and International Private Law* 615.

Meyer, C., 'Political Legitimacy and the Invisibility of Politics: Exploring the European Union's Communication Deficit' (1999) 37 *Journal of Common Market Studies* 617.

Meyer, J. and Bernsdorff, N., *Kommentar zur Charta der Grundrechte der Europäischen Union* (Baden-Baden 2003).

Meyer, J.-H., *The European Public Sphere: Media and Transnational Communication in European Integration 1969–1991* (Stuttgart: Franz Steiner Verlag 2010).

Michel, H., 'La transparence dans l'Union européenne: réalisation de la bonne gouvernance et redéfinition de la démocratie' (2018) 165 *Revue française d'administration publique* 109.

van Middelaar, L., 'Seven Brexit Propositions: Towards a Union the Protects' in B. Martill and U. Staiger (eds.), *Brexit and Beyond: Rethinking the Futures of Europe* (London 2018) 81–7.

van Middelaar, L., *The Passage to Europe: How a Continent Became a Union* (New Haven, CT 2013).

Miklóssy, K., 'Lacking Rule of Law in the Lawyers' Regime: Hungary' (2018) 26 *Journal of Contemporary European Studies* 270.

Miller, D., 'Majorities and Minarets: Religious Freedom and Public Space' (2016) 46 *British Journal of Political Science* 437.

Miller, J. M., *Constitution of Argentina: A Contextual Analysis* (Oxford 2010).

Mitchell, J. F., 'Reconsidering Murdock: State-Law Reversals as Constitutional Avoidance' (2010) 77 *University of Chicago Law Review* 1335.

Mody, A., *Eurotragedy: A Drama in Nine Acts* (Oxford 2018).

Möllers, C., *Das Grundgesetz : Geschichte und Inhalt* (Munich 2009).

Moloney, N., *EU Securities and Financial Markets Regulation* (Oxford 2014).

Monaghan, H. P., 'Supremacy Clause Textualism' (2010) 110 *Columbia Law Review* 731.

Monaghan, H. P., 'The Confirmation Process: Law or Politics?' (1988) 101 *Harvard Law Review* 1202.

Monar, J., 'Eurojust and the European Public Prosecutor Perspective: From Cooperation to Integration in EU Criminal Justice?' (2013) 14 *Perspectives on European Politics and Society* 339.

Mooney,C. and Lee, M.-H., 'The Influence of Values on Consensus and Contentious Morality Policy: U.S. Death Penalty Reform 1956–82' (2000) 62(1) *Journal of Politics* 223.

Moravcsik, A., 'Federalism in the European Union: Rhetoric and Reality' in K. Nicolaidis and R. Howse (eds.), *The Federal Vision: Legitimacy and Levels of Governance in the United States and the European Union* (Oxford 2001).

Moravcsik, A., 'In Defense of the "Democratic Deficit": Reassessing Legitimacy in the European Union' (2002) 40(4) *Journal of Common Market Studies* 603.

Moravcsik, A., 'Negotiating the Single European Act' in R. Keohane and S. Hoffman (eds.), *The New European Community: Decisionmaking and Institutional Change* (Boulder, CO 1991).

Moravcsik, A., 'Preferences and Power in the European Community: A Liberal Intergovernmentalist Approach' (1993) 31(4) *Journal of Common Market Studies* 473.

Moravcsik, A., 'Preferences, Power and Institutions in 21st-Century Europe' (2018) 56 *Journal of Common Market Studies* 1648.

Moravcsik, A., 'Reassessing Legitimacy in the European Union' (2002) 40 *Journal of Common Market Studies* 603.

Moravcsik, A., 'What Can We Learn from the Collapse of the European Constitutional Project?' (2006) 47 *Politische Vierteljahresschrift* 219.

Moro, G., *The Single Currency and European Citizenship: Unveiling the Other Side of the Coin* (London 2013).

Morwood, J. (ed.), *Oxford Latin Dictionary: Latin–English*, 3rd ed. (Oxford 2012).

Moull, D., 'Lessons the EU Should Learn from the Formative Years of the US: Challenges to EU Authority in the Areas of Legitimacy and Interpretive Competence and the Implications for the Conceptualization of the EU' (2004) 51 *Jean Monet Working Papers in Comparative and International Politics*, www.fscpo.unict.it/EuroMed/jmwp51.pdf.

Mourelo, E. L., Khatiwada, S. and Corley-Coulibaly, M., 'Overview of Employment Trends and Projections' (2013) World of Work Report 1.

Müller, J.-W., 'Defending Democracy within the EU' (2013) 24 *Journal of Democracy* 138.

von Münch, I., *Die deutsche Staatsangehörigkeit: Vergangenheit, Gegenwart, Zukunft* (Berlin 2007).

von Munch, I., *Grundgesetz-Kommentar* (Munich 1975).

von Münch, I. and Kunig, P., *Kommentar zum Grundgesetz*, 6th ed. (Munich 2012).

Murphy, W. F., 'Civil Law, Common Law, and Constitutional Democracy' (1991) 52 *Louisiana Law Review* 91.

Murray, H., *Limiting Federal Powers: The Tenth Amendment* (New York 2019).

Murray, P. and Longo, M., 'Europe's Wicked Legitimacy Crisis: The Case of Refugees' (2018) 40 *Journal of European Integration* 411.

Nagy, C. I., *The EU Bill of Rights' Diagonal Application to Member States Comparative Perspectives of Europe's Human Rights Deficit* (The Hague 2018).

Nedergaard, P., 'Borders and the EU Legitimacy Problem: The 2015–16 European Refugee Crisis' (2019) 40 *Policy Studies* 80.

Nelson, C., 'What Is Textualism?' (2005) 91(2) *Virginia Law Review* 347.

Nelson, W. E., *Marbury v. Madison: The Origins and Legacy of Judicial Review*, 2nd ed. (Kansas 2018).

Nettesheim, M., 'A Tribute to Professor Richard M. Buxbaum: Developing a Theory of Democracy for the European Union' (2005) 23 *Berkeley Journal of International Law* 358.

Neuberger, D., 'The British and Europe', Annual Freshfields Lecture, Faculty of Law, University of Cambridge, 12 February 2014, www.supremecourt.uk/docs/speech-140212.pdf.

Nicola, F., 'The European Union 20 Years after Maastricht: Transatlantic Perspectives' (2011) 20 *Tulane Journal of International and Comparative Law* 65.

Nicolaidis, K., 'A View from the Ground Up' in N. W. Barber, M. Cahill and R. Ekins (eds.), *The Rise and Fall of the European Constitution* (London 2019).

Nicolaidis, K., 'Braving the Waves? Europe's Constitutional Settlement at Twenty' (2018) 56(7) *Journal of Common Market Studies* 1614, https://doi.org/10.1111/jcms.12791.

Nicolaidis, K. and Howse, R., *The Federal Vision: Legitimacy and Levels of Governance in the United States and the European Union* (Oxford 2001).

Nic Shuibhne, N., 'Case C-361/01 P, Kik v. Office for Harmonization in the Internal Market (Trade Marks and Designs), (Kik IV)' (2004) 41(4) *Common Market Law Review* 1093.

Nic Schuibhne, N., 'What Is the Autonomy of EU Law, and Why Does that Matter?' (2019) 88 *Nordic Journal of International Law* 9.

Nolte, G. (ed.), *European and US Constitutionalism* (Cambridge 2005).

Norman, P., *The Accidental Constitution: The Making of Europe's Constitutional Treaty* (Brussels 2005).

Oakes, L. and Warren, J., *Language, Citizenship, and Identity in Quebec* (London 2007).

Öberg, J., 'The Rise of the Procedural Paradigm: Judicial Review of EU Legislation in Vertical Competence Disputes' (2017) 13 *European Constitutional Law Review* 248.

O'Brien, F. W., 'Baker v. Carr Abroad: The Swiss Federal Tribunal and Cantonal Elections' (1962) 72 *Yale Law Journal* 46.

Odermatt, J., 'When a Fence Becomes a Cage: The Principle of Autonomy in EU External Relations Law' EUI Working Paper MWP 2016/17.

Oechsli, W., Eden, P. and Cedar, P., *History of Switzerland, 1499–1914* (Cambridge 1922).

Oh, C. H., Travis Selmier, W. and Lien, D., 'International Trade, Foreign Direct Investment, and Transaction Costs in Languages' (2011) 40 *Journal of Socio-Economics* 732.

Ólafsson, T. T. and Pétursson, T. G., 'Weathering the Financial Storm: The Importance of Fundamentals and Flexibility' in M. Beblavý, D. Cobham and L. Ódor (eds.), *The Euro Area and the Financial Crisis* (Cambridge 2011).

Oliver, P. C., *The Constitution of Independence: The Development of Constitutional Theory in Australia, Canada, and New Zealand* (Oxford/New York 2005).

Oliver, P., Macklem, P. and des Rosiers, N. (eds.), *The Oxford Handbook of the Canadian Constitution* (Oxford 2017).

van Ooyen, R. C., 'Die Staatstheorie des Bundesverfassungsgerichts und Europa' in R. C. van Ooyen (ed.), *Von Solange über Maastricht zu Lissabon* (2010).

Oppermann, K., 'The Politics of Avoiding Referendums on the Treaty of Lisbon' (2013) 35 *Journal of European Integration* 73.

Orgad, L. and Lepoutre, J. (eds.), *Should EU Citizenship Be Disentangled from Member State Nationality?* EUI Working Paper RSCAS 2019.

Pacquin, S., 'Multilevel Governance and International Trade Negotiations: The Case of Canada's Trade Agreements' in G. Lachapelle and P. Oñate (eds.), *Borders and Margins: Federalism, Devolution and Multi-Level Governance* (Opladen/Berlin/Toronto 2018).

Palombella, G., 'Whose Europe? After the Constitution: A Goal-Based Citizenship' (2005) 3 *International Journal of Constitutional Law* 357.

Panara, C., 'In the Name of Cooperation: The External Relations of the German Länder and Their Participation in the EU Decision-Making' 2010 6(1) *European Constitutional Law Review* 59.

Papadopoulou, L., Pernice, I. and Weiler, J. H. H. (eds.), *Legitimacy Issues of the European Union in the Face of Crisis: Dimitri Tstsos in Memoriam* (Baden-Baden 2018).

Papadopoulos, N. A., 'Austerity-Based Labour Market Reforms in Greece vs Fundamental Rights in the Aftermath of the European Debt Crisis: An Analysis of Supranational and National Bodies' Jurisprudence' (forthcoming) *European Public Law* 24, https://ssrn.com/abstract=3276880.

Papdopoulos, Y., 'Eurozone Crisis Management and the Changing Nature of the Democratic Deficit in the European Union' in R. Careja, P. Emmenegger and N. Giger (eds.), *The European Social Model under Pressure* (Wiesbaden 2020).

van Parijs, P., *Linguistic Justice for Europe and for the World* (Oxford 2011).

Patberg, M., 'Challenging the Masters of the Treaties: Emerging Narratives of Constituent Power in the European Union' (2018) 7 *Global Constitutionalism* 263.

Payandeh, M., 'Constitutional Review of EU Law after Honeywell: Contextualizing the Relationship between the German Constitutional Court and the EU Court of Justice' (2011) 48 *Common Market Law Review* 9.

Pech, L. and Scheppele, K. L., 'EU Values Illiberalism Within: Rule of Law Backsliding in the EU' (2017) 19 *Cambridge Yearbook of European Legal Studies* 3.

Peeters, P., 'The Federal Structure: Kingdom, Regions and Communities' in G. Craenen (ed.), *The Institutions of Federal Belgium: An Introduction to Belgian Public Law* (Leuven 1996).

Perez, A. T., 'The Federalizing Force of the EU Charter of Fundamental Rights' (2017) 15 *International Journal of Constitutional Law* 1080.

Perju, V., 'On the (De-)Fragmentation of Statehood in Europe: Reflections on Ernst-Wolfgang Böckenförde's Work on European Integration' (2018) 19 *German Law Journal* 403.

Pernice, I., 'Europäisches und nationales Verfassungsrecht' (2001) Veröffentlichungen der Vereinigung der Deutschen Staatsrechtslehrer 60.

Pernice, I., 'Multilevel Constitutionalism in the European Union' (2002) 27 European Law Review 511.

Pernice, I., 'The European Constitution' (May 2001), paper presented at the 16th Sinclair House Talks in Bad-Homburg.

Perrin, B., 'Challenges Facing the EU Network of Competition Authorities: Insights from a Comparative Criminal Law Perspective' (2006) 31(4) *European Law Review* 540.

Perrone, F., 'The Judicial Path to European Constitutionalism: The Role of the National Judge in the Multi-Level Dialogue' in P. Pinto de Albuquerque, *Judicial Power in a Globalized World: Liber Amicorum Vincent de Gaetano* (Cham 2019).

Pescatore, P., 'Preface' in T. Sandalow and E. Stein (eds.), *Courts and Free Markets*, Vol. 1 (Oxford 1982).

Peters, A., *Elemente einer Theorie der Verfassung Europas* (Berlin 2001).

Peters, A., 'Global Constitutionalism Revisited' (2005) 11 International Legal Theory 39.

Petric, D., 'Game of Courts: A Tale of Principles and Institutions' (2019) 25 *European Law Journal* 273.

Peyer, H. C., *Verfassungsgeschichte der alten Schweiz* (Zurich 1978).

Pfersmann, O., 'The New Revision of the Old Constitution' (2005) 3 *International Journal of Constitutional Law* 383.

Philadelphia Inquirer, The, 'Pa. Court Rules Voters Can Cast Regular Ballots without ID' (3 October 2012), http://articles.philly.com/2012-10-03/news/34219088_1_voter-id-law-commonwealth-secretary-carol-aichele-league-of-women-voters.

Phillipson, R., 'Lingua Franca or Lingua Frankensteinia? English in European Integration and Globalisation' (2008) 27 *World Englishes* 250.

Piqani, D., 'The Simmenthal Revolution Revisited: What Role for Constitutional Courts?' in B. de Witte and others (eds.) *National Courts and EU Law: New Issues, Theories and Methods* (Cheltenham/Northampton, MA 2016).

Piris, J.-C., *The Constitution for Europe: A Legal Analysis* (Cambridge 2006).

Piris, J.-C., *The Future of Europe: Towards a Two-Speed EU?* (New York 2012).

Piris, J.-C., *The Lisbon Treaty: A Legal and Political Analysis* (Cambridge 2010).

Pirro, A. L. P., Taggart, P. and van Kessel, S., 'The Populist Politics of Euroscepticism in Times of Crisis: Comparative Conclusions' (2018) 38 *Politics* 378.

Pliakos, A. and Anagnostaras, G., 'Saving Face? The German Federal Constitutional Court Decides Gauweiler' (2017) 18 *German Law Journal* 213.

Poli, S., 'The Common Foreign Security Policy after Rosneft: Still imperfect but Gradually Subject to the Rule of Law' (2017) 54 *Common Market Law Review* 1799.

Pollack, M. A., *The Engines of European Integration: Delegation, Agency, and Agenda Setting in the EU* (New York 2003).

Pollicino, O., 'European Arrest Warrant and Constitutional Principles of the Member States: A Case Law-Based Outline in the Attempt to Strike the Right Balance between Interacting Legal Systems' (2008) 9 *German Law Journal* 1313.

Pollicino, O., 'The Conseil d'Etat and the Relationship between French Internal Law after Arcelor: Has Something Really Changed?' (2008) 45 *Common Market Law Review* 1519.

Polsby, N. W., 'The Institutionalization of the U.S. House of Representatives' (1968) 62 *American Political Science Review* 144.

Potvin, M., 'Social and Media Discourse in the Reasonable Accommodations Debate' (2010) *Immigration and Diversity* 78.

Prakash, S. B. and Yoo, J. C., 'The Origins of Judicial Review' (2003) 70 *University of Chicago Law Review* 887.

Příbáň, J., 'Constitutional Sovereignty in Post-Sovereign Jurisprudence of the Czech Constitutional Court: From the Lisbon Judgments to the Landtová Ultra Vires Controversy' in M. Bobek (ed.), *Central European Judges under the European Influence: The Transformative Power of the EU Revisited* (Oxford 2015).

Puder, M. G., 'Supremacy of the Law and Judicial Review in the European Union: Celebrating Marbury v. Madison with Costa v. Enel' (2005) 36 *George Washington International Law Review* 567.

Puetter, U., 'Europe's Deliberative Intergovernmentalism: The Role of the Council and European Council in EU Economic Governance' (2011) 19 *Journal of European Public Policy* 161.

Pufendorf, S., *Dissertatio de Republica irregulari* (Heidelberg 1668).

Puntscher Riekmann, S., Mokre, M. and Latzer, M. (eds.), *The State of Europe: Transformations of Statehood from a European Perspective* (Frankfurt 2004).

Quandt Stiftung, H., *Europe's Constitution: A Framework for the Future of the Union* (Bad Homburg 2001).

Rabl, K., Stoll, C. and Vasold, M., *From the U.S. Constitution to the Basic Law of the Federal Republic of Germany [Von der amerikanischen Verfassung zum Grundgesetz der Bundesrepublik Deutschland]* (Munich 1988).

Rasmussen, M., 'Law Meets History: Interpreting the Van Gend en Loos Judgment' in F. Nicola and B. Davies (eds.), *EU Law Stories: Contextual and Critical Histories of European Jurisprudence* (Cambridge 2017).

Rauchegger, C., 'The Bundesverfassungsgericht's Human Dignity Review: *Solange III* and Its Application in Subsequent Case Law' in L. Violini and A. Baraggia (eds.), *The Fragmented Landscape of Fundamental Rights Protection in Europe* (Cheltenham/Northampton, MA 2018).

Redish, M. H., 'Federal Judicial Independence: Constitutional and Political Perspectives' (1994) 46 *Mercer Law Review* 697.

Reh, C., 'The Lisbon Treaty: De-Constitutionalizing the European Union?' (2009) 47 *Journal of Common Market Studies* 625.

Reinhard, J., Biesenbender, J. and Holzinger, K., 'Do Arguments Matter? Argumentation and Negotiation Success at the 1997 Amsterdam Intergovernmental Conference' (2014) 6 *European Political Science Review* 283.

Reiss, A., 'Police Organization in the Twentieth Century' (1992) 15 *Crime and Justice* 51.

Requejo, F., 'Cultural Pluralism, Nationalism and Federalism: A Revision of Democratic Citizenship in Plurinational States' (1999) 35 *European Journal of Political Research* 255.

Reuter, L. R., *Constitutional Developments in Germany since 1945* (Hamburg 1994).

Reuters, 'Italy's Top Court to Rule on European Parliament Electoral Law' 9 May 2014, www.reuters.com/article/2014/05/09/us-eu-election-italy-courts-idUSBREA480KM20140509.

Richardson, E. L., 'Checks and Balances in Foreign Relations' (1989) 83(4) *American Journal of International Law* 736.

Riffel, C., 'The CETA Opinion of the European Court of Justice and Its Implications: Not That Selfish After All' (2019) 22(3) *Journal of International Economic Law* 1.

Rifkin, J., *The European Dream: How Europe's Vision of the Future Is Quietly Eclipsing the American Dream* (New York 2004).

Risse, T., *A Community of Europeans? Transnational Identities and Public Spheres* (Ithaca, NY/London 2010).

Risse, T., *European Public Spheres* (Cambridge 2014).

Röben, V., 'Constitutionalism of the European Union after the Draft Constitutional Treaty: How Much Hierarchy?' (2004) 10 *Columbia Journal of European Law* 339.

Roederer-Rynning, C., 'Parliamentary Assertion and Deep Integration: The European Parliament in the CETA and TTIP Negotiations' (2017) 30 *Cambridge Review of International Affairs* 507.

Rosas, A., 'The Interaction between the European Court of Justice and National Courts in Preliminary Ruling Proceedings: Some Institutional and Procedural Observations' in H. Ruiz Fabri (ed.), *International Law and Litigation: A Look into Procedure* (Luxembourg 2019).

Rosas, A. and Armati, L., *EU Constitutional Law: An Introduction* (London 2018).

Rose, R., 'Referendum Challenges to the EU's Policy Legitimacy – and How the EU Responds' (2018) 26 *Journal of European Public Policy* 207.

Rosenfeld, M., 'Comparing Constitutional Review by the European Court of Justice and the U.S. Supreme Court' (2006) 4 *International Journal of Constitutional Law* 618.

Rosenfeld, M., 'The European Convention and Constitution Making in Philadelphia' (2003) 1 *International Journal of Constitutional Law* 373.

Rosenfeld, M. and Sajó, A., *The Oxford Handbook of Comparative Constitutional Law* (Oxford 2012) 12.

Rosenthal, A. J. and Henkin, L., *Constitutionalism and Rights: The Influence of the United States Constitution Abroad* (New York 1990).

Rosenthal, L. H. and Joseph, G. P., 'Foundations of U.S. Federalism' (2017) 101 *Judicature* 39.

Rossi, L. S., '"Same Legal Value as the Treaties"? Rank, Primacy, and Direct Effects of the EU Charter of Fundamental Rights' (2017) 18 *German Law Journal* 771.

Roznai, Y., *Unconstitutional Constitutional Amendments: The Limits of Amendment Powers* (Oxford 2017).

Rubenfeld, J., *Revolution by Judiciary: The Structure of American Constitutional Law* (Cambridge, MA 2005).

Rush, S. E., 'Oh, What a Truism the Tenth Amendment Is: State Sovereignty, Sovereign Immunity, and Individual Liberties' (2019) 71 *Florida Law Review*, https://ssrn.com/abstract=3259988.

Russell, P. H., 'The Political Purposes of the Canadian Charter of Rights and Freedoms' (1983) 61 *Canadian Bar Review* 30.

Rutkus, D. S., 'CRS Report for Congress: Supreme Court Appointment Process: Roles of President, Judiciary Committee, and Senate' (2005) US Department of State.

Sadurski, W., *Constitutionalism and the Enlargement of Europe* (Oxford 2012).

Sager, F. and Zollinger, C., 'The Swiss Political System in a Comparative Perspective' in C. Trampusch and A. Mach (eds.), *Switzerland in Europe* (New York 2011).

Sajó, A., 'Constitution without the Constitutional Moment: A View from the New Member States' (2005) 3 *International Journal of Constitutional Law* 243.

Sajó, A., 'On Constitutional Identity and the Loyalties of the Constitutional Judge' (2019) 40 *Cardozo Law Review* 3253.

Sandalow, T. and Stein, E., *Courts and Free Markets* (Oxford 1982).

Šarčević, S., *Language and Culture in EU Law: Multidisciplinary Perspectives* (London/New York 2016).

Sarikakis, K. and Kolkytha, O., 'EU Democratic Deficits: The EU Project and a European Public Sphere', in K. Arnold, P Preston and S. Kinnerbrock (eds.), *The Handbook of European Communication History* (Hoboken, NJ 2019).

Sarmiento, D., 'Who's Afraid of the Charter? The Court of Justice, National Courts and the New Framework of Fundamental Rights Protection in Europe' (2013) 50 *Common Market Law Review* 1267.

Sbragia, A., 'Post-National Democracy as Post-National Democratization' in S. Fabbrini (ed.), *Democracy and Federalism in the European Union and the United States: Exploring Post-National Governance* (Abingdon/New York 2005).

A. Scalia, *A Matter of Interpretation: Federal Courts and the Law* (Princeton, NJ 1997).

Scharpf, F. W., 'Democratic Legitimacy under Conditions of Regulatory Competition: Why Europe Differs from the United States' in K. Nicolaidis and R. Howse (eds.), *The Federal Vision: Legitimacy and Levels of Governance in the United States and the European Union* (Oxford 2001).

Scharpf, F. W., 'Legitimacy Intermediation in the Multilevel European Polity and Its Collapse in the Euro Crisis' in K. Armingeon (ed.), *Staatstätigkeiten, Parteien und Demokratie* (Heidelberg 2013).

Schiffauer, W., *Parallelgesellschaften: Wie viel Wertekonsens braucht unsere Gesellschaft?: Für eine kluge Politik der Differenz* (Bielefeld 2008).

Schimmelfennig, F., 'Getting Around No: How Governments React to Negative EU Referendums' (2019) 26 *Journal of European Public Policy* 1056.

Schimmelfennig, F., 'Liberal Intergovernmentalism and the Crises of the European Union' (2018) 56 *Journal of Common Market Studies* 1578.

Schlosser, P., *Europe's New Fiscal Union* (Cham 2019).

Schmidt, S. K., *The European Court of Justice and the Policy Process: The Shadow of Case Law* (Oxford 2018).

Schmidt, V. A., *Democracy in Europe: The EU and National Polities* (Oxford 2006).

Schmidt, V. A., 'The Political Dynamics of EU Governance in Response to Crisis: Toward More or Less EU Legitimacy?' (2017), www.democratic-anxieties.eu/wordpress/wp-content/uploads/2017/10/Berlin-Paper-EU-political-dynamics-and-legitimacy.pdf.

Schmitt, H., Hobolt, S. B. and Popa, S. A., 'Does Personalization Increase Turnout? Spitzenkandidaten in the 2014 European Parliament Elections' (2015) 16 *European Union Politics* 347.

Schroth, P. W., 'Marbury and Simmenthal: Reflections on the Adoption of Decentralized Judicial Review by the Court of Justice of the European Community' (1978–1979) 12 *Loyola of Los Angeles Law Review* 869.

Schuck, P. H., 'Citizenship in Federal Systems' (2000) 48 *American Journal of Comparative Law* 195.

Schumacher, T., Marchetti, A. and Demmelhuber, T. (eds.), *The Routledge Handbook on the European Neighborhood Policy* (Abingdon/New York 2017).

Schütze, R., *European Constitutional Law* (Cambridge 2012).

Schütze, R., *From Dual to Cooperative Federalism: The Changing Structure of European Law* (New York 2009).

Schütze, R., 'From Rome to Lisbon: "Executive Federalism" in the (New) European Union' (2010) 47 *Common Market Law Review* 1385.

Schütze, R. and Tridimas, T. (eds.), *Oxford Principles of European Union Law: Volume 1: The European Union Legal Order* (Oxford 2018).

Schwartz, B., *The Great Rights of Mankind: A History of the American Bill of Rights* (New York 1977).

Schwartz, D. S., *The Spirit of the Constitution: John Marshall and the 200-Year Odyssey of McCulloch v. Maryland* (Oxford 2019).

Schweiger, C., 'The Legitimacy Challenge' in D. Dinan, N. Nugent and W. E. Paterson (eds.), *The European Union in Crisis* (London 2017).

Scicluna, N., 'When Failure Isn't Failure: European Union Constitutionalism after the Lisbon Treaty' (2012) 50 *Journal of Common Market Studies* 441.

Seamon, R. H., 'Supreme Court Supremacy in a Time of Turmoil: James v. City of Boise' (2017) 50 *Loyola of Los Angeles Law Review* 175.

Sedler, R. A., 'Constitutional Protection of Individual Rights in Canada: The Impact of the New Canadian Charter of Rights and Freedoms' (1983) 59 *Notre Dame Law Review* 1191.

Shalaby, O. and others, 'Transparent Selection of Judges for EU Courts: Complaint to the European Ombudsman' (2017) HEC Research Paper Series 1239, https://ideas.repec.org/p/ebg/heccah/1239.html.

Shapiro, M., 'The European Court of Justice' in P. Craig and G. de Búrca (eds.), *The Evolution of EU Law* (Oxford 1999).

Shaw, J. and Wiener, A., 'The Paradox of the "European Polity"' in M. G. Cowles and M. Smith (eds.), *The State of the European Union: Risks, Reform, Resistance, and Revival* (Oxford 2000).

Sicakkan, H. G., 'The Role of EU Policies in the Making of the European Public Sphere' in H. G. Sicakkan (ed.), *Integration, Diversity and the Making of a European Public Sphere* (Cheltenham/Northampton, MA 2016).

Siemers, D. J., *Ratifying the Republic: Antifederalists and Federalists in Constitutional Time* (Stanford, CA 2004).

Slaughter, A.-M., Stone Sweet, A. and Weiler, J., *The European Court and the National Courts: Doctrine and Jurisprudence: Legal Change in Its Social Context* (Oxford 1998).

Small, H. B., *Chronicles of Canada, or a Concise History of the Leading Events in the Old Provinces of the New Dominion* (Ottawa 1868).

Smeets, S. and Beach, D., 'Political and Instrumental Leadership in Major EU Reforms: The Role and Influence of the EU Institutions in Setting-Up the Fiscal Compact' (2019) 27(1) *Journal of European Public Policy* 63, https://doi.org/10.1080/13501763.2019.1572211.

Smith, A. D., 'National Identity and the Idea of European Unity' (1992) 68(1) *International Affairs* 55.

Smith, J., *Reinvigorating European Elections: The Implications of Electing the European Commission* (London 2005).

Smith, R. M., *Civic Ideals: Conflicting Visions of Citizenship in US History* (New Haven, CT 1997).

Somek, A., 'Postconstitutional Treaty' in R. A. Miller and P. C. Zumbansen (eds.), *Comparative Law as Transnational Law: A Decade of the German Law Journal* (Oxford 2011).

de Somer, M., *Precedents and Judicial Politics in EU Immigration Law* (Cham 2019).

Z. Somer-Topcu and M. E. Zar, 'European Parliamentary Elections and National Party Policy Change' (2014) 47(6) *Comparative Political Studies* 878.

Sowery, K., 'The Nature and Scope of the Primary Law-Making Powers of the European Union: The Member States as the "Masters of the Treaties"' (2018) 2 *European Law Review* 205.

Spevack, E., *Allied Control and German Freedom: American Political and Ideological Influences on the Framing of the West German Basic Law (Grundgesetz)* (Münster/Piscataway, NJ 2001).

Stein, E., 'Lawyers, Judges and the Making of a Transnational Constitution' (1981) 75 *American Journal of International Law* 1.

Steinberg, J., *Why Switzerland?* 2nd ed. (Cambridge 1996).

Stevenson, A. (ed.), *Oxford Dictionary of English*, 3rd ed. (Oxford 2010).

Stone Sweet, A., *Governing with Judges: Constitutional Politics in Europe* (Oxford 2000).

Stone Sweet, A., 'Judicialization and Supranational Governance' in M. Shapiro and A. Stone Sweet (eds.), *On Law, Politics and Judicialization* (Oxford 2002).

Stone Sweet, A., 'Judicialization and the Construction of Governance' (1999) 32(2) *Comparative Political Studies* 147.

Stone Sweet, A., 'The Court of Justice' in P. Craig and G. de Búrca (eds.), *The Evolution of EU Law*, 2nd ed. (Oxford 2011).

Stone Sweet, A., *The Judicial Construction of Europe* (Oxford 2004).

Stone Sweet, A., 'The Structure of Constitutional Pluralism: Review of Nico Krisch, Beyond Constitutionalism: The Pluralist Structure of Post-National Law' (2013) 11 *International Journal of Constitutional Law* 491.

Stone Sweet, A. and Caporaso, J., 'From Free Trade to Supranational Polity: The European Court and Integration' in W. Sandholtz and A. Stone Sweet (eds.), *European Integration and Supranational Governance* (New York 1998).

Stone Sweet, A. and Gehring, M., 'Environmental Protection' in A. Stone Sweet, *The Judicial Construction of Europe* (Oxford 2004).

Stras, D., 'Why Supreme Court Justices Should Ride Circuit Again' (2006–2007) 91 *Minnesota Law Review* 1710.

Streeck, W., 'The Crisis in Context: Democratic Capitalism and Its Contradictions' in W. Streeck and A. Schaefer (eds.), *Politics in the Age of Austerity* (Chichester 2011).

Sundquist, J., *Dynamics of the Party System: Alignment and Realignment of Political Parties in the United States* (Washington, DC, 1983).

Swaine, E. T., 'Subsidiarity and Self-Interest: Federalism at the European Court of Justice' (2000) 41 *Harvard International Law Journal* 1.

Swenden, W., 'What – If Anything – Can the European Union Learn from Belgian Federalism and Vice Versa?' (2005) 15 *Regional and Federal Studies* 187.

Szczerbiak, A. and Taggart, P. A., *Opposing Europe? The Comparative Party Politics of Euroscepticism*, Vols. 1 and 2 (Oxford 2008).

Taagepera, R. and Shugart, M. S., *Seats and Votes: The Effects and Determinants of Electoral Systems* (New Haven, CT 1983).

Teubner, G., 'A Constitutional Moment? The Logics of "Hitting the Bottom"' in P. F. Kjaer, G. Teubner and A. Febbrajo (eds.), *The Financial Crisis in Constitutional Perspective: The Dark Side of Functional Differentiation* (Oxford 2011).

Thatcher, M. and Stone Sweet, A., 'Theory and Practice of Delegation to Non-majoritarian Institutions' (2002) 25(1) *West European Politics* 1.

Theil, S., 'What Red Lines, If Any, Do the Lisbon Judgments of European Constitutional Courts Draw for Future EU Integration?' (2014) 15 *German Law Journal* 599.

Thorlakson, L., 'Representation in the EU: Multi-level Challenges and New Perspectives from Comparative Federalism' (2017) 24 *Journal of European Public Policy* 544.

Thurner, P. W. and Pappi, F. U., *European Union Intergovernmental Conferences: Domestic Preference Formation, Transgovernmental Networks and the Dynamics of Compromise* (London 2009).

Tömmel, I. and Verdun, A., 'Political Leadership in the European Union: An Introduction' (2017) 39 *Journal of European Integration* 103.

Torbiorn, K. M., *Destination Europe* (Manchester 2018).

Trachtman, J. P., 'International Regulatory Competition, Externalization, and Jurisdiction' (1993) 34 *Harvard International Law Journal* 47.

Tsebelis, G. and Money, J., *Bicameralism* (Cambridge 1997).

Tuori, K., *European Constitutionalism* (Cambridge 2015).

Tuori, K., 'The Eurozone Crisis as a Constitutional Crisis' in M. Fichera, S. Hänninen and K. Tuori (eds.), *Polity and Crisis: Reflections on the European Odyssey* (London/New York 2016).

Tuori, K., 'The Pluralism of European Fundamental Rights Law' in S. Douglass-Scott and N. Hatzis (eds.), *Research Handbook on EU Law and Human Rights* (Cheltenham/Northampton, MA 2017).

Turmo, A., 'A Dialogue of Unequals: The European Court of Justice Reasserts National Courts' Obligations under Article 267(3) TFEU: ECJ 4 October 2018, Case C-416/17, Commission v France' (2019) 15 *European Constitutional Law Review* 340.

Tushnet, M. V., 'Misleading Metaphors in Comparative Constitutionalism: Moments and Enthusiasm' (2005) 3 *International Journal of Constitutional Law* 262.

Tushnet, M. V., *The Constitution of the United States of America: A Contextual Analysis* (Portland, OR 2009).

UK Parliament, European Union Committee, 'The Workload of the European Court of Justice of the European Union', 29 March 2011, Fourteenth Report.

Uyttendaele, M., *Précis de droit constitutionnel belge. Regards sur un système institutionnel paradoxal*, 3rd ed. (Brussels 2005).

Verdussen, M., *La Constitution belge, lignes et entrelignes* (Brussels 2004).

Verschueren, H., 'Preventing "Benefit Tourism" in the EU: A Narrow or Broad Interpretation of the Possibilities Offered by the ECJ in *Dano*?' (2015) 52 *Common Market Law Review* 363.

de Villers, B., *Evaluating Federal Systems* (Cape Town/London 1994).

Vítolo, A. M., 'The Argentine Federal System' in D. Halberstam and M. Reimann (eds.), *Federalism and Legal Unification: A Comparative Empirical Investigation of Twenty Systems*, Vol. 28 of the Ius Gentium: Comparative Perspectives on Law and Justice book series (Berlin/Heidelberg 2014).

Vollard, H., *European Disintegration* (London 2018).

de Vries, C. E., *Euroscepticism and the Future of European Integration* (Oxford 2018).

Wahl, N. and Prete, L., 'The Gatekeepers of Article 267 TFEU: On Jurisdiction and Admissibility of References for Preliminary Rulings' (2018) 55 *Common Market Law Review* 511.

Waibel, M., 'Karlsruhe Gives Green Light for ESM Treaty Ratification' (12 September 2012), EJIL:Talk!, www.ejiltalk.org/karlsruhe-gives-green-light-for-german-esm-ratification.

Waibel, M., 'Monetary Policy: An Exclusive Competence Only in Name?' (2017) University of Cambridge Legal Research Paper No.11/2017, 15–20, https://ssrn.com/abstract=2915162.

Walker, N., 'After the Constitutional Moment' (November 2003). The Federal Trust Constitutional Online Paper Series No. 32/03. p 26.

Walker, N., 'After the Constitutional Moment' in I. Pernice and M. Maduro (eds.), *A Constitution for the European Union: First Comments on the 2003 Draft of the European Convention* (Baden-Baden 2004).

Walker, N., 'Europe's Constitutional Momentum and the Search for Polity Legitimacy' (2005) 3 *International Journal of Constitutional Law* 211.

Walker, N., 'Post-Constituent Constitutionalism? The Case of the European Union' in M. Loughlin and N. Walker (eds.), *The Paradox of*

Constitutionalism: Constituent Power and Constitutional Form (Oxford 2007).

Walker, N. and Loughlin, M., *The Paradox of Constitutionalism: Constituent Power and Constitutional Form* (Oxford 2007).

Walker, N., Shaw, J. and Stephen, T., *Europe's Constitutional Mosaic* (Portland, OR 2011).

Wallace, H., Pollack, M. A. and Young, A. R. (eds.), *Policy-Making in the European Union*, 6th ed. (Oxford 2010).

Wasserfallen, F., 'The Judiciary as Legislator? How the European Court of Justice Shapes Policy-Making in the European Union' (2010) 17(8) *Journal of European Public Policy* 1128.

Wegener, B. W., 'Commentary on TFEU Art. 267 (ex-Art. 234 TEC) [Vorabentscheidung]' in C. Calliess and M. Ruffert (eds.), *EUV/AEUV – Das Verfassungsrecht der Europäischen Union – Kommentar*, 4th ed. (Munich 2011).

Weiler, J. H. H., 'Does Europe Need a Constitution? Reflections on Demos, Telos and the German Maastricht Decision' (1995) 1 *European Law Journal* 219.

Weiler, J. H. H., 'Eurocracy and Distrust: Some Questions Concerning the Role of the European Court of Justice in the Protection of Fundamental Human Rights within the Legal Order of the European Communities' (1986) 61 *Washington Law Review* 1003.

Weiler, J. H. H., 'European Neo-constitutionalism: In Search of Foundations for the European Constitutional Order' (1996) 44 *Political Studies* 517.

Weiler, J. H. H., *Federalism and Constitutionalism: Europe's Sonderweg* (2000), https://jeanmonnetprogram.org/archive/papers/00/001001.html.

Weiler, J. H. H., 'Federalism without Constitutionalism: Europe's Sonderweg' in K. Nicolaidis and R. Howse (eds.), *The Federal Vision: Legitimacy and Levels of Governance in the United States and the European Union* (Oxford 2001).

Weiler, J. H. H., 'On the Power of the Word: Europe's Constitutional Iconography' (2005) 3 *International Journal of Constitutional Law* 173.

Weiler, J. H. H., *The Constitution of Europe: 'Do the New Clothes Have an Emperor?' and Other Essays on European Integration* (Cambridge 1999).

Weiler, J. H. H., 'The Transformation of Europe' (1991) 100 *Yale Law Journal* 2403.

Weiler, J. H. H., 'Van Gend en Loos: The Individual as Subject and Object and the Dilemma of European Legitimacy' (2014) 12 *International Journal of Constitutional Law* 94.

Weiler, J. H. H. and Winds, M., *European Constitutionalism beyond the State* (Cambridge 2003).

Wheeler, R. and Harrison, C., *Creating the Federal Judicial System*, 3rd ed. (Washington, DC 2005).

White, G. E., 'The Constitutional Journey of "Marbury v. Madison"' (2003) 89 *Virginia Law Review* 1463.

White, S., 'Rousseau and the Meaning of Popular Sovereignty' in D. Satz and A. Lever (eds.), *Ideas that Matter: Democracy, Justice, Rights* (Oxford 2019).

Widdershoven, R., 'The European Court of Justice and the Standard of Judicial Review' in S. Lavrijssen, E. H. Ballin and J. de Poorter (eds.), *Judicial Review of Administrative Discretion in the Administrative State* (The Hague 2019).

Wiener, A., 'The EU's Unbound Constitutional Quality' in S. Champeau, C. Closa, D. Innerarity and M. P. Maduro (eds.), *The Future of Europe: Democracy, Legitimacy and Justice after the Euro Crisis* (London 2015) 111.

Wiener, A., Börzel, T. A. and Risse, T., *European Integration Theory*, 3rd ed. (Oxford 2018).

Wiener, A. and della Sala, V., 'Constitution-Making and Citizenship Practice: Bridging the Democracy Gap in the EU?' (1997) 35 *Journal of Common Market Strategies* 595.

Wiener, A. and Neunreither, K., 'Introduction: Amsterdam and Beyond', in K. Neunreither and A. Wiener (eds.), *European Integration after Amsterdam: Institutional Dynamics and Prospects for Democracy* (Oxford 2000) 10.

Wiener, A. and Oeter, S., 'Introduction: Who Recognizes the Emperor's Clothes Anymore?' (2016) 14(3) I•CON 608.

Wiesner, C., *Inventing the EU as a Democratic Polity* (Cham 2018).

Wiesner, C., *Meanings of Europe: Changes and Exchanges of a Contested Concept* (Abingdon 2014).

De Wilde, P., Michailidou, A. and Trenz, H.-J., *Contesting Europe: Exploring Euroscepticism in Online Media Coverage* (Colchester 2013).

Williams, A., *EU Human Rights Policies: A Study in Irony* (Oxford 2004).

de Witte, B., 'Language Law of the European Union: Protecting or Eroding Linguistic Diversity?' in R. Craufurd-Smith (ed.), *Culture and European Union Law* (Oxford 2004).

Wolkenstein, F., 'Demoicracy, Transnational Partisanship and the EU' (2018) 56 *Journal of Common Market Studies* 284.

Wood, G. S., *Empire of Liberty: A History of the Early Republic, 1789–1815* (New York 2009).

Wood, G. S., 'The Significance of the Early Republic' (1988) 8(1) *Journal of the Early Republic* 1.

J. Wouters, H. Cuyckens and T. Ramopoulos, 'The European Union: A Federation in All but Name' in D. Halberstam and M. Reimann (eds.), *Federalism and Legal Unification*, vol. 28 (Heidelberg/Berlin 2013), 191–235.

Woyke, W. (ed.), *Stichwort: Wahlen*, 12th ed. (Heidelberg 2013).

Wright, B., 'UK Left Out of Campaign for EU's Top Job (8 May 2014), *BBC News*, www.bbc.co.uk/news/blogs-eu-27322896.

Wright, C. and Miller, A., *Federal Practice and Procedure, Jurisdiction and Related Matters*, 4th ed., Vol. 14B (Minneapolis, MN 2013) table S-7, p.46, section 3721.

Yates [Brutus], R., 'Anti-Federalist No. XI' (1788).

Young, E. A., 'Protecting Member State Autonomy in the European Union: Some Cautionary Tales from American Federalism' (2002) 77(6) *New York University Law Review* 1612.

Zaccaroni, G., 'Procedural Rights within the European Economic Constitution: Which Remedies for the Rights and Interests of Those Affected by the Legal Measures Enacted to Counter the Economic Crisis?' in H. C. H. Hoffmann, K. Pantazatou and G. Zaccaroni (eds.), *The Metamorphosis of the European Economic Constitution* (2019), 11, orbilu.uni.lu/bitstream/10993/37508/1/08_Chapter%208_Zaccaroni_Metamorphosis.pdf.

Zuckert, M. P., *Natural Rights and the New Republicanism* (Princeton, NJ 1994).

Zuleeg, M., 'What Holds a Nation Together? Cohesion and Democracy in the United States of America and in the European Union' (1997) 45 *American Journal of Comparative Law* 505.

Financial Times, 'Why a Presidency Is the Best Model for Europe', 26 February 2003.

INDEX